News from Overton, Nevada and surrounding areas (Logan, St. Thomas, Cappa, Kaolin and Moapa)

1905 - 1915

Compiled from the Las Vegas Age Newspaper and the Washington County News (Utah)

Often while working on family history (genealogy) I wonder about more than is listed on the pedigree sheets. In reading all of these articles I got more familiar with my grandparents, uncles/aunts and great grandparents and their neighbors. Some of the stories I had been told and some were wonderful surprises.

I added correct spelling several times, during a Family History Expo one of the classes mentioned that often spellings were used that would give the meaning especially if they were of of the correct letter for the plates in that edition.

Some of the old names include: Andersen, Angell, Batty, Conger, Cooper, Cox, Hannig, Ingram, Jones, Koenig, Leavitt, Lewis, Losee, Lytle, Marshall, McDermott, McDonald, Mills, Nay, Perkins, Pixton, Shurtliff, Swapp, Syphus, Turnbaugh, Wells, West, Whitehead, Whitney, Wittwer and others. 3

Some of the articles are easier to read than others, please consider they are all over 100 years old.

4

ISBN-13: 978-1495923425
ISBN-10: 1495923428

POPULATION

Las Vegas, Largest Town in Lincoln County

Following is an estimate of the population of Lincoln county, made by ex-Senator H. E. Freudenthal, of Pioche:

Las Vegas	1,000
Delamar	600
Caliente	600
Searchlight	500
Pioche	300
Panaca	250
Bunkerville	250
Crescent	200
Overton	150
St. Joseph	100
Fay and Deer Lodge	100
Eldorado Canyon	100
Mesquite	80
Eagle Valley	50
Moapa	50
Spring Valley	40
St. Thomas	40
Good Springs and Sandy	50
Scattering	375
Total population	4,775

Please notice that a majority live in the south half of the county.

5

OVERTON

Threshing Continues in the Muddy River Valley

[Special Correspondence]

We have experienced some very hot weather the past two weeks, but a cool breeze is blowing today and we are hoping it will continue.

The threshing machine is in running order again and will finish threshing all the grain in the valley before stopping again.

Mrs. John A. Lytle and baby came in from Las Vegas Thursday. They will visit friends and relatives here a few days before returning.

Miss Octavia Cobb and Miss Mary Wallace left last Monday for Los Angeles, the former to attend the State Normal School and the latter for a visit.

Miss Vinnea Angell left last Wednesday for Salt Lake City, where she will attend school this winter.

Mr. Sherman Thomas and family and Mr. A. S. King and wife have gone to the mountains for a few days until hot weather is over.

Mr. Chas. Cobb came down on Wednesday's stage from Moapa to attend a meeting of the Muddy Valley Irrigation Company.

The board of directors of the Muddy Valley Irrigation Company met yesterday at 2 p. m. to transact business of the company.   "TRIXEY."

6

OVERTON

There are six ditches at Overton, aggregating eleven miles in length and watering 770 acres in holdings averaging 30 acres. Land at Overton in 1903 was valued at $2.50 to $10.00 per acre, the latter being comparatively choice and having some improvements. Although capitalized at $1.00 per acre, water usually sold at $10.00 per acre.

LOGAN

At Logan, five miles above Overton, there are five ditches, aggregating five miles in length and irrigating 424 acres in holdings of 35 acres. Conditions and products are similar to those of Overton and St. Thomas.

OVERTON

[Special Correspondence]

We had a very nice, steady rain Thursday night and Friday morning, making the weather much cooler.

Farmers are now busy preparing to sow grain and plant early gardens.

Mrs. J. A. Lytle, who has been visiting relatives the past month, has returned to Las Vegas, where Mr. Lytle is employed.

Mr. Jed Cox and wife, of St. George, are visiting relatives here. They are en route home from Las Vegas, where they have been the past six months.

Mr. and Mrs. Ellis Turnbaugh came in on Friday's stage. They expect to make their home here in the future.

Quite a number of our young people attended an ice cream party at St. Thomas Wednesday evening. All report having had a very nice time and the ice cream was delicious.

Mr. Ed. Cox, of Bunkerville, and Francis Bunker, of Mexico, passed through town Saturday morning on their way to Bunkerville from Old Mexico.

The dance given Friday night by the M. I. A. was a decided success. All report having had a very nice time.

"TRIXEY."

8

OVERTON

Happenings During a Week in the Muddy Valley

[Special Correspondence]

Overton, March 12, 1906.

Las Vegas Age.—Spring has come at last. It was quite cold last week, the ice was nearly a quarter of an inch thick in the water trough, but this week everything is growing nicely and people are very busy planting their melons, cucumbers and other seeds.

Andrew L. Jones left here this morning with a six-horse team for Good Springs to freight for one of the mines near that point.

The State Engineer is here to measure up every man's land that is under cultivation and give him a certificate showing that he has a right to water from the Muddy river to irrigate his land.

J. M. Lytle has the contract and is putting up the buildings and sheds for the Experiment Farm.

The board of directors of the Muddy Valley Irrigation Company met yesterday and agreed to call a special meeting of the stockholders of the company to meet on the 7th of April, as quite important business is to come before the meeting. State Engineer Henry Thurtell was at the meeting, and gave an explanation of the law regarding his labors and duties in the matter of irrigation on the various streams of the State.

The postmaster here has procured and installed a cabinet in the postoffice and added a money order department, which proves to be very convenient.

MUDDY.

9

Notice of Application for Permission to Appropriate the Public Waters of the State of Nevada.

Notice is hereby given that on the 29th day December, 1905, in accordance with Sec 180 28, Chapter XLVI, of the statutes of 1905, the

Nevada Land and Live Stock Company

of Salt Lake, County of Salt Lake and State of Utah, made application to the State Engineer of the State of Nevada for permission to appropriate the public waters of the State of Nevada. Such appropriation to be made from the Muddy River at points S. E. ¼ of S. E. ¼ of Sec. 34, T. 16 S., R. 67 E., and S. E. ¼ of S. W. ¼ of Sec. 18, T. 16 S., R. 68 E., by means of a dam, and 20 cubic feet per second in to be conveyed to points in Secs. 2, 11, 12, 13, and 14 in T. 16 S., R. 67 E., and 18, 20, 29, 30, 31, 32, and 33, T. 16 S., R. 68 E., and Sections 3 and 4 in Twp 17, S. R. 68 E., by means of a ditch, and there used for irrigation. The construction of said works shall begin before Jan. 1, 1907, and shall be completed on or before Jan. 1, 1908. The water shall be actually applied to a beneficial use on or before Jan. 1, 1910.

Signed: HENRY THURTELL,
11-51   State Engineer.

OVERTON

[Special Correspondence]

May 27, 1906.

Very cold weather during the past week and rain is threatening every day. It is almost cold enough to frost.

Postmaster T. J. Jones is having lumber shipped in for a new dwelling.

The marriage of J. M. Lytle and Miss Violet Angell took place at the beautiful white stone residence of the bride's parents and the wedding dance was participated in by a large number of the friends of the happy couple last Friday evening. The fair bride was elegantly attired in a white mousseline de soie costume trimmed with lace and satin ribbons.

The fence is completed around the Experimental Farm and broad fields of green vegetation greets the eyes of the passers by.

Much fruit will be raised in the valley this season. Vegetables are so plentiful they are going to waste, and there is an abundance of rich milk, butter and honey. We have yet more room for settlers.

Preparations are being made by the people of this valley for a grand time in honor of Independence Day, July 4th.

An election was held today for school trustees, which resulted in the selection of Willard L. Jones for the long term and John A. Lytle and Stephen R. Whitehead as the other two members.

John M. Lytle is erecting a large dance hall on Main street.

Apricots are ripe and peaches and plums are ripening fast.

11

OVERTON

Grand Celebration for July Fourth

[Special Correspondence]

The people of the upper and lower Muddy Valley will all join in a big celebration at the central location of Overton. An elaborate program has been prepared. There will be firing of guns at sunrise, a grand parade, splendid literary and musical program, races and small sports, with a ball in the evening at Lytle hall. Everybody is invited.

LITTLE LOCALS

Mrs. Ann Bonelli left on the train yesterday for Kingman, Arizona. She will spend the summer there with her son, G. A. Bonelli.

Born, to Mr. and Mrs. Wm. Batty, on the 13th inst., a girl.

The large dance hall being erected on Main street by Lytle Bros. is nearly completed.

Cantaloupes are ripening and figs, peaches and apricots are being shipped out every day.

Vienna Angell has returned from Salt Lake, where she has been attending school.

Miss Maggie Thomas has been very sick for some time with typhoid fever.

We expect three wedding dances next week, those of Mr. John M. Bunker and Miss Eloise Turnbaugh, Mr. Robert O. Gibson and Miss Edith Hinton, Samuel B. Gentry and Miss Mabel Murphy.

12

OVERTON

Muddy May Have a Branch Railroad

(Special Correspondence.)

The weather is still warm along the Muddy.

Cantaloupe season is nearly at an end and the farmers are glad to have a rest after a rushing season.

Mrs. Virginia Lytle returned from the north where she has been visiting relatives and friends and enjoying the cool weather.

Mrs. John M. Bunker has returned from Los Angeles. She has spent the past month there enjoying the sea breeze.

W. L. Jones, wife and family left for a trip in the mountains to escape the intense heat.

A number of railroad and business men have been visiting the valley and report is we will have a branch railroad running down our valley by the next cantaloupe season.

Mrs. W. A. Perkins is spending the summer weeks in Salt Lake City.

Loretta McKenna, of Moapa, is spending a few days in town enjoying the dances in the new hall.

New buildings are being erected on every side; the valley is flourishing; new home-seekers seen daily and room for more.

13

Overton Notes

[Special Correspondence.]

Our fall weather has arrived, bringing with it cool breezes and turning the leaves golden.

School commenced October 1st, with Ellis Turnburgh as principal.

Frank Batty and family have recently moved into town and intend making their future home here.

Mrs. Alice Mills has been very sick for some time, but is slowly improving.

The mines in Cedar Basin seem to be attracting attention from all parts of the country, making work quite plentiful.

We have great hopes of a railroad through the valley soon and have many inducements to offer such an enterprise, such as gold, salt and whitewash mines and a rich and prolific farming communit.

Threshing is being completed and the farmers are busy putting up their grain.

14

MOAPA NOTES

Mining and General Improvement on the Muddy

(Special Correspondence.)

Mr. C. M. Temple, day operator at this place, who has been east for over a month, has returned, and after spending a few days in Cedar Basin looking over his mining interests there, will again resume work for the railroad company.

Now that cooler weather has once more arrived, Cobb Bros. are preparing to open up the Lincoln group of copper claims. These claims were located last spring by Gentry and Reese, and after doing location work showed over 40 tons of high grade ore, assaying over 64 per cent copper, 30 ounces in silver and $4 in gold.

The Grand Gulch Mining Co. want about eight or ten more men, miners and muckers. They have recently put on 25 men. The company are short of freighters and have raised the price for hauling $3 per ton over price paid last year.

The nominees on the Republican State ticket gave Moapa and Lower Valley a call last week.

We have two tri-weekly stages from this place, one to Cedar City, Utah, via Bunkerville, and one to St. Thomas, via Logan and Overton. The Government is also calling for bids for carrying mail from St. Thomas to Gold Butte (Cedar Basin).

The people here are in favor of moving the county seat, that is, if it will be located in the center of the county, viz, Moapa.

It is rumored that parties have taken options from settlers on all the lands in the upper valley of the Muddy.

About three sections of land in Meadow Valley Wash, adjacent to Moapa, have been filed on under the desert act, and parties are contemplating boring for artesian water.

Greenwater has six saloons. No danger from thirst in that new copper camp.

15

Registration by Precincts

The number of registered voters in the precincts from which returns have been received is given below:

Las Vegas	320
Searchlight	320
Crescent	39
El Dorado	18
Moapa	16
Logan	17
Ploche	132
Callente	170
DeLamar	113
Good Springs	30
Overton	20
Lake Valley	13
Sandy	11
Spring Valley (Newlands)	10
Deerlodge (Fay)	30
Stewart (Alamo)	20
Eagle Valley (Urwine)	12
St. Thomas	25
Panaca	60
Hiko	30
Stine (Power Plant)	12
Acoma	17
Bunkerville	39
Mesquite	20
Nelson	18
Total	1520

GROWING

Business Looking Up in Gold Butte, St Thomas, Overton

(Special Correspondence)

Whitehead Brothers' new store at Gold Butte, with Will A. Whitehead in charge, has done enough business in the short time it has been established to justify the move, and the indications are that the venture will prove a good one. Also the new 24x40 store building they are erecting in Overton is almost ready to be moved into and will enable them to handle the large business they are building up to much better advantage.

There has been a new store 16x24 put up in St Thomas within the past two weeks and two new ones started at Gold Butte and "Copper City" within the same time, and since the trade of the old stores is better than ever, it looks as if this country must be coming to the front. All the prospectors look happy and half the people of Overton have either work in the mountains or freighting to the mining camps.

17

OVERTON

Industrial Progress In Rich Muddy River Valley

It has been an unusually windy spring.

Whooping cough is still raging.

The big store of F. F. Gunn is doing fine business. A new addition and beautiful soda fountain will soon be added.

The Valley contains any amount of garden vegetables, waisting for want of market. Grain is now ripe and the binder is busy harvesting.

Whitehead Bros. have their new store completed, making one more nice looking building on Main street.

Men are traveling to and from Gold Butte and Copper City all the time. Work still continues there and prospecting goes on. rich ore being found all the time.

Miss Luremma Cox will leave for Salt Lake City to attend school the latter part of the week.

A. S. King and wife have sold out their home and left for Fieldrorg, Utah.

The crowd of young people who attended the circus at Las Vegas returned home feeling well paid for their trip.

Apricots and figs are beginning to ripen and peaches will be ripe in June.

The new cottage of James Huntsman is nearing completion and looks very nice.

18

MUDDY RIVER VALLEY

Wonderfully Productive Farms and Shipping Mines

MOUNTAINS OF PURE SALT AND COPPER

MOAPA STATION

The Moapa Commercial Company, C. E. Christiansen, does a big business with the farmers and miners of Muddy and Virgin rivers. F. F. Gunn also directs from Moapa a large commercial business. He handles cattle, fruits and farm products, sending them to market.

Moapa's big new Salt Lake depot has been opened with a dance, and is a credit to that town.

A saloon at Moapa sells Los Angeles and Salt Lake beer at 25c per bottle, ice cold.

Muddy River Valley is about 30 miles long and averages one mile wide, reaching from the great springs six miles west of Moapa to St. Thomas at the junction with the Virgin river.

Fifty years ago the Mormons found the valley inhabited by Piute Indians and sand storms. They dug canals, made the valley bloom by irrigation, planted trees and built up prosperous communities at Logan, Overton, St. Thomas and Bunkerville.

Being only 1,100 to 1,600 feet above the sea, the climate is semi-tropical, and peaches, apricots, almonds, apples melons, garden and field crops mature early.

In the vicinity of Moapa, Geo. C. Baldwin, D. O. Huntsman, J. M. Pickett, Mr. Conger, Mr. Storrs and others are cultivating farms.

TOWN OF LOGAN

At Logan postoffice H. H. Church runs a supply store. From his own and adjoining farms Mr. Church shipped to market before June 1st ripe peaches, apricots and apples. Other substantial farmers near Logan are W. H. Gann, large farmer and stock raiser; 500 acres; W. C. Bowman, general farmer, good land; H. B. Mills 250 acre farm and good home; A. J. Sprotes, good farm; John H. Averett, J. M. Thomas, H. N. Holt, fruit cattle and general farm and garden crops.

Dr. E. L. Benson is finishing a handsome cement block residence 34x36 at Logan. Cement blocks are made on the ground.

Manager S. H. Wells of the Moapa Improvement Company has in cultivation a large farm, and is building an imposing residence. Mr. Wells is setting an example to other farmers. He made money on canteloupes and has 40 acres of asparagus.

H. H. Church of Logan is Secretary of the Muddy Valley Telephone Company, which will cover the valley.

At Logan is located the State Experimental Farm, controlled by President Stubbs of the Nevada University, H. H. Church of Logan and E. H. Syphus of St Thomas. Manager, Chas. Arney is busy laying out the 80 acres for experimental purposes. The State will build a cement block house 35 feet square, plant fruits, garden and field crops, trees, etc. in variety. Blooded stock will be raised on the farm. By this method quality and variety will be reached.

Alfalfa hay sells from $10 to $12 per ton.

19

OVERTON

Two good supply stores are located at Overton : Whitehead Bros and F. F. Gunn, E. Turnbaugh being manager of the latter. A large brick school house speaks well for the community. J. A. Lytle owns the big dance hall, where frequent gatherings are held. Bishop Jones is also Postmaster. S. A. Angel, Brig. Whitmore and other progressive farmers have stone and brick houses. Fields of alfalfa yield five crops every year, averaging eight tons to the acre. Wheat, barley and oats make big crops in May. Canteloupes, asparagus, fruits and vegetables yield abundantly. On every hand along the irrigating ditches and roads shade trees flourish. Cottonwood fence posts sprout and make trees. Over 2,000 head of cattle graze in the valley.

Overton is headquarters for the Muddy Valley Irrigation Company. Hon. Levi Syphus President, H. A. Sparks Vice President, and A. L. F. MacDermott, Secretary and Treasurer. The land owners incorporated this company to distribute the waters fairly. Awards of water were made by the State Engineer, from the Muddy river.

Cultivated lands with water rights are worth from $25 to $100 per acre. Wild lands $5 to $25.

Quail, doves, and mocking birds abound, and rabbits are plentiful over the valley. Millions of ducks in season.

Among the leading farmers are : Brig. Whitmore, Nevada Land & Live Stock Co., H. A. Sparks, Bishop Jones and sons, D. J. Cox, S. A. Angel, Marshall Bros., Ute V. Perkins, Jos. F. Perkins, W. A. Perkins, Wm. Van Rensslaar, L. N. Shurtliff, J. M. Lytle, Crayton Johnson, M. D. Cooper, J. F. Cooper, Alvin C. Crosby, A. B. Redford, Wm. L. Batty, J. A. Swapp, and others.

SAINT THOMAS

At the junction of the Muddy and Virgin rivers St. Thomas lies at the foot of the rich Muddy valley. Garden, field and fruit crops grow luxuriantly. Here Sam Gentry ends his stage journey from the Moapa station, and another stage takes mail and passengers on 28 miles to Gold Butte Mining District. From Moapa to Logan is 12 miles, Logan to Overton 5 miles, Overton to St. Thomas 7 miles; St. Thomas to Bunkerville 35 miles; St Thomas to Grand Gulch mine 40 miles; roads rough, sandy or muddy.

Good railroad grade down the valley and out to the mines gives assurance of a railroad soon.

The great salt deposits near St. Thomas, gold and copper mines, rich agricultural lands and other resources will make an important business point at St. Thomas.

Among the prominent farmers are : Bishop J. M. Bunker, good general farmer; M. A Bunker, farmer and bee rancher; Harry Gentry, Postmaster, merchant, farmer, building brick residence; F. F. Gunn, merchandise, Fay Perkins, Manager; Wm. Francis Murphy, asparagus and general farming; M. W. Gibson, vineyard; E. H. Syphus, scientific gardener; M. W. Gibson and others.

GRAND GULCH MINES

Diversified farming, cattle, hogs, stock, pottery clay deposits, gold, copper, salt, mica, platinum and other minerals; Grand Gulch copper mines; Copper City, Gold Butte, and all the rich country east of Las Vegas will soon come in for detailed mention.

Las Vegas Age Newspaper
June 15, 2007

OVERTON

"A reader of the Age" who sent in some items this week is advised that correspondence cannot be published unless the name of the sender is signed to the same.

The Age is always glad to receive news items from any section of the county, but must insist on knowing who is responsible for the statements made.

Las Vegas Age Newspaper Ads
June 8, 15, 22 and 29, 1907

MOAPA COMMERCIAL CO.

General Merchandise

Wholesale and Retail

MINERS SUPPLIES A SPECIALTY

Branch Store Copper City, Nev.   Moapa, Nevada

MOAPA PRODUCE AND FORWARDING CO.   F. F. GUNN
Manager

SHIPPERS OF FRUITS AND PRODUCE
OF ALL KINDS

MINERS' SUPPLIES   Stores at Overton, St. Thomas and Gold Butte

WHITEHEAD BROTHERS

Carry a General Stock of Merchandise, including Miners' and Prospectors' Supplies, at
GOLD BUTTE AND OVERTON, NEVADA

FARM FOR SALE

In Muddy River Valley, near Logan P. O., Lincoln county, fine 80 acre Farm, all under barbed wire fence. Good water right with land. One of best Farms in Muddy River Valley; 31 acres in crop and 4 acres in Cantaloupes 17; acres in Alfalfa; 10 acres in Grain; flower garden, vineyard, young orchard, shade trees; teams, machinery and tools to run ranch. Large adobe house on farm. For particulars, address,   A. J. SPROLES,
To July 1   Moapa, Nevada

Las Vegas Age Newspaper
July 6, 1907

Death of Vegas Baby

Overton, July 1, 1907:—On June 25 little Genevieve, daughter of John A. and M. Virginia Lytle passed away at the family home in this place.

The little one had been ailing some time with whooping cough and on the morning of the 24th was taken with a spasm, and later with another, from which she did not recover.

She was a beautiful, loveable child, the first born in Clark's Las Vegas, nearly two years ago. The parents are heartbroken over the loss of their darling girl, and have the sympathy of a host of friends and relatives.

Las Vegas Age News[a[er
July 13, 1907

Moapa Produce Co.

The Moapa Produce and Forwarding Co., in which E. T. Maxwell recently secured one-half interest, will have headquarters for shipping and forwarding at Moapa with a general merchandise store at Overton, the metropolis of the Muddy Valley. The stores at St. Thomas and Gold Butte will be closed for the summer and the stock transferred to Overton. This fall it is their intention to build at Gold Butte, where the company owns building lots. A large warehouse will be built on the railroad at Moapa to accomodate the shipping and forwarding of the company. The company will handle all kinds of fruits and produce, live stock, etc. They have a large acreage of cantaloupes contracted for this season and shipping has already begun.

Las Vegas Age Newspaper
July 27, 1907

Uncle Bill Stewart! At Overton, July 17th, a daughter was born to Mrs. Sherman Thomas, sister of Mrs. W. J. Stewart. Mrs. Stewart is visiting her relatives in the valley.

E. T. Maxwell has been having considerable sport because he got credit for a crate of extra fine cantaloupes received by The Age, whereas the melons were sent by Geo. O. Baldwin of Moapa, former county commissioner. Up to date The Age does not know that Herr Maxwell can produce any cantaloupes equal to those grown by Mr. Baldwin. (?)

Las Vegas Age Newspaper
August 24, 1907

Oil Signs

On the Muddy river and on the lower Virgin, in Lincoln County are signs of oil. At a point near Logan claims have been located on oil bearing shale. On the lower Virgin near St Thomas rock impregnated with oil has been found.

Great petrified forests near Overton show that the country has not always been a desert. It is possible that coal and oil will yet be found in quantity on the Muddy and Virgin. Who will be the first to drill.

Fifty miles south of Moapa, across the Arizona line, Robert Dillon has just located 4000 acres of promising oil land for a party of Las Vegas gentlemen. Messrs Dillion and French returned from the section this week and bring encouraging reports of the indications there. Plans for development are being formulated.

MUDDY RIVER

Many Improvements Under Way In the Valley

Some talk of a new townsite scheme at Moapa, with ambition for a county seat.

G. E. McGilvary reports much building prospect for the Muddy river valley.

H. Gentry is planning to erect a new store building at St Thomas.

S. H. Wells will complete his new residence at Logan this fall.

Moapa Produce & Forwarding Company will put up a new store building or two in Muddy Valley.

A water contest is possible between farmers of the upper and lower Muddy river. The Muddy does not supply enough for all lands in the valley. Perhaps a system of reservoirs or artesian wells would solve the problem.

It is said the Clark's will build a railroad from Moapa down the Muddy Valley through Logan, Overton and St Thomas. Work will begin on completion of the Pioche branch. Such a line would be 25 miles long over an easy grade. It would not cost more than $12,000 per mile.

A few artesian wells in the Muddy Valley would increase the farm land area. Chances for artesian water on the Muddy are very good.

Muddy Valley may have the next oil strike, and chances are good on the lower Virgin near St Thomas.

24

Farm Notes

Farmer A. L. Murphy came to Vegas for Christmas.

W. F. Murphy raises the fine hogs at St. Thomas.

Chickens and turkeys come from the Overton farms.

W. H. Gann and Joe Perkins of the Muddy Valley furnish many good beef cattle for the Vegas market.

Only about a month and the birds will be singing spring songs in the blooming peach trees in Las Vegas.

John D. Pulsifer and son recently filed homestead with U. S. Commis- at Mesquite,

turkey that ing on was by Jacob Bauer, and was captured by E. T. Maxwell.

MUDDY RIVER

New Buildings and Improvments Below Moapa

Miss Era Conger of Muskeke is spending the week with Miss Nora Thomas.

Mr. Bert Thomas has been spending the holidays down at Overton attending the dances and enjoying a good time.

Salt Lake Hunters are spending a few days with us shooting quail. They speak very highly of the climate.

N. L. Benson, of Salt Lake is spending a few days with his brother Dr. S. L. Benson. Mr. Benson as well as the Dr. is a good "shot" and they are bagging the quail.

Mr. W. H. Gann is having some changes made in his house, G. E. McGilvary is doing the work.

Mr. Gann has gone to farming, he has about 100 acres in grain, 80 in barley and 20 in wheat.

W. H. Gann will have put in his house a Burton water system and will have some city luxuries.

John Thomas is planing to build a new house.

W. W. Perkins' large house is ready for the plasterers. Mr. Perkin's house is under the careful supervision of G. E. McGilvary.

COMMISSIONERS

Brief Summary Of Official Minutes

Commissioners met January 6th, 1907. Present, Jas. A. Nesbitt, chairman; Geo. T. Banovich, member; Chas. Lee Horsey, Dist. Attorney and Wm. E. Orr, Clerk.

Minutes of the December meeting read and approved.

Quarterly and monthly reports of the various county officers, read and approved. Salary and General County bills allowed as per register claim book.

The claim of W. L. Aplin for the sum of $63.00 was ordered laid over.

The following claims for labor performed on and supplies furnished the temporary hospital at at Las Vegas were laid over for further investigation, Paul Buol, $8.00, McPherson & Buol, $16.50, J. A. Rhoads, $36.75, Ed Von Tobel Lumber Co. $81.25.

The district attorney objected to the allowance of all bills incured by the Board of Fire Commissioners of Caliente upon the ground that said Board is without any legal authority whatever to incur any indebtedness but on the contrary are merely vested with an advisary authority to reccommend to the County Commissioners the purchase of what is necessary for a proper fire system in the town of Caliente.

The Claim of Geo. A. Bell for the sum of $4.00 was ordered laid over.

One hundred dollars was appropriated for completing the repairing of the lane leading from Bullionville to Panaca.

It was ordered that A. V. Lee and W. H. Edwards of Panaca, J. N. Holiinge, of Eagle Valley, J. I. Earl of Bunkerville, John Bunker of Overton, W. H. Gann of St. Joe, Geo. C. Baldwin of Moapa, W. T. Stewart and A. W. Geer of Pahranagat Valley and W. J. Stewart of Las Vegas, be appointed as delegates from Lincoln County, Nevada, to the Trans Missouri Dry Farming Congress to be held in Salt Lake City, Utah, January 23, 24, 25, 26 and 27th, 1908.

The county advertising for the year 1908 was awarded to Caliente Lode-Express and the county job printing contract to Pioche Record, the only bidder. [The Age bids were not received in time to be considered—Ed.]

Chairman of the board was authorized to extend lease for ground occupied by branch county jail at Caliente.

A petition from Caliente requested the lease of the Caliente fire system to individuals. Laid over.

An application was received from Las Vegas asking for the enactment of additional ordinances for the government of said town, said application was ordered laid over until such time as Commissioner Hawkins be present to act upon same.

The Sheriff was authorized to purchase and have installed an additional cage for the branch County Jail at Caliente.

It was ordered that the liquor license issued to J. O. McIntosh for a liquor business in the Meadow Valley Wash near the construction work be revoked.

OVERTON

Industrial and Personal News of Muddy Valley

[Special Correspondence]

Fine weather still prevails in the valley, farmers have begun tilling the soil and springtime is nearing. Trees are budding and fruit trees will soon be in bloom. Many improvements are being made in town as well as in the valley; new buildings being erected and much land now being put under cultivation.

Mr. White and family of Escalante, Utah, who have been visiting friends and relatives, left for their home recently.

W. W. Perkins' two-story building on his farm is nearing completion.

W. L. Jones' brick house is now being erected with Mr. Geo. Syphus as mason and Mr. McGilvary carpenter.

Joe F. Perkins and Frank Culburtson are having machinery hauled on their oil fields and will begin boring soon.

Oil excitement is now on and citizens of the valley are in and around the side hills locating lands.

Many fruit trees are being set out. Over a thousand have already been planted and others expect to put in orchards and vineyards soon.

Hon. Thomas Judd was in town a few days ago, doing business.

The citizens of the Valley met in the Overton school house on the 10th for the purpose of electing a new president and board of directors for the Muddy Valley Irrigation Co. The old board was retained with the exception of H. H. Church, who resigned. W. C. Bowman was elected in his stead. Hon. Levi Syphus was retained as president of the company.

Send in your subscription to The Age. We are trying to make the paper of interest to you and a credit to central and southern Lincoln county, and need your help. Only $2.00 a year.

28

MUDDY RIVER OIL

Standard Company Sends Drilling Tools to New Field

Reliable information reaches The Age that the Standard Oil Company is behind the scheme to drill for oil in the Muddy River Valley. Drilling apparatus has already arrived at Moapa and will be sent down the river 15 miles, between Logan and Overton.

Indications of oil have long been noted in the Muddy Valley. The great salt deposits, gypsum, oil shale and the fossils found near Logan and Overton are the best indications of oil.

Many claims have been staked on the Muddy and Virgin rivers, and active drilling will bring Lincoln county to the front as a new and important oil field Moapa on the Salt Lake, is the nearest point by rail—only 15 miles away from the oil fields.

OVERTON

Muddy River, Oil and Other Industries

[Special Correspondence]

We are having nice showers at present which makes the hearts of the farmers and stock raisers rejoice. It has rained steadily for the past 36 hours and still continues.

W. A. Whitehead made a trip recently to Gold Butte, Nev. Prospectors are still in that locality searching for gold, but at present everything is dull there. A boom in the future for this section is anticipated.

B. F. Bonelli recently returned from a trip to Kingman, Searchlight and other towns and mining camps in the south. He reports business and mines as very lively in that part of the country.

A number of men and boys left town to work oil claims in the upper valley a few days ago, under the management of J. F. Perkins and Frank Culbertson.

Owing to the breaking of an axle on the engine in moving it from Moapa to the oil grounds, work will be postponed for a few days until the same can be sent east and repaired, when boring will be resumed.

A grand masquerade ball will be given in Lytle Hall on the 22nd of Feb. Also a Leap Year party on the 14th.

Mr. Jim Heines, of Idaho, who with his family is here for his health, is improving rapidly.

J. A. Lytle has been ill for the past two weeks and no better at this writing.

Mr. Mitchell and friends from Salt Lake City are making the air ring with shots while here hunting on the Moapa river and through our wonderful valley for duck, quail, rabbit, etc, which are plentiful, making great sport for the hunters.

Mr. Lee of Moapa has taken position as clerk in F. F. Gunn's store, with Alma Shurtliff as assistant.

Fields of grain are now beginning to look very green. Vegetables, such as radishes, turnips, lettuce, have been shipped all winter, and still an abundance in the gardens.

School has again commenced after the return of teachers from county examination.

Miss Virginia Cox has gone to Beaver, Utah, to attend school.

RAILROAD NEWS

About 200 men are out on strike from Beatty to Mina on the L. V. & T., T. & T. and Bullfrog Goldfield and Tonopah railroads. Most of them are section hands who want $4 per day. Some are pumping station men and freight handlers, and telegraph operators in Goldfield have struck in sympathy. Sheriff Owens has a large force of deputies watching the situation.

Eastern storms and snows are driving tourists west. Passenger traffic managers of the Santa Fe, Salt Lake and Southern Pacific roads are unanimous in their opinion that the rush of 1908 is the largest in the history of tourist travel on the Pacific coast.

A railroad 25 miles long down the Muddy river from Moapa, via Logan and Overton to St Thomas, will be built from the Salt Lake, if the drillers strike oil near Overton. An Oil City would make a market for Muddy Valley farm produce.

During July, August and September 1340 persons were killed on railroads in the United States and 21,724 injured.

The freight rates charged in Nevada are over three times as high as those charged by the Southern Pacific road on other portions of its lines, according to the brief of Chairman Bartine, of the Nevada railroad commission, who is just now completing his final brief in the case to be filed in the United States court.

The suit for taxes which has been pending in the courts for some time against the Tonopah and Goldfield railroad, brought by Esmeralda county, has been adjusted. By the adjustment the railroad will pay into the coffers of Esmeralda county about $14,000.

The Reno Gazette says 450 men have been laid off at the railroad shops at Sparks.

Richard R. Coleman has filed suit to collect from the Tonopah & Tidewater Railroad company money for the grading along the new route in San Bernardino and Inyo counties, sums totaling over $26,000. Character and amount of work done caused the disagreement.

About 8000 men have been thrown out of employment on the Harriman railroads. The Salt Lake and Reno machine shops have closed down for the present, because of the slump in railroad business.

LIABILITY BILL

The Knox bill pending in Congress makes all railroads engaged in interstate commerce liable to their employes for injury incurred in service, and to their heirs in the event of a fatal accident. The fellow servant doctrine is overturned by the Knox bill and the rule of contributory negligence is greatly modified. Under its term the mere fact that an employe is injured or killed through the negligence of a fellow employe does not relieve the employer from responsibility. Nor does contributory negligence bar an injured employe from claiming damages. It merely lessens the amount of damage in proportion to the percentage of negligence contributed.

TROUBLE FOR RAILROADS

Attorney General Bonaparte directed that a bill in equity be filed to set aside the control of the Union Pacific Railway company and its subsidiary corporations of the Southern Pacific and the San Pedro, Los Angeles & Salt Lake roads; also to have declared illegal the ownership by the Union Pacific of the Oregon Short Line of stock in the Santa Fe, the Great Northern and Northern Pacific, all of said lines being competitors of the Union Pacific. Harriman and Clark are the big fellows principally interested.

L. V. & T. BUSINESS

The annual statement of the Las Vegas & Tonopah road for the year 1907 shows that corporation to be in a very healthy condition, the receipts being $600,031.41, and expenses, including taxes and interest, $468,162.46, leaving a net balance of $131,868.95. And the Goldfield end of the line was not completed till late in the fall.

OVERTON

Overton, Nevada, Feb 11 — Everybody is putting in potatoes, peas, beets, carrots, radishes and other seeds All kinds of grain looks nice and green, and people are still sowing grain and lucern seed A great many fruit trees of all kinds are being put out

Hon. Levi Syphus, our legislator, returned last week from Carson City, where a special session of the legislature had been called by Governor Sparks for the purpose of passing a law establishing a state police force for the protection of life and property and to quell riots

W. L Batty is superintending the building of a dam in Muddy river and taking out a canal to water the new townsite and farm lands about half-way between here and St. Thomas, under the direction of Hon Thos Judd, for the Nevada Land & Live Stock Co,

S R and W. A. Whitehead are running a large trading house and furnish wagons and sell all kinds of machinery for the farmers, and all kinds of merchandise for the miners and general public, and a dollar's worth of good for every dollar they receive.

The stork has been around this way recently and left a boy at Mr. and Mrs Edwin Huntsman's, their first, also a boy at J W. Huntsman's, and a girl at George E Perkins'. All doing well.

We need a good blacksmith here in Overton, one who can run his shop as well as work at farm and gardening, as the shop alone would not occupy all his time.

Our district schools are running very successfully with H B Redford as principal and Miss Effie Whitehead in charge of the primary department.

W. L Jones' new brick house was completed to the square on the 4th inst. George Syphus of Panaca was the stone and brick mason.

F F Gunn of Moapa has been running a store here since early last summer, but was closed by the sheriff a few days ago.

W W. Perkins of Logan has recently built him a two story eight-room frame house, now about ready to move into

W. W McDonald, a new-comer last fall, commenced a large lumber residence on the 6th inst.

Angell Bros. have been shipping lettuce, onions and other garden truck for some time

Recently we have had an unusual amount of rain which has wet up the country good.

Last, but not least! Recently a railroad company was organized in Salt Lake City, capitalized at $600,000, and have to commence work within sixty days or loose the right of way from Moapa to St. Thomas, twenty-five miles, and a few days ago some of their men were down looking over the route and say the road will be completed so as to ship this year's crop of cantaloupes We only hope it will be so

OVERTON

Almond Blossoms Are Blooming Along the Rio Muddy

(Special Correspondence)

Overton, Nevada, February 12, 1908. —Rain still continues in this vicinity and cold north winds blow continually off from the snowy peaks near by.

Dr. Benson has returned from a trip through Goldfield and northern settlements in Nevada.

Almond blossoms are beginning to put in their appearance and shade trees are leafing out; garden vegetables are plentiful, peas are in bloom and cabbage heading out on the farm of S. A. Angel and sons.

Several cases of measles are reported in our midst and throughout the valley, but all doing nicely so far.

Numerous cases of lagrippe are going around among the people which seem hard to cure.

McDonald and son have their new frame residence nearing completion on Popular Grove street.

Rev. Dr. Bain of Las Vegas is seen in our valley again the past few days.

Gentlemen of Salt Lake owning land here in the valley are at present looking over the same and anticipate a bright future here.

It is said the salt mines four miles below St Thomas, on the Virgin River are extensive enough to pay a railroad down through the valley to say nothing of the many thousands of canteloupes and large quantities of vegetables and fruit raised here.

OVERTON

Overton, Nevada, Feb 19th — The Experiment farm near Logan in this valley is being improved and put in good shape for experimental work. A large numbes of grape and other fruit cuttings will be put out The grape roots and fruit trees are being brought from California Mr. Arney has charge of the farm. Sinford A. Angell, by order of the board of directors of the Muddy Valley Irrigation company, is employing a number of men and teams making new canals and ditches for the purpose of consolidating the water so that it can be more easily controlled and save a great amount of waste. and not have so many tapping the main canal and creek.

Bert Chisholm with a Mr. Wallace a mining expert, arrived here a few days ago from Cripple Creek, Colorado John A Lytle took them down to the Colorado river between Bonelli's ferry at Rioville and Temple Bar to look at some prospects th[?] were visited by Mr. Chalmer a year ago If considered worth developing, business will start up as there is plenty of capital back of

35

them.

John A. Swapp and son returned from Copper Mountain mines with ore that runs over 30 per cent copper, 60 ounces silver, and $5 in gold They expect to continue mining and hauling the ore President White of Beaver City, Utah, owns a majority of the stock of the company.

We have one case of measles and others exposed, but hope they will not spread over the town Quite a few have had colds, or grip as some call it Cold wave from the north the past few days

James Hymas, wife and two sons of Liberty, Bear Lake county, Idaho, who have been here for some time in quest of health left for Los Angeles, California, Monday to try that climate awhile.

C. M. Peterson is running the stage line and carrying the mail from Moapa to St. Thomas three times a week.

John M. Lytle owns the dance hall and superintends the dances once or twice a month on Friday evenings

H Gentry and son are running three six-horse teams hauling ore from Grand Gulch to Moapa at $18 per ton.

Mr. McGillivary, a native of Georgia, has the carpenter job on W L Jones' new brick house.

Bishop John M. Bunker is running the mail line from St. Thomas to Gold Butte twice a week.

Brig Whitmore is out at his mine again after ore, which assays very good.

OVERTON

[Special Correspondence]

Overton, Nev., Feb. 25, 1908—Beautiful spring weather prevails after so much rain. The air is full of fragrance of perfume from the many blossom's and opening buds of spring time.

Owing to so much sickness in town and contagious deseases, both schools closed Friday and will not reopen again until sickness ceases.

The two children of Mrs. Pearl Turnbaugh have been very sick with measels.

Big land buyers arrive in town daily and continue busy buying land. Some of the old settlers have been offered $100 per acre for their land, but advice is to hold on to your land as the many who come and visit the valley report 'it just in its infancy and the boom very soon will commence.

Many families from the north and numerous places are moving in and locating here.

Mrs. C. M. Turnbaugh of Panaca, Nev., arrived here late last evening, being sent for on account of the serious illness of her grand children.

The valley has been called to mourn the death of Mrs. W. C. Bowman which occured yesterday. Deceased was well known and thought of in this county. She leaves a husband and eight children to mourn her death as well as numerous relatives and friends.

Mining men from Cripple Creek, Col. are now in town coming and going to and from the Colorado River 25 miles below here where they are doing work along the river.

B. Whitmore & Co. are working continously on the mining claims near Gold Butte and may put on more men in the near future as valuable rock has been found in great quantities.

S. A. Angell, road and water supervisor, is busy with a force of men working ditches and roads and putting them in good condition.

OVERTON

Overton, Nevada, March 5 —We have had another fine rain, it commenced on the evening of the 3rd and rained all night and until 2 p m. the next day, the finest rain for the the time of year for a long time Our creek has had flood water in it for some time and so very muddy that a good many people haul water from the spring a mile and a half away, for house use.

Bert Choloner and Mr. Wallace, who went onto the Colorado river some time ago to look over old prospects, have returned to Cripple Creek, Colorado, not finding what they expected and are quite disappointed.

Frank Culberton has men working assessments on his oil claims in the hills between Logan in the valley and the lower end of the upper valley.

The county assessor, J. H. Roeder, has appointed T. J. Jones, his deputy for Logan, Overton, St, Thomas and Gold Butte, for this year.

A. Angell, the superintendent of

water ditches, to put in head gates at the head of all the ditches coming out of the main canal and creek.

John S Lytle has a return of the fever that he was afflicted with some time ago and has gone to Barclay, Clover Valley, for awhile.

Whitehead, Bros. are receiving new supplies of goods every few days, so keep a good stock on hand continuously.

The weather has turned off very fine since the storm, everything looks fine and flourishing

The board of the Muddy Valley Irrigation company has ordered S,

Measles are thinning out so that school has started again.

pany sent a plasterer down from Salt Lake City who has just completed the work on their farm house.

MOAPA

Moapa, Nevada, March 7.— Spring is here with us. Trees are leafing out and everything looks beautiful. The Moapa Improvement company is shipping lettuce and asparagus Cantaloupe planting is in full blast.

Mrs. William C. Bowman of Logan died very suddenly a week ago last Monday. In her death the community loses one of its best members. She was an intelligent, hospitable, and progressive woman who always had a good word for every one. She leaves seven children, the oldest about eighteen years of age and the youngest between two and three years of ago Brother Bowman has now gone to Toquerville, Utah, for his mother, Mrs. Dodge, who will come and live with him.

The oil-drilling machine is still waiting for repairs, but are expecting them every day. It is the intention of the company owning it to commence work as soon as possible and they expect to go down between 2,000 and 3,000 feet.

The Moapa Improvement com-

OVERTON

Overton, Nevada, March 14 — The Key West company has commenced work on its mines, and expect to build a smelter on the Virgin river near the Badger bench crossing. The company will make a road over the mesa to Logan to ship material from and bullion to Moapa, the nearest railroad point.

The Grand Gulch teams are hauling copper ore from the mine to the railroad at Moapa right along, even 'tho copper is down to 12¾ cents

We learn that Miss Nora Thomas of Logan has been very sick with measles but is improving now.

Brig Whitmore is putting in a carload of ore at Moapa before going back to his mine.

We see notices in town that there is to be a grand ball in the hotel at Moapa tonight.

The irrigated land company's agent is around trying to buy a lot more land.

W. W. Macdonald has his new lumber house about ready to move into.

School has started up again, the measles having cleared out.

Very warm and good growing weather now.

There was a nice dance here last night.

39

MUDDY VALLEY

Overton Correspondent Complain of Public Schools

The Age has received an anonymous communication from Overton complaining of the inefficiency of school teachers in that section and charging that the trustees hire their relatives or friends regardless of qualifications. The Age must refuse to publish such complaints without knowing the writer's name, so that we may judge of his responsibility. We would suggest, however, that if the patrons of the schools have any just complaint at the manner in which they are conducted, the better way would be to bring the matter to the attention of the district superintendent of schools, Gilbert C. Ross, Tonopah, Nevada, who will no doubt be found willing to make an investigation.

40

[Special Correspondence]

Overton, March 23—Beautiful weather prevails altho the north wind blowing has been a little cold for the past few days.

Garden vegetables are plentiful in our midst such as lettuce, onions, radishes asparagus, cabbage, etc.

Peas will soon be ready for table use. Turnips and asparagus going to waste for the want of a market.

Water has been cut out of the town ditch for the purpose of moving the same and cleaning it.

Brig Whitmore and his men returned from their mine a few days ago. They just shipped a car of ore.

Reports are that Fremont Cobb will soon put on a force of men at Gold Butte to work his mining claims.

Miss Virginia Cox returned home from Beaver, Utah where she has been studying music the past three months.

Brig Whitmore has gone to Salt Lake City on important business.

Freighters still come and go from the Grand Gulch mines with loads of ore.

Land buyers are coming in daily buying up land and paying good money for the same.

Part of our townsmen are at the upper Muddy Valley with teams plowing up the soil recently purchased by the Moapa Land and Water Company.

Mr. W. Scott and wife of Moapa are visiting in the town, enjoying fresh vegetables and game.

Miss Tucker of Moapa was in attendance at the grand ball given Friday evening.

Born to Mr. and Mrs. Crayton Johnson on the 15th inst. a son. Father well and happy, mother and babe progressing nicely.

41

OVERTON

Overton, Nevada, April 8 —T J. Jones received word on the 6th inst of the death of his son-in law, George W Lee, Jr, at Morelos, Mexico, after being sick ten days

The stork has been flying around the valley again and has left a baby-boy at the home of W. W. Perkins of Logan, also a baby-boy at the home of Crayton Johnson of this place Mothers and babies getting along nicely.

We had an unusually heavy wind last Monday night which blew down a large cottonwood tree opposite the postoffice. We had rain yesterday and last night

Overton people have been clean-ing their main ditch the past ten days and are now watering their field crops, fruit and garden

The experiment farm people are rushing up their cement block house, George Syphus of Panaca being the boss mason

Lucern will soon be in bloom,

42

and barley has been headed out for the past two weeks

Honorable Thomas Judd of La Verkin was here on business one day last week.

O M. Peterson, our mail driver, has gone to Salt Lake city to attend conference

Mrs Harry Gentry of St Thomas has been very sick the past four or five days.

Whitehead Bros have just received a new stock of goods

Three babies were blessed last Sunday at fast meeting.

There will be a dance in the Lytle hall on Friday night

OVERTON

Railroad Branch Through Farming Oil and Mineral Lands.

[Special Correspondence]

Altho the weather is warm our schools still convene. Easter day was celebrated by a jolly crowd of scholars and teachers going for long walk over the flower covered hills, and dining at 12 o'clock for lunch in a huge cave west of town.

Examinations now commence and will be held for the next three weeks, which closes the term of our school until fall.

Work on the oil claims will not commence again until fall, owing to the breaking of machinery, but at the close of the warm season the hills will again be covered with busy oil seekers. Some are yet locating and keeping up their assessment work. This fall business will be revived and development rushed, for the valley certainly contains vast fields of oil.

Condition of crops fine; alfalfa is now ready to cut, green peas, radishes, onions, asparagus, cabbage and numerous other kinds of vegetables are being shipped out daily. Irish potatoes will be ready to eat by May 1st.

Apricots will ripen about the 15th of May and cantaloupes will be ready for market in June. We find market everywhere for the early vegetables, fine fruits and luscious cantaloupes and watermelons which our little valley produces.

Anyone desiring a nice little home where they can raise all the above named during any month in the year, should come to the Muddy Valley. Plenty of water, numerous shade trees to lounge under. During summer days; beautiful, cool evenings. During summer nights a breeze can always be felt to refresh the soul of the laborer.

Fine large hall where amusements are held.

Nowhere to compare with the valley for convenience in any way; anyone can make a good living and not have to work hard because of the rich soil and beautiful climate. Plenty of good feed for cattle.

A few of our noted stock men are Joe F. Perkins, W. Garnn, Whitmore brothers. The drive comences next month, when the stock raisers will all be on the rush to and fro looking over and for their cattle, which look fine.

Rumors are afloat concerning a branch railroad down our beautiful little valley. Report says work will begin in six months, grading a branch line through to Chloride, Arizona. Farm produce, cattle, copper and other ores, mountains of salt on the Virgin, acres of oil land to be developed and numerous other industries would pay a branch line.

The beautiful vineyards of seedless raisins, muscatels etc. Figs and all kinds of fine fruits, and orange trees have been put out this spring, and in the course of a few years we expect to rival California oranges.

As the stranger rides through our valley at the present date and day beautiful gardens of roses greets the eye on every side, as well as other beautiful flowers.

The handsome cement block house on the experiment farm is nearing completion.

B. Whitmore recently purchased the store owned by F. F. Gunn, and has opened the doors for business.

A. L. Jones and J. F. Cooper recently left on a trip through Idaho.

L. Shurtliff and wife just returned from a visit to Salt Lake City and other northern parts.

M. W. Gibson and wife have gone to Los Angeles to greet the fleet when it arrives.

OVERTON

Overton, Nevada, April 24 — Mrs Josephine Clark of Provo, Utah, with her four little girls arrived in Moapa the 22nd inst to visit her father, T J Jones, and other relatives at this place Mrs Clark went away a young girl from this place nine years ago and was left a widow by her husband being killed by a log rolling over him in the pine forest near LaGrande, Oregon, a year ago last January Mrs Clark and two of her sisters have been left widows within the past few years

The experiment farm house of cement blocks is up with roof on Several acres of barley on this farm will be ready for harvest inside of ten days. Some are cutting their first crop of lucern We will have a good crop of all kinds of fruit

J. S Swapp and A L F McDermott have gone on a prospecting tour into the Copper Mountain country and over into Utah along the Colorado river and may go into the Green river country before returning

Joseph H Jones of Bunkerville, son of T. J Jones of this place, was taken by his father to Moapa on the 22nd inst where he took the train for Salt Lake city on his way to the Southern States mission field

We are having fine growing weather Asparagus and peas are being shipped to Salt Lake city in great abundance Lettuce, radishes, onions, turnips, etc, are also being shipped every day

The stock and store of F F nn, whose business at this place was closed up some time since by his creditors, was bought out and opened up by Brig Whitmore a few days ago

W C Bowman of Logan, this county, has bought out the Commercial Company's store at Moapa and took possession on the 22nd inst

45

OVERTON

Overton, Nevada, April 29 —The talk here is that Senator Clark said a few days ago in Salt Lake city that he would move the station now at Moapa up to the Y this fall and start a branch road down through the valley to St Thomas

Andrew L Johnson has returned from Carey, Idaho, where he went two weeks ago today. While in Idaho he visited his sister Ella at Blackfoot He thinks Idaho is a fine country but quite cold there now.

Lucern cutting is on in earnest here now. There is about two wagon loads of vegetables shipped out of the valley every day now. It is getting very warm so we know summer is nigh.

Brig Whitmore has gone to Salt Lake city on business He has Vernon Kenney as clerk in the store he recently bought here, formerly run by F. F. Gunn, now of Moapa

The schools will be out on the first of May. The teachers, Miss Effie Whitehead of St George, and H B Redford of Idaho, will no doubt leave for their homes

S L F. McDermott returned today from Copper mountain He had been there to examine the copper mine and report for an eastern company.

J S. Swapp and a Mr Noble have gone on to the Colorado river above Lees Ferry to examine some mining property.

We expect several men here soon to buy land and homes as this country is coming to the front very fast

OVERTON

Sentiment strongly favors a standard guage railroad in preference to narrow guage.

The Nevada Land & Live Stock Company will lay out a new town called Kaolin, near the clay deposits.

E. Kinney last week became the proud father of a new daughter. He now smiles at all customers at Whitmore's store.

Haying began about May 1st. Alfalfa will yield five or six crops this season.

School will soon close at Overton, and an election for two new directors will be held the latter part of May. J. A. Lytle, W. L. Jones and S. R. Whitehead are the present directors. Terms of the two latter expire.

Overton school census shows 69 pupils between the ages of six and 18 years. Two teachers have been employed during the past term.

Messrs. Whitmore and Perkins are rounding up and branding their cattle on the lower river.

Whitehead Bros. and Brig Whitmore conduct general stores at Overton, and appear to be doing good business.

Overton people are building a big dam and making a deep cut west of town to change the flow of the wash that floods the town occasionally.

U. V. Perkins, State Water Commissioner for Muddy Valley, is busy remodeling the irrigation ditch system to economize on water. He says the summer flow at Overton is about 40 cubic feet per second.

Will Jones recently finished one of neatest brick residences in the valley. He has a bearing orchard, peaches, apricots, pears, grapes and some orange trees.

Brig Whitmore's mine threatens to make him a copper King.

Road Supervisor S. A. Angel understands early gardening. He had Irish potatoes in market May 1st.

W. W. McDonald has finished a neat residence on his 200 acre farm. Such enterprising settlers are welcome.

47

VALLEY NEWS

Live Industrial, Agricultural and Personal Items

School has closed at Moapa for the summer.

Stages leave Moapa every Monday, Wednesday and Friday for St Thomas and Bunkerville.

The Age will contain a series of articles showing the resources of the Muddy and Virgin River Valleys. Subscribe for The Age.

Friends are urging merchant W. C. Bowman to be a candidate for County Commissioner from the Muddy Valley on the Republican ticket. He would poll a strong vote.

H. H. Church and others had the first crop of alfalfa cut before May 1st. Four more cuttings—five in all—will be made this season, aggregating from seven to eight tons to the acre. This alfalfa is worth about $7 to $8 in the stack at Logan, 12 miles from the railroad.

Peaches, apricots and figs will be on the market from Muddy Valley by June 15th, about as early as they come from California.

J. H. Burtner, district freight and passenger agent for the Salt Lake, has been in the Moapa Valley, looking over the harvest that shall yield a harvest to the railroad he represents.

C. M. Peterson runs the stage from Moapa down the Muddy Valley to St Thomas every Monday, Wednesday and Friday and returns on alternate days. Henry Leavitt runs the stage from Moapa to Bunkerville on the same days.

Quail are very numerous in Muddy River Valley and farmers complain that they destroy crops.

Freight and express rates discriminate against the farmers of the Muddy river valley and favor outsiders. Car lots cost as much from Moapa to Salt Lake as from Los Angeles to Salt Lake. Express rates are equally unfair. Nevada's railroad commission should get busy.

In winter the Muddy river flows 5,250 inches of water and in summer about 4,500 inches. Evaporation and rainfall accounts for the difference. At the great springs where the river heads, the water temperature is 90 degrees.

Old County Commissioner Baldwin, on the Upper Muddy, is a progressive farmer and has a lovely place near the big springs. He says there is more money in farming than in politics.

Brig Whitmore of Overton says cattle must disappear from the Muddy Valley because the lands are wanted for small farms and gardens; that the range is a thing of the past. Hogs can be raised profitably.

Good school facilities in the valley speak well for the Muddy.

Poultry does well in the valley and home eggs should supply the county.

The big land companies west of Moapa on the upper Moapa valley are making great improvements. They are breaking ground and developing water, ditching, planting trees and harvesting crops. In this section there is something doing every month in the year, and no bad weather to interfere. In the fall they plant garden crops and market them in February and March.

Las Vegas Age Newspaper
May 16, 1908

MOAPA VALLEY

Muddy river farmers will be interested in the report that the first ripe cantaloupes were marketed in Imperial valley May 8th.

Some old adobe houses, built by the Mormons 40 to 50 years ago, are still comfortable abodes, at St Thomas, Overton and Logan.

Enough onions are grown in the Muddy River Valley to perfume the breath of every girl in the United States. Farmers are now experimenting to produce the odorless variety.

OVERTON

Overton, Nevada, May 18 —We have had some very cold, backward weather lately and considerable wind. The first crop of alfalfa is cut and stacked and harvesting is in full swing. People are shipping in cantaloupe and tomato crates. New potatoes and peas are plentiful on the market, orange trees set out this spring are growing fine and some are in bloom, tomatoes and cantaloupes are setting on the vines. A recent frosty spell killed some of our peaches, apricots and plums.

Alma Leavitt of Bunkerville is driving one of Harry Gentry's ore teams hauling ore from Grand Gulch. There are now four six-horse teams hauling ore. Cobb brothers are now working their copper mine at Gold Butte.

The stork came around recently and left a son at the home of Fay Perkins, their first, and another boy at the home of Ute V Perkins. All doing nicely.

M. W. Gibson and wife returned a few days ago from San Pedro, California, where they had been to see Uncle Sam's big warships.

Mr Mooney and son of Salem, Utah, were in the valley a few days ago and bought 47 acres of land at $50 the acre.

Alfonzo Huntsman is putting up a lumber house in view of caging his bird soon.

W. W. McDonald leaves tomorrow on a business trip to Salt Lake city.

Mrs Iva Leavitt of Bunkerville is visiting relatives in this valley.

50

OVERTON

Lonzo Huntsman has a new cottage 28x30, at Overton.

Andrew Jones recently returned from Idaho to the farm and the g—arden he left behind him. He couldn't stay 'way off in Idaho.

Mr. A. M. Fleming is a new settler, who mined in Eldorado Canyon 15 years ago. He finds more gold on the farm than in the mines.

Overton, Nevada, May 13th., 1908. Our schools closed Friday with an entertainment in the afternoon in which parents and scholars were all present; a dance was given in the evening by the teachers.

The Overton Primary association will give an entertainment on June 1st., in honor of the Prophet, Brigham Young. A grand time is anticipated by all.

T. J. Jones left for Bunkerville, Nevada today. He will bring back with him his daughter Mr. D. Clark who has been visiting there.

The Overton Primary association will give an entertainment on June 1st., in honor of the Prophet, Brigham Young. A grand time is anticipated by all.

T. J. Jones left for Bunkerville, Nevada today. He will bring back with him his daughter Mr. D. Clark who has been visiting there.

The Ward Relief Society Ladies convened last Thursday at the residence of the President, Mrs. D. Coper. Fancy work and sewing was indulged in after a lecture on " What it takes to Constitute a Home" by Mrs. W. L. Jones.

Madame Powers of Moapa will arrive in town tomorrow with a new lot of ladies spring and summer hats to sell.

Land is being disposed of quite rapidly in the valley, new parties are coming daily to invest in land and property in the valley.

Meeting will convene in the Overton school house with Joseph Atkin and Harmon Hofen as speakers.

Hyrum B. Redford, pricipal teacher of our school left for his home in Idaho on Saturday's Stage.

Brig Whitmore s disposing of the greater portion of his land in and around town.

Broyant Whitmore left for Sunnyside, Utah to be gone for an indefinite period.

51

OVERTON

Overton, Nevada, May 27.—You can see every man busy making crates. It certainly looks like there would be a great many cantaloupes leave Overton this year for northern markets

Mrs Powers came down from Moapa bringing a supply of ladies' and children's trimmed hats, which she found ready sale for. Although we have two up to date stores they do not carry any millinary goods.

Miss Sibyl Whitmore and Miss Sadie Perkins entertained about twenty-five guests at an oyster supper Monday evening. All has a lovely time

Miss Virginia Cox has been quite ill the past week. At this writing we are pleased to say, she is on the improve

Mrs Loretta Felt was down from Moapa a few days. While here she was the guest of Mrs. Whitmore

Mrs Whitmore and son, Raxton, made a flying trip to Moapa Sunday on business

Mrs Anna Cox is spending a few days here with her sister, Mrs Will Batty.

We are having an unusually windy spring, wind, wind all the time

Will Jones and wife took a flying trip to Bunkerville this week.

J W. Grace and Sam Whitmore came in on today's stage from Salt Lake city. They are here looking after the interests of their mines at Copper city

There is any amount of new potatoes in the valley now, also every other kind of garden truck one could wish for, including cucumbers

Our fruit crops will be excellent this year, apricots are now commencing to ripen, and there will be an immence crop of almonds

Mr. and Mrs Mose Gibson just returned from California points, where they went to view Uncle Sam's battleships

The little child of Mr. and Mrs Fleming is very, very ill.

52

LOGAN

Cantaloupes are looking fine, and fruits are ripening.

Mr. John Thomas and Dr. Benson will soon have ripe tomatoes in market.

Supt. Chas. Arney of the State Farm has moved into part of the new building. Under supervision of G. E. McGilvary the building is being rushed to completion. Wm. Marschall of Vegas is doing the plastering.

Miss Era Conger entertained friends at the residence of Mrs. O. G. Church. St. Thomas and Overton were represented, and all had a good time.

Recitals were given by Miss Conger and Mr. R. A. Swank. Miss Anna Syphus rendered a pretty solo. Mr. Bert Thomas parodied Shade of the Old Apple Tree. Mr. Harry Gentry sang the Whip-Poor-Will. Miss Cox and Miss Maud McDonald rendered some pretty organ music. Mr. G. E. McGilvary rendered catchy airs on his graphophone. Bert Thomas and Clif. Whitmore gave an acrobatic contest. Dave Conger was the jolly good fellow from everywhere.

53

OVERTON

A primary meeting was called for the purpose of electing trustees. Two candidates were put up for each vacancy. Ute V. Perkins and S. R. Whitehead were selected to run for the office of long term and W. W. MacDonald and Mrs. Isabel Stauffer for short term.

School election convened in the Overton school house on the 25th. Election board consisted of Fay Perkins, James Huntsman, J. A. Lytle and Vern Kinney. Polls were open from 10 o'clock a. m. until four p. m.. W. W. McDonald was elected over Isabel Stauffer for school trustee, short term, by four votes. U. V. Perkins was elected over S. R. Whitehead for long term by one vote. J. A. Lytle was held over.

The Mutual Improvement Association will close meetings with a grand program and Ice Cream refreshments on June 4th. Meetings will again convene in the fall, with Improvement still our motto.

Alvin C. Crosby has an extensive patch of green string beans, looking thrifty and will be ready for market soon.

The large canal under construction below the town is now being worked by about eight men under supervision of W. L. Batty. The purpose of the canal is to carry water over the new townsite between Overton and St Thomas, which will be called Kaolin.

Hill Bros. were in town last week looking over land, with purpose of buying. W. W. MacDonald made their visit a pleasant one by driving them through the beautiful Valley and making them comfortable at his new dwelling house.

Brig. Whitmore will start his ice cream stand and soda fountain going, on Friday.

Whitehead Bros. have a nice display of strawberries, cherries, bannanas, and oranges in stock this week.

An ice cream party will be given Wednesday evening at the home of Mrs. O. G. Church by the Misses Era Conger and Nora Thomas.

Ore teams are passing daily, hauling much ore from Grand Gulch to Moapa.

U. V. Perkins, water and Irrigation commissioner is busy putting in flumes and arranging the water in order to supply the farmers economically.

Mrs. I. Stauffer has shown what a woman can do on a farm. She has no superior in bee culture and puts up a fine quality of honey for the market in cans of any size.

Pottery Clay

On the west side of the Muddy river valley, midway between Overton and St. Thomas, is a wonderful deposit of kaolin or fine pottery clay, capable of making china.

It is white as chalk—in fact much resembles chalk. Hon. Levi Syphus says it is a magnesite, used for making fine china, pottery, tiling, fire brick, cement and for chemical purposes.

Great hills of this kaolin deposit, gleaming white as an angel wing, stand boldly out near the line of the proposed railroad down the Muddy. Located in an accessible valley, it is only a matter of time when this deposit can be worked to advantage. Works may be established at the beds or the clay mined and railroaded away.

Hon. Levi Syphus and Harry Gentry are the principal owners.

The kaolin deposits are very extensive and are covered by about a dozen mining locations. Good water flows all the season near by. A townsite called Kaolin has been surveyed in the valley and will be colonized by the Mormons soon as convenient.

SMOKER

Republicans Enjoy a Feast at the Club Rooms

At the Vegas Republican Club Tuesday evening the boys had a love feast, and a nice Dutch lunch.

Delegations from Searchlight and Caliente were present and took an active part in the entertainment.

In spite of the stormy evening every seat at the Club was occupied.

After routine business, Dr. Murray of Caliente was called for a speech and responded in good style, giving facts and figures of interest.

He said the political parties are very evenly divided, but some of the Republican fences were broken down at the last convention and need repair. For instance there is some doubt as to the principal officers, and many vacancies exist among the precinct committeemen. Dr. Murray thought the party should be reorganized and put in good working lines, by filling vacancies. He gave much information about members of the committee, furnishing names of many precinct officers.

Dr. Murray gave kindly mention to Sam Blunt, of Caliente, also present. He believed Sam could carry off the Sheriff's prize while the Democrats are fighting for it.

Frank A. Doherty next responded to call and said Searchlight had a safe Republican majority and would cast even a larger vote than last election. He spoke of the manner in which Searchlight had been overlooked politically, and paid a high compliment to a friend who accompanied him—O. H. Smith of Searchlight, Republican candidate for Sheriff. Mr. Doherty also counseled reorganization of the party on harmonious lines, and a fair distribution of the honors over the county.

Mr. O. H. Smith was called to the floor and made a brief statement of his candidacy, and believed the party had a good chance to win. Mr. Smith is a young man of good appearance and made a favorable impression.

Many members of the Club agreed with the visitors that with harmony and good organization the Republicans can succeed. Judge Thomas, Ronnow, Bracken, Beale, Stewart, Kramer, Judge Lillis and others made remarks bearing on the good of the party.

A vote of thanks was given the visiting friends from Caliente and Searchlight, after which refreshments were served in recess.

Several letters were read from members of the Committee, who could not attend. A letter from H. A. Perkins of Searchlight says they hope to organize soon and fill vacancies in the committee. Howard Perkins and Frank A. Doherty are the only ones left of the old committee.

A letter from W. C. Bowman invites Republicans to hold the county convention at Moapa.

A letter from H. H. Church says he is Committeeman at Logan; M. D. Cooper at Overton; Frank Bonelli at St. Thomas.

A letter from Bunkerville says James S. Abbott is Committeeman.

At Mesquite Arthur Bunker is said to be Committeeman.

Wm. Roberts is said to be Committeeman at Good Springs, and at Crescent the Republican member has gone away.

All through the meeting was a strong sentiment in favor of allowing Republicans a chance to elect delegates, and against the appointment system.

After a general consultation with the Committeemen present, Judge W. R. Thomas introduced the following call, which was adopted by the meeting.

CALL FOR REPUBLICAN COUNTY CONVENTION

Whereas, there appears to be an uncertainty as to the existence of a chairman for the Republican County Central Committee for Lincoln County, Nevada and as to the membership of the Committee in certain cases, therefore, we, the undersigned members of the said committe do hereby call a delegate convention of the Republicans of Lincoln County to meet at Las Vegas on the 30th day of June, 1908 at 1 o'clock p. m., to select delegates to attend the Republican State Convention to be held at Goldfield, and for the purpose of choosing a central committee for Lincoln County.

The different precincts will be entitled to one delegate at large and one delegate for every fifteen votes, or major fraction thereof, cast for C. J. Smith for Congressman at the election in 1906, as follows:

Pioche	5	Panaca	3
Eagle Valley	1	Spring Valley	2
Fay	1	Clover Valley	1
Caliente,	5	Stine	1
Delamar	4	Hiko	2
Stewart	1	Moapa	2
Logan	2	Overton	2
St. Thomas	2	Bunkerville	2
Mesquite	3	Las Vegas	5
Good Springs	1	Searchlight	7
Nelson	1	Crescent	1
Sandy	1		

We recommend and authorize that caucuses be held at the usual polling places in the different precincts on Saturday, June 27th, 1908 at 5 oclock p. m.

All Committeemen present, including those from Searchlight and Caliente, signed the call, and arranged to present it to all other Committeemen.

It was the general opinion that precincts from which the old Committeemen have removed should fill vacancies by electing new men, who can take part in the political affairs. Send names of Committeemen to Las Vegas Republican Club, so that we may know your wants and work with you. Call at the Club and get acquainted.

It was the concensus of opinion that broken fences must be restored and all factions and sections work together to the common end.

OVERTON

Overton, Nevada, June 4 —J. N Holt of Los Angeles, Cal , returned yesterday. He has bought the Dr Morrison land, about 400 acres, across the creek from Overton He will bring artesion well drills back with him and expects to develop plenty of water to irrigate his land. He expects to put a good share of his land in grain next fall

The second crop of alfalfa is being cut. Harvesting is not all done yet. The weather has been so changeable lately that quite a few are complaining of the grip

Brig and Sam Whitmore and their brother in-law, Mr Grice, have gone to their copper claims, north of Overton about thirty miles, to do assessment work

T J Jones is going north Monday to visit his sister and her children at Provo, Utah He will also visit relatives in Emery county

W W McDonald returned yesterday from Salt Lake city, where he had been talking up land sales in this valley.

A party of surveyors are running the lines for the railway from Moapa to St Thomas

Mrs George Davis of Las Vegas is visiting here

LOGAN

Wm. Marschall has contracted to do the plastering on W. W. Perkins' new house. In fact Marschall will have two or three plastering contracts soon in the valley, at Overton and St. Thomas.

MOAPA VALLEY

S. A. Angel, Road Supervisor of district No. 4, writing from Overton, says Commissioner Hawkins has requested him to repair the Muddy Valley roads before the cantaloupe season.

Mr. Angel says the road fund is inadequate; that last year the people of the valley donated nearly $1,000, and have helped on roads this year.

Mr. Angel thinks the Muddy Valley should have a Commissioner, and suggests Brig. Whitmore, who knows the wants of the country.

59

OVERTON

Farmers propose to form an association to work economically in the marketing of products. Arrangements should be made to supply the market with all kinds of garden truck and fruit speedily from various farms. Only by concentrated effort can this be done.

Muddy Valley will ask one or two places on the political slate this fall.

W. L. Batty has a nice fruit orchard and some good apples, on the Cobb orchard place. He is also agent for the Nevada Land and Live Stock Company owning 1,500 acres. The company is cropping the land, mainly to grain and alfalfa. A new dam and caunal have been built to properly water the farm.

I. E. Losee is an industrious new settler from Utah. He put the finishing touches on the McDonald residence and built a neat cottage for Lonzo Huntsman. By profession Mr. Losee is a school teacher and may apply for the Overton school.

SAINT THOMAS

St Thomas, Nevada, June 15, 1908.—During the past few weeks there has been considerable oil ground located within a short distance of this place From five to ten miles east the ground is claimed to be second to none by men who have had years of experience in oil fields. It is claimed that no better oil shale can be found anywhere than in this district The boys say the odor from the rocks as they build the monuments is so strong of oil that it is unpleasant to work.

Apricots and peaches are nearly all gone; barley, wheat and oats are in the shock and some in the stack, and the second crop of alfalfa is being cut. Tomatoes and cantaloupes will be ready for market in about two weeks.

Two parties have been fishing the past week down at the lower end of the Muddy river near St Thomas They report good success, their catch consisting of salmon, catfish and carp

Harry Gentry's freight teams arrived this evening with the usual loads of copper ore from the Grand Gulch mine The mine is reported as looking fine.

A L. T. McDermott is here interviewing parties who have mining property in this district He is working in the interest of an English company.

Warm weather is with us but not without good results. The health of the people is good, as is usually the case.

61

OVERTON

[Special Correspondence]

Very warm weather prevails in our valley and summer has put in its appearance at last although our long cool spring has been fully appreciated.

T. J. Jones has gone on a trip through the north country he will also visit in Mexico with his daughter before returning.

J. A. Lytle left for Idaho a few days ago to seek employment in that country.

Overton will celebrate the glorious Fourth, guns to be fired at day break, flag hoisted at sunrise, grand parade to take place at nine o'clock, led by the Goddess of Liberty and Uncle Sam. A grand program will be rendered in the forenoon. Numerous sports well managed by a lively and energetic committee will be the afternoon's entertainment. A grand old time ball will be given in the evening.

A dance was given Friday evening in the hall, all the male members cast a vote for the young lady to act as Goddess of Liberty; price consisted of 5c a vote, Miss Effie Whitehead winning out as Goddess. The money for the votes will go to help in the sports.

B. Whitmore and Bros. returned from their Copper mine. They will not resume work for a time at least.

Sybil Whitmore left for Salt Lake City to spend the summer.

Cantaloupes will soon be on the market and farmers are gazing about to seek employees for that business.

The old Wiser ranch under supervision of F. A. Miller has 50 acres of cantaloupes soon to be put on the market.

LINCOLN COUNTY REPUBLICANS

Perfect Organization and Select Delegates to State Convention

In pursuance to a call issued by the Republican County Central Committee, representatives of the Republican party of Lincoln County convened at Las Vegas, June 30th. The meeting, which took place at the headquarters of Las Vegas Republican Club, resulted in the perfection of the organization of the Republicans of this County and the selection of eight delegates to the State Convention at Goldfield on August 27, 1908. Harmony was the keynote of the meeting and there is no doubt but what the Republican Party of Lincoln County is now in a position to make a strong fight for first honors in the coming campaign.

The proceedings were opened by A. W. Jurden, Central Committeeman from Las Vegas, with representation from eighteen precincts out of a possible twenty-five on the floor before him. In the absence of John G. Brown, chairman of the Central Committee, who was unavoidably absent on account of illness, A. W. Jurden was selected as temporary chairman and Eugene Goodrich of Pioche, secretary, performed his duties as such in his usually capable manner.

(Concluded on last page)

REPUBLICANS

(Concluded from first page)

The first business before the meeting was the filling of vacancies existing in the County Central Committee, which was accomplished with the following result.

List of members of the Republican County Central Committee by precincts.

Alamo, J. E. Allen.

Arden, J. A. Sumner.

Barclay, Albert Woods.

Bristol, Charles Fernander.

Bunkerville, Ezra Bunker and Ed Cox.

Caliente, George E. Coxe, W. P. Murray and A. Springall.

Crescent, M. H. McClure.

Delamar, George W. Nesbitt, Bert Pace and H. W. Turner.

Eagle Valley, J. M. Hollanger.

Fay, Henry Bennett.

Goodsprings, S. E. Yount and C. E. McCarthy.

Highland, J. W. Taylor.

Hiko, David Service.

Las Vegas, W. J. Stewart, W. R. Bracken, F. W. Manuel, J. D. Kramer and A. W. Jurden.

Logan, H. H. Church.

Lake Valley, ——

Mesquite, Nephi Johnson and W. F. Abbott.

Moapa, F. F. Gunn.

Nelson, E. P. Jeans.

Overton, John W. Bunker and Maudus Cooper.

Panaca, A. G. Bladd and Chris Ronnow.

Pioche, Eugene Goodrich, John G. Brown, M. L. Lee and W. W. Stockhan.

Potosi, W. E. Smith.

Power Plant, George Baker.

Sandy, Walter McCuen and Jesse Jones.

Searchlight, Howard Perkins, W. T. Kennedy, H. A. Perkins, F. A. Doherty, Wm. Colton, H. A. Walbrecht, G. E. Burdick and Leon French.

Spring Valley, Henry Rice and A. Delmue.

Sunset, John Burns.

St. Thomas, Frank Bonelli.

As delegates to the State Convention at Goldfield to be held August 27th the following were selected:—George Baker, Delamar; A. Bladd, Panaca; H. H. Church, Logan; F. A. Doherty, Searchlight; Eugene Goodrich, Pioche; C. E. McCarthy, Goodsprings; Dr. W. P. Murray, Caliente and C. C. Ronnow, Las Vegas.

As alternates to the State Convention the following were selected:—J. G. Brown, Pioche; Stephen Bunker, Bunkerville; George Coxe, Caliente; H. A. Perkins, Searchlight; W. Geer, Hiko; H. M. Lillis, Las Vegas; George W. Nesbitt, Delamar and S. E. Yount, Goodsprings.

Ordered that the County Convention be held at Caliente on Thursday, September 17, 1908.

Ordered that the representation at the County Convention be on the basis of one delegate at large from each precinct and one additional delegate for every 15 votes and major fraction thereof cast for Oscar J. Smith for Congress in the election of 1906.

Ordered that the primaries to select delegates to the County Convention be held on Thursday, September 3rd, 1908, between the hours of 1 p. m. and 8. p. m.

Election officers to serve at the above primaries in the various precincts were selected as follows.

List of precinct election officers and polling places for primaries, Sept. 3, 1908:

Alamo: J. E. Allen, W. T. Stewart, A. Niebecker; school house.

Arden: J. A. Sumner, A. Simmons; boarding house.

Barclay, Albert Woods, J. Woods, H. Empy; school house.

Bristol: O. Fernander, A. Bishop, A. VanEmon; Fernander's.

Bunkerville: J. S. Abbott, Frank Cox, Ed. Bunker; school house.

Caliente: J. W. Smith, George Coxe, O. M. Moody; Ward's Hall.

Crescent: H. M. McClure, J. S. Morgan; McClure's.

Delamar: J. Johnson, Bert Pace, H. W. Turner; school house.

Eagle Valley: J. M. Hollanger, Ed Lytle, Wm. Werem; school house.

Fay: Henry Bennet, E. H. Hackett, O. Stokes; school house.

Goodsprings: C. E. McCarthy, Harvey Hardy, Jr., P. H. Springer; school house.

Highland: J. W. Taylor, I. Hinkle; Menduli Mine office.

Hiko: David Service, Lewis Stern, A. W. Gear; school house.

Las Vegas: A. W. Jurden, H. M. Lillis, C. C. Ronnow; Republican Club Rooms.

Logan: H. H. Church, W. T. Bowman, J. Wells; school house.

Lake Valley: School house.

Mesquite: Nephi Johnson, W. F. Abbott, Allen Waters; school house.

Moapa: A. T. Sharp, F. F. Gunn, W. C. Bowman; Bowman's Hotel.

Nelson: H. Spanogle, E. P. Jeans, J. Smith; Vanna's.

Overton: S. A. Angel, T. J. Jones, Maudus Cooper; school house.

Panaca: A. G. Blad, Chris Ronnow, H. Mathews; school house.

Pioche: Jesse Peaslee, F. W. Dickle, H. E. Freudenthal; Hotel Cecil.

Potosi: W. E. Smith, Clayton Smith, J. Poznasky; mine office.

Power Plant: George Baker, M. Matasky, J. Jones; school house.

Sandy: Walter McCuen, Jesse Jones, Nickolas Kuntz; McClanahan's.

Searchlight: F. A. Doherty, Wm. Colton, H. A. Perkins; Doherty's office.

Spring Valley: Henry Rice, Chas. Millet, A. Delmue; school house.

St. Thomas: Frank Bonelli, Jacob Bauer, W. Murphy; school house.

Sunset: John Burns, L. Butterfield, Wm. Bright; mine office.

Adjourned subject to call of chairman of County Central Committee.

Overton, Nevada, June 29.—Melons, cantaloupes and cucumbers are being shipped right along and are bringing fair prices. Apricots are all gone, peaches are being marketed. The third extracting of honey is out and is of splendid quality.

T. J. Jones returned yesterday from a visit to his sister and daughter in Provo, and son in Salt Lake city and daughters in Emery, Utah. He found weather cold in the north and crops backward.

Horace Jones and Tom Johnson have gone into the butcher business and are furnishing beef to the valley people, and to Moapa citizens twice a week.

W. W. McDonald returned from Salt Lake city a few days ago bringing with him Joseph Conner to see and boost this country.

Andrew and Albert Jones sold one of their forty-acre lots to Mr. Hesler, a new comer, a few days ago for $75 per acre

Whitehead Bros. have recently put in wagon scales in front of their store.

Everybody is busy making crates for shipping fruit and vegetables,

65

LOCAL NOTES

A. W. Jurden made a business trip to Moapa Saturday last.

M. E. Clayson, who left here quite ill, is improving in Corona, Cal.

Dr. Roy W. Martin visited Los Angeles and coast resorts this week.

Mrs. F. H. Clayson and baby are visiting with Mrs. Clayson's parents in Riverside, Cal.

Mrs. Peter Buol writes from Reno that the weather is cool and pleasant and the surroundings delightful.

Coolest place in town; electric fan. J. D. Kramer, barber, Thomas blk. Best baths, hot or cold, three for $1.00. tf

For rent—Two room furnished house. Apply to Geo. H. Coffey, Las Vegas Livery. tf

The Moapa Improvement Company is making daily shipments of cantaloupes from the Muddy Valley.

The Eagle's lodge will meet the first and third Tuesday nights of each month during the summer season.

Mrs. Joe Smith is visiting in Salt Lake City. She will spend some time in Montana before returning.

Miss Marie Thomas has returned from Los Angeles and will spend the summer with her parents, Mr. and Mrs. W. R. Thomas.

Mrs. Will Stewart arranged a very delightful affair in honor of her guest Miss Elizabeth Perkins of Searculight. The entertainment consisted of a ride and picnic dinner in the shade of the giant cottonwoods in Stewarts meadow. To their great regret no gentlemen were invited.

for an extended visit through the west before returning east.

James Thomas has returned to Vegas from Phillips Acadamy, Andover, where he graduated with honor in June.

The family of Z. S. Tranthan, news agent on the L. V. & T. has arrived from Los Angeles to make their home in this district.

The ladies of the Catholic Church gave a social at Fife's Hall Thursday evening. Refreshments were served and music, games and dancing enjoyed by all.

There is a small supply of garden seeds sent by the government for distribution, still remaining at The Age office Call for a supply and keep things growing.

B. M. Davis has opened the Star Saloon with R. H. Shaffer in charge of the bar. At the opening Thursday night patrons were treated to a fine lunch.

A number of the boys enjoyed a camping trip to the Kyle ranch last Saturday night and Sunday, endulging in rabbit mulligan and other near-to-nature refreshments.

Miss Elizabeth Perkins, of Searchlight has been a visitor in Vegas for the purpose of taking the State teachers examinations. She is remaining here for a few days as the guest of Mrs. Stewart at the ranch.

Mr. and Mrs. J. O. McIntosh are again in Caliente after settling up their wholesale liquor business here. Al James has taken charge of the Eastside beer agency. Many friends hope to see Mr. and Mrs. Mc. back again in Vegas.

A post office will be established by Uncle Sam at Lyons station. Mrs. Tuttle, wife of the agent of the Salt Lake Route will be the postmistress. This will be a great convenience to the Lucy Gray and other properties in that vicinity.

Overton, Nevada, July 21 — Everybody busy shipping cantaloupes, they are going from Moapa by the carload lot every day. Tomatoes, grapes and peaches are also being shipped. The fourth crop of alfalfa is being cut. The weather is very hot now, the thermometer running up to 111 frequently.

Steve Whitehead and wife have gone to St. George to visit relatives and friends. Steve took his sister, Effie, who has been visiting here, back with him.

Horace Jones and young Macdonald have gone to Bunkerville to celebrate Pioneer day, also to return the visit of their best girls who spent the 4th here.

W. W. Macdonald and some Salt Lake people have formed a company and are buying land here to improve and sell to new comers.

A big horse race is to come off Saturday next for a $100 bet, the animals being Joe Perkins' horse and J. M. Bunker's mare.

Vernon Kenney and wife left yesterday on the stage for Blackfoot, Idaho, expecting to be gone till the beginning of next year.

Mrs. W. W. Macdonald left on the stage yesterday morning for the north to avoid the hot weather for awhile.

Gentry's teams continue hauling ore from the Grand Gulch mine even though it is hot.

Nora Thomas and Eva Conger have gone to Salt Lake city to visit there awhile.

The stork visited W. L. Batty on the 17th inst. and left a boy; all doing well.

All are celebrating Pioneer day at St. Thomas today.

W. L. Jones is having his house plastered

DISTANCES

In Lincoln County, to Pioche and Las Vegas

Mileage given is by ordinary convey-ance route. Note the remarkable equal-ization of distances in the proposed div-ision on the Third Standard Paralell.

Township	Miles to Pioche	Miles to Las Vegas
Searchlight	233	77
Nelson	257	101
Crescent	219	63
Jean	187	31
Goodsprings	195	39
Sandy	207	51
Potosi	195	30
Las Vegas	156	...
Moapa	107	49
Logan	119	61
Overton	122	64
St. Thomas	131	73
Bunkervill	147	89
Mesquite	152	94
Gold Butte	157	99
Caliente	33	
Ursine (Eagle Valley)	16	
Newlands (Spring Valley)	22	
Fay (Deer Lodge)	22	
Barclay (Clover Valley)	55	
DeLamar	68	
Alamo	98	
Hiko	100	
Panaca	12	
Geyser (Lake Valley)	60	
Stine	41	
Jack Rabbit	18	
Bristol	23	
Tem Piute	130	

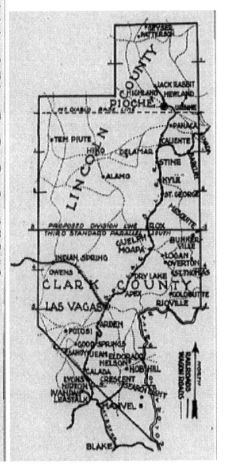

TO THE
Citizens of Southern Lincoln County:

The time has come when it is neccessary for us to bring about the division of Lincoln County.

The machinery for waging a most vigorous campaign to this end is now in working order.

The Lincoln County Division Club, with headquarters at Las Vegas desires the active co-operation of all favoring this movement. Funds must be raised to meet the large expenses of an active and vigorous campaign.

We invite your subscriptions for this purpose and guarantee that all moneys contributed shall be expended in a careful and economical manner and a strict accounting thereof made.

Let no man shirk his duty or his just obligation.

Fill out the coupon below and mail to C. P. Squires, Chairman Finance Committee, Las Vegas, Nevada. Make all checks payable to John S. Park, Treasurer, at First State Bank of Las Vegas.

SUBSCRIPTION COUPON

....1908

*I hereby subscribe the sum of............................
Dollars to the Lincoln County Division Club, to be
used for the purpose of carrying on the campaign
for the division of Lincoln County.*

Name ....

Address ....

OVERTON

Overton, Nevada, Sept. 3.—The rush to market with cantaloupes is over for this season, and many are preparing to put in a good large crop of lettuce, some as high as thirty-five acres, for the Chicago market. The income from lands in this valley has greatly increased this summer, from $600 to $1000 per acre being cleared after paying all expenses, so you can see there is money in lands here, yet good land may be bought at from $50 to $100 per acre.

T. J. Jones returned on the 29th of August from Sonora, Mexico, where he visited his daughter, Mrs Patience Lee, who lost her husband at Colonia Morelos on the 31st day of March last. He also visited his nephew, J. H. Langford, at Oaxaca, both places on the Vabiepa river. Since the summer rains in that country the hills and mountains are as green as a meadow and in some parts the people are cutting the grass for hay.

The stork has been around again and left a boy at the Walberg home, and a girl at the M. D. Cooper nome. All concerned doing nicely.

Will Whitehead, Crayton Johnson and others have gone to Gold Butte to work at the Mica mine for a New York company.

J. A. Swapp and Justice McDermott have just returned from a trip to Copper mountain and other mining property on route.

70

LINCOLN COUNTY WINS

First Prize For the Best Horticultural Exhibit at the State Fair

Twenty-four Blue Ribbons for the Muddy and Virgin

People of the State Amazed at Splendid Showing of Products

The State Fair at Reno last week was a success and Lincoln County carried off the honors.

A splendid exhibit of products was taken to Reno under the supervision of Chas. Arney of Logan. Our County booth was the center of attraction and people from all parts of the country expressed amazement that any section of so called arid Nevada would produce such a wonderful variety and perfection of products. [adapted both to temperate and semi-tropic climates. It was a matter of universal wonder that any portion of the State produced lemons of the fine quality of those shown and the statement that both oranges and lemons could be successfully grown in the Muddy Valley gave our fellow citizens of Northern and Central Nevada new ideas of the extent and diversity of our state.

Out of thirty-five products from Lincoln County on exhibition twenty-four were awarded first prizes. This is in addition to the silver medal awarded as first prize for the display as a whole.

We take pleasure in publishing the list of blue ribbons coming to Lincoln County with the names of the exhibitors.

Grapes—All varieties—J. H. Averett, Logan; M. W. Gibson, St. Thomas; L. Whitney, St. Thomas; M. D. Cooper, Overton.

Watermelons—H. H. Church, Logan.

Sweet Potatoes—H. A. Sparks, Overton.

Pomgranates—John Bunker, St. Thomas and S. A. Angel,

Overton.

Beets, three varities, turnip table, blood table and sugar beet—S. H. Wells and Aug. Koenig, Logan.

Sorgum cane—Aug. Koenig, Logan and Sam Gentry, St. Thomas.

Pumpkins—Experimental Station, S. H. Wells and Aug. Koenig, all of Logan.

Canned fruits—Peaches, apricots, preserved seedless grapes, muscat grapes and Black Hamburg grapes—Mrs. Wm. Jones,of Overton and Mrs. M. W, Gibson, St. Thomas.

Peaches—John Thomas, Logan.

Lemons—H. H. Church, Logan. (It is interesting to note that these are the first lemons ever grown in the state.)

Irish Potatoes--four varieties, Aug. Koenig, Logan.

Peanuts, two varieties--Aug. Koenig, Logan.

Pears--L. N. Shurtliff, Overton.

Almonds--H. B. Mills and D. P.Hargus of Logan.

Apples--D. P. Hargus, Logan.

Cantaloupes---John Thomas, Logan and S. A. Angel, Overton.

Egg plant---M. D. Cooper, Overton.

Tomatoes---H. H. Church, Logan.

Cucumbers, Okra, Squash and Cotton---Experimental Station.

The full blooded Holstein bull calf recently presented by the University Experimental station to the State Experimental Station at Logan was awarded first prize in the six months old class in the live stock department.

This will encourage the farmers of the Muddy to improve the breed of cattle raised there and means much to the future of the stock raising industry.

The officials who for thirty years past have had charge of the exhibits at the State Fairss, tate that this Lincoln County exhibit was the finest ever seen there.

M. W. Gibson's wonderful Thompson seedless grapes and John Thomas's beautiful Indian Cling peaches together with the cotton, lemons and pomgranates attracted more attention than any other product shown and it was necessary to place them in glass cases to protect them from the curious and greedy.

Great credit is due to Chas. Arney for his tireless efforts in collecting and arranging the products for exhibition. During the entire week he was constantly on hand with a steady stream of information as to this locality for the thousands of visitors. This is Lincoln County's first appearance at a State Fair and it is to be hoped that another year will see all sections of the County alive to the value of uniting in a display which will eclipse if possible the splendid showing of 1908.

Overton, Nevada, Sept. 16 —The state fair being held at Reno this week is a howling success Lincoln county excels in the exhibits, and best of all the seedless raisins attract wide attention. Lincoln county seedless raisins grown at St. Thomas lead the world; the Thompson seedless raisins were better than ever before shown at a county fair, averaging three-fourths of an inch in thickness and nearly an inch long. These grapes were grown by M. W. Gibson at St Thomas, and raisins made from the Gibson product are pronounced by experts to excel in size, flavor and firmness any such product known. Mr Gibson who is a leader in the St. Thomas Mormon settlement has put in several acres of these grapes, some clusters of which weigh four pounds.

Ellis Turnbaugh and wife have returned from Sparks, where they have resided, for several months. He is to teach our school the coming winter.

Our neighbor, Hon. Levi Syphus, of St. Thomas, got the nomination for state senator at the county convention held at Delamar on the 10th inst

W, L, Jones, wife and mother have gone to the fair and conference at St. George.

Bishop Bunker and Samuel H. Wells were visiting preachers here last Sunday.

Brig Whitmore started for Salt Lake City on business yesterday morning.

Threshing has commenced. We had a fine rain last week.

Overton, Nevada, Sept. 19 — Apostles Geo A. Smith and A. W. Ivins with Presidents Ed. H. Snow and Geo. F. Whitehead of the St. George Stake came in and held meeting on the evening of the 17th inst. and another at 10 a m. the 18th inst From here they went to St. Thomas and held meetings there and organized the new ward of St. Thomas with J. M. Bunker of Overton Bishop and M. W. Gibson and G. L Whitney as his counselors They then came to Overton and appointed William L. Jones bishop of the Overton ward with M. D. Cooper and S. R. Whitehead as his counselors and Elmer Loose as ward clerk, after which they took supper at T. J. Jones' place and went on to Logan, holding meeting there at 7.30 p m The party then went with S H. Wells to the Moapa Improvement company's place, remaining there that night and were driven by S. H. Wells on the morning of the 19th to Moapa, where they took train for Panaca to hold ward conference. Their teachings were very good and timely and were given to full houses at all places

We are having nice fall weather now. Everybody is preparing land for next year's crops, planting onions, lettuce, and other garden truck. We have had some fine rains lately.

The threshing machine owned by Bishop J M Bunker, W. L. Jones and others is now running successfully and is doing good work.

T. J. Jones has gone to Bunkerville for a few days

74

Farmer's Association in the Muddy Valley

Several meetings have been held in the Muddy Valley looking toward the formation of a growers association for the purpose of handling the agricultural products of the valley.

A committee consisting of Levi Syphus, of St Thomas, W. A. McDonald, of Overton and W. J McBurney, of Logan have been appointed to get information about the methods of organization of similar associations in California, also their by-laws and methods of handling products.

As soon as these matters can be investigated and information thereon be obtained, another meeting will be called and the organization completed.

The idea of forming an association is to get better markets, handling the crops more economically, getting a more uniform pack.

ITINERARY

Democratic Meetings

The Democratic Campaign has opened in ernest and from now on candidates will go sleepless. Meetings have been arranged as follows:

Oct.
17 Overton
18 St. Thomas
19 Bunkerville
20 Mesquite
21 Caliente
22 Delamar
23 Alamo
24 Hiko
25 Delamar
26 Panaca
27 Eagle Valley
28 Spring Valley and Fay
29 Pioche
30 Jack Rabbit
31 Las Vegas

The meeting at Las Vegas Oct 31st will be an enthusiastic wind up of the campaign and the feature of great interest will be the grand ball at which the candidates will do the honors.

Overton, Nevada, Nov. 18,—J. P. Anderson of Fountain Green, Utah, has bought Brig Whitmore's store business and is running it o k. More settlers are coming to the Muddy valley to help build the country up. We are glad of it, the old settlers will welcome all good people.

Bp E Bunker and wife left here this morning having been here and at St. Thomas in the interest of the Sunday schools

Bp. J. M. Bunker and Elder Martin from St Thomas visited us as home missionaries last Sunday.

Correct spelling is Andersen

75

Overton, Nevada, Nov 21 —Mrs Rachael Laub Perkins died on the 20th inst after an illness of two or three weeks Funeral services were held Sunday at 2 p m , the speakers being Elders Thomas Judd, G, L Whitney, J M Bunker and Bishop Jones She left six sons, four daughters, and seven grandchildren.

Bp L. Bunker has the contract to put in 250 acres of barley for the Nevada Land & Live Stock Co W W. Perkins has a contract to fence land for the same company.

The Grand Gulch has increased its ore hauling force by one six-horse team and one four-horse

Fall garden truck is looking fine

Overton, Nevada, Jan 2 —The Moapa Valley Farmers association has been organized recently for the purpose of handling the crops of all kinds, so that they can be put on the markets to the best advantage of all concerned

Burt Mill and company of Logan, Nevada, are putting in a mill on the Colorado river near Scanlon's ferry to work their gold ore through and expect to have it ready to run in a few days He only pays $2 per day with board and several of the boys have quit work on account of the low wages

The stork has been flying around St Thomas lately and left a boy at Guy Gardner's home, their first child; also left a pretty boy at Robert Gibson's place, their second one; all parties concerned are doing well

Garden truck put in last fall is growing very slowly. The Nevada Land and Live Stock Co , under Thos Judd, have put in nearly two hundred acres of barley and have more to put in yet.

The Cannon Bros Co have a lot of men in the valley improving their land, building houses and getting ready for this year's crops

Harry Gentry of St Thomas is having his brick home finished up as it has been standing several years unfinished.

Some talk of puting up a telephone line from St Thomas to Moapa, a distance of seventeen miles.

The stork visited Edwin Marshall's home and left a boy there January 1st, all doing well

The experiment farm house at Logan is having a porch put all around it.

76

Early fall grain crops look well and some are putting in grain yet.

Our coldest weather this winter went down to 19 above zero

Overton, Nevada, Jan 4 — Holidays over and everybody tired out after so many good parties

The little daughter of S Gentry, who has been very low, with pneumonia is slowly recovering, which we are all glad to learn.

The stork has been busy of late, and has left new babies at the homes of Robert Gibson, Mark Murphy and S. Gentry.

Joe Perkins and Roxton Whitmore shipped a car of beef cattle last week to the Los Vegas market

Miss Whitehead gave her school children a party which they all enjoyed very much.

Brig Whitmore has gone to Salt Lake City on business connected with his mines

Everybody busy putting in early gardens

.Overton, Nevada, Jan 13 —The stockholders of the Moapa Valley Farmers association organized and had their annual meeting on January 11th, and elected Levi Syphus, Sam Gentry, W L. Jones, W. J. McBurney, and Brig Whitmore as the board of directors for the ensuing year This company is organized for the purpose of marketing the products of the farmers in the most improved manner and for the best prices to be obtained, and putting the middle men out.

At a meeting of the Muddy Valley Irrigation Co on the 9th inst , Levi Syphus, S A Angell, Samuel H Wells, Luke Whitney, and Aug Koenig were elected as the board of directors for the ensuing year. The secretary of the company read a report of the last year's business of the company, showing the expence for one year was one dollar per acre

S R Whitehead is visiting the citizens of the valley taking subscriptions to put in a telephone line from Moapa to St Thomas, about 25 miles. There is every prospect that the line will be built

Sam M. Whitmore has returned from the north, and with his brother, Brig, are working their copper mine in the Gold Butte country.

FOR ITALIAN SUFFERERS

(He Gives Twice Who Gives Quickly)

The following amounts have been received at this office

Seth A Pymm, St George,		$1 50
Eliza J Pymm,	"	1 00
H. Marvin Pymm,	"	.25
J R Wallis	"	1 50
Cash	"	50
Sarah J. Atkin,	"	1 00
Maggie Cragon,	"	1 50
Edna Cragon,	"	1 50
J. A Crosby	"	1 00
E M. Brown	"	1 00
Jos S Snow	"	1 00
Wm T. Perkins	"	1 00

Relief Society, St. George D ,		5 00
"	Enterprise	1 00
"	Mesquite	1 00
"	Bunkerville	1 00
"	La Verkin	1 30
"	Overton	1 00
"	Toquerville	1 00
"	Preston	1 25
"	Pine Valley	2 50
"	Gunlock	1 00
"	Rockville	1,00
"	Panaca	1 00
"	Littlefield	2 25
"	Washington	2 00

78

"Too Young to Marry"

without her parents consent, was what County Clerk Woodbury told a blushing damsel at the courthouse Tuesday. The young lady, Miss Elizabeth Cornelia Swapp, of Overton, Nevada, who is just sweet seventeen, appeared with her intended husband, Alonzo Huntsman, also of Overton, Nevada, and her sister, and requested a license to marry. Miss Swapp said she had her father's consent, and was borne out in this by the others who accompanied her, but, alas, the consent was verbal and the hard-hearted county clerk (who takes a keen delight in torturing the unfortunate young victims that come before him on such errands) insisted on a written consent The discomforted young couple left the presence of the heartless county clerk, and have taken means to have the necessary writing sent up as early as possible.

NOTICE OF ASSESSMENT

MUDDY VALLEY IRRIGATION COMPANY

At the regular monthly meeting of the Board of Directors of the MUDDY VALLEY IRRIGATION COMPANY, held at Overton, Nev. on February 6th 1909, an Assessment of One Dollar ($1.00) per share on all Preferred stock was levied, payable, 50c per share on or before March 15th, 1909, and 50c per share on or before April 15th 1909.

By order of the Board.
A. L. F. MacDermott,
Secretary Treasurer.

First publication Feb. 18th 1909.

OVERTON

Newsy Notes From the Muddy Metropolis

Cool, pleasant weather is still with us and the people are rejoicing, as the summer days will last long enough and be sufficiently warm when they appear.

Mrs. Sloan of Monpa is visiting a few days in town looking over the beautiful gardens.

Schools closed yesterday with a nice entertainment in the evening in which the students did honor to the parts assigned them. The teacher deserves credit for work and interest in the scholars. Certificates were presented to each scholar by School Trustee U. V. Perkins at the close of the exercises.

May day was celebrated here in the usual manner. A nice program was well carried out with Miss Sadie Perkins Queen of May, and Misses Etta Hewitt and Myrtle Whitmore maids of honor, all doing justice to their parts. Picnic dinner was partaken of under the trees.

Mary V. Lytle has returned from the north where she has been for the past year, for a short visit.

Ralph Perkins has returned from Logan, Utah, where he went to ship a car load of cattle to D. J. Cox, formerly of Overton.

Cantaloupes are doing well considering the cool weather. Hundreds of acres have been planted and times will soon be busy.

H. B. Mills, an old resident of the Muddy Valley, has recently sold his farm and will move with his wife into the state of Washington soon.

Senator Levi Syphus, with Mr. B. Whitmore, is in Monpa holding a miners meeting in order to form rules and adopt them that mining may be better regulated.

NOTICE

To Whom it May Concern:

The Moapa Valley Telephone Company, a corporation organized under the laws of the State of Nevada, has made application to the Board of County Commissioners of Lincoln County Nevada, for a franchise to construct, maintain and operate a telephone line, over and across the public lands of Lincoln County, Nevada, such authority and franchise to confer the right to erect and maintain poles upon the right of way and along the course of such line and to string wires upon the poles, for the use of public telephone service, in, along and upon the following described course to-wit:

The proposed line will commence at Moapa and be carried thence south-easterly over the vacant public lands, all of which are barren gravel hills and mesas, and nearly as practicable in a straight course to the farming lands now held and occupied by the settlers of the valley, who have all agreed to give the right of way over their lands, as may be necessary and convient for the proper construction and use of the proposed line, the whole distance from Moapa to the first private land being under six miles; and the present termination of the line to be at St. Thomas. The entire distance of the line to be twenty-five miles.

And further, that the width of such right of way shall be so as to admit of the convient setting and establishing of the poles necessary for the construction of said telephone line.

Notice is hereby given that such application will come up for hearing before the Board of County Commissioners of Lincoln County, Nevada, at the meeting of the Board to be held at the Court House in Pioche, on Monday the Seventh day of June, A. D., 1909; at which time and place any and all persons interested in the granting or refusing to grant such authority, franchise and right of way, shall have the right to be heard either in person or by attorney, and at which time and place the said Board of County Commissioners will receive bids for such franchise and right of way.

Date of First Publication, April 17th, 1909.
Date of Last Publication, May 15th, 1909.

J. M. Lytle, one of Overton's enterprising business men, was a welcome caller at the Age office Thursday. Mr. Lytle reports that the Muddy Valley is in a very prosperous condition, the cantaloupe crop especially being very promising.

Deputy Sheriff Sam Gay was called to Moapa Friday last to serve a warrant on W. J. Powers and wife, on the charge of battery on the person of one of the residents of the Muddy Valley. The victim's arm is reported to have been broken and other serious injuries inflicted.

Preparing For The Big Cantaloupe Crop

Overton, Nevada, June 14.—Second crop of lucern is stacked and harvest is about over. Everybody is busy now preparing for the cantaloupe crop, one carload of cantaloupe crates is in and distributed to the growers, and teams are going after the second carload this afternoon, 2500 crates have been ordered for cantaloupes alone, and several thousand crates for tomatoes, peaches and apricots. A good many teams will be needed to haul cantaloupes; the price for hauling is twenty cents per crate from Overton to Moapa, thirty to forty crates are a load and a trip can be made every 24 hours. Lots of cantaloupe pickers will be needed at $1 25 to $1 50 per day with board

The weather is getting quite warm, the thermometer registering from 104 to 109 in the shade several days lately. Crops of all kinds are very good

Miss Clara Perkins returned home a few days ago from Logan and other Utah points, where she had been visiting relatives

Elder Sam H Wells visited us and preached last Sunday and predicted a grand future for the valley.

Jesse Odenol and wife of St. Thomas lost their first and only child about ten days ago

Brig Whitmore and daughter returned from Salt Lake City last week

82

A FINE COUNTRY

Splendid Crops Raised on Virgin Soil in The Rich Muddy River Valley, Near Overton

---

William L. Batty and wife of Overton, Nevada, were here Wednesday en route to their former home, Toquerville, where Mrs Batty will visit for several days

Mr Batty is the foreman for the Nevada Land & Live Stock Co., and speaks in glowing terms of the wonderful fertility of the soil about that point (Overton) of the Muddy valley, its climate, and the progress being made by the company and by settlers.

The grain crop has just been taken off the company's land, and yielded 8000 bushels from 200 acres. This is the first crop ever taken off the land, which was not even plowed being simply cut and covered. The total grain crop of the Muddy Valley this year is about 10,000 bushels, or more than twice as much as has hitherto been raised.

The cantaloupe crop prospects were never better, said Mr. Batty. Our company alone has 25 acres in cantaloupes and we will ship 5,000 crates. This crop of cantaloupes is from virgin soil, nothing having been planted in it before. Mr. Batty said he could not get teams down the valley to haul the crops to the railroad at Moapa, and one of the objects of his visit here was to try and get teamsters to contract the hauling of the crop at 25 cents per crate.

The productiveness of the soil in that section is wonderful, as these crops from soil cultivated for the first time amply prove. There are no vacant lands left now, but land can still be bought at a reasonable figure, and Mr. Batty says no young man could ask for a better opportunity to win and build up a home than exists in the Muddy valley.

SUMMONS

In the Justice's Court of Overton Township, County of Lincoln, State of Nevada.

Wm. J. Powers, Plaintiff, vs. Frank Bowlin, Defendant.

The State of Nevada sends Greeting to Frank Bowlin, Defendant:

You are hereby directed to appear before me at my office, in Overton, in the County of Lincoln, and answer the complaint in the above entitled action within five days, if the summons be served in the township or city in which the action is brought, ten days if served out of the township or city, but within the County in which the action is brought; "and within twenty days if served elsewhere;" and unless you appear and answer, the plaintiff will take judgment for any money or damages demanded in the complaint, as arising upon contract, or will apply to the Court for the relief demanded in the complaint.

The said action is brought to recover the sum of $73.00, alleged to be due from defendant to plaintiff, for goods and merchandise sold and delivered by plaintiff to defendant, as more particularly set forth in the complaint on file in this cause, to which reference is hereby made. And you are hereby notified that if you fail to appear and answer the said complaint, as above required, the said plaintiff will take judgment against you for the said sum of $73, and costs.

To the Sheriff or any Constable of said County, Greeting: Make legal service and due return hereof.

Given under my hand this 23rd day of April, A. D., 1909.   A. L. F. MacDERMOTT,
        Justice of the Peace of said Township.

First publication, May 22, 1909.
Last publication, June 26, 1909.

85

Notice of Application for Permission to Appropriate the Public Waters of the State of Nevada.

Notice is hereby given that on the 29th day of May 1909, in accordance with Section 26, Chapter XVIII, of the Statutes of 1907, one Nevada Land & Live Stock Company of Salt Lake City, County of Salt Lake, and State of Utah, made application to the State Engineer of Nevada for permission to appropriate the public waters of the State of Nevada. Such appropriation is to be made from Muddy River, Lincoln Co., Nevada, for concentration of water right and manner of use agreeable to Logan and Overton Canals by means of canals and 20 cubic feet per second is to be conveyed to points of use by means of canals and there used for irrigation and domestic purposes. Water not to be returned to stream.

Date of first publication June 5, 1909.
Date of last publication June 26, 1909.
Signed: FRANK R. NICHOLAS,
State Engineer.

Washington County News
June 28, 1909

Overton Now Shipping Tomatoes

Overton, Nevada, June 26—We have just got all the poles set for a telephone line from Moapa to St Thomas. John Riding of St George has been here several days stretching the wire, and today put a phone in Whitehead Bros store, one at the Wells ranch, and some others. All the wire will be stretched in about twelve days, and thirty phones are already spoken for.

Tomatoes are being shipped, watermelons are about ready for use, and cantaloupes will be ready for shipping by July 10th.

Washington County News
July 8, 1909

Mrs. Wm L. Batty of Overton, Nevada, was in the city this week, having her baby operated on by Dr. Woodbury for some trouble with one of its feet.

Las Vegas Age Newspaper
July 17, 1909

Senator Levi Syphus arrived in Vegas Sunday evening from a trip to Reno. He left for the Moapa valley Monday morning.

Harold Sparks of Overton, was a visitor to Vegas Tuesday last. Mr. Sparks is looking after the interests of the cantaloupe growers at Moapa during the shipping season.

A. M. Mortensen, manager of the Pacific Fruit Express company, was in the city this week. Mr. Mortensen, accompanied by J. W. Weeks, the local manager, visited Moapa Monday to arrange for handling the crop of cantaloupes just coming on the market.

MOAPA VALLEY PARTICIPATES

In Prosperity of the American Farmer

Many are the jokes that are perpetrated at the expense of the supposedly slow-witted farmer, and many persons share in the opinion that he is just a little behind his city cousin in knowledge and attainments, and that anything is good enough for him. But let us consider what he is really worth.

The American farmer earns enough in seventeen days to buy out the Standard Oil Company; in fifty days to wipe Carnegie and his steel trust from off the commercial map. Compared with such facts as these, the story of the money made corporations seems like "the short and simple annals of the poor."

Talk of swollen fortunes. With the setting of every sun, the money bag of the American farmer bulges with the weight of twenty-four new millions.

Place your finger on the pulse of your wrist and count your heart beats, one, two, three, four. With every four of those quick throbs, day and night, one thousand dollars clatter into the gold-bin of the American farmer.

How incomprehensible it would seem to Pericles, who saw Greece in her golden age, if he could know that the yearly revenue of his country was no more than one day's pay for the man who tills the soil of this infant republic. Or how it would amaze a resurrected Christopher Columbus if he were told that the revenues of Spain and Portugal were were not nearly so much as the farmer's hens.

More crumbs that fall from the farmer's table, otherwise known as agricultural exports, have brought in enough of foreign money since 1892 to enable the American farmer, if he so wished to settle the railroad question once for all, that is, to buy every foot of railroad in the United States.

We can readily see that the American farmer is really the backbone of the earning power of our country.

88

The Moapa Valley Telephone Company of Overton, Nevada, have spared no effort to provide for the farmers of that community the best facilities for instant communication, not only with their neighbors, but with the large trade centers. In fact, if they so desire, they can reach the most distant points, such as Chicago, New York and Boston, over the lines of the American Bell Telephone Company. Their equipment is what is known as Standard Bell apparatus, having been purchased from the Western Electric Company, who are pioneers in the furnishing of telephone equipment.

We show in these columns a cut of the telephone set that is being used. This set represents the most up-to-date type that has been put on the market, and the officials of the Moapa Valley Telephone Company are to be commended upon their good judgment in purchasing this type of equipment.

The wires enter this set from the rear to concealed binding posts. This prevents trouble caused by tampering with the connections and accidentally putting the telephone out of business, as may happen should the line wires be connected to exposed binding posts on top. A great many other companies have experienced trouble in this respect by the subscribers placing small metal articles such as scissors and steel rimmed spectacles, etc. on the top of the telephone cabinet.

This telephone instrument is self-contained, that is, the different compartments are large enough to hold all the accessories, such as batteries, etc. A writing shelf is mounted below the transmitter, so as to make it convenient to take notes or messages received over the wire.

89

All the world is at one of these telephones. The telephone should not be considered a luxury. In this busy twentieth century of ours, time is money, and residents of this community will save much time by the use of one of these telephones. In an emergency, one telephone call may be worth the entire cost of the telephone service for a lifetime. You cannot afford to be without it.

It shops in all weathers,
 Corrects all mistakes,
 Hastens deliveries,
 Saves your time,
 Saves letter writing,
 Lengthens your life,
 Invites the guests,
 Makes appointments,
 Cancels and renews them,
 Invites company, and
 Asks them to stay away,
 Asks them to hurry, and
 Enables them to invite you,
 Calls the constable or sheriff,
 Calls help in case of fire,
 Calls the doctor, and
 Saves emergencies.
 Lengthens your days,
 Reduces your worries,
 Is useful every day,
 Is helpful very often,
 Is indispensible on occasions,
 Is always on duty,
 Saves your temper,
 Makes living easy, and
 "WHAT IS HOME WITHOUT A PHONE."

COUNTY COM-MISSIONERS

Proceedings of the Board of Clark County

Business taken up from adjourned meeting of July.

Meeting called to order August 2, 1909, Chairman W. E. Hawkins, Samuel H. Wells, W. H. Bradley present. Harley A. Harmon, clerk.

The levy of $3.00 special school tax on Bunkerville district was taken up and passed. Motion by Bradley, seconded by Wells.

On motion by Wells and seconded by Bradley, the application of the Las Vegas Land and Water Company for a franchise to lay water mains in the streets and alleys of the town of Las Vegas was presented and the hearing on the same was set for September 7, 1909, the Clerk of the board was instructed to have same advertised to comply with the law.

A petition was presented from Searchlight, Nelson and Crescent asking for the consolidation of the three road districts under the name of the Searchlight road district and the appointment of B. F. Miller as road supervisor. Carried.

A petition was presented from Nelson asking for the appointment of L. E. Sowers as deputy sheriff. Upon motion of Wells, seconded by Hawkins, same was laid over until such time as funds are in a condition to consider same.

The taxes as levied by the Searchlight city council was certified to by the Board.

Jurors selected by the Board for the balance of the term.

Las Vegas; Frank A. Buol, E. J. Clark, Walter Greening, John W. Horden, F. B. Hawn, A. W. Jurden, A. L. Murphy, A. J. Sommer, H. J. McGowan, A. H. Kramer, A. D. Bishop, C. P. Ball, F. H. Clayson, G. A. Case, Geo. Cronse, R. A. Ferguson, Wm. S. Park, C. C. Ronnow, W. J. Stewart and J. J. Tuckfield.

Arden; W. Wilson, G. E. Sherman and D. O. Houston.

Crescent; Chas. S. Sheerer, M. J. Sullivan, M. J. Flanigan, Wm. O. Matchett, A. L. Burr, Henry F. Daniels, J. L. Hallam and Geo. W. Morgan.

Nelson; Thos. Bartogee, A. J. Peak, Frank L. Feighan, E. P. Jeanes, Nicholas J. Touroff, A. N. Watson, H. W. Weineke, I. W. Allcock, O. A. Ellis, C. T. Fish, Geo. D. Freeborn and H. L. Harris.

Searchlight; E. R. Bowman, K. M. Beattie, W. H. Bainbridge, A. C. Burlingame, E. F. Carleson, Jas. H. Hicks, Walter A. Hopkins, Wm. W. Burt, Chas. D. Jones, C. W. Lund, Roderick S. Morrison, Jas. H. Maguire, H. E. Spanogle, Alton A. Wait, John Howe, John H. Albright, Walter M. Brown, C. E. Burdick, Paul Barlock, Mark P. Blaumire, Wm. Black, Wallace W. Blair, Frank Byrd, M. F. Emerson, L. W. Godin, H. A. Wallbrecht, H. A. Perkins and John W. Stark.

Sandy; John B. Cryer, Jesse Jones and Nicholas Kunz.

Goodsprings; John A. Eager, John Fredrickson, Geo. A. Fayle, Harvey Hardy Jr., H. J. Jarman and A. J. Robinson.

Overton; Sanford Angell, Richard Cooper, Sherman Thomas, Lyman Shurtleff, W. L. Batty, Mendes D. Cooper, Geo. M. Hayden, Jas. W. Huntsman, W. L. Jones, Creighton Johnson, August

(Continued on Page 8)

COUNTY COMMISSIONERS

(Continued from Page 1)

Koenig and John M. Little.

Mosquite; Ashley Barnum and Lemley Leavitt.

Bunkerville; Parley S. Hunt, Conrad Waite, Benjamin Bunker, Ezra Bunker, Edward L. Cox, Frank L. Cox, Joseph I. Earl, Heber H. Hardy, Calvin H. Jones, Albert Leavitt, Dudley Leavitt Jr., Orange W. Leavitt and Harmon Wittwer.

Moapa; W. L. Sprunt and Geo. C. Baldwin.

St. Thomas; Martin Bunker, Jas. H. Hardy, Wm. F. Murphy and Stowell Whitney.

Logan; Henry Dodson, J. H. Averett, Harry Huntsman and W. W. Perkins.

The following tax levy was ordered for the year 1909. State fund 60c, general county 45c, contingent 15c, indigent 10c, school 45c, interest 42c, current expense 8c, jury 10c, state school 5c, Total $2.40.

Board adjourned.

Las Vegas Age Newspaper
October 9, 1909

Joe F. Perkins, a large stock raiser of Overton, was in the county seat on business Monday last.

S H Wells, who represents the Moapa valley country on the board of county commissioners, was on hand at the board meeting this week

B. F. Bonelli, one of the prominent ranchers of the Overton country, was in Vegas on business during the session of the county commisseoners.

George C. Baldwin, of Moapa, a former county commissioner of Lincoln county, served on the grand jury during the week.

S. A. Angell, one of the prominent ranchers of Overton, was a welcome caller at the Age office this week. Mr Angell is a member of Clark county's first grand jury.

Washington County News
October 14, 1909

A marriage license was issued by the County Clerk on October 13th to Albert Jones of Overton, Nevada, and Miss Era Conger of Moapa, Nevada.

Trial Jurors

The following is a list of the trial jurors who have been summoned to appear in the District Court Monday morning.

A D Bishop, Harry J McGown, W J Stewart, Walter Greening, A H Kramer, F A Buol, F D Hahn, Las Vegas; Harry Dodson, Perry Huntsman, W W Perkins, Logan; Joe H Hardy, Stowell Whitney, St. Thomas; A J Sumner, Arden; Wm Black, W H Bainbridge, E F Carlson, H A Perkins, Chas W Lund, Wm W Huitt, E R Bowman, Chas D Jones, John M Albright, H A Wallbrecht, Wallace Blair, John Howe, Frank Byrd, Herman Spanogle, John W Stark, Paul Barlock, E M Beattie, Searchlight; Chas S Sheerer, John L Hallam, Harry F Daniels, Wm O Matchett, Crescent; Geo Freeborn, O A Ellis, O T Fish, Thos Bartogee, Nelson; Sherman Thomas, Jas Huntsman, Geo M Hayden, Lyman Shurtleff, A N Watson, Wm L Batty, Richard Cooper, John M Lytle, Creighton Johnson, Overton; Frank L Cox, Calvin H Jones, Ezra Bunker, Herbert Hardy, Benj Bunker, Albert Leavitt, Bunkerville; W P Sprunt, Moapa; Harvey Hardy, Jr., John A Egger, A J Robbins, Goodsprings; Lem Leavitt, Mesquite; John B Cryer, Jesse Jones, Sandy.

Washington County News
December 14, 1909

Washington, Dec. 14.—Ezekiel Conger of Overton, Nevada, is here visiting his sister, Mrs. Ezra Jolley.

Moapa Valley To Build Railroad

A branch railroad taking off from Moapa, on the line of the Salt Lake Route, and extending as far southeastward as the Colorado river, tapping a wonderfully fertile territory, will in all probability be built after the first of the new year.

Information about the proposed line has been received by the Moapa Fruit Land company, of which Cannon Brothers are the heaviest stockholders, from H L, A MacDermott, secretary of the Muddy Valley Irrigation company.

A mass meeting of representatives of various interests and people of the Muddy valley generally has been called for Saturday, December 18, at Overton, Nev. At that time it is thought that decisive action will be taken with regard to the building of the branch.

It is maintained by those who are boosting the new line that railroad facilities are absolutely necessary for the proper development of Muddy valley and of surrounding localities It is intended to systematize the efforts now being made for the building of the branch railroad.

The line will extend from Moapa station southeast through Logan, Capalapi and Overton down to St. Thomas, and perhaps as far as the Colorado river. In addition to developing a rich agricultural country, the railroad will be the means of opening up great copper fields — Herald-Republican.

Teachers' Examinations

Teachers' examinations were conducted by Judge Thomas on Monday, Tuesday and Wednesday of this week. There were four candidates for teachers' certificates—Bert Mills, of Logan; Miss Garbury, of Crescent; Mrs. Leavitt, of Mesquite, and E. Thornbaugh, of Overton. The papers have been forwarded to the superintendent of public instruction, who will award the coveted certificates.

COMMISSIONERS

April Meeting Devoid of Sensational Features

The regular meeting of the board of county commissioners was held April 4, 1910. Those present were Chairman W. E. Hawkins and Samuel H. Wells, members, and Harley A. Harmon, clerk. All bills were allowed as per claim book except the following: A. L. F. McDermott, justice of the peace at Overton, $5, and Orayton Johnson, constable, for $4.50, which bills were held awaiting the filing of report of the proceedings in which said court costs were incurred.

Reports of officers were read and approved as read.

On motion the clerk was instructed to write the proper officers of Lincoln county and ask that they forward to the clerk of this county the bond of Frank Manuel, former night marshal of Las Vegas town. Also that Ed C. Ross, present night marshal of Las Vegas town, be required to furnish a bond in the sum of $1,000, to be approved at next meeting.

In the matter of caring for the county indigents, the same was laid over until a meeting of the full board.

An engineer's license was granted to Albert Nelson.

In accordance with the action of the board of county commissioners of Lincoln county fixing the tax levy for the interest fund at 60c it is ordered that the tax rate for the interest fund for Clark county be fixed at the same figure as required by law. [This is a reduction of 5c, leaving the total Clark county rate as fixed at this date $2.95.—Ed.]

The new bond of H. M. Lillis, justice of the peace, with Roy T. Lockett and Chas. P. Ball as sureties, was approved.

In the matter of the plat of Ladd's Addition to Las Vegas, the chairman was authorized to accept the same when it is executed and filed as provided by law.

An allowance of $12.50 per month was made for the relief of W. H. Sherman, to be in the shape of a credit at the store of Harry O. Russell at Crescent.

Water Commissioner

State Engineer Emmet D. Boyle has appointed I. H. Jacobs, of Overton, water commissioner for district No. 5 of the Muddy river. The appointment met with the approbation of the county commissioners, who ratified it at the meeting of the board Monday.

Washington County News
April 13, 1910

Overton, Nev, April 13.—An interesting debate was held Sunday evening, the subject being "Resolved, That, on the whole, strikes are a benefit to the laboring man." W. L Perkins, V. A. Kenney and Bert Mills taking the affirmative, and Willard Jones, S R Whitehead and H P. Hught the negative side of the question. The judges, U. V. Perkins, Ellis Turnbaugh and Geo L Whitney, rendered a decision in favor of the affirmative. The opening program consisted of a solo, "In the Purple Twilight," by Miss Mabel Lewis, and a quartet, "Who Built Dat Ark?" by A. L F. McDermott, Sam. Pixton, S. R. Whitehead and Wm McDonald.

Miss Carlie Perkins took the train at Moapa Sunday evening en route to Tonapah, Nevada, where she will be married to Mr. Bert Marshal, a one time resident of the Muddy valley, but for the past two years engaged in the forestry service for Uncle Sam

Miss Clara Perkins has resigned her position as clerk in the Whitehead Bros' store and central at the telephone office after nearly a year's service. Miss Minerva Swapp has taken her place as "hello" girl

The Ladies' Sewing club met at the home of Mrs Ellen Perkins Wednesday. Refreshments were served and all enjoyed a pleasant afternoon.

A son was born to Mr. and Mrs George Ingram on the 10th; all concerned doing nicely.

Mrs Nellie Brown and Mr Van Renseller were married at Moapa last week.

96

Overton, Nev., April 22—The Y. L M. I. A. girls met at the home of Miss Effie Whitehead Monday evening and listened to the closing chapters of "Six Girls." a book which has been read as a serial in the regular meetings, now closed Light refreshments were served also

E. J. Robertson of Salt Lake City, who is interested in the Moapa Fruit Lands Co., was in the valley the fore part week attending to business connected with their ranch here

Under the supervision of Commissioner Samuel Wells, the farmers of the valley are repairing the road to Moapa which was greatly damaged by the big flood.

This week the schools closed Ellis Turnbough has had charge of the higher grades, Miss Effie Whitehead the Primary grades, and Samuel Pixton the Capalapa school.

Miss Clara Syphus of Panaca, Nev., has spent several months at St Thomas and was visiting friends in Overton Wednesday

Horace Jones returned Monday from Arizona, where he has been working since the Christmas holidays

H. J Doolittle of St George was in town this week on business Mrs Doolittle accompanied him

The Ladies Sewing club was entertained on Wednesday at the home of Miss Nellie Frampton

Mr. and Mrs. L A. Pace, prominent residents of New Harmony, were city visitors the latter part of last week, visiting friends and transacting business. Mr Pace reports everything looking well at New Harmony, though frost had nipped some of the fruit They enjoyed their visit, and left for home Sunday.

97

Overton Talks of Ice Plant and Flour Mill

Moapa, April 18—The season for planting the famous Moapa cantaloupes is about over now, there having been in the neighborhood of one hundred twenty-five acres planted this spring The decrease from last year's acreage of cantaloupes being due to the uncertainty of shipping facilities this summer.

The Y. L and Y. M. M I A. concluded their winter's work with an interesting program Sunday evening Crayton Johnson and Miss Effie Whitehead as presidents of the two associations have been efficient workers and the winter's course has been a very successful one

Mrs. Kate Alphin Deeble and daughter, Miss Allie, enroute from Los Angeles to Caliente, Nev , spent a week in the valley visiting relatives and renewing old acquaintances

They are the guests of their aunt, Mrs Sallie Thomas of Logan.

S A Bunker, Jr , of Bunkerville came over Monday to deliver a load of young hogs at the Capalapa ranch. Hog raising is the coming industry in the valley, some believe, and a number of the ranches are now raising a herd of them

A meeting of the farmers of the valley was held on the 18th at Overton to discuss the possibility of erecting a flour mill and ice plant A committee was appointed to investigate and report at an early date.

Mrs. Mary V Lytle leaves on the 20th for Arizona, where she will join her husband and there make their home for some time. Her sister, Miss Clara Perkins, will accompany her for a visit

Farmers are now harvesting their first crop of hay. Green peas have been on the home market for a couple of weeks, but none are being shipped Growers of asparagus have quit shipping now

Overton, Nev , April 30—On Sunday evening an interesting debate was held before a crowded house on the question· "Resolved that competition affords greater progress than cooperation " Robert Gibson, John Perkins and John M Bunker, all of St Thomas, spoke on the negative, while Samuel Pixton, S R Whitehead and Crayton Johnston of Overton spoke on the affirmative. By mutual consent the debate was held without judges The preliminary program consisted of vocal and instrumental quartets

Postmaster T. J. Jones went over to Bunkerville Wednesday in company with his son-in-law, Orange W. Earl of that place

Warren Cox of St George and Edward Cox of Bunkerville are here this week on business.

New potatoes has been added to the list of vegetables now ready for table use.

Frank S Leavitt of Mesquite was seen on our streets this week.

Overton, Nevada, May 5—The ladies, of the M I A. spent the evening in a farewell social for their president on Wednesday. Miss Whitehead left the following morning for her home in St George with David Conger and Miss Mabel Lewis

Mr. and Mrs Samuel Lytle were the guests of their cousins, Mr and Mrs John M. Lytle at Overton this week. They were returning to their home in Fay, Nevada, after a visit of several months in California.

Wm. Bowman and family have returned to their ranch for the summer. The family spent the winter in Bunkerville, their children attending the school there

A public lecture was given Sunday evening under the management of the M I. A. on the "Book of Mormon," Elder Jessie T. Cooper being the speaker

Mrs S. H. Wells accompanied her husband to the county seat to attend the monthly meeting of the Clark Co commissioners, of which he is a member.

The Ladies' Sewing club was entertained on Wednesday afternoon at the home of Mrs S. R Whitehead.

George S Bunker and family of Morelos, Mexico, spent a few days visiting relatives in the valley this week.

The majority of our townspeople have risen early enough to enjoy a glimse of Halleys comet.

Born, to the wife of Fay Perkins, a daughter on May 2nd

Mrs Effie Whitehead returned Saturday from Overton, Nevada, where she had been teaching school.

County Clerk Woodbury issued marriage licenses on the 9th inst, to Thorald H Truman and Miss Edith Viola Leavitt, both of Gunlock, Samuel David Conger and Miss Mabel Rosalie Lewis, both of Overton, Nevada

99

Overton, Nev., May 13 —The Primary association gave the children a character ball in the Lytle hall Tuesday evening Officers of the Sunday school conducted an ice cream stand in Anderson's store during the evening.

Mrs Lena Stewart of Las Vegas is the guest of her sister, Mrs. Mary Thomas She spent part of last week visiting her sister-in-law, Mrs. Doctor Benson, of Logan, Nev.

Norman Shurtliff has returned from the north, where he has been attending school the past winter.

Cabbage and cauliflower are on the local market this week

U. G. Morse is taking the census in Overton this week

100

The hardest windstorm in many years struck the valley Sunday afternoon coming from north and east It raged all through the night doing some damage to tent homes and shade trees.

Vernon Kenny and family left Tuesday evening for Blackfoot, Idaho, where they will make their home in the future William McDonald left the same evening for Salt Lake City.

The hum of the binder is heard in the grain fields, the second cutting of lucern is also being harvested. Small fruits, such as berries, plums and apricots, are now ripening.

Mrs Albert Jones entertained a number of her lady friends on the afternoon of May 18.

Levi Syphus, Averett Syphus and Brig Whitmore returned Wednesday from Salt Lake City.

Overton, May 20 —Miss Elsie Lewis returned to her home this week after spending the past winter in Salt Lake City. She came via Modena and St George, coming from the latter city with her sister and husband, Mr. and Mrs David Conger, who were recently married at that place.

The hardest windstorm in many years struck the valley Sunday afternoon coming from north and east It raged all through the night doing some damage to tent homes and shade trees.

RUSSIAN THISTLE

Experiment Farm Declares War on Pest in Moapa Valley

Roy M. Filcher, superintendent of the State Experiment Farm located at Logan, in the Moapa valley, has declared war on the Russian thistle, and has appointed today, May 28, as the time for a general campaign. It is possible to entirely eradicate the weed, before it gains a firm hold on the community, if vigorous action is taken by the people.

The Russian Thistle, *Salsola Kali Tragus*, also known as Russian Cactus and Russian Tumble, is considered by most all recent writers upon weeds as our most dangerous. The following from Bulletin No. 15, 1894, Division of Botany, U. S. Department of Agriculture, by Lyster Hoxie Dewey, will give an idea of its destructive nature:

"A weed new to America made its appearance a few years ago in the wheat-raising regions of the Northwest, and has already caused damage to the estimated amount of several millions of dollars. Spreading rapidly as it is over new territory, and becoming more destructive in the regions already infested, it threatens serious consequences unless prompt measures are taken to subdue it.

"A single plant of average size, two or three feet in diameter and weighing two or three pounds at maturity when dry, is estimated to bear 20,000 to 30,000 seeds.

"The most important mode of distribution of the Russian Thistle and the principal one furnished by nature is the wind. When the seed breaks loose from the plant the paper-like flower parts surrounding it act as a sail so that it may be carried a long distance."

Mr. Filcher is to be commended for his action in attacking the pest so systematically and it is expected that the people throughout the valley will give every assistance in the good work. There will be specimens of the plant on exhibition at the postoffices in Logan, Overton and St. Thomas and at the Experiment Farm, so that all may familiarize themselves with this thistle.

Overton, Nev., June 3—Elder Robert Bunker of St. George was released from his mission on May 24, and reached Panaca this week, where his wife has been living with her parents during his absence. His field of labor was the Central states. They will come back to their home as soon as the railroad track is completed to Caliente

David Anderson and family left last week, returning to their old home in Fountain Green, Utah. Mrs Andersons health was very poor and was the cause of their moving away.

Sunday evening Samuel H. Wells of Logan, Nev., spoke upon "The Power of the Mind." The lecture was delivered under the managment of the local Y. M. M. I. A.

On May 30 the Primary children with their president, Mrs. Martha C. Swapp, were among those visited the cemetary to decorate the graves of loved ones

The Ladies' Sewing club was entertained at the home of Mrs. Geo Ingram on June 3 Refreshments were served and an enjoyable afternoon spent

Harvey Gentry, Jr., returned on the 29th from Provo where he has been attending the B. Y. university the past winter.

Born, to Mr. and Mrs George Perkins, a son on May 22, all concerned doing nicely.

Correct spelling should be Andersen

Overton, Nevada, June 10—About 500 bushels of fine wheat belonging to August Koenig was burnt up on the afternoon of June 9 He was burning brush beside his field of about fifteen acres of wheat in the shock and in some way the stubble caught fire and spread all over the field, burning the entire crop.

While driving down a steep hill en route home from Moapa with a load of melon crates, John Thomas was thrown out of his wagon and badly bruised and a rib broken Dr. Benson dressed his wounds and he is now recovering as fast as could be expected.

Orange and Ira J. Earl came over from Bunkerville Saturday. The former returned Monday with a load of salt and the latter went to work for N. L. Larson on the Cox ranch

Guy Gardner and family left the Valley on Saturday for Kingman, Arizona, where they will reside for some time.

Albert Frehner's threshing machine commenced work at St Thomas on June 9th.

Elmer Losee is building an addition to his residence this week.

104

Overton, Nev, June 18—Mrs Bryant Whitmore has been seriously ill with brain fever and other complications since Sunday Dr Benson and Mrs Harry Gentry have been at her bedside for several days. Her sister and husband, Mr and Mrs Harry Howell, of Lehi, Utah, came Wednesday evening

Mrs Sanford Angell came home on the first train from Salt Lake City, where she went to spend the Christmas holidays with her daughters, Rachel and Vinnie, who are married there. The washout on the road deferred her return until now.

Mr and Mrs A. G Nelson have returned for the summer to their home at Mt Pleasant, Utah They have spent the last two winters here for Mr Nelson's health. He has rheumatism and returns to his home much improved

Christian Woenig and family, who have been leasers on the Capalapa ranch the past year, expect to leave Friday for Salt Lake City

Mrs Alonzo Huntsman entertained a party of lady friends at luncheon Wednesday afternoon

Mr. and Mrs Daniel Leavitt of the Weiser ranch have a baby boy, born June 8th.

Mrs Herbert Waite of Bunkerville is a visitor at the Weiser ranch.

105

Overton, June 24 —Mrs. Bryant Whitmore, who has been very ill with brain fever, was taken to the hospital in Salt Lake City, leaving here Sunday morning. Her husband and sister, Mrs Harry Howell and husband accompanied her. A telegram was received here Monday stating that she had been pronounced insane. Brig Whitmore left the same evening for the city. It is generally thought here that her insanity is but temporary.

While turning round the point of a hill south of town, a buggy belonging to W. L Batty was suddenly upset, a bolt having come apart in the tongue. Horace Walker, Mrs W. L Batty and three children, Misses Amelia Ingram and Zilla Peterson, the occupants, escaped with only slight bruises

Willard Pixton of Taylorsville, Utah, paid a visit to his son, Sam, this week. Sam, with his brother, N. Ray Pixton, purchased Mrs Stauffer's, ranch east of the big creek near Overton. The latter is now filling a mission in England

The Primary will close Saturday for the months of July and August. The officers and teachers have planned to serve cake and lemonade to their pupils at the close of the program

The threshing has been completed at Kaolin, (the Church Farm), three thousand and ninty three bushels of grain having been raised there this season

Andrew L Jones and Jesse F. Cooper left Friday for Salt Lake City. They intend spending the summer in the north

Mrs. Crayton Johnston has been very poorly for some time, her health is now thought to be improving, tho slowly.

Farmers are now shipping a few crates of cantaloupes, the season coming about two weeks earlier than last year.

Sylvia Shurtliff has been employed as clerk in Whitehead Bros. store.

Overton, Nevada, June 30—Mrs Isaac Turnbaugh of Panaca, Nev., with her children, Francis and Florence, spent the week visiting her son Ellis and daughter Mrs J. M. Bunker. They left Thursday for San Diego, California, to visit Mrs. Turnbaugh's mother. Mrs. J. M Bunker and children accompanied them

C J. Robertson of Salt Lake City is at his ranch here this week. A carload of hogs has recently arrived from Millard Co, Utah, for his ranch. Orin Jarvis of Provo is also at Capalapa on business.

The Ladies Sewing club met at the home of Mrs. Ethel Anderson Wednesday afternoon. Lunch was served and an enjoyable time spent.

A fire was started in the cellar under Harry Gentry's store last week but was put out before any serious damage was done.

Ben Swapp came in Tuesday from Parashant, where he has been working for some time He will return Friday.

Bp Thos Judd spent the Sabbath and the day following looking after the interests of the Church farm here

Mr. and Mrs James Anderson left Friday to spend the 4th in their old home in Fountain Green, Utah.

Mrs. W. H. McDonald left Tuesday for Salt Lake City to join her husband and spend the summer.

Cantaloupes are ripening very fast these warm days, and are being shipped out as fast.

The settlements in the valley will join in one celebration for July 4th at Overton

Correct spelling should be Andersen

Overton, Nev., July 8—July 4th was celebrated at Overton with a program in the morning; sports, races and a children's dance in the afternoon, and a ball for adults in the evening. Ice cream was on sale at both stores. Twenty-one hundred pounds of ice was shipped over from Las Vegas for the celebration.

Brigham Whitmore and son Bryant returned Friday from Provo, Utah, where they placed the latter's wife in the asylum for the insane. It is a very sad case, she being about twenty years of age and a bride of less than a year, a bright and talented young woman. It is sincerely hoped she can soon be cured.

Crayton Johnson and wife have gone to Beaver, Utah, for a visit and to get medical aid for the latter, whose health has been very poor for some time.

Andrew L Jones has returned from a trip to Salt Lake City, having decided not to remain there through the summer as he first intended.

Misses Laura Leavitt and Louisa Jones of Bunkerville are working here, the former for Mrs. S. H. Wells and the latter for Mrs. W. L. Batty.

Mrs. Al. Young and daughters, Mrs Pymm and Mrs. Bert Nay, came in from Nay's ranch to spend

An unusually large crowd of Indians came into town to celebrate the Fourth from the surrounding country. They were orderly and well behaved and seemed to have as fine a time as any body.

Roxton Whitmore of this place and Miss Della Gentry of St. Thomas were married Sunday at the home of the bride's parents. Judge A. L F. McDermott performed the ceremony.

Mr. and Mrs. Robert Bunker returned Saturday from Panaca to their home in St. Thomas. Mrs Bunker has lived in Panaca during her husband's absence on a mission.

came in from Nay's ranch to spend the Fourth.

W. W. McDonald is here on business from Thatcher, Ariz., where he moved his family last fall.

Miss Lottie Angell returned last week from northern Utah where she has spent the past year.

Miss Clara Perkins returned Sunday from Arizona.

SUMMONS

In the Justice's Court of Overton Township, County of Clark, State of Nevada.

Summons. Act of 1907, Stats, p. 27.

WM. J. POWERS, Plaintiff, vs. FRANK BOW-LIN, Defendant.

The State of Nevada sends greeting to Frank Bowlin, Defendant.

You are hereby directed to appear before me at my office in Overton, in the County of Clark, and answer the complaint in the above entitled action within five days, if the Summons be served in the township or city in which the action is brought; ten days if served out of the township or city, but within the county in which the action is brought; "and within twenty days if served elsewhere;" and unless you appear and answer, the plaintiff will take judgment for any money or damages demanded in the complaint, as arising upon contract, or will apply to the court for the relief demanded in the complaint.

The said action is brought to recover the sum of $73.00 due and unpaid from said defendant to this plaintiff for goods and merchandise.

To the Sheriff or any Constable of said county, Greeting:

Make legal service and due return hereof.

Given under my hand this 1st day of July, A. D. 1910.

A. L. F. MACDERMOTT,
Justice of the Peace of said township.

First publication July 9, 1910.
Last publication July 30, 1910.

SUMMONS

In the Justice's Court of Overton Township, County of Clark, State of Nevada.

Summons. Act of 1907, Stats, p. 27.

WM. J. POWERS, Plaintiff, vs. GEO. HOCK-ERY, Defendant.

The State of Nevada sends greeting to Geo. Hockery, Defendant.

You are hereby directed to appear before me at my office in Overton, in the County of Clark, and answer the complaint in the above entitled action within five days, if the Summons be served in the township or city in which the action is brought; ten days if served out of the township or city, but within the county in which the action is brought; "and within twenty days if served elsewhere;" and unless you appear and answer, the plaintiff will take judgment for any money or damages demanded in the complaint, as arising upon contract, or will apply to the Court for the relief demanded in the complaint.

The said action is brought to recover the sum of $90.00 due and unpaid from said defendant to this plaintiff for goods and merchandise.

To the Sheriff or any Constable of said county, Greeting:

Make legal service and due return hereof.

Given under my hand this 1st day of July, A. D. 1910.

A. L. F. MACDERMOTT,
Justice of the Peace of said township.

First publication July 9, 1910.
Last publication July 30, 1910.

Bp. J. I. Earl has gone to Moapa on business His daughter, Vida, accompanied him and will go on to Overton to visit with her sister, Mrs. Willard Jones

Overton, July 15—J I Earl and daughter, Vida, came over from Bunkerville Tuesday. After spending a day in Moapa he returned, leaving Miss Vida to visit her sister, Mrs W L Jones His son, Milton, returned with him

F R. Snow, Pres. of the Utah-Nevada Distributing Co , is in the valley this week on business His company are handling part of the crop of cantaloupes now being sent to market in shipments of two and three cars a day.

Mrs. Sarah Perkins left this week to visit her daughter, Mrs Emma Cox, at Logan, Utah. Her daughter, Vivia, accompanied her.

A. J. Barnum of Mesquite, Nev , has opened an eating house in Moapa, greatly to the accommodation of the cantaloupe haulers

Mr. and Mrs. Alma Leavitt of Bunkerville are at Capalapa, where Mr Leavitt is working

Mr. and Mrs W. J. Po ers of Moapa had a baby girl born to them recently.

Mr. and Mrs. Van Renseller returned last week from a trip to the coast

S. R Whitehead has installed a soda water fountain in his store.

Mr and Mrs Albert Jones have a baby boy, born July 15.

110

July 23—The rush of the cantaloupe harvest is over in Overton for the season, a few crates are yet being gathered daily. While it is not definitely known what the crop will pay it is generally believed that a good price will be paid the farmers for this year's crop.

Mr. Squires of Las Vegas met with the voters of the valley Friday evening to select men from this section for the county ticket of the coming election in the fall.

Mrs. Vernon Anderson will take the train at Moapa Thursday for a visit with her relatives in Fountain Green, Utah.

Mrs Birdie Pernell and family have moved back to her home in northern Utah.

Miss Clara Perkins has taken her old place as sales lady in Whitehead's store.

Ira J. Earl left this week to spend the 24th of July at Grass Valley, Utah.

Born, to Mr. and Mrs. James Huntsman, a girl on the 16th.

111

Overton, July 29—A meeting of Democrats held in Las Vegas on the 23rd was attended by Bp. J. M. Bunker of St. Thomas and S R. Whitehead, Harold Sparks and Joseph Perkins of Overton.

Vernon Anderson has gone to Fountain Green, Utah, to make his home in the future. He left on the 29th inst., Joseph Ingram accompanying him, for a trip, as they will go by team.

Alvin, the youngest son of J. P. Anderson, was thrown from a wagon Wednesday and run over by the hind wheel; he was not seriously injured however.

W. O. Bowman, A. L. F. McDermott and By. W. L. Jones of this place attended a meeting of Republicans on the 26th inst. in Las Vegas.

Misses Lovisa Leavitt and Lottie Hansen of Bunkerville, have employment here in the homes of Mrs. Robinson and Gann of Logan.

Will Cooper is visiting his family here after an absence of several months in the mines out in Nevada.

Wm. Stewart of Las Vegas spent a few days in the valley this week, returning Wednesday.

Mr. and Mrs. W. L. Batty have a baby boy, born July 26.

Correct spelling should be Andersen

112

CANDIDATES OUT

Firing Line Manned for Battle of the Primaries by Men of Both Parties

Republican Party Represented by Strong Men, From Whom the People Will Choose Winning Ticket Sept. 6

Many candidates for nominations at the primary election Sept. 6 have appeared in both parties and the line-up, as it appears from the list of those seeking nominations, is nearly complete. The state tickets, of course, are not fully represented in this county, many of the candidates not deeming it necessary to send their nomination petitions here. Those who have circulated nominating petitions in Clark county to date are as follows:

STATE TICKET

REPUBLICAN		DEMOCRATIC
George S. Nixon, Reno	U. S. SENATE	Key Pittman, Tonopah
J. F. Douglas, Reno	CONGRESSMAN	Chas. A. Sprague, Goldf'd
T. L. Oddie, Tonopah	GOVERNOR	D. S. Dickerson, Carson
W. A. Massey, Reno	"	
Wm. Easton, Reno	LIEUT.-GOV.	Frank Williams, Goodsprings
F. H. Norcross, Reno	JUSTICE SUPR. COURT	
	SEC'Y OF STATE	Geo. Brodigan, Goldfield
Hugh H. Brown, Tonopah	ATT'Y GENERAL	
W. W. Booth, Tonopah	STATE PRINTER	
W. R. Thomas, Las Vegas	DISTRICT JUDGE	Chas. Lee Horsey, Pioche
E. J. L. Taber, Elko	" "	

County Ticket

REPUBLICAN		DEMOCRATIC
Chas. P. Squires, Las Vegas	STATE SENATOR	George Bergman, Nelson
E. W. Griffith, Las Vegas	" "	
Leon French, Searchlight	ASSEMBLYMEN	H. H. Sparks, Overton
Willard L. Jones, Overton	"	
W. J. Stewart, Las Vegas	COMMISS'R (long term)	John M. Bunker, St. Th'a
Edward I. Cox, Bunkerv.	" "	
T. A. Brown, Searchl't	COMMIS'RS (short term)	W. E. Hawkins, L. Vegas
C. C. Ronnow, Las Vegas	" "	
Sam Gay, Las Vegas	SHERIFF	C. C. Corkhill, Las Vegas
	"	Jos. F. Perkins, Overton
	CLERK	Harley A. Harmon, L. Vegas
Frank A. Doherty, Searchl't	RECORDER & AUD.	I. W. Botkin, Las Vegas
	" "	C. L. Aug Mahn, Searchl't
Ed. Von Tobel, Las Vegas	TREASURER	Ed. W. Clark, Las Vegas
Frank A. Buol, Las Vegas	ASSESSOR	S. R. Whitehead, Overton
W. J. McBurney, Logan	"	
Richard Busteed, Las Vegas	DIST. ATTORNEY	O. J. Van Pelt, Las Vegas
Lloyd D. Smith, Las Vegas	PUB. ADM'R	Chas. Ireland, Las Vegas
C. E. McCarthy, Goodspr'gs	SURVEYOR	
Henry M. Lillis	J. P., Las Vegas Twp.	
	J. P., Searchlight	John J. Vogel
W. L. Colton	CONSTABLE, Searchl't	Robert A. Wilson

DEMOCRATS COGITATE

Bunch of the Faithful Plan for Division of Offices Among Themselves

Several visitors from out of town, all candidates for office except A. E. Babcock, of Nelson, met with the local office holders at the county court house Saturday evening to consider the best plan of dividing the offices without disrupting the party. In addition to Mr. Babcock, the visitors were C. L. Aug. Mahn, of Searchlight, George Bergman, of Nelson, John M. Bunker of St. Thomas, S. R. Whitehead of Overton, Henry Rice of Logan and H. H. Sparks and Joe. F. Perkins of Overton.

The sentiment seemed to be that in order to win it is necessary for the party to put its very best timber in the field. In order to promote party harmony each of the visitors except Mr. Babcock, as above stated, offered to sacrifice himself by becoming a candidate before the primaries, and the meeting broke up with a hopeful feeling which lasted almost until Tuesday evening.

A. L. F. MacDermott, of Overton, took an active part in republican deliberations this week.

W. C. Bowman was the Logan representative at the republican meeting Tuesday evening. Mr. Bowman is considering the purchase of land in the artesian belt.

Willard L. Jones, one of the prominent citizens of the Moapa valley, came down from Overton Tuesday to attend the republican meeting.

114

REPUBLICANS HARMONIZE

Enthusiastic Meeting Tuesday Evening Promotes Good Feeling in the Party

In response to the invitation sent out from Vegas last week, a goodly bunch of republicans from various portions of the county came to Vegas and attended the meeting held at the Age office Tuesday evening. Judge Lillis presided and Frank A. Doherty acted as secretary. About 60 energetic republicans were present.

In his opening remarks Judge Lillis declared it to be the desire of Vegas republicans that both the north and the south should be given a full share of representation on the ticket. In response to a request the guests from the north and the south made recommendations of names to be placed before the primaries as representing those sections.

The utmost harmony prevailed, the result of the meeting being to still further cement the party for the coming campaign. A desire that the party primaries should result in the selection of the best possible men to fill the places on the ticket was expressed by all and a determination to work for that end was manifest.

Among those from out of town attending the meeting were the following prominent republicans: H. A. Perkins and Leon French, of Searchlight; Edward I. Cox, James S. Abbott and S. W. Darling, of Bunkerville; Willard L. Jones and A. L. F. MacDermott, of Overton; Wm. Francis Murphy, of St. Thomas; W. O. Bowman, of Logan.

Overton, Aug. 5—Mrs. J. C. Jones and Albert Jones have gone to Idaho to visit Mrs. Ella Jones Callister of Blackfoot. The latter will also look over that country with a view of finding a home.

Mr. and Mrs Clinton McDonald left here on the 1st for a trip to the coast; they will also go up the coast to San Francisco and Oakland before returning.

Crayton Johnson and wife returned Monday from Beaver, Utah. Mrs Johnson is much improved in health.

Andrew L Jones has begun the erection of a cement block cottage on his lot one block west of Main.

Samuel Pixton and Miss Nell Frampton of Logan were married Aug 3 in the Salt Lake temple.

John Averett of Logan and Miss Lottie Angell of this place were married Aug. 2 at Las Vegas.

Mr. and Mrs. Willard L Jones will leave Tuesday for a trip to Southern California.

Mrs John Thomas of Logan and son Bert have gone to Salt Lake City.

Sherman Thomas has gone to Idaho to look for a home.

Miss Armelia Ingram is visiting relatives in Lehi, Utah

Stanley Jones left Friday for his home in Provo, Utah.

116

COMMISSIONERS

Appoint Election Officers and Transact Two Months' Business

At the meeting of the Commissioners held last Monday, Aug. 1, those present were chairman W. E. Hawkins and S. H. Wells, with Clerk Harley A. Harmon.

The minutes of last meeting were approved and bills allowed as per claim book.

Clerks and judges were appointed for the primary election Sept. 6, as follows:

Mesquite: Abram N. Woodberry, W. E. Abbott and Jas. E. Hughes.

Overton: S. A. Angell, H. A. Sparks and Ellis Turnbaugh.

Moapa: W. O. Fullshays, J. M. Pickett, W. L. Moore.

Bunkerville: Henry Adams, Frank I. Cox, Orange W. Leavitt.

St. Thomas: Jacob Bauer, Wm. Murphey, M. A. Bunker.

Logan: J. H. Averett, John Thomas, Sr., S. L. Benton.

Las Vegas: Chas. Ball, J. J. Tuckfield, H. J. McGown.

Goodsprings: J. G. Armstrong, H. J. Jarman, J. F. Kent.

Searchlight: Paul Berlock, L. Gilroy, Howard Perkins.

Nelson: Clark Alvord, J. E. Babcock, J. H. Humphrey.

Crescent: J. H. Joat, H. O. Russell, J. B. Horne.

Arden: R. C. Lochridge, W. Wilson, Ed. Brown.

The resignation of C. W. Patterson, as registration agent at Moapa was accepted and C. F. Feldt appointed to fill the vacancy.

J. N. Hunter was appointed road overseer of Bunkerville Mesquite road district in place of E. Bunker, Jr.

The appointment of Ed. C. Ross as night policeman and fire marshal of Las Vegas town was revoked and R. A. Ferguson appointed to fill the vacancy, and his official bond approved.

The treasurer was authorized to sell any of the property sold to the county for taxes upon giving legal notice.

On application of H. J. McGown to purchase lots 14 to 18 town of Las Vegas, the treasurer was ordered to sell said lots after legal notice.

On petition of more than 50 tax paying electors it was ordered that the question of establishing a county high school be submitted to the electors at the general election.

Chas. Carr was granted an engineer's license.

The report of Peter Buol and J. T. McWilliams as road viewers of the Sandstone road was accepted.

On petition of Frank Williams certain lands were ordered stricken from the delinquent tax list.

$250 was transferred from the general fund to the Bunkerville road district, and $2,000 to the salary fund.

The clerk was instructed to ask a report of 1909 poll tax collections from the tax collector of Lincoln Co.

The applications of O. B. Landon, W. B. Cooper, C. E. Brown and Bert Mize for engineers' licenses were granted.

MARRIED

AVERETT-ANGELL.—At the Overland hotel in this city, Monday evening, August 1, 1910, John Henry Averett, of Logan, aged 26 years, and Lottie Angell, of Overton, aged 19 years, Judge Lillis officiating.

The many friends of the contracting parties extend their congratulations. The happy couple left for home Tuesday.

117

J. P. Andersen should be the correct spelling
Alvin was 11 years old at the time.

OVERTON

[Special Correspondence]

Vernon Anderson and family have gone to Fountain Green, Utah, to make their future home.

Joseph Ingram has gone on a trip to Northern Utah.

Wm. J. Stewart, of Las Vegas, spent the fore part of last week in this valley, returning home Wednesday.

Wm. Cooper is visiting his family here after an absence of several months in the mines out in Nevada.

Born—To Mr. and Mrs. James Huntsman, a daughter, and to Mr. and Mrs. Albert Jones, a son, on the 15th of July.

Misses Lovisa Leavitt and Lottie Hansen of Bunkerville are working for Mrs. Robinson and Mrs. Gann of Logan.

J. P. Anderson's son, Alvin, was thrown from a wagon on the 26th ult., a hind wheel passing over him. He is recovering nicely from his bruises.

A meeting of democrats held at Las Vegas on the 23d ult. was attended by J. M. Bunker, of St. Thomas, and S. R. Whitehead, Harold Sparks and Joe Perkins, of Overton. They returned home Sunday evening.

Mr. and Mrs. W. L. Batty are rejoicing over a son born July 26th. Mother and babe are doing nicely.

W. C. Bowman of Logan, W. L. Jones and A. L. F. MacDermott of this place and Wm. Francis Murphy of St. Thomas represented the valley at the republican meeting in Las Vegas on the 26th ult.

An ice cream party was held in St. Thomas on the evening of July 25th.

Geo. L. Whitney, of St. Thomas, was in Vegas on business Wednesday last.

Mr. and Mrs. W. L. Jones, of Overton, passed through Vegas Tuesday evening for a month's outing at the coast.

OVERTON

[Special Correspondence]

Mr. and Mrs. Clinton McDonald left here on the 1st for a trip to the coast. They will visit Southern California, also San Francisco and Oakland, before returning.

John Averett, of Logan, and Miss Lottie Angell of this place were married on August 2d at Las Vegas.

The following persons left Friday on the north-bound train for various points in Northern Utah and Idaho: Mrs. John Thomas, Bert Thomas, Sherman Thomas, Albert Jones, Stanley Jones and Mrs. J. C. Jones.

Crayton Johnson and wife returned Monday from Beaver. Mrs. Johnson's health is much improved.

Miss Amelia Ingram is visiting relatives in Lehi, Utah.

Sam Pixton, of Overton, and Miss Nell Frampton, of Logan, were married August 3d in Salt Lake City.

Andrew L. Jones has begun the erection of a cement block house.

Mr. and Mrs. W. L. Jones left Tuesday for Los Angeles and other Southern California points.

119

Joe F. Perkins of Overton, one of the democratic candidates for the nomination as sheriff, has been in Vegas several days.

Washington County News
September 2, 1910

Overton, Sept. 2—Pres E G. Wooley, Sec. F. R Snow and directors Muir, Murphy and Hobson, of the Moapa Improvement Co , came down from Salt Lake City to hold their annual directors meeting on the farm this week.

Mrs Wm Batty left on the 1st for Provo, Utah, where she expects to get medical attention for her little son, Arlo, whose foot has been turned from birth

Mr. and Mrs Sam Pixton have returned from northern Utah, where they have been visiting relatives since their marriage, August 3.

Since his return from Idaho, Albert Jones has purchased the Wm Cooper home and farm from Mr. Gunn of Moapa

W L Jones and family have returned from California. They report having had a very nice trip.

Mrs Lydie Squires of Long Beach. California, is visiting her grandchildren at the Bowman ranch.

W R Thomas and E. W. Griffith of Las Vegas were over on political business this week.

Mrs. Ves Nay returned Wednesday from Gold Field, where she has spent the summer.

Bp. Thos. Judd was here this week in the interest of the Church farm at Kaolin

Mr. and Mrs. M. D. Cooper have a baby boy, born on the 18th of August

Horace Jones has gone to Provo to attend the B. Y. U the coming winter

Edward and Warren Cox spent a couple of days in the valley this week

Bert Thomas left on the 23rd for a trip to the coast

Las Vegas Age Newspaper
September 10, 1910

120

H. H. Sparks, of Overton, democratic nominee for the assembly, was in the county seat several days this week.

OVERTON

[Special Correspondence]

Mr. and Mrs. Samuel Pixton have returned from Northern Utah, where they have been visiting relatives since their marriage Aug. 3d.

Bert Thomas left on the evening of the 23d for Los Angeles and other California points.

Born, Aug. 18th, to Mr. and Mrs. M. D. Cooper, a son. All concerned doing nicely.

Since his return from Idaho, Albert Jones has purchased from Mr. Gunn of Moapa the Wm. Cooper home and farm in Overton, and will make his home here in the future.

Horace Jones left Tuesday for Provo, Utah, where he will attend the B. Y. university this winter.

Mrs. Mary Batty left on the 31st for Provo, Utah, where she will secure medical attention for her little son Arlos, whose foot has been slightly turned since birth.

Bishop Thos. Judd of La Virkin, Utah, spent a couple of days recently at Kaolin on business connected with the church farm.

The telephone company has installed a line from Overton to Logan, improving the main line service.

Mrs. Lydia Squires of Long Beach, Cal., visited her grandchildren at the Bowman ranch recently.

The Moapa Improvement Co. held its annual meeting Aug. 27, there being present from Salt Lake President E. G. Wooley, Secretary F. R. Snow and directors Hobson, Muir and Murphy.

Mr. and Mrs. W. L. Jones have returned from a pleasant trip to Southern California.

Party Organizations

The members of the republican and democratic county committees elected at the primaries, so far as returns have been received, are given below. At Arden and Mesquite precincts no democratic votes seem to have been cast and no democratic committeemen elected. Our returns from Logan and St. Thomas do not show committeemen.

PRECINCT.	REPUBLICAN.	DEMOCRATIC.
Nelson	Clark Alvord	J. E. Babcock
Searchlight	B. F. Miller Jr.	O. S. Reeder
Crescent	S. C. Whipple	Jeff Davis
Goodsprings	C. E. McCarthy	J. C. Armstrong
Arden	A. G. Sherman	
Las Vegas	Dr. R. W. Martin	Frank A. Clark
Moapa	J. S. Sprague	J. S. Sprague
Overton	S. A. Angell	Brig Whitmore
Bunkerville	S. W. Darling	J. I. Earl
Mesquite	Wm. E. Abbott	
Logan	W. J. McBurney	Henry Rice
St. Thomas	Wm. F. Murphy	M. A. Bunker
	SOCIALIST	
Las Vegas	M. F. Richter	

ST. THOMAS

[Special Correspondence]

Sam Gentry, Jesse O'Donell and Martin Bunker, Jr., who have a fine bunch of cattle at their ranch at Pahcoon spring, report their stock in fine condition.

An action in replevin brought by Brig Whitmore to recover two donkeys resulted in judgment for plaintiff in Judge McDermott's court at Overton and a warrant was issued for the arrest of Bert Nay, who will be asked to explain what right he had to sell Whitmore's burros.

Milder weather prevails in this section, ending an unusually long and hot summer.

Jake Beckley had the misfortune to injure his left hand in the gear of the new drilling rig Friday.

Overton, Sept. 19—A change has been made in our mail service, the stage not leaving Moapa until after the arrival of the 4 o'clock train from California. The stage will bring the mail down Sunday instead of Monday after this week.

A goodly number of the farmers of Logan and St Thomas met with the farmers of Overton to discuss methods for the continuance of the Farmers' association, on the afternoon of the 17th.

Our representatives at the recent stake conference in St. George, nine in number, have returned in excellent spirits and report having had a good trip.

Ves Nay has purchased the Vernon Anderson home two blocks west of Main and will take possession soon.

Born, Sept. 18th. a son to Mr. and Mrs Wm. Marshall of Logan; all concerned doing nicely.

After a vacation of two months the Primary association has begun its regular meetings again.

Miss Fanny Hughes of Mesquite is visiting her cousin, Mrs. Bert Whitney.

Mr. and Mrs O B. Nay of Tonopah are spending a few weeks here

We enjoyed a fine rain on the 13th and 14th insts

The school at Logan commenced a week ago.

123

DISMAL DEMOCRATS

Anxiously Await Word From the North Before Adopting Platform

The Democratic County Central Committee met in an extremely perfunctory and polite manner, said how-de-do and adjourned Tuesday afternoon. They did get up enough life to appoint an executive committee, probably being moved thereto by the rebellious name of Jeff Davis, the Crescent member; those appointed being F. A. Clark, chairman, M. A. Bunker and said Jeff Davis.

George Bergman, the democratic nominee for the state senate, was present, bearing the proxy of J. E. Babcock, of Nelson. The others were O. S. Reder, Searchlight; Jeff Davis, Crescent; Joe Armstrong, Goodsprings; F. A. Clark, Las Vegas; Henry Rice, Logan; Brig Whitmore, Overton, and M. A. Bunker, St. Thomas.

The keynote of the democratic campaign not having been transmitted from the north by the leaders of democracy, the matter of adopting a platform was laid over until after the meeting of the state central committee Tuesday next, after which the executive committee will enunciate the platform for the rest of the bunch.

REPUBLICAN PLATFORM

County Central Committee Puts Forth Sound Doctrine for Voters' Consideration

At the meeting of the Republican County Central Committee in this city on Tuesday last a platform was adopted which we publish in full below. The spirit of the document is earnest and it will commend itself to the thinking voter.

The Republican County Central Committee of the county of Clark, state of Nevada, reaffirms its allegiance to the principles of the Republican party, which is now, as it always has been, the party of progress and achievement.

We glory in the history and traditions of the Republican party, and believe that, as in the past it has been the leader in every great movement tending toward the improvement of conditions under which men live, so it always will lead in those reforms that make for progress, prosperity, the welfare of the people and the advancement of the race.

We heartily endorse the administration of President William H. Taft. We commend his administration as having redeemed, in little more than one year, the promises contained in the platform on which he was elected by the people. In all matters of important legislation, as well as in volume of work accomplished, the 61st congress is without parallel.

We declare our adherence to the doctrine of protection, without which the American standard of living and wages cannot be maintained. We especially commend the attitude of President Taft in demanding revision of the tariff by schedule only, upon data furnished by a competent, permanent tariff commission.

We commend the policy pursued by the past and present Republican administrations in placing under government control all corporations doing an interstate business and prohibiting them from making contributions to campaign funds.

We rejoice in the impetus given to the cause of civic righteousness by Theodore Roosevelt and other leaders of the Republican party, and commend their courage and diligence in prosecuting to conviction violators of the law irrespective of high position held in the political, business or social world.

We believe that the same morality, courage, honesty and common sense should be demanded from those aspiring to office and the same integrity, fidelity and efficiency demanded in the execution of official duties by those occupying official positions as are exacted from those seeking or occupying positions of trust in private life.

125

We heartily commend the general features of the primary law, placing as it does the nominating power in the hands of the people, where it rightly belongs. We recommend to the next legislature such modifications and simplifications of the present law as are found practicable.

We recommend to our senator and representative in congress that they make every effort to secure the enactment of a law establishing a Department of Mines in the general government, along lines similar to those of the Department of Agriculture.

We heartily favor and urgently recommend that our commissioners inaugurate a system of permanent county roads and that the same be improved systematically from year to year through the careful expenditure of the road funds. We further recommend the expenditure of sufficient money by the county commissioners to sink wells or otherwise develop water in such locations as may be necessary along county roads for the benefit of the traveling public.

We recommend that the state senator and members of the assembly be instructed to institute such legislation as shall establish the county of Clark into three Commissioner Districts. The first district to extend from the north boundary line of the county to a line drawn east and west and south of the Muddy river, to include the precincts of Mesquite, Bunkerville, Moapa, Logan, Overton and St. Thomas. The second district to extend from the south boundary of the first district to a line drawn north of Goodsprings, so as to include the precincts of Arden and Las Vegas. The third district to include the precincts of Crescent, Searchlight, Nelson and Goodsprings. Each district to elect a commissioner who shall have the immediate supervision of affairs in his district, to recommend the appointment of road supervisors and to introduce all matters connected with his district to the consideration of the board of county commissioners.

We hereby pledge the nominees of the Republican party on the county ticket to a careful and economical conduct of their respective offices, especially in the expenditure of public money.

In the whole course of the Republican party its watchwords have been education and progression. We heartily urge the establishment of a County High School to meet the educational requirements of the county of Clark.

REPUBLICANS ORGANIZE

County Central Committee Plans Winning Campaign--Harmony Prevails

The meeting of the Republican County Central Committee was called to order Tuesday afternoon at the court house by S. C. Whipple, who placed in nomination Dr. R. W. Martin for temporary chairman. The choice was unanimous and Dr. Martin immediately took up the duties of his exacting office. On motion of B. F. Miller, Jr., Frank A. Doherty was made temporary secretary.

The county committee was declared to be composed of the following precinct committeemen:

Nelson—Clark M. Alvord.
Searchlight—B. F. Miller, Jr.
Crescent—S. C. Whipple.
Goodsprings—C. E. McCarthy.
Las Vegas—R. W. Martin.
Logan—W. J. McBurney.
Overton—S. A. Angell.
St. Thomas—Wm. F. Murphy.
Bunkerville—S. W. Darling.

J. T. Sprague was made committeeman for Moapa, James E. Hughes for Mesquite and A. G. Sherman for Arden. The temporary organization was then made permanent.

An executive committee, consisting of W. J. McBurney of Logan, C. E. McCarthy of Goodsprings and R. W. Martin of Las Vegas, was provided for and W. J. McBurney, B. F. Miller, Jr., and R. W. Martin were recommended to the nominees for the legislature for appointment on the state central committee, with the understanding that if the county should be entitled to a larger number of committeemen the chairman should recommend the appointments. The secretary was instructed to inform Messrs. C. P. Squires, Leon French and Willard L. Jones of above action.

On motion of Clark Alvord the entire state and county and all local tickets nominated by the republicans at the primaries were endorsed.

The name of Jesse Knight was placed on the ticket as nominee for justice of the peace of Goodsprings.

Each nominee on the county ticket was assessed $10 as a preliminary campaign fund and the further raising of funds was left to the executive committee.

S. W. Darling, S. C. Whipple and J. T. Sprague were appointed a committee on platform and an adjournment was taken until 7:30 p. m., at which time the committee again convened and adopted the platform published in another column.

The proceedings throughout were marked by a business-like attention to the details of the business and were very harmonious.

Senatorial Committee

The republican candidate for the state senate, Chas. P. Squires, has appointed a republican senatorial committee as provided by law. The members of the same are: Dr. Roy W. Martin, Las Vegas precinct; J. E. Hastings, Nelson; H. A. Perkins and C. H. Jones, Searchlight; K. N. Bright, Crescent; S. E. Yount, Goodsprings; J. T. Sprague, Moapa; M. D. Cooper, Overton; B. F. Bonelli, St. Thomas; W. C. Bowman, Logan; Edw. I. Cox, Bunkerville; Wm. E. Abbott, Mesquite.

OVERTON

[Special Correspondence]

Born, Sept. 18, to Mr. and Mrs. Wm Marshall, of Overton, a son. All concerned doing nicely.

We are pleased to have Mr. and Mrs. W. J. McBurney return to their home in the valley after an absence of some months in Las Vegas.

Mr. and Mrs. S. H. Wells have been visiting in Salt Lake City.

W. C. Bowman has moved his family over to their winter home in Bunkerville, where the children will attend school the coming winter.

W. L. Jones, Crayton Johnson and M. D. Cooper, also a number of young people, who attended the Dixie Field Sports and Stake Conference in St. George, all returned home last week.

Threshing has been resumed, as only a part of it was done when they quit running for lack of help during cantaloupe season.

Mr. and Mrs. O. B. Nay are here visiting for a few weeks.

The Children's Primary Association has begun again after a two months' vacation during the heated term, and holds every Saturday afternoon. Mrs. Martha Swapp is president of the association.

Andrew L. Jones and Wm. Batty left this week for the north, the former going to Salt Lake City and the latter to join his family, now visiting in Provo.

Mrs. David Conger has recently returned from a visit to Salt Lake City.

Mr. and Mrs. Orin Jarvis arrived here Wednesday from Provo, coming by way of St. George to visit relatives there. Mr. Jarvis has business interests here. His family will spend the winter at Overton.

Tom Osborne, of Salt Lake City, is looking after business interests here.

Our district school began Monday with Ellis Turnbaugh of Overton and Miss Hattie Brown of Los Angeles as teachers.

Mrs. W. H. McDonald has returned from Salt Lake City, where she and her husband spent the summer.

Stage driver Wm. Hutchings having recently married in St. George, Utah, C. M. Peterson is driving the stage down the valley from Moapa a few trips.

129

Overton, Oct 3 —District Attorney Thomas for the State and Attorney Van Pelt for the defense were called to Overton from Las Vegas on the 29 to attend the trial of Herbert Nay before Justice McDermott on the charge of grand larceny. Nay was charged by Brig Whitmore with driving away a burro belonging to the latter; Nay also claimed the burro as his property and the criminal action follows a civil action in which Whitmore made claim for delivery of the animal Nay was bound over to the grand jury but secured bail and is at liberty.

Andrew L Jones of this place and Miss Sevilla Henderson of Salt Lake were married in the Salt Lake Temple Wednesday Sept 28. They will visit relatives in Idaho and attend the general conference in Salt Lake before returning

Mr. and Mrs Hinckley of Logan are visiting in northern Utah. Mr. and Mrs. Sam Pixton are living on their ranch and taking care of the store and postoffice during their absence.

Jacob Rhoner came last Saturday from Wasatch Co, Utah, for a few days with his daughter, Miss Gertrude Rhoner of this place.

Mrs W. J. Conger is visiting her children in the valley for a few weeks

Mr. and Mrs S Wells and family are visiting in Salt Lake City.

130

Overton, Oct 10—The Y M M
I. A. and Y. L M. I A. commenced
their winter's work with a joint
program Sunday evening The
house was filled beyond its seating
capacity and an excellent program
rendered Crayton Johnson, Andrew L Jones and Ellis Turnbaugh,
with Albert Jones for Secretary,
have charge of the young men's department, and Misses Mildred Anderson, Elise Lewis and Sadie Perkins
are the presidency of the young
ladies' department.

Two daughters of August Koenig
of this place, Clara and May, and
their husbands have recently returned from Idaho and will spend the
winter here

Willard L Jones went over to Las
Vegas to attend the Republican
rally held there on the evening of
the 10th.

OVERTON

[Special Correspondence]
October 17, 1910.

Mr. and Mrs. Andrew L. Jones and Mrs. J. Jones came home Tuesday from conference and the state fair in Salt Lake city.

Nevada's republican senator, George S. Nixon; T. L. Oddie, for governor and E. L. Roberts, for congressman, also several other republican candidates for state offices held a rally here Wednesday evening. The party came in the first two automobiles ever brought down the valley, and of course attracted considerable attention. They gave the children of the town some fine rides while here. The party made the run back to Moapa after the rally Wednesday evening.

W. H. McDonald returned home from Salt Lake city this week.

Messrs. French, Brown and McBurney, republican candidates for assemblyman, commissioner and assessor spent Friday in the valley calling on the voters. W. L. Jones, of this place, who is also out for the assembly, accompanied them to St. Thomas.

Mr. and Mrs. W. L. Batty returned home from Provo Saturday. They came by way of Toqueville, where they spent a few days visiting relatives.

The Y. L. M. I. A. have placed a gas light in each of the school rooms for use in their meetings.

Mr. and Mrs. Albert Jones have moved into their home in the northern part of town, until recently owned by Will Cooper.

Orange W. Earl, Edw. I. Cox and S. Darling, of Bunkerville, were in the valley this week, the two latter to attend the republican rally held Wednesday evening.

There has been some sickness here of late, with fever, both old and young being afflicted, but your correspondent has learned of no serious cases.

May and Clara, two daughters of August Koenig, who have recently married in Idaho, have returned with their husbands to spend the winter in our delightful climate.

The Young Men's Mutual Improvement association, with Crayton Johnson, Andrew L. Jones and Ellis Turnbough as president, have commenced their winter's work. They will hold regular weekly sessions and will take up the subject, "The Making of a Citizen." The junior department will take up lessons on conduct and the development of character.

The Young Ladies' Mutual have also commenced their weekly meetings with Misses Mildred Anderson, Elsie Lewis and Sadie Perkins in charge. Jointly with the young men they gave an excellent program Sunday evening, consisting of musical numbers, both instrumental and vocal, also readings and recitations, and an outline of the work planned for the winter by Crayton Jonson.

132

Moapa Valley Farmers' Association

A meeting of the stockholders of the Moapa Valley Farmers' Association has been called by the Board of Directors, for SATURDAY, NOVEMBER 5TH, 1910, at 2 o'clock p. m., at Lytle's hall in Overton, Nev. The meeting is called to consider the question of amending the Articles of Incorporation so as to reduce the face value of the shares, and the redemption price of stock received in exchange for the stock of the Association, and to amend the by laws accordingly, and for the transaction of such other business as may come before it.

By order of the Board of Directors.

A. L. F. MacDERMOTT, Secretary.

First publication Oct. 1, 1910.
Last publication Oct. 22, 1910.

Washington County News
October 29, 1910

Overton, Oct 29.—Mrs Emily C Brooks and Mrs Paralee Miles in the interest of the Relief societies of the stake and Mrs Zilla Lund of the stake Primary held a convention here Monday. They were accompanied by Hyrum Larson of Washington who spent the time visiting his sister, Mrs. J. C. Jones, and family of this place

A moving picture show was given in the Lytle hall Friday and Saturday evening. After they hold forth a couple of evenings in St. Thomas they will hold again here Wednesday evening

Thos Judd and A. B Andrus came in from St George Tuesday. The former will spend a few days looking after matters connected with the Kaolin farm.

Judge E. J. L. Taber of Elko, regular Republican nominee for district judge with several other Republican candidates came down the valley Sunday.

The case of the state against Bert Nay of this place for felony was thrown out of court by the grand jury in Los Vegas this week.

J. L Linton has recently returned from a trip to Los Angeles and the surrounding beaches

W. W McDonald of Thatcher, Ariz , is looking after his interests here

133

Hon. E. J. L. Taber

Word has been received that Hon. E. J. L. Taber, republican candidate for district judge, has this week been touring Lincoln county, and has been received with great favor. Very enthusiastic meetings were held in Alamo, Wednesday night, Caliente Thursday, Panaca Friday and tonight the final meeting in Lincoln county will be held in Pioche.

Judge Taber will meet a number of the local candidates in Clark county at Moapa Sunday afternoon, and the party will then proceed to Overton, where a meeting will be held Monday evening, to be followed by a visit to Bunkerville and Mesquite. After the return from the north, the party will visit Searchlight, Goodsprings Crescent, Nelson and other places in the southern end of the county, ending the campaign with a rousing rally in Las Vegas Saturday or Monday evening.

Judge Taber is an entertaining and forceful speaker and will create much enthusiasm wherever he speaks.

134

Accords Republican Candidates Splendid Reception Monday

The hospitable people of Overton came out in force Monday night to hear the republican county candidates and Judge E. J. L. Taber speak at the dance hall.

The street was illuminated by an immense bonfire. Within, the building was tastefully decorated with bunting. Good music was furnished by the orchestra. Mr. S. A. Angell acted as chairman of the meeting, introducing the various candidates fittingly.

Short, neaty talks were made by Rich ard Busteed, candidate for district attorney, Chas. P. Squires, for state senator, Frank A. Doherty, for auditor and recorder, and Judge Taber, for district judge. All were well received, the address of Judge Taber being especially entertaining.

Following the meeting, the various candidates were introduced to the people and a dance served to while away the hours until midnight. The candidates left the following morning with many pleasant words for their kindly reception and the assurances of support which they received.

135

Overton, Nov. 14 —Election day passed off quietly and after several days of anxious waiting, the following candidates from our section are reported elected by the total unofficial count: John M. Bunker of St. Thomas for county commissioner, Stephen R Whitehead for assessor, and Willard L. Jones for assemblyman.

The Parents class of the Sunday school has appointed a committee to arrange for sports every Saturday afternoon. Clinton McDonald is chairman, and a basketball ground has been prepared, also pole vaulting and base ball grounds.

Manager Thomas Judd of the Nevada Land & Live Stock Co. is busy with a corps of men and teams building an extension on the Overton canal about two miles long to Koalin to cover the higher lands of the company.

The postoffice has been moved from S. R. Whitehead's store to J. P. Anderson's store on Main street and the latter will now act as postmaster. T. J. Jones has served as postmaster about 12 years.

Wm. L. Batty, Sanford Angell, J. W. McBurney, Mr. Sparks, Sen, and W. L Jones were summoned to Las Vegas on the 14th as jurymen.

Harold Young, shoe drummer for Z. C. M. I., came down the valley Thursday visiting the merchants of the valley

George Syphus of Panaca, Nev, is here doing mason work for Andrew L. Jones on his cement block house.

S. H. Wells is at Las Vegas on business connected with his office as county commissioner

On the 13th and 14th insts. we were treated to a fine rain.

136

OVERTON

[Special Correspondence]

Manager Thos. Judd, of the Nevada Land and Live Stock Co., is busy with a corps of men and teams building an extension on the Overton canal about two miles long to Kaolin, to cover the higher lands of the company.

Z. C. M. I.'s genial drummer, Harold Young came down the valley this week taking orders from the merchants for shoes.

The parents' department of the Sunday school has appointed a committee, with Clinton McDonald as chairman, to arrange for sports every Saturday afternoon. Basket ball, pole vaulting and base ball grounds have been prepared and several afternoon's sport enjoyed by old and young.

We enjoyed a fine rain on the 13th and 14th inst.

Geo. Syphus of Panaca, Nevada, is here doing mason work for Andrew L. Jones, who is building a cement block house.

Wm. L. Batty, Sanford Angell, W. J. McBurney, Mr. Sparks, Sr., and Willard L. Jones left Sunday for Las Vegas, where they were summoned to appear as jury men on the 14th inst.

Postmaster T. J. Jones has resigned his position, and J. P. Anderson is our new postmaster. The office has moved to the latter's store last week.

Overton, Nevada, Nov. 21—Prof. Hickman of the Murdock Academy, Beaver, Utah, spoke here on Friday and Sunday evenings and at St. Thomas Saturday evening He spent some time among the young men encouraging them to attend the school at Beaver.

Mrs Issac Lossee and two children from Tropic, Utah, are here visiting her son, I. E Lossee and family of this place They will remain through the winter.

Miss Etta McMullin of Leeds, Utah, spent two weeks visiting her sister, Mrs. J. A. Fleming of this place, leaving here by way of Moapa Sunday.

Thos. Judd left Sunday for his home in St. George to spend Thanksgiving day with his family. J. L. Linton accompanied him.

Jurymen W. L Jones, Luke Whitney, Wm Perkins and Sanford Angell returned from Las Vegas Monday.

E. B. Snow of St. George spent Sunday here. He came in the interest of the Religion Class work.

Albert Frehener left Monday for Littlefield, Arizona. He has made up about 325 gallons of molasses at St. Thomas this fall.

138

Correct spelling should be Frehner

Overton Offerings

Overton, Nov. 28—Thanksgiving day passed off quietly here. Games of base ball and basket ball were played in the after noon and a dance was given in the Lytle hall in the evening

Mr. and Mrs. May of Elko, Nev., were guests of Mr. and Mrs Sanford Angell Saturday. Mr. May has purchased land in the lower part of the valley and expects to locate here.

Sherman Thomas, George Ingram and others have gone with Brig Whittmore to work on his mine for a month.

Mr. and Mrs O B Nay and Mr. and Mrs Bert Nay left here Monday en route to Washington, Utah.

The Mutual Improvement association played "The White Lie," to a crowded house Saturday evening.

John Swapp, who has been ailing for some time with rheumatism, is improving

George Perkins and Frank Jones left Monday for the Grand Gulch mine.

139

OVERTON

(Special Correspondence)

Bishop Thos. Judd and L. L. Linton left on the 20th for St. George, to be gone about two weeks.

Juryman W. L. Jones, Luke Whitney, Wm. Perkins and Sanford Angell returned from Las Vegas Monday.

Mrs. Isaac Losee and two children from Tropic, Utah, are here visiting her son, Elmer Losee and family.

Prof. Hickman, of the Murdock academy at Beaver, Utah, spoke here on Friday and Sunday evenings, and at St. Thomas Saturday evening. He left for his home on Monday morning, Crayton Johnson accompanying him to the depot.

Albert Frehner has made up 325 gallons of excellent molasses in the valley this fall. He and his son and daughter left this afternoon for their home in Littlefield. Mr. Frehner expects to make his home in the valley in the near future.

E. B. Snow, State Councelor of the Religious Class, visited the St. Thomas and Overton wards this week, leaving for his home in St. George Monday.

Miss Etta McMullen of Leeds, Utah, is visiting her sister, Mrs. A. J. Fleming, of this place. She gave up her school in northern Nevada on account of poor health, but is much improved in this warm climate.

Overton, Nov. 28.

Thanksgiving day passed off very quietly here. Base ball and basket ball were played in the afternoon and a dance given in the hall in the evening.

Dr. Lewis Marco of Caliente, Nevada, spent several days here last week doing dental work.

Bishop Thos. J. Jones left Wednesday for Bunkerville.

Orange Earl passed through here Saturday from Gold Butte, going to Fayette, Utah, where his mother is seriously ill.

John Swapp, who has been ailing for some time with rheumatism is improving.

The Mutual Improvment association played "The White Lie," to a crowded house Saturday evening.

Overton, Dec 4.—There is some sickness here, colds and the grip. Among those afflicted are the infants of Mr. and Mrs M. D. Cooper and Mr. and Mrs Ves Nay also Mrs. Bert Whitney. All are improving now.

Miss Ethelyn Bennion is the guest of Mr. and Mrs Samuel Pixton Her father, Bp Heber Benion of Taylorsville, Utah, who came down with her has returned to his home but Miss Bennion will remain for some time.

Bp Edw. Bunker of Bunkerville was over to a directors meeting of the Experiment farm on the 5th He spent Sunday visiting in Overton.

At the conjoint session of the Mutual Improvement association held Sunday night a very spicy program was rendered to a full house.

A committe with Clinton McDonald as chairman has been appointed to arrange a program and sports for the coming holidays.

Mr. and Mrs. Henry Kocherhans and Stephen Swapp came in Sunday from a trip to the Parashant ranch and saw mill.

Mrs. S H. Rich of Centerville, Utah, spent a few days looking over the valley last week.

Bp Thos. Judd and John Linton came down from St. George Sunday evening.

Carpenters are busy roofing the new house of A. L Jones this week.

141

Overton Offerings

Overton, Dec 17.—We are very pleased to have in our midst at this time a party of surveyors for the Salt Lake Route who are surveying a road from Moapa to St. Thomas There is talk of the road being finished to Logan in time for the shipment of next season's crop of cantaloupes

On the evening of the 11th a debate was held under the management of the M I. A. Subject: "Resolved that United States Senators be elected by popular vote" Samuel Pixton, S. R. Whitehead and Miss Ethelyn Bennion were for the affirmative, and Orin Jarvis, A. L F. McDermott and Mrs W. L Jones for the negative The debate was held without judges.

Mrs. Albert Jones and Mrs. Sam Pixton entertained a number of their friends in honor of Mr and Mrs S R. Whitehead Friday evening at the home of the latter. Mr. Whitehead will take up his residence at Las Vegas when he assumes the duties of assessor on the first of the New Year.

Abram Woodbury of Mesquite sold out a load of honey here last week. With Stephen Bunker and others from Bunkerville he made a trip to the salt mine before returning

Moses Gibson of St Thomas passed through here Saturday en route to Salt Lake City, where he goes for medical help as he has not been well for some time Mrs Gibson accompanied him.

Levi Syphus of St Thomas passed through here Sunday en route to Panaca.

Mr and Mrs Bert Mills have a son born to them recently.

142

Ellis Turnbaugh, of Overton, is in the city. Mr. Turnbaugh is teaching in St. Thomas this year.

Roy T. Lockett, undersherriff, left on Tuesday for the Moapa Valley and the Virgin, to serve those who have been chosen as grand and trial jurors for the coming term of court.

W. A. Whitehead of Overton spent New Years in Vegas as the guest of his brother.

Washington County News
January 9, 1911

Overton, Jan. 9.—The annual meeting of the Moapa Valley Farmers association was held here Monday, Jan. 9, for the election of officers and discussion of plans for handling the coming season's crops F. R. Snow and W. W. Muir, president and manager respectively of the Utah-Moapa Distributing Co, were present from Salt Lake City.

Mrs. Wm Mathews, her son Alonzo and daughter Dora, of Panaca, passed through here Saturday, returning to their home after a two weeks visit at St Thomas. Her daughter, Mrs Robert Bunker, accompanied her, the latter's husband having gone to Kingman, Arizona, to work for some time

S. R Whitehead went over to Las Vegas to assume the duties of county assessor on the first. He also went to Carson City to attend a meeting of the assessors of the state last week. Norman Shurtliff and Miss Minerva Swapp have charge of his store and the telephone office during his absence.

John M Bunker and S H. Wells were over at the county seat last week, the former to take the oath of office of county commissioner for coming two years and the latter to attend the last meeting of the retiring board of county Commissioners of which he is a member.

Mrs. Annie J. Cooper has resigned her place as president of the Relief society and Mrs. Elizabeth Anderson was chosen to fill the vacancy. Her councilors are Mrs. J. C. Jones and Mrs Ellen Perkins.

143

Mr. and Mrs. W. L. Batty have purchased the home of J. P. Anderson, one block west of Main and now make their home in town, Mr. Batty still having charge of the work at Kaolin, the Church farm.

The annual meeting of stockholders of the Muddy Valley Irrigation Co, was held here Saturday, Jan. 7, for the purpose of electing officers and attending to other business for the company.

The Primary association gave the children a dance Saturday evening in Lytle's hall and collected the Primary nickle fund. There was a fine attendance of little folks

Ralph Leavitt and the Misses Elsie and Ethel Lewis of Capalapa have returned from spending the holidays in Bunkerville. Miss Mabel Leavitt accompanied them.

A. Chandler of Santa Cruse, California, was here Jan. 1 and 2 on business for Uncle Sam, connected with irrigation

Born, to Mr and Mrs. I. E Los see, a daughter Dec. 31; and to Mr. and Mrs Fred Bischoff a daughter, Jan. 2.

The J. P. Anderson family have taken up their residence in the David Cox home two blocks west of Main.

Thos. Judd of St. George and Thos Osbone of Salt Lake are here on business

Mrs Mary V. Lytle of Eager, Arizona, is visiting here.

"What's the matter with that child now?" "They're playing house and George won't let her go through his pockets "—Brooklyn Life.

Correct spelling should be Andersen

Las Vegas Age Newspaper
January 14, 1911

Mr. and Mrs. A. L. Jones of Overton, spent the week in Vegas.

Joe Perkins of Moaya, was in Vegas a few days during the week.

Teachers examinations were held in Vegas the past week. Those undergoing the ordeal were Mrs. A. L. Jones, of Overton, Miss Katherine Keller, of Moapa, Miss Laura Wright, of Logan, Miss Mary Sadler, of Arden, Mrs. Burns and Miss Squires of Las Vegas.

OVERTON

The children of the town were given a dance Sat. evening in Lytle's Hall.

Mr. and Mrs. W. L. Batty of Kaolin, have moved into their new home one block west of Main recently purchased of J. P. Anderson. The Anderson family having taken up their residence in the David Cox home two blocks west of Main.

Born Dec. 31, to Mr. and Mrs. I. E. Lossee, a daughter, and Jan. 2, to Mr. and Mrs. Fred Bischoff, a daughter.

Thos. Judd of St. George, and Thos. Osborne of Salt Lake, are here on business.

Ralph Leavitt and the Misses Elsie and Ethel Lewis have returned from spending a part of the Xmas holidays in Bunkerville. Miss Mabel Leavitt returned with them.

Mrs. Mary Wythe and Geo. Lytle of Eager, Ariz., spent holidays visiting realitives and friends here.

Mrs. Wm. Mathews and two children were guests of her daughter Mrs. Robt. Bunker, during holiday week. They returned to their home in Panaca last week. Mrs. Bunker accompaning them her husband having left recently to work in Kingman, Ariz.

The Muddy Valley Irrigation Company elected officers Jan. 7.

The annual meeting of the M. V. F. A. was held here Monday Jan. 7. Officers were elected. F. R. Snow and W. W. Muir, of Salt Lake, were ppesent.

During the absence of S. R. Whitehead. Norman Shurtliff has charge of the Whitehead Bros. store.

Orange Earl passed through here Thursday.

The district school began again this week after a two weeks vacation.

145

OVERTON

We are favored with a fine rain here today.

Wm. C. Bowman left his ranch here this morning to return to his home in Bunkerville.

Mr. and Mrs. A. L. Jones returned Thursday from Las Vegas where Mr. Jones took the teachers' examination.

Ezra Bunker came down the valley Wednesday from Bartner, Utah. He left for Bunkerville on Friday.

John Swapp came in from Parashout Sat. evening where he has been overseeing some assessment work. Mr. and Mrs. Henry Kocher have come in with him.

Mr. and Mrs. John Avarett were in town Sat. from their ranch near Logan. Mr. Avarett is attending the farmer's meeting in Lytle's Hall Sat. afternoon. A number of other farmers were in for this meeting.

A. Ruby, of Washington, Utah, is a visitor here this week.

Prof. John T. Miller, of Salt Lake, gave two lectures here Jan. 6, one at 3:30 to mothers and daughters on Human Culture and one in the evening to fathers and sons. Prof. Miller is editor of the Character Builder, a human culture magazine, published at Salt Lake.

The Ladies' Relief Society gave a social and lunch in the school house Friday evening.

146

Overton, Jan. 23.—Funeral services were held here on the 21st for A S King, who died on the 17th in California, of blood poison and pneumonia. His family were visiting here and reached his bedside four hours before he passed away. His wife was Rachel Perkins, daughter of Wm. Perkins of this place, and is left with a family of three small children.

Wm. Conger came Saturday from his home in Sevier Co., Utah, to visit members of his family here His son, Ezekiel has been sick with fever several days

Mrs Bryant Whitmore returned from Provo on Thursday looking well. She was taken to the state mental hospital after a severe attack of brain fever last July.

Albert Jones, Sherman Thomas and Crayton Johnson are doing assessment work near Gold Butte.

Mrs W. J. Stewart of Las Vegas is visiting her sister, Mrs Sherman Thomas at this place

LOGAN

Soft warm rains have attended us with some snow on the mountain, the air is bracing and fine. With heavy floods in the Virgin not long since.

William Liston and Scott Allen of Caliente are busy developing their gold mine at Gold Butte, hoisting the water with gasoline power.

A large surveying party from Arizona passed through the Gold Butte mining country for Iron county Utah. It is not known just where they crossed the Colorado river or what they were surveying for.

Mr. King, a resident of this valley passed away in California. The remains were brought here for interment. The entire community extend their sympathy and condolence to the bereaved widow and little children.

A Farmer's meeting was held at the Logan school house last night for the benefit of the progressive farmers.

A railroad meeting was held in Overton Friday to find out ways and means of a railroad down through Moapa valley. A bonus was asked or discussed at $4 per acre on tillable land. I believe the majority is in favor of giving a right of way.

Roy Filcher of the experiment farm has returned from Berkley, Cal., where he has been for some weeks. Roy informs us he is the head of a family, has a fine boy weighs ten pounds. Mother and baby are doing fine. Roy is as proud as a Peacock before losing his plumage.

We hear that some time in February there will be several car loads of exhibits from Idaho and Utah. I hear these exhibits are very interesting entertainment with picture shows and hope every one will visit Moapa when they arrive.

A petition is being passed in the valley by a representative of the Nevada Liquor League. The petition is for a law to vote for local option. A good thing I believe.

OVERTON

There is quite a bit of sickness of colds and lagrippe among the people here at present.

Ezekiel Conger is ill with typhoid fever at the home of his sister, Mrs. Albert Jones. His parents and Dr. Benson are caring for him.

We have had lots of stormy weather, a little rain and a lot of flood this week. The later playing havoc with regularity in the mails.

French the photographer is here.

Funeral services were held here January 21, for A. S. King, who died on the 17th in California. His wife, who was Miss Rachel Perkins of this place reached his bedside a few hours before he died and returned with the corpse Friday. She was accompanied in her trip by her three small children, her brother, Wm. Perkins met her at Nipton and returned with her to Moapa.

148

Overton, Feb. 5 —Bertha, the little daughter of Mr and Mrs Lyman Shurtliff, has been ill with scarlet fever, thought to have been carried in a letter from relatives in Ogden, Utah, who had the disease She is recovering nicely and so far there has been no other cases

Mr. and Mrs S R Whitehead left on Friday for their new home in Las Vegas to live there during Mr Whitehead's term of office as assessor of Clark Co.

Mr and Mrs Geo B. Whitney of St George, who are visiting their children in St Thomas and the Muddy valley, were in Overton Sunday.

The infant son of Mr. and Mrs. Albert Jones has been quite ill this week but is now recovering

ment Farm at Logan Saturday and then went to St Thomas to spend the Sabbath.

Horace Jones of this place who is attending school at Provo, Utah, has the measles

Assessor S. R. Whitehead is assessing the tax payers of the valley this week.

Ezekiel Conger who has been ill with typhoid fever is now much better.

149

Mrs Andrew L Jones has taken charge of the Logan school for the remainder of the term

Floods from the Meadow Valley wash have greatly hindered travel and mails this week.

We had a fine rain here Feb 3rd which will do much good to crops.

Overton, Feb 12 —Bp Thos Judd, J. W. Linton and Elder Wm. A Whitehead arrived here from St. George Friday evening. The latter will take charge of Whitehead Bros. store at this place He has many friends in the valley who will be pleased to have him home again from his mission

Bp Edw Bunker and daughter, Mrs Lillian Corry, arrived here Friday evening from Bunkerville. Bp Bunker and Edw. H Syphus of St Thomas visited the Experiment Farm at Logan Saturday and then went to St Thomas to spend the Sabbath.

Horace Jones of this place who is attending school at Provo, Utah, has the measles

Assessor S. R. Whitehead is assessing the tax payers of the valley this week.

Ezekiel Conger who has been ill with typhoid fever is now much better.

Washington county News
February 20, 1911

Overton, Feb 20 —Bp. Jos I Earl of Bunkerville spent Sunday visiting his daughter, Mrs. W. L Jones, of this place He attended church and he and Elder Wm Perkins of this place delivered exellent discourses at the afternoon services

The Mutual Improvement Association gave a basket and lunch ball in the Lytle hall Friday. They realized a neat sum from the sale of the baskets

A welcome home social was given Elder Wm A Whitehead in the school house Tuesday evening. Lunch was served and all enjoyed a good time

John Laub of Fielding, Utah, is visiting his sister, Mrs, Sarah Perkins and her family of this place

The weather has been exceptionally cold for this section the past week with some storm

Ves Nay has been ill with quinsy this week. He is now recovering.

Overton, Feb 27 —Edwin S Hinckley and Frank Hinckley of Provo, Utah, are visiting their brother, Lucian Hinckley, and sister, Mrs Robinson, both of the latter of Logan, Nev. They were down to Overton to attend church Sunday and the two former spoke to us in the afternoon services E. S Hinckley also spoke to the young people in the Mutual Improvement association in the evening

Harry Church and wife, who was Miss Jessie Henderson of California, has recently returned from the coast state and will remain here some time looking after his interests at Logan.

Misses Minerva Swapp and Viva Perkins, teachers of the Sunday School Primary class gave their class a picnic outing Sunday afternoon.

N E Miller of Logan, Utah, was here a few days last week looking over our valley with a view of bringing in a large colony of bees.

Mrs Vinnie Bennett of Salt Lake City is visiting her parents, Mr, and Mrs Sanford Angell and their family of this place

Samuel H. Wells and Robert Gibson returned last week from a home missionary trip to Parhanagut valley.

Mrs Mary Whitehead and daughter, Winnie, arrived here Saturday evening from St George.

Joseph H. Jones of Bunkerville spent a few days visiting his relatives here this week.

W L Batty has recently built a porch on the front of his residence

George Swapp of Kanab, Utah, is visiting relatives here

151

OVERTON NEWS

What the Moapa Valley People Are Doing

George Swapp of Kanab, Utah, is visiting relatives here.

Harry Church and wife, who was Miss Jessie Henderson of California, have recently returned from the coast state, and will remain in the valley some time looking after interests here. Mr. Church has an asparagus farm in Logan.

Joseph H. Jones of Bunkerville spent a few days visiting relatives here this week. Mr. Jones has recently returned from a mission of nearly three years in Georgia and Florida.

N. E. Miller of Logan, Utah, was looking over our valley for a few days last week with a view of bringing in a large colony of bees.

Samuel H. Wells and Robert Gibson have recently returned from a home missionary trip to Paranaghat valley.

Stephen Swapp of this place is visiting relatives in Kanab, Utah.

Dentist Lewis Marco, of Caliente, was here for a few days last week. Mrs. Marco accompanied him.

Edwin S. Hinkley and brother, Frank, are visiting their brother, Lucian Hinckley and sister, Mrs. Rolinsen of Logan, Nevada.

They were at Overton to attend church Sunday and the two former spoke in the afternoon services. E. S. Hinckley also addressed the young people in their Improvement association Sunday evening.

152

Overton Offerings

Overton, March 6 —A number of laborers and teams arrived at Moapa Saturday to build the branch line from Moapa down the valley two and one half miles to the gypsum mine.

Warren Cox of St George spent several days in the valley this week in the interest of the Studebaker Bros Co , leaving here Friday for Paranaget valley.

Miss Winnie Whitehead is our "Hello" girl now in place of Miss Minerva Snapp, who has graciously answered our calls for the past year.

Horace Jones came home from Provo this week. He has been attending the B Y. U. the past six months

The mail schedule has been changed to arrive here from Moapa several hours earlier than formerly.

J. W. Imlay, the sheep-man of Hurricane, passed through here Tuesday en route to Las Vegas

E. J. Robinson of Moapa is in Vegas.

O. W. Jarvis of Overton was in Vegas on Tuesday.

OVERTON NEWS

[Special Correspondence]

Mr. Imley, the sheepman of Hurricane, Utah, passed through here Tuesday, enroute to Las Vegas.

Warren Cox, Studebaker's agent at St. George, Utah, spent several days in this valley in the interest of his company this week, leaving here Friday for Pahranagat valley.

The mail schedule has been changed to arrive here from Moapa several hours earlier than formerly.

Horace Jones came home this week from Provo, Utah, where he has been attending school the past six months.

Miss Winnie Whitehead is clerking in Whitehead Bros. store here. Miss Minerva Swapp has occupied the position for the past year.

Drummers for the Z. C. M. I. of Salt Lake visited valley merchants last week.

154

Joe F. Perkins, of Overton, is down this week wearing the green.

OVERTON NEWS

The telephone line has been out of service between Overton and Moapa since Friday's flood.

Fruit trees are in full bloom and shade trees are coming into leaf.

The Relief society will celebrate its anniversary day here March 17 with a public dinner in the afternoon and a program at night. The following ladies are acting as committee: Mesdames Nora McDonald, Nellie Lossee, Ethel Perkins and Emma McDonald.

Mr and Mrs. Orin Jarvis were at Las Vegas a few days last week.

The asparagus crop will soon be ready to ship. Enough is now being gathered for home use.

Joseph and Orange Earl of Bunkerville were up to the salt mines for loads of salt this week. They were delayed two days at Overton on their return trip on account of flood.

Mail service has been demoralized this week. None at all from Wednesday until Saturday, the mail carrier coming down horseback on that date.

Ute V. Perkins and Geo. L. Whitney are recovering from lagrippe.

The flood changed the creek channel, leaving the Overton channel dry.

An enormous damage has been done to crops by last week's flood.

Wash Leavitt left here for Bunkerville Monday.

Freighters are seriously hindered on account of some small bridges being washed out.

155

Overton, March 20 —C J. Robertson and Mr Shattuck, principal contractors on the high line, met the landowners of the valley in the Lytle Hall Saturday evening with a plan to build a grade gown the valley to St Thomas if the people of the latter place would give a mortgage on their land for $90,000 as security and then turn it over to the railroad company to put on the rails and rolling stock and operate. The people did not approve the plan, but put in a committee, S. H. Wells and Mr. Robinson of Logan, who with Robertson and Shattuck left Sunday for Los Angeles on business connected with the building of a railroad down the valley.

The Relief Society celebrated their annual day Saturday with a sumptuous dinner in the school house at 2 p m followed by sports and a short program Everybody had a fine time

Bp T J Jones came over from Bunkerville this week. His daughter, Mrs Annie Cox, came with him

Drummers Tabin and McCune for Schocroft & Sons Co of Ogden were here this week

Bert Thomas has recently returned from California, where he spent the past winter

156

OVERTON NEWS

[Special Correspondence]

T. J. Jones came over from Bunkerville this week. His daughter Mrs. Annie Cox, accompanied him, and brought a shipment of ladies and children's hats down from the station for sale here.

Schocroft and Sons' drummers visited the merchants here this week.

Bert Thomas, of Logan, has returned from California, where he has been since August, 1910.

The Relief Society celebrated their annual day Saturday with a sumptuous dinner in the afternoon followed by sports and a short program.

Messrs Wells and Robinson, of Logan, left Sunday for Los Angeles on business connected with a prospective railroad down the valley.

C. J. Robertson, and Mr. Shattuck, principal contractor on the high line, held a meeting here Saturday evening to present plans for building a line down the valley, the people to give a mortgage on their land as security for the road. The land owners did not approve of the plan and will anxiously await the return of Messrs. and Wells and Robinson from Los Angeles.

Overton, March 27.—The railroad company has decided to extend its line as far as Logan in time for the shipment of this season's cantaloupes Engineers Tilton and White came down the valley today to secure right of way for the road from Logan to St. Thomas and committees of the Commercial club are busy obtaining the same. The line has already been surveyed and there is every reason to believe that the road will be completed this season.

The telephone line has been extended to the northern part of town, commonly known as "String town," and several phones have been installed there One was also installed at the Gypson mine near Moapa last week.

Assemblymen Willard L Jones of this place and Senator Levi Syphus of St. Thomas returned from the capital city Thursday, where they have been attending the legislature. They returned via Salt Lake City.

A Commercial club was temporarily organized here Friday evening and will boost for the building of the railroad down the valley. Orin Jarvis was elected president.

Jos H Jones came over from Bunkerville last week and will work at Kaolin for some time.

Tobe Whitmore of Salt Lake City is visiting his brother, Brig. Whitmore, of this place.

Bp Thos Judd of St George came down from Salt Lake City Thursday.

Sylvester Nay has gone into Arizona to work for some time

S H Wells left Friday for Salt Lake City.

158

Railroad to Build Down Moapa Valley This Season

(Special Correspondence)

Sylvester Nay has gone into Arizona to work for some time.

Jos. H. Jones came over from Bunkerville this week and will work at the Kaolin Farm.

Bishop Thomas Judd came down from Salt Lake City Thursday.

Mr. J. Whitmore, of Salt Lake City, is visiting his brother Brig Whitmore of this place.

Samuel H. Wells left here Friday for Salt Lake City.

The telephone line has been extended to the northern part of town, commonly known as "Stringtown" and several 'phones installed there. One was put in at the Gypsum Mine also last week.

Assemblyman Willard L. Jones of this place and Senator Levi Syphus of St. Thomas returned via Salt Lake City from the State Legislature at Carson City last week.

A Commercial Club was temporarily organized here Friday evening and will boost for the building of the railroad down the valley. Orin Jarvis was elected president.

The Railroad Company have decided to extend their line as far as Logan in time for the shipment of this season's cantaloupes. Engineers Tilton and White came down the valley today to secure right of way for the road from Logan to St. Thomas, and committees of the Commercial Club are busy obtaining the same. The line has already been surveyed and there is every reason to believe that the road will be completed this season.

159

OVERTON NEWS

[Special Correspondence]

S. D. Conger has moved his family into the Redford house and is working for C. J. Robertson & Co. on the Overton Ranch.

Mrs. Albert Jones entertained a party of ladies at her home Friday afternoon.

Bishop Thomas Judd left by stage on Saturday for his home in St. George.

The Overton and Logan Basket Ball teams played a game at Logan Sunday, the latter winning the game.

Miss Helen Bunker of St. Thomas spent Saturday and Sunday visiting friends here.

The Home Dramatic Co. played "The Red Rosette" Saturday evening.

Miss Amelia Huntsman is visiting her sister, Mrs. James Huntsman of this place. She came down from Cane Springs Saturday.

Bishop Thomas J. Jones left for Provo, Utah Friday where he will visit his daughter, Mrs. Josephine Clark.

Overton, April 10 —Mr and Mrs. E J Robertson of Salt Lake City are spending a few days in the valley. Mr. Robertson is one of the largest stock holders in the Capalapa ranch. They have some fifty men employed and will encrese the force as the cantaloupe season advances

John Swapp and Mr. Jones came in from Parshant where they went with a band of horses, the feed being all gone compelled them to drive the horses back into the valley, which was hard on the men as well as the horses

Cliff Whitmore and Ralph Perkins have returned from Sheep mountain where they have been looking after their cattle. They report cattle in fine shape

Mr. Murphy has two teams on the road from St Thomas to Moapa shipping asparagus which is selling for 12½ cents per pound

Mrs A. S King will leave shortly for Texas, she will go to visit Mr. King's sister, Mrs Bruce, and will remain all summer

In playing basket ball Sunday one of the boys, Elmer Bowman by name, belonging to the Logan team had his wrist broken

Mrs Rob Gibson has returned home after an absence of several months She has been visiting relatives in the north.

Everybody is busy planting and hoeing cataloups There will be some good shipments leave the valley this summer.

Banker J M Whttmore from Price, Utah, has been looking after his mining claims which are out near Gold Butte

Our M. I A continues for all it is very warm It looks like the officers were afraid their job would run out.

✱There is a great deal of small garden stuff in the valley and has been all winter, plenty of green peas now.

Mrs Brig Whitmore with her three small daughters will spend the summer at Long Beach, California.

Mr Ivins, a son of A. W. Ivins of Salt Lake City, is spending a few days here looking over the valley.

Harold Sparks has returned from Carson City, where he has been for the past few months on business

Mr Roxton Whitmore and wife of St Thomas were visiting in town a few days last week

There is strong R R talk, and if talk will build a road we will certainly have one

County Commissioner J M. Bunker made a flying trip to Las Vegas last week

Bryant Whitmore is having a neat frame house built on Main street.

T. J. Jones has gone to spend the summer with his daughter at Oasis, Utah

Miss Clara Perkins will spend the summer at Eagar, Arizona.

M W Gibson, Sr , is very low, and has been for some weeks.

The Sunday school will have a picnic outing Easter

Overton, April 16.—The Mutual Improvement associations give a social and lunch in the school house Tuesday evening in honor of Mr. and Mrs Clinton McDonald and Miss Ethelyn Bennion, who left Thursday for northern Utah, the former to Ogden and the latter to Taylorsville. Miss Bennion has spent the winter here for her health and returns to her northern home much improved.

O. P. Miller of Salt Lake City and Thos Judd of St. George came down the valley Friday to the Church farm at Kaolin on business connected with the farm, there is about five hundred acres of barley in very good condition there.

As the result of a "good roads" movement, there was a goodly number of men and teams at work on the roads in the valley last Saturday.

Mrs Mary V. Lytle came in from Eager, Arizona, this week. Her husband, J. A. Lytle, is coming by team and will arrive later.

Mr and Mrs C. J. Robertson of Salt Lake are here this week. Mr. Robertson having business interests in the valley.

Mrs. Mary C Batty entertained a party of lady friends in honor of Mrs Emma McDonald Wednesday afternoon.

Bryant Whitmore is having a frame house built on his lot east of Whitehead Bros. store on Main street.

The children of the town spent Saturday in Easter picnic parties

The roses and carnations are out in full bloom here now

163

Overton, April 25 — W L Jones, S A Angell, Crayton Johnson, W H. McDonald, O W Jarvis and L J Robertson, the committee appointed by the Overton Chamber of Commerce, to secure the right of way for the railroad from Logan to St Thomas, are very busy and will soon have the right of way secured.

Thos J Osborne and daughter, Miss Isabel Osborne of Salt Lake City, and Mr Frank Thompson and his mother came down the valley Friday. Mr Osborne has a ranch below town a couple of miles The party spent Saturday looking over the valley and returned Sunday, George Perkins accompaning them to the station

The mutual give a debate Sunday evening, the subject being "Resolved that wealth brings happiness," W L Jones, Jesse F, Cooper, Isaac L Losee, W H. McDonald, Sadie Perkins, Mildred Anderson and Hattie Brown being the debaters

Dennis and Patrick Ryan and John McCarty of Salt Lake City were in the valley a few days this week They have business interests here

The lady friends of Mrs Agnes Marshall gave her a pleasant surprise last Monday, the event being her 24th birthday

Crayton Johnson and William Whitehead went to Bunkerville Saturday to fill a home missionary appointment

Messrs Ivers and Daily of Salt Lake were here the fore part of last week looking over their business interests

Mr and Mrs S H Wells were down from the Moapa Improvement Co. ranch for services here Sunday.

John Swapp and Henry Kocherhans left today with a band of horses for Parashaunt

Mrs W L Jones entertained a party of lady friends Friday afternoon

Fred Rushton has returned from a short trip to Salt Lake City.

J A Lytle came back from Eager Arizona, last Tuesday.

VALLEY IMPROVES

Railroad Assured from Logan to St. Thomas

Mr. E. J. Robertson of the Moapa valley, favored the Age with an interesting interview on the Moapa valley country Thursday. Mr. Robertson was in Vegas by appointment with Senator Wm. A. Clark to discuss the railroad question as pertains to the valley.

Mr. Robertson said:

"The conditions in the valley are more prosperous than ever before. The value of combined effort has been demonstrated by the success of the movement to secure the extension of the railroad to St. Thomas. By co-operation of the people of the valley and the formation of the Chambers of Commerce at Overton and St. Thomas, the railroad company has been induced to to extend the road through to St. Thomas instead of stopping at Logan as at first proposed. This will make the branch 26 miles in length instead of 12 miles. The advantage to the valley by this move is apparent in view of the fact that eight tenths of the cultivatable area lies south east of Logan and the valuable kaolin deposits and mountains of salt will be opened up by railroad transportation.

"When the real facts were brought before Senator Clark he lost no time in authorizing the construction of the line on from Logan, and a spirit of enterprise has thereby been awakened in the people.

"The area of cantaloupes planted this year will exceed three times the total area ever before planted. The Moapa Fruit Land Co. and the Irrigation & Development Co. now have 140 acres up and are planting 60 acres additional. This will mean the shipment of at least 200 cars from the lower portion of the valley and should bring the total, including the upper valley to 350 cars for the season.

"In addition to the above, vastly increased shipments of asparagus and early vegetables will be made. The raising of hogs is also rapidly becoming a very important industry, the markets of Caliente, Las Vegas and Goldfield being now supplied with pork from the valley.

OVERTON NEWS

[Special Correspondence]

S. D. Conger has moved his family into the Redford house and is working for C. J. Robertson & Co. on the Overton Ranch.

Mrs. Albert Jones entertained a party of ladies at her home Friday afternoon.

Bishop Thomas Judd left by stage on Saturday for his home in St. George.

The Overton and Logan Basket Ball teams played a game at Logan Sunday, the latter winning the game.

Miss Helen Bunker of St. Thomas spent Saturday and Sunday visiting friends here.

The Home Dramatic Co. played "The Red Rosette" Saturday evening.

Miss Amelia Huntsman is visiting her sister, Mrs. James Huntsman of this place. She came down from Cane Springs Saturday.

Bishop Thomas J. Jones left for Provo, Utah Friday where he will visit his daughter, Mrs. Josephine Clark.

Judge Taber Postpones Term One Week

Word has been received that Judge Taber has found it impossible to be present May 16th and has postponed the term of court one week.

Tuesday, May 16 1911, Judge Taber will open the regular spring term of the District Court in the Majestic Theatre. The Grand Jury has been sudpoenaed for the opening day of court, and will, upon being empanelled, proceed to consider the charges against John Livingstone, colored, for assault with a deadly weapon, and W. J. Williams for assault with a deadly weapon, both of whom were bound over by Judge Lillis. The various county offices will be examined by committee of the grand jury as well as the jail, all county property, etc.

On Monday, May 22, the trial jury will be on hand to hear such cases as may be ready for disposal by jury trial. There are numerous cases which may be set for this term although there are none of great public interest now pending except the case of B. F. Miller against The County of Clark, to recover money expended on roads, the bill for which the county commissioners refused to allow.

We print below the list of grand and trial jurors drawn for this term.

GRAND JURORS

Nelson, Clark M. Alvord.

Searchlight, Launchelot Gilroy, Walter M. Brown, E. Macready.

Crescent, Jeff Davis

Goodsprings, A. J. Robbins

Las Vegas, O. C. Boggs, C. C. Corkhill, Frank Grace, W. E. Hawkins, L. Holcomb, I. C. Johnson.

Mesquite, Frank S. Leavitt, Wm. E. Abbott.

Bunkerville, Orange B. Leavitt, Thomas H. Adams.

St. Thomas, R. E. Bunker, Robert O. Gibson.

Overton, Mandas D. Cooper, Orrin W. Jarvis.

Logan, Sam Wells, John H. Averett.

Moapa, W. C. Bowman, Geo. C. Baldwin.

TRIAL JURORS

Las Vegas, G. A. Case, W. E. Arnold, C. A. French, Geo. Swadner, Harry R. Beale, J. J. Coughlin, Julius F. Fox, W. D. Worrell, J. D. Kramer, R. E. Lake, Geo. Crouse, Wm. Laubenheimer, A. D. Bishop, Wm. S. Park, Wm. O'Brien, Robt. Ferguson, E. W. Griffith, A. N. Pauff, J. E. Westlake, John F. Miller, I. W. Botkin, J. W. Seiders, John S. Wisner, C. P. Squires.

Logan, David Conger, John R. Hewitt, Perry D. Huntsman.

Bunkerville, Geo. H. Hunt, Alfred D. Leavitt, Joe I. Earl, Alma D. Leavitt, Alfred J. Tobler, Albert Haffen, Hector Bunker.

St. Thomas, B. F. Bonelli, Wm. E. Hutchins, Alfred L. Syphus.

Overton, Fred J. Rushton, I. E. Losee, Geo. F. Perkins, August Koenig, Clinton D. McDonald, Allen M. Fleming, H. H. Sparks, Sherman Thomas, Andrew L. Jones.

Searchlight, Thomas P. Davis, Guy Corson, A. F. Jennings, J. A. Turner, Frank M. Fry, Walter W. Wells, Fred Pfander, S. S. Irvin, B. F. Miller, Jr., Raymond Rice, G. H. Wilkings, Rudolph Voos.

Crescent, Kenneth N. Bright, Fred E. Toberg, John Paden, G. H. Morrison.

Moapa, Louis M. Grant.

Goodsprings, James Jarman, S. C. Root, J. E. Armstrong.

Nelson, F. L. Millen, H. H. Wesselhoft.

Mesquite, A. J. Barnum, Daniel A. Potter, James E. Hughes, Carlos Knight, A. N. Woodbury.

166

MARRIED

KOENIG-ANGELL: In this city, April 29, 1911, Arthur Koenig, aged 21, a resident of Overton, Nevada, to Miss Minnie Angell, aged 18, of the same place, Judge H. M. Lillis officiating.

The ceremony was performed in the parlor of Hotel Nevada in the presence of a few friends. Mr. Frank R. Nicholas played the wedding march and County Clerk Harmon and U. S. Land Commissioner Buol were the witnesses. The young couple received many congratulations, in which the Age takes pleasure in joining.

Come On, Muddy

Now that the Las Vegas Chamber of Commerce has taken up the matter of maintaining an exhibit of products at the Salt Lake depot for the coming summer, it would seem to be well worth while for the Moapa Valley to share in the benefits to be derived from the same. If the Chambers of Commerce of Overton and St. Thomas as well as any other private interests in the valley will send samples of their products at intervals to the Chamber of Commerce, the same will be placed on exhibition here and will be viewed by thousands of people, many of whom will be induced to inquire further into the resources of that section. Send on your exhibits, Muddy.

Overton, May 8 —Engineers White and McGuire were here Sunday on matters connected with the railroad. A number of engineers are expected to pitch camp tonight near the right-of-way in the western part of town. There are four grading and surveying outfits at work on the grade between the gypsum mine and Overton

Mr. and Mrs Bird Murphy of Salt Lake City came down the Valley on the 1st to visit relatives in St Thomas, Mr Murphy having business interests both in St. Thomas and Logan. Mrs Murphy went from here on Tuesday to Bunkerville and returned the latter part of the week to Moapa.

Arthur Koenig and Miss Minnie Angel surprised their friends last week by slipping over to the county seat and being wedded while there Mr and Mrs Koenig will live at the Koenig ranch which has been recently sold to E J. Robertson.

Orin Jarvis and family have taken up their residence in one of the cottages at Capalapa. Mr. Jarvis has been employed as foreman of the ranch, Fred Rushton having recently given up the position.

Paul, the little son of Mr and Mrs. John A. Lytle, was ill with measles, contracted in Arizona last week. He is now much better and there has been no other cases.

The families of James Huntsman and Alex Swapp spent the last week at the Gypson mine where Messrs Huntsman and Swapp are at work

By invitation from Mr Felcher, many of the farmers spent Saturday afternoon looking over the experiment farm at Logan

Levi Syphus and Robert Gibson were up yesterday to attend the board meeting of the Moapa Valley Farmers' association.

A number of people went to St. Thomas on the afternoon of May 1 for a game of base ball and other sports

Mr and Mrs Alonzo Huntsman are visiting Mr. Huntsman's mother at Cane Springs ranch near Moapa

Mr and Mrs Calvin Barnum of Mesquite are here and may spend the summer

Joe F. Perkins and Miss Keeler of Moapa were visiting here Saturday

Warren Cox of St George came over from Bunkerville Saturday.

George Lytle of Enger, Arizona, was a visitor here last week

Mrs Rachel King is visiting relatives in Texas

OVERTON BUSY

Building Railroad Wakes Up Moapa Valley

[Special Correspondence]

Overton, May 8, 1911.

Paul, the little son of Mr. and Mrs. John A Lytle was ill with measles, contracted in Arizona last week. He is now much better and there have been no other cases.

Mr. and Mrs. Bird Murphy, of Salt Lake City came down the valley on the first, Mr. Murphy having business interests both at Logan and St. Thomas. Mrs. Murphy went from here on Tuesday to Bunkerville and returned the latter part of the week to Moapa.

Joe F. Perkins and Miss Keeler, of Moapa were visiting here Saturday.

By invitation from Mr. Filcher many of the farmers spent Saturday afternoon looking over the Experiment Farm at Logan.

George Lytle, of Eager, Ariz. was a visitor here last week.

Mr. and Mrs. Calvin Barnum, of Mesquite, are here and may spend the summer.

Engineers White and McGuire were here Sunday on matters connected with the railroad. A number of engineers will pitch camp tonight near the right of way in the western part of town.

Mr. and Mrs. Alonzo Huntsman are visiting Mr. Huntsman's mother at Cane Springs near Moapa.

The families of James Huntsman and Alex Swapp, who are working at the Gypsum mine, spent the last week visiting at the mine.

Warren Cox came over from Bunkerville Saturday.

Mrs. Rachel King is visiting her husband's people in Texas and will spend the summer there.

Orin Jarvis and family have taken up their residence in one of the cottages at Capalapa. Mr. Jarvis has been employed as foreman of the ranch, Fred Rushton having given up the position some time ago.

Arthur Koenig and Miss Minnie Angell were over to the county seat last week and returned as Mr. and Mrs. Arthur Koenig. They will take up their residence at the Koenig ranch which has recently been sold to E. J. Robertson.

Levi Syphus and Robert Gibson were up yesterday from St. Thomas to attend the Board Meeting of the Moapa Valley Farmers' Association of which Mr. Syphus is president.

A number of our people went to St. Thomas on the 1st of May for a game of base ball and other sports.

There are four grading and surveying outfits at work on the railroad between the Gypsum Mine and Overton.

Overton, May 15 —The district school closed Friday with a program in the evening given by pupils of the school. Miss Hattie Brown, who has had charge of the Primary department left Saturday for her home in Pasadena, Cal

Mrs Annie Cox and children, Mariner and Kathleen, of Bunkerville also Miss Lillian Jones came over Wednesday. Mrs Cox and children returned Monday but Miss Jones will remain for some time

Engineer Ryus and a corps of five engineers are located in Overton and have charge of about ten miles of road. There is a grading camp 1½ miles north of town

Bp Thomas Judd and Bp Isaac Macfarlane of St George came in Saturday and are doing some surveying on the church farm at Kaolin

Mrs Dezie Perkins of Salt Lake City came in last week to keep house for her brother Wm. Perkins this summer.

Elders Calvin Barnum of Mesquite and Jos H Jones of Bunkerville were here as home missionaries Sunday.

Mrs Lewis of Capalapa has been very ill the past week but is somewhat improved the last two days

Mrs Fred Rushton and family expect to leave this week for Salt Lake City for a visit

Born, a daughter to Mr. and Mrs David Conger May 10, all concerned doing nicely.

Andrew L Jones is painting the roof of his new cement block house this week.

Mr and Mrs Sylvester Nay made a trip to Bunkerville last week.

E. J. Robertson, of Moapa, was at Hotel Nevada Wednesday.

M. D. Cooper was representing Overton on the Grand Jury this week.

Samuel H. Wells of Logan, was attending court as a member of the grand jury during the week.

Oevrton Happneings

[Special Correspondence]

Mrs. Lewis at Capalapa, has been very ill the past week, but under the care of Dr. Benson she is now recovering.

Our schools closed on Friday, the pupils giving an entertainment in the evening. Miss Hattie Brown, who had charge of the Primary Department, left Saturday for her home in Pasadena, California.

Mrs. Annie Cox and children, Mariner and Kathleen, and Miss Lillian Jones, came over from Bunkerville Wednesday

Mr. and Mrs. Sylvester Nay made a trip to Bunkerville last week.

Andrew L. Jones is painting the roof of his new house this week.

Engineer Ryus, who has charge of about ten miles of road, with a corps of of five engineers is located at Overton. There is a camp of graders at work one and one half miles north of town.

BORN,- To Mr. and Mrs. David Conger, a daughter, May 10. All concerned doing well.

Mrs. Fred Rushton and family are going to Salt Lake City this week for a visit.

Bp. Thos. Judd and Bp. Isaac McFarland came in Saturday from St. George They are doing some surveying on the church farm at Kaolin this week.

Elders Calvin Barnum and Jos. H. Jones were here as home missionaries and delivered excellent addresses at church Sunday.

Overton, June 4 —The committee that is securing the right of way for the railroad have succeeded in persuading the engineers to charge the survey through the town of Overton a few hundred feet to the west, thereby the homes and property of Sanford Angell and Geo Ingram will not be damaged and the cost of the right of way lessened a thousand dollars.

A committee has been appointed to arrange for a Fourth of July celebration, and the birth of our nation and the coming of the railroad down the Moapa valley this summer will be fittingly celebrated.

Mrs Christie Turnbough of San Diego, Cal , is visiting her son, Ellis, and daughter, Mrs J M. Bunker, and their families in the valley for a few weeks

Horace Jones, Wm. Cooper and Brig Whitmore returned Friday from the latter's mine where they have been working for some time

John Swapp and Henry Kockerhans returned yesterday from the range south of here where they have been with a band of horses

The Y. L M I A and the junior class of the Y. M. M I A. closed their meetings for the summer last Sunday evening

Mr and Mrs Albert Jones entertained a number of their friends at an ice cream party Sunday afternoon.

Elmer Losee has a header at work in the harvest fields, there is a number of binders at work also

Albert Frehner's threshing machine is at work threshing at Kaolin this week

Mrs S H. Wells will leave this week for a visit to Salt Lake City.

Miss Sarah A. Barnum of Mesquite is visiting here

Peaches and Apricots Ripe and Threshing Nearly Over In Moapa Valley

(Special Correspondence)

Overton, Nevada, June 7, 1911.

Weather has been extra warm the past few days.

Threshing has begun and the hum of the busy machine can be heard on all sides. Much grain is the estimate this year.

Clara Perkins left last week for Logan, Utah. She will spend the summer there.

Ripe apricots and peaches are now in the market. Apricots are more plentiful than peaches.

A base ball game will take place on the 7th inst. between the Overton and St. Thomas nines. The losing team will give a dance and supper.

Mrs. Sarah Perkins and little granddaughter, Pearl, have gone to California to spend a few weeks on the beach.

Mrs. J. W. Swapp and Mrs. Albert Jones, in company with others of the Primary Association, have gone to Bunkerville to attend a Primary convention.

Preparations are being made for a glorious Fourth of July. The young ladies who are in the voting contest for Goddess of Liberty are the Misses Etta Hewett, Winnie Whitehead, Mildred Anderson, Viva Perkins, Sybil Whitmore and Helen Bunker.

Spelling should be Mildred Andersen

Overton, June 14 —Miss Clara Perkins has gone to Logan, Utah, where she will spend the summer.

The following young ladies are in the voting contest for goddess of liberty on July 4th: Etta Hewett, Winnie Whitehead, Mildred Anderson, Vivan Perkins, Sybil Whitmore and Helen Bunker.

Mrs Martha Swapp, Mrs Albert Jones and Sylvia Shurtliff went to Bunkerville to attend a Primary convention held there last week.

Mrs Sarah Perkins and little granddaughter, Pearl, have gone to California to spend a few weeks on the beach.

Jefferson Jones and Harold Earl came over from Bunkerville last week, the latter returning home on the 7th.

Bp W. L Jones entertained a goodly number of the townspeople in his apricot orchard Sunday afternoon.

The Primary officers and teachers met Tuesday evening at the home of Pres. Martha Swapp for an ice cream party.

Miss Minerva Swapp went over to Las Vegas Monday expecting to remain for some time.

We were favored with a cooling shower on the 14th after a number of very warm days

Brig Whitmore and daughters, Sybil and Myrtle left Wednesday for Salt Lake City.

Mrs Alice Jones and daughter, Louisa came over from Bunkerville Tuesday.

175

Route of Railroad Slightly Changed

(Special Correspondence)

June 8, 1911.

Horace Jones, Wm. Cooper and Brig Whitmore came in Friday from the latter's mine, where they have been working for some time.

Miss Sarah H. Barnum, of Mesquite, is visiting here.

Mr. and Mrs. Albert Jones entertained a number of their friends at an ice cream social Sunday afternoon.

Rance Shurtlif has moved to a lot recently purchased of M. D. Cooper on Main street, and has a neat barber sign hung out.

John Swapp and Henry Kocherhaus and the ladies who accompanied them, returned Sunday from Mr. Swapp's cattle ranch in the mountains south of St. Thomas.

A committee has been appointed to take charge of the celebration for July 4. A fine time is expected.

Mrs. S. H. Wells will leave this week for a visit to Salt Lake City.

Elmer Losee has a new harvest header at work in the grain fields the past two weeks. There are also a number of binders at work.

Albert Frehner's threshing machine has been running for a week, threshing grain at Koolin and the ranches this side of there.

A threshing machine from Mesquite, is threshing grain in the upper end of the valley. A casting was broken a few days ago and the men have been waiting for extras which are expected here by today's train.

The committee on right of way for the Moapa Valley railroad have succeeded in getting the surveyors to move the line a few hundred feet west of the first survey as it passes the town of Overton. The homes and property of Sanford Angell and George Ingram were undamaged by the new survey and a thousand dollars saved on the cost of the right of way.

Mrs. Christie Turnbaugh of San Diego, is visiting her son and daughter here.

176

Overton, June 20 —Olive Vaughn, age 23, oldest daughter in a family from Idaho that are working on the grade down the valley, died here June 15th of typhoid fever. The body was buried in Overton cemetry. Contractor Banks, who is a L D. S, elder and friend of the family, and Bp W. J Jones spoke at the funeral services, Elder W. A. Whitehead having charge of the singing

At a dance in the hall Friday evening a voting contest was held for goddess of liberty for the 4th. Miss Mildred Anderson received 95 votes, Miss Sybil Whitmore 143 and Miss Vivian Perkins 149. A neat sum was realized from the sale of votes and will go to defray the expenses of the celebration.

Mr. and Mrs Calvin Barnum have gone to St. Thomas where Mr. Barnum has employment driving teams to the Grand Gulch mine for Mr. Gentry.

Miss Sadie Perkins went over to Las Vegas Sunday to attend the Teachers' examination being held there this week

Mrs Sarah Perkins returned from California Sunday. Her son, Joe F Perkins, and wife will arrive later

Correct spelling should be Andersen

177

Miss Clara Perkins, of Overton, was in Vegas this week taking the state teachers examination.

Joe F. Perkins, of Moapa, who has been in California for a time, was in Vegas early in the week.

Moapa Valley Metropolis Shows Evidences of Prosperity-- Early Fruit Ripe

(Special Correspondence)

Our summer showers the past week have improved the weather and made it considerably cooler.

Funeral services were held yesterday over the remains of Miss Olive Vaughn who died of typhoid fever. Deceased, with her parents, had lately moved in to the valley. A large crowd attended the services and the beautiful casket was covered with a profusion of flowers. The sympathy of the valley goes out to the bereaved family who are strangers in our midst.

A grand ball was given in Lytle Hall last evening. Ballots for the voting contest for Goddess of Liberty were closed, Miss Vivian Perkins being the lucky goddess.

Miss Sadie Perkins attended the teachers' examination held at Las Vegas June 19th and 20th.

Fruit season is now on and everybody is busy putting up early fruit. A later crop will be on near Sept. 1st when our valley hopes to make the grand Fruit Festival a noted success.

Cantaloupes are growing rapidly and quite a variety are now netting and it is feared the track will not be completed in time to ship them unless a more rapid movement is made.

The officers and teachers of the Primary Association enjoyed a pleasant ice cream party at the home of Mrs. J. W. Swapp, the president of the Primary Organization.

Renee Shurtliff is doing lively business in his new barber shop which is now located on Main street.

The general committee, together with the Finance and Amusement Committees are rushing business and intend to make our Fourth of July celebration one of the grandest. Everybody is extended a hearty invitation to join in our natal day.

Mrs. Alice Jones and daughter, Lousa, came over last week to see her daughter, Lillian, who has been ill but is now recovering.

Brig Whitmore left Wednesday for Salt Lake City. His daughters Sybil and Myrtle accompanied him.

Miss Minerva Swapp has gone to Las Vegas for a few weeks visit.

Bishop W. L. Jones entertained the people of Overton in his apricot orchard Sunday.

Jefferson Jones and brother, Jos. H. Jones came over from Bunkerville last week.

Moapa Valley Will Enjoy Big Time At the Metropolis

Overton has arranged to celebrate the Glorious Fourth in regular old fashioned patriotic style. A Goddess of Liberty has been cho-en in the person of Miss Vivian Perkins, who will lend her grace and beauty to the day.

Games and races will occupy a large share of the day. A big barbecue will be prepared so that no one need be hungry.

The Overton people have invited their friends from various portions of the county to celebrate with them and extend to them every hospitality without money and without price.

Washington County News
June 28, 1911

Overton, June 28 —Cantaloupes are beginning to ripen, also tomatoes and watermelons. Work has not progressed as expected and the railroad will only be completed to the Narrows below the Weiser ranch for this summer's shipments of cantaloupes.

The Primary association has closed its weekly meetings during July and August. A children's dance was given at the close of their last meeting Saturday afternoon in the Lytle Hall.

Mr. and Mrs Arthur Koenig and their sister May and her husband left here this week for southern California where they will make their home

Joseph H. Jones with his mother and sister, Lillian, left for Bunkerville Monday. Miss Lillian was much improved in health.

The committee for the 4th of July celebration has arranged for a barbecue and public dinner after the morning exercises

Born, to Mr and Mrs John A. Lytle a son on the 23rd, and to Mr. and Mrs Sam Pixton, a daughter on the 24th

Misses Sybil and Myrtle Whitmore returned on the 24th from a trip to Salt Lake City.

Luke Whitney was in town Sunday from his ranch in the mountains east of here.

Mr. John Fagan is confined to his bed threatened with fever.

Judge A. L. F. MacDermott, of Overton, spent Friday in the county seat.

Las Vegas Age Newspaper
July 8, 1911

Contractor Wm. Marshall is about to begin the construction of a handsome home for H. L. Bruce at Overton, and is now at Moapa checking over the car of lumber purchased by Mr. Bruce for the building. Mr. Marschall will also probably take charge of the new school house building planned for Logan.

OVERTON WINS

Vegas Ball Team Meets Hot Surprise and are Defeated 10 to 7

Owing to the unavoidable delay in going to press with this week's issue, the AGE is able to give its readers the result of the Sunday game.

The scofe was 10 to 7 in favor of the Overton team. Errors, Vegas 6, Overton 18. Hits, Vegas 4, Overton 21. The game was played at Overton.

180

Overton Won

At a baseball game played on the 9th inst between Las Vegas and Overton, the latter won with the following score

	Las Vegas	Overton
Runs	7	15
Hits	4	21
Errors	6	18

Pitch, McDonald
Catch, Leavitt

Overton, July 13 —Harry Brown died here on the evening of July 4 after an illness of several weeks, which, however had only been considered serious for a few days. He was a young man of good habits who came here in December, 1910, to visit his uncle, James P. Anderson and family, and decided to spend the summer and raise a crop of cantaloupes His home was in Bear River City, Utah, but his father and other relatives live in Sanpete county Utah Funeral Services was held July 5th and the body was interred in the Overton cemetry, it being impossible to ship the corpse to his home. The young man had made many friends here who regret to see his untimely death.

On the morning of June 29, a frame house belonging to W. W McDonald of Thatcher, Arizona, was burned to the ground with all its contents. The house was occupied at the time by W. H. McDonald and family who lost all their clothing bedding and furniture. A piano and other furniture belonging to Clinton McDonald of Ogden was also lost in the fire. W. W. McDonald received word of the fire by telegraph and arrived here Sunday,

H. L Bruce of Keene, Texas is

Ths railroad track has been completed from Moapa down the valley to the Narrows and they are now prepared to load cantaloupes at that point, thus cutting off several miles of bad road for the freighters

here to build a house for his sister-in-law, Mrs Rachel King, who is spending the summer in Texas

181

OUR BOYS TRIMMED

"Cantaloupe Pickers" of Moapa Valley Put It Over Vegas Base Ball Team

As announced briefly in last week's AGE, the Moapa Valley boys took the Vegas pets in and did all kinds of things to the defenseless babes. Whether it was the sleepless nights of travel, the quality of the water, etc., or what, we have as yet had no explanation as to why the crack Vegas base ball experts should let the valley lads rub their noses in the dirt. It is said that the Vegas lads unwittingly hit on the true solution of the puzzle when they blamed each other. However since this explanation is not entirely satisfactory, we would prefer to lay the defeat to the fact that the Overton boys are the best players.

The line up for the Overton team is, Leavitt, c.; McDonald p.; D. Thomas ss; Conger 1b; Jacobs 3b; Rice 2b; M. Thomas Ccf.; Stone lf; Anderson rf.

The Vegas boys played as follows: Fennell, 3b; Hauk p and 1b; Black 2b; Voriss ss; Emerick p. and 1b; Thomas rf; Alter lf; Oswalp cf; Goodrich c.

The Overton boys are credited with 10 runs, and 21 hits and charged with 6 errors. The Vegas boosters got 7 runs 6 hits and are charged with 16 errors. It looks as if that man McDonald were a little too classy for our boys. But cheer up. There is yet left Goldfield to beat.

OVERTON VERY BUSY

Fire, Fourth of July, Base Ball and Cantaloupe Keep People Jumping

On June 29th a frame house belonging to W. W. McDonald, of Thatcher, Ariz., and occupied at the time by W. H. McDonald and family burned to the ground with all its contents. The fire was accidental, starting in the kitchen, and owing to the strong wind and lack of water it was impossible to save anything it burned so quickly. W. W. McDonald received word by telegraph of the accident, and arrived here Sunday. His son and family will return for the summer with him to Arizona. There was a small insurance carried on the house. A piano and some other furniture belonging to Clinton McDonald, of Ogden, also burned.

H. L. Bruce arrived here Monday July 3, from Keene, Texas to put up a house for his sister-in-law, Mrs. Rachel King, who is now spending the summer in Texas but will return in the fall.

Harry Brown died here July 4 after an illness of several weeks of malaria fever which became serious only a few days before his death and some thought turned to typhoid fever. Deceased came here from Bear River City, Utah to visit his uncle, J. P. Anderson, and decided to remain there the summer and raise cantaloupes. He was a young man of excellent habits and had many friends.

Ellis Turnbaugh has purchased an outfit for a moving picture show and gave several exhibitions there last week.

Rance Shurtliff has opened an ice cream parlor under a bower near his residence.

The Fourth of July celebration passed off very well here; everybody had a fine time and the committee in charge deserve credit for their excellent management of the celebration. There was a program in the morning in which Miss Vivian Perkins acted as Goddess of Liberty and Crayton Johnson as Uncle Sam. Ellis Turnbaugh read the Declaration of Independence. A number of fine musical selections were rendered as also some other parts after which there was a public dinner on the grounds followed by various sports for old and young, among which was the Pole Pillow fight. Bert Thomas proved the champion of the day by retaining his seat while he knocked eleven men— one at a time off the pole with a pillow.

A base ball game between Overton and St. Thomas concluded the day's amusements.

The Overton and Las Vegas base ball teams played an interesting game of ball here Sunday afternoon resulting in a score of 10 to 7 in favor of Overton, the latter team playing only eight innings. The Las Vegas boys returned the same evening to Moapa to take the train for home. We trust the completion of the line down the valley will make it convenient for many like contests in base ball and the various sports between the valley boys and their friends from the county seat.

Las Vegas Age Newspaper
July 29, 1911

Fragrant Beauties

The Editor of the AGE is indebted to County Assessor S. R. Whitehead for a crate of Moapa Valley cantaloupe which are, indeed, fragrant beauties. The spicy melons were grown on the ranch of Mr. Whitehead at Overton and are just about the ripest, sweetest, juciest, most fragrant specimens ever brought from the soil. We extend our hearty thanks.

Washington County News
August 8, 1911

Overton, Aug 8 —The boys from settlements who were here to assist in harvesting the cantaloupe crop have returned to their various homes There was a dance in the hall Thursday evening which was attended by many of them

Alma Shurtliff returned recently from the Central States where he has been employed for three years past He will return to his work there in October

Mr. and Mrs Albert Jones and Mr. and Mrs Ves Nay returned Monday from a trip to the mountain for a rest in the cool

Mr and Mrs Fay Perkins and Clifford Whitmore and Etta Hewett left this week for a trip to the Timber mountain.

The weather has been exceptionally cool here the past two weeks for this season of the year.

Misses Myrtle and Sibyl Whitmore entertained at an oyster supper Saturday evening

Born, a son to Mr. and Mrs Alonzo Huntsman, Aug 6.

184

OVERTON NEWS

Various Happenings in Moapa Valley Metropolis

Mrs. Doxie Perkins has returned to Salt Lake City.

Miss Minerva Swapp is home again from Las Vegas.

Misses Thelma and Irene Cox, of Bunkerville are here.

Ellis Turnbaugh gives a moving picture show every Saturday evening at the school house.

Wm. Conger lost a horse by its being struck by lightning in one of last week's electrical storms.

Mrs. Rachel King returned this week from Texas. The cottage being built for her is nearing completion.

Mr. and Mrs. John Swapp and Mrs. Alex Swapp and small children have gone out to their ranch near the saw mill.

Last week was delightfully cool and somewhat stormy, a pleasant change from the intense heat of the few weeks previous.

Miss Mildred Anderson is visiting in Fountain Green, Utah. Miss Grace Bischoff has taken her place behind the counter in Anderson's Store.

Bishop Jos. I. Earl of Bunkerville was here a couple of days this week visiting his daughters, Mrs. W. L. Jones and Miss Vida; his son, Harold also who is at work on the Overton ranch.

A number of farmers at Overton are through harvesting their crop of cantaloupes and the pickers and some of the farmers are assisting with the cantaloupes up the valley as their rush is now on and at some of the ranches melons are wasting for lack of enough pickers to go over the patches more than once a day.

OVERTON ITEMS

Moapa Valley People Look for Cooling Breezes with Close of Harvest

Joe F. Perkins is in Southern California for a few weeks.

Miss Ellen Shurtliff is at Swapp's ranch for her health.

Born August 6th, a son, to Mr. and Mrs. Alonzo Huntsman.

Misses Myrtle and Sybil Whitmore gave an oyster supper Saturday evening.

Ellis Turnbaugh was at Panaca last week to give a moving picture show.

Miss Vida Earl, Will Wittwer, Jefferson Jones and a number of others have returned to their homes in Bunkerville.

Alma Shurtliff returned recently from the Central States where he has been for three years in the employ of the Chicago Portrait Company. He will return in October.

The weather man seems to have forgotten what month it is and is giving us a real treat in the way of exceptionally cool nights and pleasant days. Heretofore we have regarded August as a real old "scorcher."

The close of the cantaloupe season finds many of our people wending their way to cooler climes for a few weeks. Among those returning or going are Mr. and Mrs. Albert Jones and Mr. and Mrs. Wes Nay to the Whitney and Nay ranches on the Bunkerville mountain; Mr. and Mrs. Fay Perkins and Etta Hewett to the Timber mountain; Wallace Jones, George Ingram, Woodruff Perkins and others to Whitney's ranch.

Overton, Aug. 14 —Several families of converts to the L D S church from Armenia came into the valley a few weeks ago to look for homes and are temporarily located at the Moapa Improvement Co's ranch at Logan, Nevada

Mrs Bert Marshall who was Miss Carlie Perkins of this place, returned Wednesday from northern Nevada, where she has been living since her marriage

Mr. and Mrs Sherman Thomas and family have gone to Gold Butte for an out

Mr and Mrs Joe F Perkins returned last week from southern California

Born, Aug 14, a daughter to Mr and Mrs Andrew L Jones

Overton, Oct 15 —Mutual Improvement meetings were begun Sunday with a joint program. William A Whitehead and Miss Mildred Anderson are presiding over the two associations

Recent newcomers are sons to Mr and Mrs Crayton Johnson, Mrs Bert Marshall and Mr and Mrs Alex Swapp

John A Lytle is building himself a new frame house Elmer Losee is also adding a number of rooms to his home.

Elder Heintze was here last week in the interest of the Armenian families now here in the valley.

J T Perkins is at Mormon well with his cattle

86

OVERTON ITEMS

Interesting Notes from Moapa Valley Metropolis

The weather has moderated considerably; a fall breeze fans the valley and the nights are cool and comfoatable.

Cantaloupe season is over, but there is still a considerable amount of fruit which is being used by the Valley people although some are shipping fruit yet.

Mrs. Bert Marshall (formerly Miss Carlie Perkins) of Tonopah, is visiting her relatives here.

The residence of Mrs. A. S. King is nearing completion and gives an attractive appearance to the town.

Engineer White and Contractor Smith have now moved their grading employees in and below town; rapid work is being done on the grade and reports state it will soon be completed to St. Thomas the end of the line.

Born to Mr. and Mrs. Alonzo Hnntsman a boy.

Quite a number of our town people have gone on excursion trips for a few weeks out in the mountains until the warm days are over.

Shurtliff Bros. and J. M. Lytle now have a deal on. The Shurtliff Bros. intend purchasing the lot of Mr. Lytle in town together with his dance hall and improvements on the same.

Mr. Joe F. Perkins and wife have returned from California where they have spent the summer.

Delinquent Notice

Muddy Valley Irrigation Co. Location of principal place of business, Overton, Nevada Location of Irrigation System and works Moapa Valley, Clark County, Nevada.

NOTICE.

There are delinquent upon the following described preferred capitol stock on account of assessment No. 17 levied on the 13th day of Feb. 1911 the several amounts set opposite the names of the respective shareholders as follows:

No. of et.	Name	Shares	Amount
436	Thos. J. Main	11½	$1.50
365)			
384 }	W. J. McBurney	14¾	5.31
522)			
439)	Henry Rice	1¾	2.31
309)			
359	Mrs. I. Stauffer	14	14.00
374	W. F. Murphy	46¾	37.17
404	Mark Murphy	31	31.00
462	J. E. Murphy	12	12.00
461	Hyrum Murphy	23 2-5	23.40

There are also delinquent upon the following described common stock on account of assessment No. 18 levied on the 13th day of Feb. 1911, the several amounts set opposite the names of the respective shareholders as follows:

	Name	Shares	Amount
77	Jacob Blodel	300	75.00
58	Kate A. Frampton	141¾	35.42
135)			
136 }	C. H. S. Morris	100	25.00
137)			
99	Irrigated Lands Co.	200	50.00
47	I. Stauffer	33	8.25
119	Hyrum Murphy	16.4	4.10
120	J. E. Murphy	10½	2.63
155	L. N. Shurtliff	12	3.00

And in accordance with law and an order of the board of directors made on the 5th day of Aug. 1911 so many shares of each parcel of each class of such stock as may be necessary will be sold at public auction at the office of the company in Overton, Clark County, Nevada, on the 16th day of Sept. 1911 at the hour of 3 o'clock p. m. of said day to pay delinquent assessment together with cost of advertising and expense of sale.

ISAAC E. LOSEE
Secretary.

First publication Aug. 19, 1911
Last publication Sept. 9, 1911.

OVERTON NEWS

(Special Correspondence)

Overton, Aug. 22.

Misses Minerva Swapp and Sylvia Shurtliff accompanied Alex Swapp to the Swapp ranch in Penn Valley last week.

Born, August 14, a daughter to Mr. and Mrs. Andrew Jones. All concerned doing nicely.

Mr. and Mrs. Sherman Thomas have returned from a trip to Gold Butte. While they were there a prospector named Chas. D. Crosby died at his camp near Gold Butte. Justice of the Peace McDermott went out from here and an inquest was held. His death was due to natural causes.

Bishop W. L. Jones left Friday for Salt Lake on business.

County Assessor Whitehead was in the valley a few days last week.

VALLEY HAPPENINGS

Overton. Aug. 21.

Mrs. Loretta Feldt, of Moapa, is in

town as the guest of Mrs. Kathryn Perkins visiting friends.

Shurtliff Bros. who recently purchased the town property of John M. Lytle, are now taking possession of the same.

Mrs. Lee Bruce, of Texas, is expected here this week, and will spend the winter with her sister-in-law Mrs. A. S. King.

W. C. Bowman has recently sold his ranch for $10,000. Mr. Fred Rushton, formerly of Capalappa Ranch will take charge of the same.

Mrs. Lee Bruce and Woodruff Perkins are now in Los Angeles. Mrs. Bruce is ordering material to build the new school house at Logan.

The home of B. Whitmore is being repainted and papered; the employees doing the same will prepare our school house with a nice painting soon.

U. V. Perkins and family are spending a few weeks in the mountains with Mr. and Mrs. Bryant Whitmore and Mr. and Mrs. Joe F. Perkins.

Warren Cox, of St. George, Utah, is in town selling wagons, carriages, etc.

OVERTON NEWS

Doings of People in Moapa Valley Metropolis

(Special Correspondence)

Overton, Aug. 28.

Warren Cox and son Melvin, of St. George, Utah, were here last week.

Fred Rushton and family have returned to the valley and are located at the Bowman Ranch, Mr. Rushton having charge of the ranch for a company of Salt Lake people who have purchased it.

Bishop Thos. Judd and W. L. Jones came down from Salt Lake City Wednesday.

Charles Ross has finished repainting the Whitmore residence of Wm. L. Batty.

The Overton base ball team have been playing a few games this week by way of practising up for the game scheduled at the Dixie Homecoming in St. George next September, where they will play the ball team from Hurricane, Utah.

Bishop Thos. J. Jones has gone to Bunkerville.

John M. Lytle has sold his home and other buildings on his lot including the dance hall to Rance Shurtliff and the latter took possession last week.

John Linton who has been ill is now some better thongh not entirely recovered.

OVERTON PERSONALS

What People Are Doing In The Moapa Valley Metropolis

(Special Correspondence)

Overton, Sept 4.

Brig Whitmore left this morning for Lehi, Utah.

W. D. Ford is at work painting the school house here.

Wm. L. Batty and family have gone to Toquerville, Utah to visit relatives.

Miss Irene Cox, Harold Earl, Lyman Leavitt, also Miss Thelma Cox have returned to their homes in Bunkerville.

Allen Fleming, who has been ill for some time left today for Salt Lake City for medical treatment. Crayton Johnson accompanied him.

John Swapp and family returned last week from their ranch in the mountains near Grand Gulch.

Chas. Ross and Joe Snyder have almost completed painting the residence of Wm. L. Batty.

Miss Sadie Perkins has gone to Panaca to attend the High School there this winter.

MOAPA VALLEY NEWS BRIEFS

Intesesting Notes from the Metropolis of the Cantaloupe Country

(Special Correspondence)

Overton, Sept. 20, 1911

After a very hot summer we welcome cooler days and the crisp evening air which calls for warmer bed clothing.

Our schoolhouse is beautifully finished inside and out with a nice painting finish and school will begin Monday the 26th, with Mr. Leonidas Hickman as principal and Miss Carrie Richards as Primary teacher.

Our town has been quite deserted the past ten days as a great majority of our citizens have been enjoying a vacation at the Dixie Home Coming in St. George, Utah, but the streets are full of buggies bringing in the returning crowds.

The surveying parties together with all construction crews and contractors have now vacated the Valley as the grading is completed, and it is hoped the rails will be laid at once and that no further delay will be endured.

Miss Clara Perkins has returned from a summer's outing in Utah and Wyoming and has taken her old stand behind the connter at Whitehead's store.

Mrs. Andrew L. Jones who is employed as teacher of the Logan school, has now commenced the same. Her husband will leave shortly for Utah to attend school the coming winter.

The Grand Ball given as a Free opening in the Shurtliff Hall was enjoyed by all. New improvements are being made by the Shurtliff Amusement Company and we wish them much success.

Will MacDonald is home from Arizona. We are always glad to see Will again.

The Base Ball game between the Moapa Valley Boys and those from up the Virgin river settlements in Utah was a good game in favor of Moapa Boys.

E. J. Robertson of Aspara ranch in the Moapa Valley, was in Vegas for a short time early in the week.

John M. Thomas, one of the best known ranchers of the Moapa Valley, is down from Logan renewing acquaintanceship with old friends.

T. H. Osborne of Salt Lake City, accompanied by his son Charles D. arrived in Vegas Thursday morning after spending two days in the Moapa Valley looking after their land holdings.

Miss Helene Reed of Moapa is now attending the High School. She is making her home at the residence of conductor Tibbens.

J. Bouse of Moapa, head of the Moapa Gypsum Company, passed through Vegas Thursday on his way to the property. He was accompanied by Mr. A. S. C. Forbes of Los Angeles who is also interested in gypsum.

O. W. Jarvis, of Overton, was a Vegas visitor Tuesday last. Mr. Jarvis was superintending the shipment of a car of hogs over the L. V. & T. road to the Goldfield market.

192

TOWNSITE OF KAOLIN

Big Holding Company to Place 1,000 Acre Tract on Market in 10 Acre Plots

The Nevada Land and Livestock Company, which has been engaged for the past three years in clearing and bringing under cultivation about 1000 acres of land which it holds about two miles below Overton, in the Moapa Valley, now has a party of surveyors on the ground, and is subdividing its holdings into ten acre plots.

These plots it is said will be offered for sale at $100 per acre, each plot carrying five shares of primary water right and ten shares of secondary.

A new townsite called Kaolin is also being laid out; the old townsite was cut squarely in two by the railroad grade.

The new location is a little to the south and east of the old one. The company obtained its certificate from the State Engineer for water right several weeks ago. This right is to be merged in the Muddy Valley Irrigation Company. This action assures the peaceful settlement of differences in the Valley relative to the use of the river water and clears the way for rapid and certain development.

Las Vegas Age Newspaper
October 7, 1911

The Overton Base Ball team will arrive in Vegas tonight and play the local team Sunday at 2 o'clock. Thr Canteloupers are now the champions of the County and an interesting fame should result.

County Assessor Whitehead has returned from a weeks stay in Overton.

OVERTON BREVITIES

What the People are Doing In the Moapa Valley

(Special Correspondence.)

Overton Oct. 16, 1911.

Assessor Stephen R. Whitehead of Las Vegas is here for a few days.

A. M. Dwight has been here several days taking orders for groceries for the firm of Loverin & Brown of Chicago.

Recent new comers are sons to the following: Mr. and Mrs. Crayton Johnson, Mr. and Mrs. Bert Marshall and Mr. and Mrs. Alex. Swapp.

John A. Lytle is building a frame house.

Elmer Losee is adding a couple of rooms to his home.

Orson Sprague of Bunkerville was violinist at a dance here Friday evening.

Dentist Lewis Marco of Caliente was here for three days last week.

The Mutual Improvement Associations began their winter sessions Sunday evening, with William Whitehead and Miss Mildred Anderson as presidents of the two associations.

Mr. Silver, the optician came down the valley Sunday.

Elder Heintze of Salt Lake City was here this week in the interest of the Armenian families now here in the valley.

A few of the people of Overton went to Moapa Monday to see the Railroad Show.

Ellis Turnbough, who is teaching school at St. Thomas, was here Saturday evening with a picture show.

194

Overton, Oct. 24 —Mrs. Nellie Pixton was called last week to the bedside of her husband, Samuel Pixton, in Taylorsville, Utah, where he went some time ago for medical treatment

Engineer Jacobson returned to his home at Provo, Utah, this week He has been in the employ of the irrigation company all summer

Miss Armelia Ingram returned home last week after a year's absence in Idaho and northern Utah

Farmers are planting fall grain. The sweet potato crop is ready to harvest.

Ves Nay left Sunday for Kingman, Arizona, accompanied by his family.

Mr and Mrs William Grann have a daugher, born last week

H L Bruce has returned to his home in Keene, Texas

Married

WHITMORE—HEWITT:- At Hotel Nevada, in this city, Wednesday evening October 25, 1911, Clifford Whitmore, aged 21 years, to Mary E. Hewitt, aged 18 years, both residents of Overton.

Judge Lillis officiated at the ceremony in his usual happy manner and Messrs. M. M. Riley and Harley A. Harmon acted as witnesses to the ceremony. The happy couple left for their home in Overton Thtrsday morning and are now receiving the congratulations of their many friends.

W. W. Angell of Overton was in this city Wednesday.

NEWS FROM OVERTON

Interesting Personals From the Center of Most Fertile Country on Earth

(Special Correspondence.)

Overton, Oct. 24, 1911.

Miss Amelia Ingram returned Friday from Idaho and Northern Utah where she has been for the past year.

H. L. Bruce left last week for his home in Keene, Texas.

Ves. Nay, accompanied by his family, left Sunday for Kingman, Arizona.

Farmers are busy planting the fall grain. The sweet potato crop is now ready to harvest.

Mrs. Nellie Pixton left Saturday to join her husband in Taylorsville, Utah, where he went some time ago for medical treatment.

Mr. Jacobson, a civil engineer who has been here through the summer in the employ of the Irrigation Company, leaves this week for his home in Provo Utah.

196

OVERTON MAKES MERRY

Moapa Valley Metropolis Enjoys a Very Busy Week

(Special Correspondence.)

Overton, Nev. Nov. 1, 1911. Commissioner Charles S. Norcross, State Engineer W. M. Kearney and Chief of Police Capt. Jack Donnelly were here Saturday. They attended a meeting of the Moapa Valley Irrigation Company held here Saturday afternoon.

We had a nice rain Friday. There has been no frost yet. Roses and other flowers are still blooming and chrysanthemums of every color are coming into full bloom.

Under the management of the Mutual Improvement Association a Hallow-e'en Character Ball was given in the Hall Tuesday evening. The hall was prettily decorated with festoons and Jack-O-Lanterns. Many fine characters were represented by the dancers. The young people from the Valley and also a number from Bunkerville were present. Among the latter were the Misses Lovira Leavitt, Rhoda Wittwer and Thirza Leavitt, and Messrs Conrad Adams, William Leavitt, Orson Leavitt, Harold Earle and Washington Leavitt.

OVERTON LOCALS

Personal Items of Interest to People of Moapa Valley

Jesse Cooper has a beautiful residence just completed on his land by the banks of the Moapa River.

Word has just been received of the death of Samuel Pixton, of this place, at his parents' home in Taylorsville, Utah.

Several Armenian families have arrived in town and intend to locate in this valley.

A new family, Grisham by name, have moved here from Texas and intend to purchase land.

The Character Ball given on Hallow-e'en night was a decided success. The hall was lighted in the old Hallow-e'en manner, with pumpkin faces, and decorated with yellow and white chrysanthemums and green and autumn foliage.

A few of those whose costumes were worthy of mention were Will Whitehead personating a Greek god; Ralph Leavitt as Buster Brown; John Lewis as Happy Hooligan, Mildred and Fay Anderson as Jack and Jill, Gertrude Rhoner as Queen of Hearts, Ethel Lewis as Priscilla, and Eloise Lewis as the Pumpkin Girl. Chichu Dotson acted her part as Night in a beautiful black dress with silver trimmings.

The dramatic Club will present a play on Thanksgiving Eve.

There was a fine attendance at the moving picture show Saturday night. An illustrated song is given with every show. The next show will be on Thanksgiving.

197

Spelling should be Andersen

Overton, Nov 1 —Under the management of the Mutual Improvment associations a Hallowe'en Character ball was given Tuesday evening in the Shurtliff amusement hall The hall was prettily decorated with festooning and jack-o-lanterns and a merry time was had. A number of young people from Bunkerville who have come here for employment attended, among them being Misses Rhoda Wittwer, Thirza Leavitt, Louisa Leavitt, and Messers Conrad Adams, William Leavitt, Washington Leavitt, Harold Earl and Orson Leavitt

Commissioner Charles S. Norcross, head of the state commission of agriculture and irrigation, State Engineer W. M. Kearney, and Capt. Jack Donnelley, Chief of the state police, came down the valley Friday returning to Moapa Sunday. They attended a meeting of the Moapa Valley Irrigation Co Saturday at Overton

Chrysanthemums of every shade and hue are coming into full flower There has been no frost yet and the valley looks as beautiful as on a day in spring We had a fine rain last Friday.

Mrs Jesse Murphy of St Thomas was in town Sunday

The W. L Jones home is being painted

198

Overton, Nov 13 —Mr Robinson of Logan and his neice, Mrs Nellie Pixton, have returned from Taylorsville, Utah, where they were called on account of the illness and death of Mrs Pixton's husband, Samuel Pixton of this place, who died Oct 30th, 1911, at the home of his parents in Taylorsville, of meningitis of the brain He leaves a wife and one child, also parents, brothers, sisters and a host of friends, both at his old home and in the Moapi valley, where he has resided about four years

The Relief society has held a "quilting bee" recently, the one held last Thursday was at the home of Mrs Nellie Lossee.

We have experienced unusually cold weather since Nov. 9th, at which time there was the first severe frost this fall.

John Swapp returned last week from a trip to his ranch in Penn valley,

The Primary association will give a chrysanthemum ball this evening.

Overton Items

(Special Correspondence.)

Overton Nov. 18, 1911.

John Swatt returned last week from his ranch in Penn Valley.

The Shurtliff Amusement Company have recently set up a doll rack in their grounds.

The weather has been unusually cold here for several days, with lots of wind but no rain. Frost was quite severe Nov. 9th and 10th.

Under the management of the Primary Association a Chrysanthemum Ball will be given for the children in the hall tonight.

The Ladies Relief Society have held a number of "quilting bees" recently, the one Thursday being given at the home of Mrs. Nellie Lossee.

Mr. Robinson of Logan and his niece, Mrs. Nellie Pixton have returned from Taylorsville, Utah, where they were called by the illness and death of Mrs. Pixton's husband, who passed away at the home of his parents Oct. 30. He leaves a wife and infant daughter, his parents, brothers, sisters, and a host of friends, both in his old home and in the Moapa Valley where he has resided for the past four years.

200

Overton Items

(Special Correspondence)

Mr. and Mrs. John Felt of Huntsville, Utah, are here this week. Mr. Felt owns a tract of land in the valley and may decide to make his home here.

Miss Mabel Leavitt is visiting at Hichton's.

Mrs. Annie J. Cox and daughter Mrs. Alma Leavitt of Bunkerville are guests of Mrs. Cox's sister, Mrs. W. L. Batty of this place. Mrs. Cox has millinery for sale.

Mrs. Agnes Marshall is visiting her sister Mrs. Albert Jones a few days this week.

Pres. E. H. Snow and D. R. Forsha of St. George, Utah, came over from Bunkerville Saturday. They will hold ward conference here Sunday afternoon and at St. Thomas the same evening. They will speak at Logan Monday.

Fay Perkins and John A. Lytle are doing assessment work on a claim near the Colorado.

An agent for a New York company was here last week to contract cantaloupes for the coming season.

201

Pres C H. Snow and D. R. Forsha held ward conference here Sunday afternoon. They will hold meeting Sunday evening at St. Thomas and Monday evening at Logan

Mr. and Mrs John Felt of Huntsville, Utah, are here this week. Mr Felt owns a tract of land in the valley about two miles north of town and may decide to make his home here.

John L Linton of this place who is at Las Vegas under the care of Dr. Martin is not improving as it was hoped he would do.

An agent for a New York company was in the valley last week to contract cantaloupes for the coming season

Fay Perkins and John A Lytle are doing assessment work on a claim near the Colorado river

Mrs Agnes Marshall of Logan is visiting her sister, Mrs Albert Jones a few days this week.

Mrs Annie J. Cox and daughter, Mrs Alma Leavitt are here from Bunkerville

Miss Mabel Leavitt is visiting at the Bowman ranch.

202

Overton, Nov. 27.—John Linton of this place died at Las Vegas Nov. 22 after an illness of several months He was sent by his friends here to the Las Vegas hospital for medical treatment in September. Mr. Linton was a native of Belfast, Ireland, and was a sailor for many years He became converted to the Gospel in the state of Washington and came to Overton in 1908 in company with Elder Wm H McDonald, who was returning from a mission in the north western states He had no relations in the church but has made many friends who regret to see his untimely demise

A number of families here have raised peanuts this summer and are now harvesting the crop They report a good yield and a profitable crop for every family to raise

Elders Myron Abbott and Raymond Abbott of Mesquite were here as home Missionaries Sunday. They went on to St Thomas to speak there Sunday evening.

Mr and Mrs Bert Nay of———— are visiting their brother, Ves Nay and family of this place

Overton Items

(Special Correspondence.)

Overton Nov. 27, 1911. The many friends of John L. Linton of this place regret his untimely death which occurred at Las Vegas Nov. 23, after an illness of several months.

Elders Myron Abbott and Raymond Abbott of Mesquite were present at church services Sunday and addressed the congregation.

Bishop W. L. Jones and J. P. Anderson held a cottage meeting at the home of Mr. Lewis at Capalapa Sunday.

A number of families who have raised a crop of peanuts this season report a good yield and excellent quality of nuts.

Mr. and Mrs. Bert Nay are visiting relatives here.

Mrs. Sophia Cooper and family are now living in their new home, which is a handsome addition to the town.

Overton Items

(Special Correspondence.)

Overton Dec. 5, 1911.

A debate was held Friday evening, the subject being, "Resolved, that modern canals on each side of the Valley would eventually be a cheaper and more efficient system of irrigation for this valley than the one now in use." Orvin Jarvis and Elmer Lossee were for the affirmative and Crayton Johnson and William Whitehead for the negative. The judges were J. P. Anderson, Joe F. Perkins and Leonidas Hickman. They judged for argument and delivery and gave 83 points to the affirmative and 84 to the negative.

Mr. and Mrs. Chas. Felt of Moapa spent Thanksgiving here as the guests of Mr. and Mrs. Joe. F. Perkins.

Wednesday evening the Home Dramatic Club presented the comedy, "The Girl from Porti Rico", the following taking part in the play: Elmer Lossee, W. A. Whitehead, Leonidas Hickman, Clarence Lewis, Jesse Cooper, Clara Perkins, Mildred Anderson and Ethel Lewis.

Thanksgiving day was one of peaceful enjoyment, family dinners being the order of the day. Games of base-ball and basket-ball were played in the afternoon and a moving picture exhibition was given in the evening, followed by a dance.

The officers of the Primary Association gave the children a Thanksgiving dinner in the school house Saturday afternoon.

Mrs. Bert Marshall has been ill for the past few days.

The stock holders of the Muddy Valley Irrigation Company met in Overton Dec. 2d to consider a bond issue for the purpose of developing the irrigation system.

Mr. and Mrs. Henry Kocherhans, who have both been working for some time at the Grand Gulch mine, came in from there Saturday. The Company have cut down the force, retaining only two men.

SUMMONS

In the Justice's Court of Overton Township, County of Clark, State of Nevada.

J. P. Anderson, Plaintiff,

vs.

H. L. Bruce, Defendant.

The State of Nevada sends greeting to H. L. Bruce, Defendant.

You are hereby directed to appear before me at my office at Overton, in Overton Township, in the County of Clark, and answer the complaint in the above entitled action within five days, if the Summons be served in the Township or city in which the action is brought; ten days if served out of the Township or City, but within the County in which the action is brought, and within twenty days if served elsewhere, and unless you appear and answer, the plaintiff will take judgment for any money or damages, demanded in the complaint, arising upon contract, or will apply to the Court for the relief demanded in the complaint.

This action is brought to recover the sum of $134.20 of which amount $4.75 is for goods and merchandise sold and delivered to you, $42.00 for cash paid out on checks issued by you and refused by the bank drawn upon and $87.45 for money lent to you by Brig Whitmore and which account has been assigned to plaintiff by said Brig Whitmore.

To the Sheriff or any Constable of said County, Greeting: Make legal service and due return hereof.

Given under my hand this 29th day of November, A. D. 1911.

A. L. F. MacDermott,

Justice of the Peace of said Township.

First Publication Dec. 2, 1911.

Last Publication Dec. 30, 1911.

SUMMONS

In the Justice's Court of Overton Township, County of Clark, State of Nevada.

W. C. Bowman, Plaintiff,

vs.

H. L. Bruce, Defendant.

The State of Nevada sends greeting to H. L. Bruce, Defendant.

You are hereby directed to appear before me at my office at Overton, in Overton Township, in the County of Clark, and answer the complaint in the above entitled action within five days, if the Summons be served in the Township in which the action is brought; ten days if served out of the Township, but within the County in which the action is brought, and within twenty days if served elsewhere, and unless you appear and answer, the plaintiff will take judgment for any money or damages, demanded in the complaint, as arising upon contract, or will apply to the Court for the relief demanded in the complaint.

This action is brought to obtain judgment against you for the sum of Forty-six and seventy one-hundredths Dollars ($46.70) for balance of account for lumber and building material sold and delivered to you by the plaintiff at your request, at Moapa, County of Clark, State of Nevada, during August and October, 1911, and amounting to Fifty-six and seventy one-hundredth dollars ($56.70), of which amount Ten dollars ($10.00) has been paid only.

To the Sheriff or any Constable of said County, Greeting: Make legal service and due return hereof.

Given under my hand this 10th day of November, A. D., 1911.

    A. L. F. MacDermott,

    Justice of the Peace of said Township.

First publication Nov. 18, 1911.

Last publication December 9, 1911.

REPORT

Of the Condition of the First State Bank of Las Vegas, in the State of Nevada, at the Close of Business on the 5th day of Dec., 1911.

RESOURCES

Loans and discounts	$ 124,293 11
Overdrafts	98 30
Bonds, stocks, securities, etc.	3,090 06
Lot and Banking House	8,000 00
Furniture and Fixtures	2,000 00
Other Real Estate	8,000 54
Due from Banks and Bankers	78,237 00
Checks and other Cash Items	395 00
Cash on hand: Gold Coin	9,625 00
Silver Coin	8,579 48
Currency	20,047 00
	252,015 49

LIABILITIES

Capital Stock paid in		$ 25,000 00
Surplus Fund		5,000 00
Undivided Profits	$ 5,469 69	
Less Expenses	3,246 50	2,223 19
Individual Deposits subject to check		193,302 28
Time Certificates of Deposit		22,998 96
Certified Checks		
Cashier's Checks outstanding		3,491 06
		$252,015 49

STATE OF NEVADA }
  County of Clark } ss.

I, John S. Park, Cashier of the above named bank, do solemnly swear that the above statement is true to the best of my knowledge and belief. JOHN S. PARK, Cashier.

Correct—Attest:

  W. R. Bracken } Directors.

  W. E. Hawkins }

Subscribed and sworn to before me this 9th day of December 1911.

    DAVID FARNSWORTH, Notary Public.

[SEAL]

Mining Expert Here

J. A. Swapp, of Overton, Nev., who owns copper property at Copper Mountain, and S L Pearce, a mining engineer of the firm of Pearce and Pearce of Alamos, Mexico, and Los Angeles, Cal, arrived here Saturday. Mr Pearce is investigating mining properties and conditions all through this section and appears to be making a thorough examination, for what purpose the gentleman does not care to state He has made a careful inspection of the Copper Mountain and other properties down that way, and on Monday went out to the copper deposits near Bloomington On Tuesday morning he left with Mr, Swapp to make an investigation of the Bull Valley mining country, expecting to return here in about five days

207

OVERTON EVENTS

Social Happenings at the Moapa Valley Metropolis

Mrs. A. S. King entertained at her home on Wednesday evening in honor of Mrs. J. A. Abbott, of Portland, Oregon, who is visiting here, a guest of Mrs. U. V. Perkins. Several vocal selections were successfully rendered by Mrs. R. E. Marshall and Mary Virginia Lytle. Katherine delighted the guests with "Shuberts Serenade", played on the piano. Miss Carrie Richards of Logan, Utah also rendered two beautiful selections. An elaborate dinner was served at 4 o'clock, the rooms being very prettily decorated with pink and white chrysanthemums and mistletoe.

Those invited to meet Mrs. Abbott were, Mrs. Roy Fileher of Berkely, Cal., Mrs. Katherine Perkins, of San Diego, Cal., Mrs. R. E. Marshall, of Austin, Nevada, Miss Carrie Richards, and Miss Nettie Williams, of Logan, Utah, Anna Cooper, Mary Virginia Lytle, Mrs. S. B. Thomas, Francis Johnson, Jennie Perkins, Mrs. W. L. Batty, Mrs. W. L. Jones, Mrs. S. B. Ney, Mrs. Geo. L. Perkins and Mrs. U. V. Perkins. The evening was greatly enjoyed by all present. Much honor is given to the charming hostess.

Extensive preparations are being made for holiday amusements. The Western drama, "Rocky Ford", will be presented here Saturday evening.

A Christmas Program will be rendered Sunday evening by the scholars of the public school under the direction of Prof. L. M. Hickman and Carrie Richards.

Mrs. W. L. Batty will entertain Friday evening in honor of Mrs. Abbott.

Miss Sadie Perkins who is attending High School at Pannen, will be home Friday to spend the holidays.

The Misses Sybil and Myrtle Whitmore, who are attending school at Nephi, Utah, will also spend their holiday vacation at Overton

Business houses have agreed to close between the hours of 3 and 4:30 Wednesday afternoon on account of the basket-ball game between the Clark County High School boys and the Goldfield boys.

Overton, Dec. 23 —The town boys played a game of base ball with St. Thomas boys on Dec 16 at the latter place, the victory was for St Thomas

Mrs Rachel King entertained at a luncheon Wednesday afternoon in honor of Mrs Chrissie Abbott of La Grande, Oregon, who is visiting relatives here

Horace and Albert Jones, have come in for the holidays from Whitmore's mine where they have been at work for some time.

Warren Cox of St George who has been looking after his cattle in this locality for some time, returned to his home this week

Ellis Turnbeaugh and family have returned for holiday week from St. Thomas, where Mr. Turnbeaugh is teaching school

Joseph and Orange Earl and Mark Laub of Enterprise are here on their way out to Gold Butte to do assessment work.

Bp W. L Jones made a trip to Caliente this week on business connected with the right of way for the railroad.

Mrs W. L Batty entertained a party of lady friends Friday afternoon.

A picture show and dance was held in the hall Friday evening

John Swapp returned from St. George today.

Miss Carrie Richards of Logan, Utah, who is teaching at Overton this winter is in Vegas as a guest at the Whitehead home.

OVERTON EVENTS

Newsy Notes from the Moapa Valley Metropolis

Overton, Dec. 23, 1911.

At the base ball game at St. Thomas on Saturday, Dec. 16th, the Overton boys were defeated by the St. Thomas team.

Warren Cox, who has been looking after his cattle in this locality has returned to his home in St. George.

Bishop W. L. Jones made a trip to Caliente this week on business connected with the right of way for the railroad.

Horace and Albert Jones have come in for the holidays from Whitmore's mine, where they have been at work for some time.

Mrs. W. L. Batty entertained a party of friends at a social on Friday afternoon.

John Swatt returned today from St. George.

Ellis Turnbaugh and family have returned for the holidays from St. Thomas where Mr. Turnbaugh is teaching school.

Andrew L. Jones who is attending the B. Y. University at Provo, and Sadie Perkins who is at the Lincoln County High School are expected home for the holidays.

Joseph and Orange Earl and Mark Laub, all of Enterprise, Utah, are here on their way to Gold Butte to do assessment work.

A moving picture show was held in the hall Friday evening followed by a dance.

OVERTON EVENTS

Newsy Notes from the Moapa Valley Metropolis

Overton, Dec. 23, 1911.

At the base ball game at St. Thomas on Saturday, Dec. 16th, the Overton boys were defeated by the St. Thomas team.

Warren Cox, who has been looking after his cattle in this locality has returned to his home in St. George.

Bishop W. L. Jones made a trip to Caliente this week on business connected with the right of way for the railroad.

Horace and Albert Jones have come in for the holidays from Whitmore's mine, where they have been at work for some time.

Mrs. W. L. Batty entertained a party of friends at a social on Friday afternoon.

John Swatt returned today from St. George.

Ellis Turnbaugh and family have returned for the holidays from St. Thomas where Mr. Turnbaugh is teaching school.

Andrew L. Jones who is attending the B. Y. University at Provo, and Sadie Perkins who is at the Lincoln County High School are expected home for the holidays.

Joseph and Orange Earl and Mark Laub, all of Enterprise, Utah, are here on their way to Gold Butte to do assessment work.

A moving picture show was held in the hall Friday evening followed by a dance.

Name probaby Swapp

Overton Jan 19 —Bishop O P Miller of Salt Lake City spent a few days here last week in the interest of the Church property in the valley He spoke in afternoon services here Sunday also held a meeting in St Thomas the same evening

Born Jan 15 a daughter to Mr and Mrs Herbert Nay of this place to Mr and Mrs Bert Mills of Logan a son Jan 14 the latter child only lived a few hours

Roy C Felcher and family who have been at the experiment farm the past two years left on the 1st for California O W Jarvis is temporarily in charge

D H Snedeker is here looking up the interest of the valley for publication in the Publicity Edition of the Las Vegas Age which will be issued in February

Mr Leonidas Hickman and Miss Carrie Richards report having enjoyed the Teachers Institute recently held in Las Vegas very much

A haystack and corral belonging to Sylvester Nay was burned Jan 7, the fire originating from a cigarette spark

Mr and Mrs Bryant Whitmore have a baby girl born Dec 29 Mother and babe doing nicely

Jessie Cooper and Jos Prince left Monday for the western part of the county to seek employment

T J Osborne is here looking after business interests this week

Calvin Nay and family of Alamo Nev are visiting relatives here

A D Bishop came over from Las Vegas Wednesday

Mrs James P Anderson is ill with pneumonia

Correct spelling should be Andersen

HIGH SCHOOL ACTIVITIES

Many Interesting Events Scheduled for Clark County High

The high school pupils have rented the pavilion at Ladd's Resort and will use the same for a basket ball court until the end of the season. The purpose of this is to give the local basket ball team practice in playing on a floor so as to enable them to cope on equal footing with the Goldfield team.

Arrangements have been made for a game at Goldfield between the Clark County girls team and the girls team of the Goldfield high school. This will occur about February 24, and much interest and rivalry has been aroused in the matter. School teachers and pupils and school officials will be entitled to half rates on the L. V. & T. road.

The second semester of the school year opens Monday January 22d. A class from the eighth grade will graduate into the high school. The present regular attendance of the high school is 20, there being ten girls and ten boys.

The new semester will see several new studies taken up, among them being a course in American Government, and a course in Physiology. A beginners class in algebra will also be taken up.

Last Thursday afternoon, the first debate of the year occurred between the boys and girls of the junior class. The question was "Resolved that the Study of Science is of more practical value than the study of English." The boys took the affirmative and the girls the negative. The judges decided the debate in favor of the negative, giving the girls the victory.

Plans are being made for the formation of a literary society to encourage debating and public speaking. Much interest is being shown by the pupils in this line.

The boys basket ball team will leave Vegas Saturday morning, Juny. 27, to play with the town team at Overton. The Moapa Valley boys claim to have the fastest team in the state, and while it will put the high school boys on their mettle to win the game, the loss of it will not prevent them from winning the state high school championship as the Overton team is not a school team.

Word has been received from the coach of the Goldfield High school team that they wish to play Clark County High again this season. They feel practically sure of winning in the north end of the state and are anxious to have one more tussel with our team.

You Can Be a Better Cook

TEA KETTLE

It isn't *all* in the "knack." The utensils you use go a long way toward making your food fine and appetizing or ill-cooked and indigestible.

It's impossible to make the best cookery in utensils that quickly scorch or crack and scale off, rust and corrode. And such utensils are dangerous. Authorities say that cancer comes of eating particles of glass chipped off from ordinary enamel ware when hot.

The heat expands the iron frame but the coating of glass—which is all enamel ware is—does not expand so fast, consequently it breaks and gets mixed with the food.

There is no such danger from food cooked in up-to-date

SAUCE PAN

"1892" Pure Spun Aluminum Ware

It *can not* crack, peel nor chip. It *will not* rust, corrode, nor spoil food, and with harder use it lasts years longer than any other ware.

COFFEE POT

We Guarantee It for 15 Years

"1892" PURE SPUN ALUMINUM is the ideal ware for all kitchen utensils—permanently bright and beautiful as silver, but many times lighter—making it convenient to handle. Heats quickly but does not quickly burn dry. Easy to clean and care for.

"1892" Pure Aluminum utensils have all the advantages of every other kind besides several that are exclusive.

And with all these added advantages over all other utensils "1892" Pure Spun Aluminum Ware costs but a trifle more.

BERLIN SAUCE PAN

Look for the Maltese Cross on Every Piece

It is for your protection and benefit. Its a guarantee that you are getting the genuine and only original "1892" Pure Spun Aluminum.

FOR SALE BY

J. P. ANDERSON,
Overton, Nevada

Call and get a Pure Aluminum Souvenir FREE while they last.

MUFFIN PAN

The correct spelling should be Andersen

Overton News

(Special Correspondence.)

Overton Jan. 19, 1912.

Bishop O. P. Miller of Salt Lake City was here on business and spoke at the afternoon services Sunday. He also held a meeting the same evening at St. Thomas and returned to Moapa Monday.

Born Jan. 14, a son to Mr. and Mrs. Bert Mills of Logan. The babe died the same day. The mother is doing nicely.

Born Jan. 15, to Mr. and Mrs. Herbert Nay of this place, a daughter. Mother and child are doing nicely.

A. D. Bishop of Las Vegas was here on a business trip this wEek.

D. H. Snedeker is here in the interest of the Publicity Edition of the Las Vegas Age, to be issued soon.

Jesse Cooper and Jos. Prince left on Monday for the western part of the country where they will seek employment.

T. J. Osborne of Salt Lake made a trip through the valley this week to look after his property.

215

Las Vegas Age Newspaper
February 3, 1912

Wm. L. Batty of Overton was greeting Vegas friends this week while on grand jury duty.

Bert Mills of Logan has been spending the week in the county seat as a member of the grand jury.

Joe. F. Perkins, one of the prominent men of Overton, was in the county seat on grand jury duty the past week.

Washington County News
February 3, 1912

Overton Feb 3 --The Industrial train came in to Moapa on the even ing of the 16th and the afternoon of the next day the following profess ors came to the experiment farm at Logan L N Winsor of Utah Ir rigation and Drainage G rdon H True of the University of Nevada Agriculture Mr. Homer of the Utah agricultural college Horticulture an1 Mr Mac of the Uni ersity of Nevada Veterinary Dept Here they met the farmers of the valley held a meeting, followed by stocl judging and demonstrations They held a meeting the same evening in Overton

A game of basl et ball was playel in the hall Safur lay evening between the Overton and I os Vegas teams I N Hicl man principal of the district school here acted as umpire and C E Overman of the Clarl County High school at Las Vegas was referee The score was 26 to 39

M. D. Cooper of Overton spent court week as a guest of the Overland hotel.

L. M. Grant of Moapa was among the prominent citizens of the Moapa valley in attendance upon court this week.

Overton Basket Ball

In writing the account of the basket ball game at Overton last week, we inadvertently omitted to state the final score.

At the close of the game, notwithstanding the improvement in play which the Clark County High School boys showed during the last ten minutes, the score stood 39 to 26 in favor of Overton. The next game is looked forward to with interest.

Overton Feb 10 — Mrs Fred Rushton died Feb 8 of pneumonia on their ranch in the upper end of the valley about six miles from Overton Funeral services were held at the residence yesterday Mr Rushton leaving the same evening with the corpse for Salt Lake City their former home Mrs Rushton was a sweet woman and her demise is mourned by all who knew her She leaves a husband and seven children with parents brothers and sisters in northern Utah

Several of our citizens were called over to Las Vegas this week on jury service among them are W I Batty J F Perkins M D Cooper and Perry D Huntsman

Jacob Rohner of Myton Utah is visiting his daughter Miss Gertrude Rohner here this week

OVERTON NEWS NOTES

Happenings of Interest to the People of the Moapa Valley

(Special Correspondence.)

Overton Jany. 29, 1912.

Professors Winsor, True, Homer and Mac, of the Industrial train were at the experiment farm on the 24th and at 2 p. m. held a meeting followed by demonstrations and stock judging. They also held a meeting on the same evening with the farmers in the Overton schoolhouse.

Bishops Edw. Bunker and Jos. I. Earl were over from Bunkerville to hear the lectures given by the professors from the Industrial train.

Mrs. James P. Anderson is recovering from an attack of pneumonia.

The infant son of Mr. and Mrs. Alex. Swapp died on the 26th, after an illness of several days.

Calvin and Sylvester Nay are trapping for furs at the head of the Muddy.

A game of basket ball was played in the hall Saturday evening between the Overton and Las Vegas teams. L. M. Hickman acted as umpire and C. E. Overman of Las Vegas as referee. The score was 26 to 39 in favor of the Overton team. The game was followed by a dance.

Overton Feb. 3, 1912.

Born January 30th, to the wife of Ellis Turnbaugh, a baby daughter. Mother and child doing nicely.

John Swatt accompanied by his daughter Minerva has gone to St. George.

J. M. Jolly is here this week in the the interest of the Contirental Life Insurance Co. of Salt Lake City.

Mr. and Mrs. Henry Kocherhans are working at the experiment farm this week.

Mrs. Jos. F. Perkins has gone for a visit to California.

Ferdinand Hienze, J. Wilford Booth and J. Holdaway came down from northern Utah this week to look over land at Kaolin.

The Farmers' Association met here today to discuss plans for the coming season.

Mr. and Mrs. Ves. Nay have returned from the upper Muddy.

John Swatt, the little son of Alex Swatt, had his finger badly cut by an axe in the hands of his little brother last Tuesday.

The correct spelling in the third paragraph is Andersen
I believe the correct spelling is Swapp in the past paragraph

218

HAPPENINGS IN OVERTON

Items of Interest to the People of the Moapa Valley

(Special Correspondence.)

Overton, Feb. 10, 1910.

Jacob Rohner, of Myton, Utah, is visiting here with his daughter, Miss Gertrude Rohner.

M. D. Cooper and Perry D. Huntsman were over to the county seat this week on business connected with the trial jury there.

There is considerable sickness here caused by colds and la grippe.

Mrs. Fred Rushton died Feb. 8th of pneumonia, after an illness of about five days. She leaves a husband and seven children. Her parents and relatives live in northern Utah.

Funeral services were held at their residence on the Bowman Ranch yesterday afternoon, Mr. Rushton leaving the same evening with the remains for Salt Lake City, their former home. The family have a host of friends who sympathize with them in this great bereavement.

219

Items from Overton

Overton Feb 14, 1912.

The trees begin to have a green appearance and fruit trees to bloom. Although the days are warm and pleasant the nights remain quite cold.

There is at present much sickness in our valley in the line of bad colds and pneumonia, especially among the children.

The people of the Valley are delighted over the rapid work of the steel gang. Track is now laid to the bridge and it is reported will be down as far as Overton next week. The 15th of March will find it completed to St. Thomas.

Mrs. J. P. Anderson is now slowly recovering from an attack of pneumonia which has lasted four weeks.

J. Ross Clark and W. A. Clark paid the valley a hurried visit yesterday. Engineer McGuire is busy along the line at present ushering on the good work.

The many friends and loved ones of M. W. Gibson of St. Thomas, are grieved over his death, which occurred at his home today. He has been ill for some time, and suffered much. All that could possibly be done was done in his behalf.

Dr. Morrison of California is in town on important business. He has recently shipped 25 tons of freight, consisting of machinery, teams and a large pumping engine, into town, for the purpose of farming and pumping water on to some 400 acres of land owned by himself and others interested with him in this place.

Our schools received a fine Valentine today and one which was indeed very much appreciated by all, in the personage of our Superintendent, B. G. Bleasdale. His visit, though short, was very much enjoyed.

The Home Dramatic Club have put on the play, "A Noble Outcast", and intend that the same shall be played on the 22nd.

Presbyterian Church services at Mesquite Hall Sunday morning at 10:30 and in the evening at 7:30. "What is the Gain of Prayer?" and "What a Well in the Desert Suggested" will be discussed by Rev. J. M. Swander. A cordial welcome to all.

The correct spelling should be Andersen

Notes from Overton

(Special Correspondence.)

Overton, Feb. 22, 1912

A game of basket ball played Saturday evening between the Regulars and Scrubs resulted in a victory for the Regulars. The team will leave this evening for Las Vegas to meet the Las Vegas and Panaca teams in a series of games there.

The infant daughter of Mr. and Mrs. Pixton is very sick at their home in Logan.

Drummers Tobin and Eggleston were here this week representing northern Utah houses.

Franklin, the oldest son of A. F. Bischoff had the misfortune to dislocate his arm at the elbow. Dr. Benson set it and he is getting along nicely.

Senator Levi Syphus and Assemblyman Willard L. Jones left on Tuesday to attend the special session of the legislature.

The schools are celebrating Washington's birthday with a holiday today.

A number of our citizens were at St. Thomas Friday the 16th to attend the funeral of Moses W. Gibson, who passed away on the 14th after an illness of some time. He leaves a wife and the following children, Moses W. Gibson, Jr., now in Arizona, Mrs. Annie Schelken of Cottonwood, Utah, Robert O Gibson and Edith Gibson, all of whom except Moses W. Jr were at his bedside when the end came.

In the demise of Mr. Gibson the valley loses an energetic citizen, a man who has spent his life on the frontier, coming as a small boy to Salt Lake City from Missiasippi in 1848. In the early sixties he came to southern Utah and lived for a number of years at Virgin City, moving to St. Thomas in 1896. At the time of his death he was first councilor in the Bishopric of the St. Thomas ward, a position which he has faithfully filled for a number of years.

, Overton Nev Feb 29 —The whistle of the Iron Horse is heard with much pleasure in our quiet little town The track has been completed to the outskirts of town and to morrow March 1st the track will be laid through the town of Overton Our people are delighted at the early completion of the road and will turn out en mass the rails placed on the grade by the track laying gang tomorrow

Afton the infant daughter of Mrs Nellie Pixton died last Thursday evening Funeral services were held at their home in Logan the following afternoon after which Mrs Pixton left with the corpse for Taylorsville Utah where interment will be made by the side of the grave of its father Samuel Pixton who died a few months ago The many friends of Mrs Pixton sym pathize with her in this double be reavement Her father in law Willard Pixton who came to the little sufferer s bedside from Taylorsville accompanied Mrs Pixton

Miss Gertrude Rohner entertained a party of her friends at a social last evening

Wm A Whitehead has returned from a business trip to Salt Lake City

John Swapp is preparing to erect for himself a neat little cottage

222

Overton News

Afton, the infant daughter of Mrs. Nellie Pixton died last Thursday evening at their home in Logan. Funeral services were held at their home Friday afternoon, after which Mrs. Pixton left with the corpse for Taylorsville, Utah, where interment will be made in the cemetery beside the grave of its father, Samuel Pixton, who died a few months ago. The many friends of Mrs. Pixton sympathize with her in this double bereavement. Her father-in-law, Willard Pixton, who came to the little sufferer's bedside from Taylorsville, accompanied Mrs. Pixton.

Mrs. Sanford Angell and daughter, Miss Effie are visiting in Salt Lake City.

Horace Jones has gone out to Mr. Brig Weitmore's mine to work for some time.

Our young people who went with the Basket Ball team last week returned Sunday having enjoyed a fine time.

Frank Smith came over from Las Vegas with the Basket Ball team Sunday.

Mrs. John T. Brown left on Tuesday to join her husband in Delta, Utah.

Bishop O. P. Miller was here on business Monday returning on Tuesday to Moapa. He came via Caliente and Paranaget Valley. Frank Allen, of the latter place, accompanying him on the trip by team down the wash.

N. Ray Pixton arrived here this week. He has but recently returned from a two years' mission in England.

Miss Gertrude Rohner entertained a party of her friends at a social last evening in honor of her eighteenth birthday.

Miss Armelia Ingram who has been ill for several days is around again.

We have had several days of extremely cold north winds this week.

The whistle of the iron horse is heard with much pleasure in our quiet little town the past few days. The track will be laid through the town of Overton on the last day of March, and our townspeople will turn out en mass to enjoy the sight.

John Swapp is preparing to erect for himself a neat little home in the near future.

Wm. A. Whitehead has returned from a business trip to Salt Lake City.

Overton, Mar 6 —The railroad construction company has now moved its camp train consisting of about fifty cars from Logan to the siding near Kaolin They will reach St Thomas in a few days Plans are being formulated for a celebration in honor of the completion of the line down the valley

The local base ball team are preparing for a game with Las Vegas on railroad day It will be a championship game as there has been two games played resulting in one victory for each team

Enos Baust of Salt Lake City with his family passed through here to day going to St Thomas to visit relatives They may decide to make their home in the valley

Born Mar 2 a daughter to Mr and Mrs Perry D Huntsman

Mr and Mrs Bert Nay have returned to their ranch

Railroad Through Moapa Valley Almost Ready for Operation

The Railroad Construction Co. have moved their camp train consisting of about 50 cars from Logan to Kaolin. Track will be laid to St. Thomas in a few days. Plans are being formulated for a celebration in honor of the completion of the line down the valley.

The local base ball team are practicing for a game with Las Vegas 'soon.

Mr. Enos Baust and family of Salt Lake City, passed through here today going to St. Thomas.

Senator Levi Syphus and assemblyman W. L. Jones have returned from Carson City.

Mr. and Mrs. Bert Nay have returned to their ranch.

Born, March 2, to Mr. and Mrs. Perry D. Huntsman, a daughter.

Dr. Martin and Sheriff Gay came on today's train from Las Vegas.

Mr. and Mrs. Bert Marshall are living at the Weiser Ranch.

225

Overton Mar 11 —Under the management of the old folks committee a social was given in the school house Friday afternoon A program was nicely rendered including reminicent tall s by John Thomas John Swapp and T J Jones on the subject What I have seen in the Moapa Valley each of whom had been in the valley at an early date and gave experiences showing the development of the valley from a time when many acres of choice land were untraversable swamps a few white people were living in forts at West Point now Moapa Logan Overton and St Thomas and thousands of Indians made the valley their home up to the time when every acre is owned and fast being brought under cultivation and the swamp reclaimed make the choicest farms in the valley and a railhoad has bought us in touch with the world s markets An excellent lunch was served at the close of the program and in time for all to attend the picture show and dance given in the hall

A fire at the Bowman ranch Friday destroyed a granary and impliment shed belonging to Mr Rushton and caused a loss of over a thousand dollars in impliments grain and groceri s etc that were stored in the building The fire was lighted by a little boy who had found a match

Mr and Mrs David Moss of St George are at the Experiment farm where Mr Moss is painting the farm house

Mrs Andrew Jones and Miss Rhoda Wittwer of Logan were visiting friends here Saturday and Sunday

with rheumatism but is now improving

Carpenters are putting the roof on the new Swapp residence this week

We had a fine rain Sunday

226

Rushton Ranch Loses Granary, Farming Implements Etc., Friday Last

[Special Correspondence]

Overton, March 12, 1912.

There was a fire at the Rushton ranch Friday which destroyed a granary and implement sheds, also grain, stores of groceries, implements, harness etc., to the valuation of over a thousand dollars. The fire was lighted by a small boy who had found a match.

J. P. Anderson is preparing to drive a well 200 feet for water for culinary purposes.

Mr. and Mrs. David Moss of St. George, Utah, are at the Experiment Farm where Mr. Moss is doing some painting.

Mrs. Andrew L. Jones and Miss Rhoda Wittwer of Logan spent Sunday visiting here.

Miss Lottie Hansen of Bunkerville came over last week. She is working at the home of Mrs. Birdie Gann.

Miss Zilla Peterson is recovering from an attack of rheumatism.

Under the management of the Old Folks Committee a social was given for old and young in the school house Friday evening. An interesting program was rendered consisting of songs, instrumental music, recitations, readings and reminiscent talks by John Swapp, T. J. Jones and John Thomas of Logan, of old, old times in the Moapa Valley when the nearest rail road station was hundreds of miles away, when the valley inhabited by thousands of Indians, and many acres of the best land of to-day were dense swamps and a few white people lived in forts for protection from the Indians. At Moapa was then a small fort called West Point. The town of Overton was a small fort, about a mile east of the present site on the foot hills, and forts were at Logan and St. Thomas. This was in 1865.

227

The correct spelling should be Andersen

Overton Mar 23 —The steel has been laid into the town of St Thomas The advent of the iron horse into that town was celebrated with a salute of 21 guns and followed by sports through the day The report of the guns was plainly heard in Overton During the recent wet weather a good deal of work has had to be done on the grade owing to its settling When the line is complete the towns of the valley will join in a railroad day celebration which will probably occur on the 1st of May

Warren Cox of St George was here this week in the interest of the Studebaker Impliment Co Mrs Cox accompanied him on the trip and will take the train at Moapa for Panaca Nevada

A game of base ball was played on the 17th between the steel gang of railroad boys and the valley team which resulted in a victory for the latter team

Bird Murphy of Salt Lake City passed through here this week returning to his home from a visit to St Thomas where he owns a tract of land

The Relief Society s seventieth anniversary was celebrated with a program and social Monday evening

A game of basket ball will be played tonight in the hall between the Logan and Overton teams

F, Hienze of Salt Lake City is here this week in the interest of the Armenian colony at Kaolin

Brig Whitmore has gone to Salt Lake City

Overton Mar 25 — Wm Kemp of St George died at the home of S H Wells of Logan Saturday night and was buried at the Logan cemetery today His mother and brother Chester Kemp arrived here from St George a few hours after his death having been telegraphed of his serious condition on the 22nd Mr Kemp had been working at the Wells ranch for two weeks having come here from Caliente Nevada He was afflicted with Delamar dust and contracted a cold which developed into pneumonia and caused his death Funeral services were held in Logan Bishop W L Jones councilor Wm Perkins and Elder N Ray Pixton being the speakers Elder Pixton also sung beautifully I Know That My Redemer Lives

assisted in the chorus by Mrs Harry Pierce and Miss Mildred Anderson Mr Kemp was 34 years of age and unmarried He was the son of Walter and Adeline Kemp and was born and lived in St George except the last five years of his life

Correct spelling should be Andersen

Current Events of Interest in Moapa Valley Metropolis

(Special Correspondence)

Overton, Nev., Mar. 21, 1912.

Under the supervision of Sherman Thomas a number of men and teams are at work on the roads through and near the town.

A game of Basket Ball played in the Hall Saturday evening between the Logan team and the Overton "Scrub" team resulted in a victory for Logan. The game was an interesting one and was witnessed by a crowded house. N. Ray Pixton acted as referee and Fay Anderson as umpire.

The Seventieth Anniversary of the organization of the Woman's Relief Society by the Prophet Joseph Smith in Nauvoo, Ill., was celebrated by the local organization March 17th with a program and Social in the school house. A delicious lunch was served by the ladies during the evening.

Warren Cox and wife of St. George spent a few days here this week.

Wm. Kemp, aged 34 and unmarried, a resident of St. George, Utah, died on the 23d at the Wells' Ranch where he had been working for about two weeks. His death was caused by pneumonia and Delamar Dust. Word of his illness was sent to his relatives in St. George, and his mother and brother Chester arrived here a few hours after his death on Sunday morning. The funeral service was held on the 25th at Logan. Bishop W. L. Jones and Elders Wm. Perkins and N. Ray Pixton were the speakers. Elder Pixton also sang beautifully "I Know that My Redeemer Lives," assisted in the chorus by Mrs. Harry Pierce and Miss Mildred Anderson. Interment was made in the Logan cemetery. Deceased was a son of Adeline and Walter Kemp, his father having fallen a a victim of Delamar dust several years ago.

230

Overton April 3 —Mr Clifford Cochran and Miss Minerva Swapp were married at the county seat Monday Bp John M Bunker officating in the ceremony They returned on the Tuesday evening train down the valley and were given a reception the same evening at the home of the bride s parents The bride s father John Swapp accompanied the young couple to Las Vegas

The schools here were visited Wednesday by Robert Butler of the Weber School Furniture Co C E Overman of the Las Vegas high school assistant Supt of public instruction B G Bleasdale and Edw I Cox a trustee of the Bunkerville district school

A Sunday School was organized last week at the Kaolin branch of the Overton ward there being now forty residents there Brigham Hardy, who has recently moved there from Mesquite was appointed Supt of the school

The children of S R Whitehead who have been ill at Las Vegas with scarlet fever are recovering Mrs Mary Whitehead of this place has been there with her son during the illness of the children and will return home soon

Among the newest arrivals in our city are a son born to Mr and Mrs U V Perkins and a daughter to Mr and Mrs Albert Jones

The ward choir was entertained on the evening of March 29th by Mr and Mrs W L Jones in a social at their home

Rupert Best of Salt Lake City was here Tuesday looking over the valley with a view of investing in Moapa valley lands

Mrs Sanford Angell and daughter Effie returned last week from a visit to Mrs Angell s daughters in Salt Lake City

J A Hollaway left on the 2nd for his home in Provo and to attend conference in Salt Lake City

Miss Mildred Anderson is ill with chills and fever

N Ray Pixton has gone to St George, Utah

231

Las Vegas Age Newspaper
April 6, 1912

J. F. Cooper of Overton was in this city Saturday last.

E. J. Robertson of the Moapa Valley was in Vegas Saturday last.

J. C. Cochran and bride, of Overton, registered at Hotel Nevada Monday.

J. A. Swapp, one of the prominent residents of Overton was in this city Monday last attending the wedding of his daughter.

Washington County News
April 8, 1912

Overton April 8 — Election was held here Saturday for school trustees. Crayton Johnson was reelected and Isaac Losee was elected in place of Ute V Perkins whose term had expired J P Anderson is the long term trustee

Miss Roxie Leavitt has taken the place of Miss Thriza Leavitt at the Rushton ranch the latter having returned to Bunkerville Mr Fred Rushton is in Salt Lake where he went to take his infant son Ferrill whose health has not been good since the death of the babe s mother

The harvesting of the asparagus crop is now well under way The Moapa Improvement company is shipping two wagon loads a day There are a number of other farms shipping also

Saturday evening there was a game of basket ball between the local teams the scrubs winning a victory over the regulars the game was followed by a dance

A concert was held in the school house Monday evening under the management of the Parents class assisted by the ward choir the program was excellent

Bp John M Bunker spoke on the meaning and proper observance of Easter in the mutuals Sunday evening

Mr and Mrs Chas Felt came down from Moapa on a speeder to attend the Saturday evening amusements

Mr and Mrs Joe F Perkins and their infant son returned Saturday from California

Ithamer Sprague and son Orson of Mesquite are working at Capalapa

Stephen Swapp has returned from Kanab Utah

232

News Items of Interest to Moapa Valley Folk

[Special Correspondence]

Overton Nev. Apr. 3, 1912.
Mrs. Sanford Angell and daughter Effie returned last week from a visit to her daughter in Salt Lake City.

Among the late arrivals in our city are a son born to Mr. and Mrs. Ute V. Perkins and a daughter to Mr. and Mrs. Albert Jones.

Messrs. James Thorne and John C. Smith were here last week in the interest of Hewlet Brothers of Salt Lake City and the Startup Candy Co. of Provo.

The schools here were visited Wednesday by Robt. Butler of the Weber School Furniture Co., C. E. Overman of the Las Vegas High School, Assistant Superintendent of Public Instruction B. G. Bleasdale, and Edw. I. Cox, a trustee of the Bunkerville disnrict school.

The ward choir was entertained on the evening of March 29th with a social at the home of Mr. and Mrs. W. L. Jones.

N. Ray Pixton has gone to St. George Utah.

Mr. Clifford Cochran and Miss Minerva Swapp slipped over to the county seat last Monday and were married the same afternoon, Bishop John M. Bunker officiating. The bride's father, Mr. John Swapp accompanied the happy couple. They returned Tuesday and a reception was held that evening at the new residence of the bride's parents, where the couple were presented with numerous gifts both useful and amusing. Ice cream, cake and lemonade were served during the evening.

J. A. Holdaway left on the 2d for his home in Provo and to attend Conference in Salt Lake City.

Rupert Best of Salt Lake City was here Tuesday looking over the valley with a view of investing in Moapa Valley lands.

Miss Mildred Anderson is ill with chills and fever.

A Sunday School was organized last week at Kaoli, with Brigham Hardy as superintendent. There are now about forty people living there. We have now four Sunday Schools in the valley.

233

Overton April 10, 1912.

A dance was given for the children in the school house Friday evening, with school trustee Crayton Johnson in charge.

The election for school trustees was held here Saturday. Crayton Johnson was re-elected and Isaac Losee was elected in place of U. V. Perkins whose term had expired. J. P. Anderson is the long te.m trustee.

Saturday evening there was a basket ball game between the local teams, the "Scrubs" winning a victory over the "Regulars" The game was followed by a dance.

A company of young folks went for an Easter outing to the salt mine below St. Thomas Sunday.

At the Conjoint Session of the M. I. A. held on Sunday evening, the following program was carried out; Current Events, Leonidas Hickman; Quartette, "Sweet Sabbath Eve", by Leonidas Hickman, W. A. Whitehead, A. L. F. McDermott and Fay Anderson; Prognostication, Alma Shurtliff; Instrumental music, Carrie Richards; Lecture, "The Meaning and Proper Observance of Easter" by Bishop John M. Bunker of St. Thomas.

Stephen Swapp has returned home after several months stay in Utah.

Fred Rushton went to Salt Lake a week ago to take his infant son Ferrill whose health has not been good since the loss of the babe's mother.

Miss Roxie Leavitt has taken the place of Miss Thirza Leavitt at the Rushton ranch, the latter having returned to Bunkerville.

Ithamer Sprague and son Orson of Mesquite are working at Capalapa.

A concert was held in the school house Monday evening under the management of the Parent's Class, the ward choir assisting. The program was exceptionally good.

Mr. and Mrs. Bert Marshall of the Weiser Ranch are visiting here.

Mr. and Mrs. Joe F. Perkins and their infant son returned from California Saturday.

Mr. and Mrs. Chas. Felt came down from Moapa on the speeder Saturday evening.

234

The correct spelling should be Andersen

Overton April 17 —We enjoyed a treat the past week in a series of three lectures from Professor E S Hinckley of Provo Friday Saturday and Sunday evenings His subjects were The Business End of Farming " Formation of the Soil " and The Closing of Christ s Ministry "

Mis May Thurston has gone to Mesquite to visit relatives Miss Armelia is cooking at the Koenig ranch in her absence

Mr and Mrs J A Holdaway came Friday from Provo They will make their home at Kaolin

Elmer Losee is at the experiment farm this week where he has charge of the construction of a barn

Mis Mary V Lytle has gone to join her husband who is working at Bull valley

John Swapp has gone out to his ranch in Penn valley

We had a good storm followed by light frost last week

235

Schools of the Northern Settlements Second to None in The County

Deputy Superintendent of Schools, R. G. Bleasdale was both pleased and surprised at the high standing of the schools of all the towns of the Moapa and Virgin Valleys, which he visited recently. This being Mr. Bleasdale's first visit to these schools since he was appointed to take charge of this district he did not expect to see schools of such high character as to scholarship and physical requirements.

The Bunkerville schools employ four teachers and give instruction in nine grades, including the first two years of high school work arranged by Mr. Bleasdale, and for which the County Commissioners have wisely made an allowance of $500.

There are now 14 pupils taking the high school work there, all being girls except one.

As an indication of the interest taken in the schools there it may be said that they have purchased additional land for the school grounds until they now have eight or ten acres about the school house which they are beautifying.

In Mesquite also great interest is shown in the schools. It has been decided to increase the school year from six months to eight months. There are three rooms and three teachers. The rooms are much crowded and plans are being discussed for a commodious new schoolhouse.

In the Moapa Valley settlements Mr. Bleasdale also reports the schools to be in a very prosperous condition. At Overton the present school house is proving too small and preparations are being made to build a school house large enough to accommodate all. Mr. Bleasdale speaks very highly of the character of the young folks attending the schools of the Moapa and Virgin valleys, they being unusually bright and well advanced in their studies.

Personal Mention of Interest in the Moapa Valley

(Special Correspondence)
Overton, April 17, 1912.

Mrs. Mary V. Lytle has gone to join her husband who is working in Bull Valley.

Mr. and Mrs. Holdaway came Friday from Provo. They will make their home at Kaolin.

Mrs. Mary Thurston has gone to Mesquite to visit relatives. Miss Armelia Ingram is cooking at the Koenig ranch in her absence.

I. E. Losee is at the Experiment Farm this week where he has charge of the construction of a barn.

Prof. E. S. Hinckley of the Brigham Young University gave three lectures here last week. His subjects were: "The Business End of Farming," "The Formation of the Soil," and "The Closing of Christ's Ministry."

John Swapp has gone out to his ranch in Penn Valley.

We had a good storm and light frost the last week. It did but little damage however.

236

RAILROAD CELEBRATION

Moapa Valley Will Rejoice Over Completion of Branch Line June 7 and 8

After many weary months of waiting the people of the Moapa Valley are enjoying the happy experience of having a real railroad.

Construction was begun a year ago and the hope was entertained by the officials of the road and by the people of the Valley that the road would be completed in time to handle last seasons crops. Owing to unforseen difficulties this hope proved futile and not until February last was the work of laying the rails on the grade again taken up.

Leaving the main line at Moapa, the road traverses the length of the Valley about 26 miles, passing through the thriving towns of Logan and Overton, and having its terminus at St. Thomas.

On June seventh and eighth the whole valley will be alive with activity. Excursions will be run from the surrounding towns of Nevada and it has been arranged to put reduced rates into effect both from Utah and California points. The occasion will be of great value to the Moapa valley in making its wonderful undeveloped resources known to the world. There is, so far as the writer knows, no place on earth where the soil and climate are so completely adapted to the successful growth of valuable products as the Moapa Valley. For fifty years and more, while railroad communication was remote and hundreds of miles of forbidding desert lay between it and civilization, this valley has been partially settled and cultivated and known as one of the richest spots on the globe.

Now, with railroad transportation brought to their doors, and the desperately hard wagon haul necessary to put their products on the market eliminated, the Valley will experience a wonderfully rapid growth and add greatly to the wealth and prosperity of Clark County.

Many excursionists from outside the state will take advantage of the reduced rates to visit this section. Las Vegas should and probably will send several hundred people to enjoy the delightful hospitality which the valley people will extend to all their visitors, and to assist in spreading the knowledge of the opportunities opened by the completion of the railroad. We are assured that the railroad company will do all in their power to assist in making the occasion a notable one. Make your plans now to join in the big celebration.

Overton May 1 —John A Swapp has recently returned from the Copper Mountain mine where he went to tale mining men from Los Angeles W A Rowe and Mr Mc Maine He says the gentlemen looked over the Grand Gulch mine the Copper Mountain and other mining property in the district and say the Copper Mountain is the biggest mine in northern Arizona Transportation has been its only drawback With the railroad now completed to St Thomas and the price of copper on the advance it could be worked very profitably Mr Swapp has now gone to St George and upon his return he will bring in some sample ore from the Copper Mountain to be on exibition here on railroad day in June Ferdinand Hienze accompanied Mr Swapp on his trip to St George

Miss Lillian Jones came over from Bunkerville recently and after visit here a few days went to Delta Utah where she will spend the summer

The Y L and Y M M I A have completed their course of study for the winter and will close for the summer with a program and dance May 1

Mrs Luisa Nay was here several days recently visiting her sons Sylvester and Calvin Nay She returned to Las Vegas Monday

Orin Jarvis of the experiment farm recently went to California to select some dairy cattle to be kept at the farm at Logan

Mrs Chas Felt of Moapa is the guest of Mrs J F Perkins

S R Whitehead came over from Las Vegas Wednesday

Mrs Andrew L Jones has gone to Provo, Utah

238

VALLEY HAPPENINGS

May Day Letter From The Moapa Valley Metropolis

(Special Correspondence)

Overton, May 1, 1912.

John A. Swapp has recently returned from the Copper Mountain Mine where he went to take Mr. W. A. Kowe and Mr. McManis, mining men from Los Angeles. The gentlemen looked over the Grand Gulch mine, the Copper Mountain and other property in the district and they say the Copper Mountain is the largest mine in northern Arizona, the only drawback being the difficulty of transportation. With the railroad now completed to St. Thomas and the price of copper on the advance it could be worked very profitably. Mr. Swapp will return from St. George where he has how gone and have some ore from the Copper Mountain on exhibition here on Railroad Day in June.

Ferdinand Hienze accompanied Mr. Swapp on his trip to St. George.

Mrs. Louisa Nay was here several days recently visiting her sons Sylvester and Calvin Nay and their families. She returned to Las Vegas Monday.

Mrs. Andrew L. Jones has gone to Provo, Utah.

Miss Lillian Jones came over recently from Bunkerville and after visiting here a few days went to Delta, Utah, where she will spend the summer.

S. R. Whitehead came over from Las Vegas Wednesday.

Orin Jarvis of the Experiment Farm went to Southern California with Prof. True of the State University. They will select a few dairy cows to be kept at the farm in Logan.

Mrs. Chas. Felt of Moapa is visiting here as the guest of Mrs. J. F. Perkins.

W. L. Jones returned Monday from a trip to Salt Lake City where he went in the interest of the Moapa Valley Farmers Association.

The Y. L. and Y. M. M. I. A. have completed their course of study for the winter and will close with a program and dance on May 1st.

239

Overton May 9 —The schools will close for the summer on Friday, the 10th The following program will be carried out in the evening by the pupils of the school

Medley Chorus   Students

Prayer

Rec   Moo Cow Moo "
                    Vernon Cooper

Musical Play, Red Riding Hood "
          pupils of the Lower Grades

Rec   Last Day of School '
                    Ellen Shurtliff

Operetta Gypsy Festival '
          pupils of the Higher Grades

Song My Own Nevada ' Students

Under the management of the Parents class the 9th of May will be observed as a street cleaning day W L Batty David S Conger Sherman Thomas and Thomas Anderson are committeemen in charge of the work in the four sections of town into which the work is divided The ladies will serve dinner for all the workers in the Shurtliff hall

Leonidas Hickman of Beaver Utah has been the principal of our schools and Miss Carrie Pichards of Logan Utah has had charge of the Primary department They have done efficient work through the past winter in our schools

The following are candidates for graduation from the eighth grade returns from their examination papers not having been received yet Grace Bischoff Jean Anderson Lydia Cooper Ellen Shurtliff and Zilla Peterson

Mrs Ratie King entertained a party of six young ladies Monday evening in honor of Miss Carrie Pichards who will leave for her home at Logan Utah after the close of her school here Friday

Miss Mildred Anderson who is president of the local Y L M I A entertained the mutual girls at her home Wednesday evening Cake and ice cream was served and all enjoyed a fine time

The officers and teachers of the Primary association met on the 6th at the home of Miss Jean Anderson for their regular monthly meeting a social followed the close of the session

240

OVERTON HAPPENINGS

Activities Attend Closing of School Year This Week

Mrs. Racie King entertained a party of six young ladies Monday evening in honor of Miss Carrie Richards who leaves for home in Logan, Utah after the close of school this week.

The officers and teachers of the Primary association met on the evening of the sixth for their regular monthly meeting at the home of Miss Jean Anderson. A social and candy lunch followed the close of the session.

Miss Mildred Anderson, who is president of the local Y. L. M. I. A. entertained the Mutual Girls at her home Wednesday evening. A luncheon of ice cream and cake was served and all enjoyed a delightful time.

Under the management of the Parents' Class of the Sunday School the 9th of May will be observed as Street Cleaning day. W. L. Batty, David S. Cooper, Sherman Thomas and Thomas Anderson are committeemen in charge of the work in the four sections of the town into which the work has been divided. The ladies will serve dinner for all the workers in the Shurtliff hall.

Our schools will close on Friday 10th. The teachers the past winter were Leonidas Hickman as principal and Miss Carrie Richards, primary teacher. They have done efficient work in our school.

The inclosed program will be carried out in the Lytle Hall in the evening, and the following pupils will pass out of their grades:

Beginners, Thelma Grieon, Erma Jones, Vernon Cooper, Cameron Swapp, David Huntsman, Royce Ingram.

First Grade, Elizabeth Bischoff, Zella Losee, Elwood Perkins, June Lewis, Lynn Batty, Helen Thomas, Donald Huntsman.

Second Grade, John Swapp, Ether Bischoff, Zona Cooper, Nevada Thomas, Grace Cooper, Bertha Shurtliff, Nettie Ingram.

Third Grade, Ether Swapp, Bernice Perkins, Ruel Bischoff, Pearl Perkins, Grace Lewis, Vera Perkins, Nellie Losee.

Fourth Grade, George Whitmore, Lillian Ingram, Alma Huntsman, Zaida Losee, Linette Huntsman, Elsie Cooper, Russel Holdaway, Rex Perkins, Lucile Shurtliff, Robert Perkins, Lionel Lewis.

Fifth Grade, Sibyl Swapp, Effie Huntsman, Alvin Anderson, Fenton Whitmore.

Sixth Grade, Carl Shurtliff, Earnest Lewis.

Seventh Grade, Franklin Bischoff, Irva Whitmore, Adlie Ingram.

The following are candidates for graduation from the eighth grade returns from their examination, not having been received yet: Grace Bischoff, Jean Anderson, Lydia Cooper, Ellen Shurtliff, Zilla Peterson.

PROGRAM

By students of Overton School May 10.

1. Medley Chorus — Students
2. Prayer
3. Recitation—Moo—Cow—Moo, Vernon Cooper
4. Musical Play—Red Riding Hood — Lower Grades
5. Recitation—Last Day of School — Ellen Shurtliff
6. Operetta, Gypsy Festival — Higher Grades
7. Song, My Own Nevada — School
8. Benediction

241

Correct spelling should be Alvin Andersen

Characters of Red Riding Hood

Red Riding Hood	Bernice Perkins
Red Riding Hood's Mother	Vera Perkins
Red Riding Hood's Father	John Swapp
Fairy Queen	Pearl Perkins
	Grace Lewis
	June Lewis
	Jettie Losee
	Nellie Losee
	R001 Bischoff
Fairies	Elizabeth Bischoff
	Nevada Thomas
	Helen Thomas
	Zona Cooper
	Nettie Ingram
	Bertha Shurtliff
	Grace Cooper

Characters of Gypsy Festival

Gypsy Queen	Grace Bischoff
Gypsy Jane	Irva Whitmore
Yankee Peddler	Alvin Anderson
	Lillian Ingram
	Earnest Lewis
	Elsie Cooper
	Lionel Lewis
Gypsies	Lucille Shurtliff
	Turl Ingram
	Bernice Perkins
	Alma Huntsman
	Zaida Losee
	Robert Perkins
Invisible Chorus	Rest of School
Accompanist	Mildred Anderson

Adams F. Brown, a prominent Goldfield attorney who has been spending the week in Los Angeles, is viewing the Vegas valley. He is much pleased with the prospects.

Judge Lillis is enjoying the Shrine week in Southern California.

NOTICE

Notice of application for permission to appropriate the public waters of the State of Nevada.

Application No. 243

Notice is hereby given that on the 19th day of February, 1912, in accordance with Section 25 Chapter XXXI, of the Statutes of 1909, one John Herbert Nay of Overton, County of Clark and State of Nevada, made application to the State Engineer of Nevada for permission to appropriate the public waters of the State of Nevada. Such appropriation is to be made from Timber Creek at points approximately in the NE¼NE¼ Sec. 1, T. 16 S. R. 70 E., M. D. B & M. by means of a dam and ditch and 3-40 cubic feet per second is to be conveyed to points upon three acres of land situated approximately in the NE¼NE¼ Sec. 1, T. 16, S, R. 70 E., M. D. B. & M. by means of ditches, and there used for irrigation and domestic purposes, water not to be returned to stream.

Date of first publication May 18, 1912
Date of last publication June 15, 1912

Signed:

W. M. KEARNEY
State Engineer.

243

MOAPA VALLEY RAILROAD DAY

Committees Have Arranged Big Celebration For June 7 to 8

Occasion Will Be the Most Notable In History of Clark County

The completion of the Moapa Valley Branch of the Salt Lake Route is to be made a big day for the valley.

The program has been arranged for the two days' celebration. All the settlements on the Moapa and Virgin Rivers are to help out with the time. Las Vegas is coming to the front with enthusiasm and will join in making the time a big success. A ball team from Vegas will play with the Valley team and the band will go along to dispense little "joys" and drive away any "glooms" that may have been lurking in the Valley.

The Committees have been at work on the program and things are shaping up for a good big time.

A voting contest to elect the most popular lady of Clark Co. to drive a copper spike at the opening ceremony of the celebration will go on from now until the first of June or thereabouts.

The Grand Gulch Copper Mining Co. have donated the copper spike and the Salt Lake Hardware Co. have donated the hammer with which to drive it and the lady who does the driving will take the hammer and the spike home as a souvenir of the event.

All who imagine they can write good advertising matter will have a chance to win a prize of $50 for the best write-up of the valley accompanied with photos taken to be used for cuts to advertise the valley later on. Any person desiring to undertake the job may enter the contest. None is barred. The entrance fee will be $5.

There will be Base Ball games, Basket Ball games, real wild west steer roping contests, foot and horse races, a real old Southern barbecue, theatre, dancing and seeing the Valley. There will be exhibits of the Valley and of the mines in the vicinity, some thing for the credulous to look at and some competent person to explain why Moapa Valley lands are superior.

A good time is expected and a great many people are already inquiring about the celebration from Northern points.

Balloting places for the voting contest and other particulars of interest will be announced in some form or other.

Some items of experiment show that Moapa Valley is one of the most fertile spots on the globe but there are not enough people the to do the work needed to develop the Valley. Companies ownin large tracts of land are preparing to place the lands on the mark and home seekers and investors will find something worth lookin after in a visit to Moapa Valley.

Rates will be in effect over the Salt Lake Line from all poin and you should either join in to make the time a success or visit th valley if interested in making a home or an investment.

The following program has been arranged.

First Day

Teams will meet the train at Logan and take the visitors over th

Continued on Page Eight.

Continued from Page One.

upper part of the Valley showing the growing crops and the grain in the shock. Then the train will proceed to St. Thomas where the copper spike will be driven by the most popular lady.

The big barbeque will then be pulled off and all will have meat barbecued in the good old Southern way for the asking. Two big beeves will be ready for the crowds. Then will follow a base ball game between teams to be announced later. There will be an admission fee of 25 cents to the ball game, some visiting team to play with the local team. A steer roping contest of the "wild west" will follow with a prize of a lariat and an entrance fee of $2, the rope to cost not less than $7.

The day will finish with a dance at night.

Second Day

The day will begin with foot and horse races. A 300 and a 600 yard race will be pulled off for the horses with an entrance fee of five dollars, the winner to get the purse. Base ball between Bunkerville and the Valley, admission 25 cents.

Meeting at 2 p. m. Bronco riding contest, entrance fee $2.50. Prize, $15 silver mounted bridle. Basket Ball, St. George vs. Valley team, tickets 25 cents. A play at night, name to be published later.

The committees are as follows for the celebration with sub-committees; General Committee, Saml. H. Wells, Chairman; W. A. Whitehead, Secy; J. M. Bunker, S. R. Whitehead, O. W. Jarvis, Sam Gentry, W. J. McBurney and Senator Levi Syphus. Committee on Finance; J. M. Bunker, Henry Rice and Dave Conger. Committee on Transportation and Advertisement, S. H. Wells and S. R. Whitehead. Committee on Program, O. W. Jarvis, Crayton Johnson, Dr. S. L. Benson, Wm. F. Murphy and John Perkins. Committee on Sports, Sam Gentry, Chas. Ross, George Perkins, W. L. Batty, L. V. Hinkley and Ben Robison. Committee on Refreshments and Entertainment; W. J. McBurney, John H. Averett, W. L. Jones, S. A. Angell, R. O. Gibson and C. Gentry. Committee on Exhibits, Hon. Levi Syphus,

B. Whitmore, Bert Mills, Ed. Syphus, J. M. Lytle and E. Marshall.

Any parties desiring general information about the celebration may write to the secretary, W. A. Whitehead at Overton, Nevada.

The General Committee suggests that parties from outside points expecting to attend the celebration to remain more than one day write to the Committee on Entertainment notifying them in order to get accommodation, as large crowds are expected.

245

Overton May 20 —The follow ing ladies visited the Primary convention in Mesquite on the 15th Mrs Eliza Ingram Mrs Lois F Jones and the Misses Grace Bischoff Jean Anderson Gertrude Rhoner Zilla Peterson and Addie Ingram Thomas Johnson and George Ingram acompanied them as drivers

Railroad officials came down the valley in a special car on the 16th to inspect the road A number of citizens were invited to join them in the run down to St Thomas and return

Mr and Mrs Andrew L Jones are home again from Provo where Mr Jones has attended the Brigham Young university the past winter

Mrs Mary V Lytle and children have gone to Clover valley to spend the summer Mr and Mrs Harry Howe are now living in the Lytle home

Carl McMullin of Leeds Utah is here to spend the summer with his sister and family Mr and Mrs Allen Fleming

John Swapp and Mr and Mrs Henry Kocherhans have gone to the Copper Mountain

246

Personal Items of Interest to People Of Moapa Valley

(Special Correspondence.)

Carl McMullin of Leeds, Utah, is here visiting his sister, Mrs. Martha Fleming.

Mr. and Mrs. Andrew L. Jones have returned from Provo, Utah, where Mr. Jones has attended the Brigham Young University the past winter.

Miss Carrie Richards left on the 12th for her home in Logan, Utah.

The following ladies visited the Primary Convention in Mesquite on the 15th, Mrs. Eliza Ingram, Mrs. W. L. Jones and the Misses Grace Bischoff, Jean Anderson, Gertrude Rhoner, Zilla Peterson and Addie Ingram. George Ingram and Thomas Johnson accompanied them as teamsters.

Officials of the railroad came down the valley on the 16th in a special car to inspect the road. S. H. Wells, S. R. Whitehead, W. L. Jones and others joined them in a run down the valley to St. Thomas and return.

Mrs. Mary V. Lytle and children have gone to Clover Valley to spend the summer. Mr. and Mrs. Harry Howe are now living in the Lytle home.

Mrs. Nellie Pixton has returned from northern Utah where she has been for several months.

John Swapp and Mr. and Mrs. Henry Kocherhans left last week for Copper Mountain.

The Primary officers gave the little folks a dance Friday evening.

Ellis Turnbaugh went to Mesquite and Bunkerville with his moving picture show last week.

Crayton Johnson has gone to Good Springs to work for some time. Woodruff Perkins and Trueman Cooper have gone to Goldfield for employment.

Bishop John M. Bunker and John Perkins of St. Thomas were at Logan as home missionaries on the 19th.

247

R. R. Day at Moapa

The News has received the program of the celebration to be held at Moapa June 7th and 8th in honor of the completion of the Moapa branch of the Salt Lake Route of which the following is a copy

Dear Sir —The people of Moapa Valley will celebrate the completion of the Moapa Branch of the Salt Lake Railroad June 7th and 8th 1912 The Committee extends you and your friends a hearty invitation to be with us on these dates

S H WELLS Chairman

The Program as outlined for the two days follows

FIRST DAY

Teams will take the visitors over the upper part of the Valley showing the lands of that portion At Logan the train will pick up the crowds and proceed to St Thomas where the lady will drive the Copper Spike There will be a great big old Southern Barbecue that will occupy some time

A Baseball Game Las Vegas vs Valley teams Admission 25c

A real Wild West Steer Roping and Tieing Contest will follow The entrance fee will be $2 00 and the prize to the person who ropes the steer and ties him down first will be a fine lariat

The crowds will then take the trains to Overton to look over the

Exhibits and enjoy the evening either in dancing or at a play given by the local Dramatic Club

SECOND DAY

There will be Horse Races for those who have fast ones—a 300 yard and a 600 yards race. The entrance fee will be $5 00 and the winner will take the purse.

Baseball Bunkerville and Valley teams. Admission 20 cents

There will be a meeting at 2 00 p m and prominent people will give ten minute talks

A Broncho Riding Contest. En trance fee $2 50 prize $15 00 silver bridle

Basketball St George vs Over ton

The day will end with a play by local talent

Overton, May 31 —Allen Martin Fleming who has been ill for some time died here May 28th Funeral services were held the following day the speakers being J P Anderson M D Cooper W L Batty and Bp W L Jones Wm A White head sang I Have Read of a Beau tiful City" and the choir sang I Need Thee Every Hour"and Some time Somewhere," also at the cem etery ' Nearer My God to Thee ' There were many beautiful floral offerings Deceased was born Dec 7 1861 at Olney Richland county Illinois and was the son of Robert Fleming and Christena Caley in Jan 1905 he married Martha Mc Mullin daughter of Ira and Helen McMullin of Leeds Utah they came to make their home in Over ton in Dec 1907 Mr Fleming was an honorable upright citizen He leave a wife and three children also his aged father and a number of brothers and sisters now living in Illinois as well as a host of friends who mourn his departure

The Parents class of the Logan Sunday school gave a social Tues day evening at the home of Orin W Jarvis About sixty guests were played in the moonlight on the lawn Everybody enjoyed a merry time

The Misses Sybil and Myrtle Whitmore have returned home from Nephi Utah where they have been to attend school the past winter

Horace Jones of this place and Miss Dora Mathis of Panaca Nev were married at the home of the bride on May 28th

Mrs Arthur Koenig who was Miss Minnie Angell is here visiting her parents Her home is near San Diego Cal

Mrs Bryant Whitmore has gone to visit her father at Lehi Utah

WHO DRIVES THE SPIKE?

Contest for Railroad Day Queen Waxes Warm. Results Will Be Close

Bunkerville, St. Thomas, Overton and Las Vegas, all have candidates in the field for the honor of being voted the most popular young lady and driving the copper spike at the celebration of the completion of the Moapa Valley railroad at St. Thomas next Friday. Although the localities are scattered, the leading candidates are well bunched making the contest one of great interest.

The latest returns place the St. Thomas candidate, Miss Clara Perkins, at the head of the list with 2280 votes. Miss Jessie Bishop of this city is second with 2250, Miss Martha Kramer third with 2035, and Miss Mildred Anderson of Overton, Miss Ethel Bunker, of Bunkerville, Miss Luella Wengert and Miss Marie Sheppard of this city following in the order named. As it stands today the vote is as follows:

Clara Perkins	2280
Jessie Bishop	2250
Martha Kramer	2035
Mildred Anderson	1710
Ethel Bunker	1630
Luella Wengert	1630
Marie Shepherd	580
Pauline Sparlin	525
Gladys Boggs	530
Margaret Potts	200
Olive Masten	150
Margaret Keets	185
Alys Saunders	175
Pearl Thomas	120

In this city the contest is carried on through the Majestic Theatre, each fifteen cent ticket sold entitling the purchaser to 15 votes and each ten cent ticket to 10 votes. In addition to this the theatre is giving a percentage of receipts from all sales of tickets during the contest to the Moapa Valley committee having the contest in charge. Those having in charge the vote counting are Ed W. Clark, S. R. Whitehead and Harley A. Harmon.

A conference will be held at Overton Nevada next Sunday June 9th of all wards and settlements in the Muddy valley Panaca Alamo Mesquite and Bunkerville Nevada and Littlefield Arizona Elders Francis M Lyman and Geo F Richards intend being there from Salt Lake City and Presidents E H Snow and Thos P Cottam of the St George stake will also be present

252

Happenings of Interest in Moapa Valley Metropolis

(Special Correspondence)

The Misses Sybil and Myrtle Whitmore are home again from Nephi, Utah where they have been the past winter to attend school.

Mr. Harrison Houseworth of the London, Liverpool and Globe Fire Insurance Co, was here last week.

Horace Jones of this place and Miss Dora Matthews, of Panaca, Nev. were married at Panaca on May 28.

Mrs. Bryant Whitmore has gone to spend the summer with her father in Lehi, Utah.

Allen Martin Fleming of this place, died May 29th, after an illness of several months, though he was not confined to his room until the last few weeks. Funeral services were held the following day. The speakers were J. P. Anderson, M. D. Cooper, W. L. Batty and Bishop Willard L. Jones, all of whom testified to his sterling qualities. Wm. A. Whitehead sang "I have Read of a Beautiful City," and the choir rendered "I Need Thee Every Hour," and "Sometime, Somewhere." They also sang "Nearer, My God, to Thee," at the cemetery. There were many beautiful floral offerings.

Deceased was born December 7, 1861 at Olney, Richland, Co. Ill., and was the son of Robert Fleming and Christena Caley. In January, 1886 he married Martha McMullen, daughter of Ira and Helen McMullen, of Leeds, Utah. They came to make their home in Overton, in December, 1897. Mr. Fleming leaves a wife and three children, also his aged father and a number of brothers and sisters now living in Illinois, as well as a host of friends to mourn his departure.

The Parents' Class of the Logan Sunday School gave a social Tuesday evening at the home of Supt. Orin W. Jarvis of the Experiment Farm. There were about sixty guests. The party was held on the lawns and porches of the Farm House and an excellent program was rendered followed by cake and ice-cream; games were played in the moonlight on the lawn. Everybody had a merry time.

RAILROAD DAY GREAT SUCCESS

Enthusiastic Crowds Invade Moapa Valley Fri and Enjoy the Day

High Officials of Railroad Present at Celebration

At 6:15 Friday morning the special train bearing nearly 200 Vegas business men with their wives, daughters and sweethearts, left Las Vegas to join with the people of the Moapa Valley in the celebration of the most momentous event in the history of that country— the completion of the Moapa Valley railroad from Moapa on the main line to St. Thomas, a distance of about 26 miles.

The run was quickly and pleasantly made to Moapa, where the entire population joined the excursion. Thence the run over the upper portion of the new line to Logan brought the throng to their first stopping place. Here the committee had supplied teams and conveyances and a trip through that portion of the valley was made and the State Experiment farm visited, much interest being shown in the many things seen.

Thence to Overton the run was quickly made and the big throng waiting for the train was taken aboard and the run made to St. Thomas where the principal events of the day were arranged.

Soon after the arrival the feast of barbecued beef was ready, followed by the ceremony of driving the copper spike by Miss Mildred Anderson, the base ball game between Las Vegas and the Valley team, the steer roping contest and other sports. Not the least in interest was the opportunity to visit some of the fine ranches and observe the wonderful fertility of the soil here.

At 5 o'clock the train returned to Overton, where, after supper, the railroad officials addressed the crowd at the schoolhouse and examined the exhibit of products arranged there. James G. Givens of the Las Vegas Chamber of Commerce also delivered an address. Those who so desired engaged in the dance until a late hour and the train left for the return trip at 12:30 a. m. arriving in Vegas about 3:30 with a tired but happy crowd of people.

One of the big features of the celebration was the Las Vegas brass band which livened up every occasion with melody which was a pleasure to both visitors and the valley people.

Among the officials present were General Passenger Agent T. C. Peck, General Freight Agent, Thos. Sloan, Industrial Agent Douglas White, Dr. H. L. Howetson, F. F. Gunn and others.

Samuel H. Wells, S. R. Whitehead and John M. Bunker, the committee are entitled to great credit for the arrangements to care for the big crowd, estimated at perhaps 800 or 1,000 people.

We organized a new stake known as the Moapa stake comprising the wards Overton St Thomas Panaca Mesquite Bunkerville and Almo Former Bishop William L Jones of Overton was appointed president of the new stake The people are pleased with the organization and they express confidence that their wards will grow and prosper

Las Vegas Age Newspaper
June 15, 1912

Mrs. S. P. Whitehead and children are spending several weeks with relatives in Overton.

Bryan Whitmore of St. Thomas, the winner of the roping contest in the Moapa Valley celebration is registered at the Overland.

MOAPA VALLEY NOW A STAKE

Officials of Church of Latter Day Saints Make New Jurisdiction

A meeting that proved of utmost importance to the members of the Church of Latter Day Saints, was held at Overton last Sunday. The meeting was presided over by Apostle Lyman, assisted by President Snow of the St. George Stake, and Bishop Nephi Wadsworth of Panaca.

The occasion was the establishment of the Moapa Valley Stake, comprising the communities of Mesquite, Bunkerville, Overton, Logan, Moapa and St. Thomas. These thriving communities have been recognized by the chief administrators of the church, tne Twelve Apostles, to the extent of instituting, this the only stake of the church in the

Church of Latter Day Saints is similar to a diocese in other Christian churches and is independent of any superior power, except the Twelve Apostles at Salt Lake City.

The officials of the new stake, elected at the meeting are:

President of Stake, Willard L. Jones
First Counsellor, John M. Bunker
Second Counsellor, Samuel H. Wells
Patriarch Priest, Joseph I. Earl
Bishop of Mespuite, William E. Abbott
Bishop of Bunkerville, Edw. I. Cox
Bishop of Overton, W. A. Whitehead
Bishop of St. Thomas, Robert O. Gibson

All of the above-named officials are well-known in Clark county and are prominent in public, local and business affairs. Willard L. Jones, the president of the stake is one of the members of the Nevada legislature representing Clark County. John M. Bunker is a prominent farmer and is a member of the Board of County Commissioners. Samuel H. Wells is one of the most active business men in the Moapa Valley, representing large Salt Lake interests; he was a member of the original Board of County Commissioners appointed by Governor Dickerson at the time of the subdivision of Lincoln county into Lincoln and Clark counties. W. A. Whitehead is a member of the firm of Whitehead Brothers, owners of a general store at Overton. Joseph I. Earl was prior to his election as Patriarch Priest, the bishop of Bunkerville, and in that capacity acted as a father to his people and bears the respect and admiration not only of his own people, but of all who know and come in contact with him. He was selectnd as foreman of the first Grand Jury that sat in Clark County. With this admirable selection of officers to govern it, the Moapa Valley Stake will exert most favorable influence in the success and progress of Clark County's most flourishing agricultural section.

Overton Notes

Miss Myrtle Watson of St. George, Utah, and Miss Ethel Bunker of Bunkerville, came over with Warren Cox to spend Railroad Day and attend conference.

Miss Neami Wood of Kanarra, Utah is visiting here.

The following bishops were in attendance at conference Sunday, Nephi Wadsworth, of Panaca, Wm. E. Abbott, of Mesquite, J. I. Earl, of Bunkerville, John M. Bunker, of St. Thomas, W. L. Jones, of Overton and Bishop Allen, of Alamo, Nev. The bishops of Bunkerville, Overton and St. Thomas were released and Edward I. Cox, Wm. A. Whitehead and Robert Gibson appointed to fill the vacancies.

President Francis M. Lyman and Geo. F. Richards of the chorus of Apostles, and Bishop O. P. Miller also Edward H. Snow and Thos. P. Cottam of the St. George stake attended Conference. The six Nevada wards of the St. George stake were organized into the Moapa stake with W. L. Jones, John M. Bunker and S. H. Wells as the presidency.

Mrs. Caroline Little of Provo, Utah, returned Tuesday having spent several days visiting her brother, Thos. J. Jones and family of this place.

Mr. and Mrs. Thos. H. Adams were over from Bunkerville for the celebration last week. Mr. Adams returned Monday and Mrs. Adams took the train for a visit to Southern California.

Overton June 13 —The confer ence which followed the railroad day" celebration was well attended by visitors from our neighboring towns Among them were Bishop Allen from Alamo Nephi Wadsworth of Panaca W E Albott of Mesquite and J I Earl of Bunkerville The bishops of Bunkerville Overton and St Thomas were released and Edward I Cox Wm A Whitehead and Robert Gibson chosen to fill the vacancies A stake was organized of the six Nevada wards of the St George stake to be known as the Moapa Stake with W L Jones John M Bunker and S H Wells as the presidency

Miss Myrtle Watson of St George and Miss Ethel Bunker of Bunkerville came down with Warren Cox to attend the celebration and conference

Miss Naomi Wood of Kanarra Utah is visiting here the guest of Miss Armelia Ingram

Mrs Caroline Little of Provo Utah is visiting her brother Thos I Jones and family

Overton June 26 —Pres W I Jones and Councilor J M Bunker of the Moapa stake were over to hold a ward conference at Bunkerville last Sunday and also to visit the Mesquite ward

The following were appointed as a committee to arrange for a 4th of July celebration in Overton Albert F Bischoff Andrew L Jones and N Ray Pixton

Ellis Turnbeaugh is erecting a building on main street opposite Anderson s store in which he will run an ice cream stand and soda fountain

David R Forsha clerk of the St George stake is here this week to attend to some matters concerning the records of the wards and stake

Mr and Mrs Horace Jones have gone to keeping house in the residence of Bert Angell in the northern part of town

Mrs W I Jones entertained the Primary Girls Sewing class in a sewing bee on the lawn Thursday afternoon

Miss Sadie Perkins is clerking in Whitehead Bros store in the place of her sister Miss Clara Perkins

A son born Saturday to Mr and Mrs Poy Barlow died last night at Logan where they are living

T J Osborne went north Monday having spent a few days here looking after his farm

The threshing machine belonging to Albert Frehner is threshing grain in town this week

Mrs Sherman Thomas has been quite ill for several days but is now recovering

Miss Mabel Leavitt of Bunkerville is working at the Swapp hotel

Bishop T J Jones went over to Bunkerville last Friday

Ernest Wadsworth of Panaca is here on business

260

Fourth of July

The Moapa Valley is to have a good old-time Fourth of July celebration. It will be held at Overton, the metropolis of the valley, and will include horse races, steer tieing, foot races and many stunts for the kids. Excursion rates will be in force on the new railroad and the whole valley will be there.

Overton Doings

T. J. Osborne was here a few days this week looking after his farm.

Pres. W. L. Jones and John M. Bunker of the Moapa Stake went over to visit the Bunkerville and Mesquite wards last week. Bishop Thos. J. Jones accompanied them over but did not return with them.

Ellis Turnbaugh is erecting a building on Main street opposite Anderson's Store in which he will conduct an ice-cream parlor and soda fountain.

Insurance agent Ernest Wadsworth, representing the Beneficial Life Insurance Co. of Salt Lake City, was here during the week.

Miss Mabel Leavitt, of Bunkerville, is working at the Swapp Hotel.

Miss Sadie Perkins returned last week from Las Vegas where she went to attend the district teachers' exam and is now clerking in Whitehead Bros' store in the place of her sister, Miss Clara Perkins.

Mr. and Mrs. Horace Jones have gone to housekeeping in the Bert Angell house in the northern part of town.

Mrs. Sherman has been quite ill for

Commissioners Meet

There was little of interest at the regular meeting of the Commissioners last Monday. Justice of the Peace, Newell tendered his resignation which was accepted and C. L. Aug. Mahn appointed to fill the vacancy. Boundaries of the Searchlight, Goodsprings, Moapa, St. Thomas and Overton school districts were defined and approved. The sanitation of Vegas creek was brought up and referred to the board of health.

Washington County News
July 6, 1912

Overton July 6 — July 4th passed off pleasantly here. The celebration began at sunrise with hoisting of the flag and a salute of guns. A program was rendered in the forenoon lunch in the bowery' at noon and sports in the afternoon for old and young. A picture show and dance in the Shurtliff hall concluded the day's exercises. The following were the guests of honor at the morning program and were driven to the bowery in a coach with four horses splendidly decorated Albert L Jones being coachman Uncle Sam A L F McDermott Goddess of Liberty Jean Anderson Miss United States Armelia Ingram Columbia Gertude Rhoner Nevada Zilla Peterson

Misses Rose Leavitt Thelma Cox and Lottie Hansen of Bunkerville were here for the 4th of July celebration They are working on ranches in the upper part of the valley

W W Muir and Pies F R Snow of the Utah Moapa Distribut Co were in town on the 4th looking over the cantaloupe crop

Samuel H Wells and family have recently returned from a vacation on the beach' '

A baby girl was born July 2 to Mr and Mrs Clifford Whitmore

Miss Amelia Huntsman of Cane Springs is visiting relatives here

Ellis Turnbeaugh opened his ice cream parlor this week

Brigham Whitmore went last week to Salt Lake City

262

Overton July 16 —Thomas John son Andrew L Jones and W A Whitehead were over to Bunkerville last week as a committee to offer some inducements to the Virgin River people to make Overton their nearest depot A meeting will be held tonight to consider their report

Bishops Edw Bunker Jr and Jos I Earl of Bunkerville came over Saturday to attend a session of the high council of which they are members they remained over Sun day and with Bp William Abbott of Mesquite occupied the time in the afternoon service

Ralph Leavitt Fay Anderson and Benjamin Robinson and the Misses Alice Lewis Armelia Ingram and Mildred Anderson went Saturday afternoon for an outing to the springs at the head of the Muddy river near Baldwin s ranch

Cantaloupes are ripening fast and the farmers are making express shipments most of these melons are being hauled by team to Moapa as the train does not come down the valley more than twice a week yet

The railroad company has com pleted the erection of a platform and shed for loading melons at the de pot They will erect similar ones at Logan and St Thomas

A baby girl was born last week to Mr and Mrs Marl Blake of St George Utah who are living at the well s ranch The child died at birth

The Logan Sunday school gave a dance in their school house Thurs day evening A crowd of Overton young people were in attendance

Miss Laura Leavitt is working at the Rushton ranch in place of Miss Thirza Leavitt who has returned to Bunkerville

Mrs Sarah Perkins and daughter Miss Vivian returned from the coast Thursday

Harold Earl came over from Bunkerville Wednesday

263

Correct spelling should be Andersen

Overton Locals

Overton, July, 16, 1912:— The Logan Sunday School gave a dance in their school-house Thursday evening.

Harold Earle came over from Bunkerville Wednesday.

Mrs. Sarah Perkins and daughter returned from a visit to the coast last week.

Tomas Johnson, Andrew L. Jones and W. A. Whitehead were over to Bunkerville last week as a committee to offer some inducements to the Virgin River towns to make Overton their nearest depot, and to book

264

OVERTON ITEMS

July 4th passed off pleasantly here. The celebration began at sunrise with the hoisting of "Old Glory" greeted with a salute of guns. The string band serenaded through the principal streets of the town. A program was rendered in the Bowry built on the public square. Just at the beginning of the program a coach and four horses decorated in the national colors drove up and the guests of the day alighted and were shown to seats on the stand. They were:

Uncle Sam	A. L. McDermott
Goddess of Liberty	Jean Anderson
Miss United States	Armelia Ingram
Columbia	Gertrude Rhoner
Nevada	Ella Peterson

The following program was then carried out, Bishop W. A. Whitehead as master of ceremonies.

Chorus by Choir	America
Prayer by Chaplain	Andrew L. Jones
Speech of Welcome	Orin W. Jarvis
Speech by Uncle Sam	
Duet "My Dream of the U. S. A." by Jay McAllister and W. A. Whitehead.	
Speech	Goddess of Liberty
Instrumental Music	String Band
Solo, "The Star Spangled Banner,"	Miss Armelia Ingram
Reading, "Barbara Frietchie" in Dutch	Leon Hickman
Instrumental Music	String Band
Toast	W. L. Jones
Chorus, "Red, White and Blue"	Choir

Prayer by Chaplain.

Orin Jarvis then led in three cheers for Uncle Sam. The Goddess of Liberty, Columbia, The United States, Nevada and the Moapa Valley.

Mrs. Birdie Gann suggested three cheers for woman's suffrage in Nevada and the crowd followed her lead with three rousing cheers. At the close of the program lunch was served on tables under the Bowry and races and other sports for the children and young people followed. The day closed with a picture show and a dance in the the Shurtliff Hall.

Miss Amelia Huntsman of Cane Springs is here visiting for a few days.

Samuel H. Wells and family have recently returned from a vacation on the beach.

W. W. Muir and Pres. F. R. Snow, of the Utah, Moapa Distributing Co., were in town on the 4th looking over the cantaloupe crop.

A baby girl was born July 2, to Mr. and Mrs. Clifford Whitmore. The babe had two teeth at birth; all concerned doing nicely.

Misses Roxie Leavitt of Bunkerville is working at the Wells ranch and Miss Thelma Cox of Bunkerville is at the Experiment Farm.

Ellis Turnbaugh opened his ice-cream parlor this week.

Brigham Whitmore has gone to Salt Lake City.

Overton July 29 —Today s ship ment of cantaloupe amounted to seven cars from the valley one from St Thomas three from Over ton and three from Logan Grow ers have been shipping in carload lots since the 16th The Farmers association has employed a number of packers who pack at the com pany s shed at the depot an l grow ers only have to pick their melons and haul them to the depot This makes it much easier for the farm er than it has been other years

Mr and Mrs Brigham Whitmore returne l Saturday from a trip to Salt Lale City where they have been to purchase a h me as they have sold tl eir l ome and Main street property here to James P Ander son of this place They expect to leave for Salt Lale City in August

We enjoye l a fine shower on the 29th much to the dismay of the cantaloupe growers as the rain l in ders the ripening of melons and tends to spread aphis throughout the field

Born July 23 a son to Mr and Mrs David Conger July 2[a son to Mr and Mrs George Perkins All concerned doing nicely

Correct spelling should be Andersen

266

Overton, Aug 13 —Word was received here Sunday that Mrs Mark Bleak who had been taken to Salt Lake City early in the week on account of complications having developed from her recent confinement had died Saturday in that city   Mr Bleak's mother who was at the Wells ranch where she and her son and his wife had been living this summer has gone to St George where funeral services and the burial will take place   Much regret is felt among their many friends here for her untimely death

Cantaloupe shipments are falling off now the melons from St Thomas being shipped by express as they haven't enough to load a car now Overton still ships a car a day Overton's best record this season was three cars a day

Mrs Lizzie Gibson and Misses Helen Bunker and Mary Syphus spent the day visiting here yesterday returning to St Thomas by evening train

Wilford Ingram and Frank Jones went to Idaho last week   Woodruff Perkins accompanied them to Salt Lake City and continued on to Colorado

Presidents Willard L Jones and John M Bunker of the Moapa stake returned Monday evening from a visit to the Panaca ward

Mr and Mrs Albert Jones entertained a number of their friends at an ice cream party Sunday afternoon

Ralph Leavitt and Miss Alice Lewis and Roxie Leavitt went over to Bunkerville Tuesday

Brigham Whitmore and family left this week for their new home near Salt Lake City

Miss Sadie Perkins is clerking in the Wm Matthews store in Panaca

S R Whitehead moved his family here from Las Vegas last week

Las Vegas Age Newspaper
August 31, 1912

Assemblyman Jones

Willard L. Jones, of Overton, the present incumbent is a candidate for nomination for the assembly on the republican ticket. Mr. Jones is well and favorably known throughout the county. He has already served one term thereby becoming well acquainted with the duties of the position. If nominated and elected he may be relied upon to do his duty towards his constituents and the interests of the County in general.

Washington County News
September 2, 1912

Overton Sept 2 —Frank Cox of St George passed through here Monday enroute to the timber mountain He has purchased the Perkins Thomas sawmill and will remove it to Mt Trumbull and put the old mill into operation again

People who think apples will not grow in the valley should visit the apple orchard of A F Bischoff He has a fine crop of lucious beauties now ready for the market

Harry Gentry, jr of St Thomas has received a call to go on a mission to the Society Islands He will leave for his field of labor in a few weeks

A number of Overton people went to Kaolin to a dance Wednesday evening They were served to a feast of watermelons and lemonade

N Pay Pixton is visiting at his old home in Taylorsville his brother Robert Pixton has charge of the ranch during his absence

Mrs Alonzo Huntsman entertained the officers and teachers of the Primary association at an ice cream party Monday evening

The friends of Mrs H Sparks gave her a surprise party last Thursday afternoon the occasion being her 66th birthday

Jay McAllister and Fay Anderson left last week for Lehi Utah They will attend school there this winter

Mrs Sarah Thomas returned Sunday from a visit with relatives in Caliente Nev

Miss Louisa Jones of Bunkerville is here and will remain until after conference

Cal Nay of Logan has been quite sick but is now recovering

Wallace Jones is visiting his sister in Idaho

E. E. ROBERTS IS ENDORSED

Voters of State Give Him Splendid Testimonial of Approval

Tuesday's Primaries Devoid of Sensations -- Much Local Interest

More than passing interest was manifested in the primary election last Tuesday as was shown by the fact that considerably over 50 per cent of the registration in this city voted.

The present system whereby all tickets are printed on the same ballot was proven defective and misleading and resulted in the voiding of 20 per cent of the ballots cast, through "crossfiring" as it is called, being the attempt of voters to support candidates in two or more parties at the same time. Three hundred and twenty three votes were cast in this city, 63 of them being declared void by the election board. Especially noticable is the fact that the Socialists, who are supposed to devote a profound study to the ballot and questions connected therewith, cast only two valid ballots out of the 16 votes cast by them.

The feature of the day was the phenomenal vote cast for Congressman E. E. Roberts and the enthusiasm which greeted his name at all times. The resultant vote in this city of 166 for Roberts to 7 for Frohlich tells the story. A similar result was noted in some of the outlying districts.

The three cornered contest for the two assemblyman nominations on the Republican ticket also caused considerable activity among the respective friends of Jones of Overton, and Buol and Smith of Las Vegas. The result was the nomination of Smith and Buol.

269

The closest contest, and one in which much interest developed at the last moment, was that between C. E. McCarthy of Goodsprings and J. T. McWilliams of this city for the nomination as County Surveyor on the Republican ticket. As the votes were reported from outlying precints, the count showed a tie, at times veering in favor of one or the other candidate as the returns came in. However, with the receipt of the Bunkerville and Mesquite returns the count gave McCarthy seven advantage over McWilliams.

The table below shows the correct total of the county on all candidates

U. S. Senate: W. A. Massey (rep) 242; Key Pittman (dem) 116; G. A. Steele (soc) 13

Congressman: E. E. Roberts (rep) 262; Clay Tallman (dem) 111; John Worden (soc) 12

Supreme Justice: James M. Lockhart (rep) 238; A. A. Heer (dem) 65; P. A. McCarren (dem) 47

Long Term Regent: A. A. Codd (rep) 222; W. E. Pratt (dem) 114; John W. Reeves (soc) 10; Thos. Woodliff (soc) 12

Short Term Regent: Jas. W. O'Brien (rep) 222; S. B. Pray (soc) 13

Assemblyman: Peter Buol (rep) 243; Willard Jones (rep) 154; L. D. Smith (rep) 182; J. E. Babcock (dem) 96; Frank Williams (dem) 117.

County Clerk: Harley A. Harmon (dem) 115

Sheriff: Sam Gay (rep) 288; H. H. Sparks (dem) 116

Assessor: S. R. Whitehead (dem) 110

Treasurer: Ed. W. Clark (dem) 109

District Attorney: O. J. Van Pelt (dem) 121

County Surveyor: C. E. McCarthy (rep) 163; J. T. McWilliams (rep) 156

Recorder and Auditor: Frank A. Doherty (rep) 255

Commissioner (long term) C. C. Ronnow (rep) 244

Commissioner [short term] Geo. Fayle [dem] 75; G. D. E. Mortimer [dem] 43

Board of Education [long term] S. W. Darling [rep] 239

Board of Education [short term] E. W. Griffith [rep] 218; W. B. Mundy [dem] 114

Public Administrator: John Kramer [rep] 233

Justice of the Peace (Searchlight Twp.) C. L. Aug. Mahn (rep) 28
Justice of the Peace [Moapa Twp.] Lew. Grant (rep) 7; A. H. Leach (rep) 6

Items Of Interest From Our Correspondent In The Valley

(Special Correspondence)
Overton, Nevada, Sept. 2, 1912.

Mrs. Alonzo Huntsman entertained the officers and teachers of the primary at an ice cream party Monday evening.

Frank Cox, of St. George, passed through here Monday enroute to the Timber Mountain to remove the Perkins-Thomas sawmill, which he has recently purchased, to Mt. Trumbull, where he will operate it.

Miss Lousa Jones of Bunkerville is here and will remain until after conference.

271

Calvin Nay, who has been very sick is now recovering. He is in Moapa.

Jay McCallister and Fay Anderson have gone to Lehi, Utah, to attend school this winter.

Harry Gentry Jr., of St. Thomas, has received a call to go on a mission to the Society Islands. He will leave for his field of labor in a few weeks.

Mrs. Sarah Thomas returned Sunday from a visit with relatives in Caliente Nevada.

Ellis Turnbaugh has given his ice cream parlor a coat of paint, adding much to its appearance.

Wallace Jones is visiting his sister in Idaho.

People who think apples will not grow in the Valley, should visit the apple orchard of A. F. Bischoff. He has a fine crop of luscious beauties now ready for the market.

A number of Overton people attended the dance at Kaolin, Wednesday evening. They were treated to a feast of watermelons and ice cold lemonade.

N. Ray Pixton is visiting at his old home in Taylorsville, Vt. His brother Robert Pixton has charge of the ranch in his absence.

The friends of Mrs. H. Sparks gave her a surprise party last Thursday afternoon, the occasion being her 66th birthday.

273

NOTICE OF APPLICATION FOR PATENT

Mineral Application No. 07204

In the United States Land Office at Carson City, Nevada.

United States Land Office, Carson City, Nevada, August 5, 1912.

NOTICE IS HEREBY GIVEN that in pursuance of the act of Congress approved May 10, 1872, and of the act of Congress entitled "An Act Extending the Mining laws to Saline Lands" approved January 31, 1901, L. C. Fox and William McGuire, the Postoffice address of e ch of whom is Ventura, Ventura County, California, and T. O. Toland and C. A. Toland, the Postoffice address of each of whom is Los Angeles, Los Angeles County, California, by and through their duly authorized Agent, LEVI SYPHUS, who resides, and whose Postoffice address is St. Thomas, Clark County, Nevada, have made application for a mineral patent for the Fairview salt placer mining claim situate in St. Thomas Mining District in Clark County, Nevada, containing eighty (80) acres and being the Southwest quarter of the Southwest quarter, the South half of the Northwest quarter of the Southwest quarter, the Southwest quarter of the Northeast quarter of the Southwest quarter and the Northwest quarter of the Southeast quarter of the Southwest quarter of Section 32 Township 18 South Range 68 East M. D. M., and including all that part of mineral surveys 37 and 38 situate within the exterior boundaries of the Governmental subdivision above described; and that all of said land for which patent is hereby applied is public lands of the United States.

L. C. Fox
William McGuire
T. O. Toland
C. A. Toland

By Levi Syphus, their duly authorized agent.

Louis J. Cohn,
Register.

First publication August 16, 1912
Last publication October 12, 1912

Washington County News
September 9, 1919

County Clerk Woodbury has is
sued marriage licenses as follows
Nephi Hunt and Lydia Amelia Bar
locker of Enterprise Sept 9th
Byron Ahlstrom of Cedar City and
Gena Neilson of Washington Sept
11 Thomas D Leavitt jr and
I ho la Wittwer of Bunkerville Sept
12th Thomas M Anderson and
Annie G Rohner of Overton Sept
1_ Daniel Purney of Monroe and
Julia A Taylor of Harmony, Sept
18

Correct spelling should be Andersen

Washington County News
September 12, 1912

Overton Sept 12 — The first
quarterly conference of the Moapa
Stake of Zion convened here Satur
day and Sunday Sept 7th and 8th
Jos F Smith Jr of the council
of the twelve and Ruth May Fox of
the presidency of the Y I M I A
were in attendance from Salt Lake
City with a good attendance from all
the wards of the stake

The following young people have
gone to Las Vegas to attend the
county high school Benjamin
Robinson Everett Syphus Bryan
Bunker Laura Gentry Mary Sy
phus Helen Bunker Dollie Pearson,
Jean Anderson Lydia Cooper and
Zilla Peterson

Young men s and young ladies
M I A conventions were held Sat
urday and also a conjoint session
Sunday evening Stake conference
was held Sunday The Shurtliff
hall was furnished free by its own
ers for use during conference

Pres S H Wells has moved his
family from the Improvement Co
ranch where he has acted as Supt
of the ranch for a number of years
to St Thomas where he has prop
erty and will build a home there
soon

A social and dance was given last
week at St Thomas in honor of
Harry Gentry Jr who has been
called to fill a mission to the Society
Islands Elder Gentry left on the
10th for Salt Lake City

Albert Frehner and a crew of
thieshing machine hands of St
Thomas passed through here Wed
nesday going to Moapa and the up
per Muddy to thresh grain

Mrs Mary Whitehead and daugh
ter Winnie and son Bishop W
A Whitehead have gone to St
George to attend the Dixie Fruit
festival

Friends of Isaac E Losee gave
him a surprise party Wednesday
evening the occasion being his 8th
birthday

Miss Ethel Lewis has gone to Salt
Lake City

275

Bishop William Arthur White
head of Overton Nevada and Miss
Clara Myrtle Watson of Parowan
were married in the St George
temple Thursday September 12th

The bride is a daughter of Mrs
S M Watson and the late L D
Watson a charming and accomplish
ed young lady who for a considerable
time was employed as clerk in the
Bank of St George vacating that
position for the purpose of being
married   The groom is a son of Mrs
Mary Wells Whitehead and the late
A R Whitehead of this city   an
estimable young man who has re
cently been appointed bishop of the
Overton Nevada ward

The young couple have a host of
friends who will wish them all hap
piness

276

Democratic Committee

At the meeting of democratic candidates Tuesday, they appointed the following county central committee:

Nelson—J. E. Babcock.
Crescent—Jeff Davis.
Searchlight—C. L. Aug. Mahn.
Goodsdrings—Frank Williams.
Arden—James Gorin.
Las Vegas—W. E. Hawkins.
Moapa—Geo. C. Baldwin.
Logan—Henry Rice, Sr.
Overton—Joe. F. Perkins.
St. Thomas—M. A. Bunker.
Bunkerville—J. I. Earl.
Mesquite—A. J. Barnum.

W. E. Hawkins was made chairman and J. I. Earl secretary of the committee.

Republican Committee

At their meeting at the court house Tuesday afternoon, the republican candidates as required by law, named a member of the republican county central committee from each precinct. No changes were made except in the cases of Murphy of St. Thomas, McBurney of Logan and Sprague of Moapa. The new committee is as follows:

Nelson, Clark Alvord; Searchlight, B. F. Miller, Jr.; Crescent, S. C. Whipple; Goodsprings, C. E. McCarthy; Las Vegas, Roy W. Martin; Moapa, W. C Bowman; Logan, Bert Mills; Overton, S. A. Angell; St. Thomas, B. F. Bonelli; Bunkerville, S. W. Darling; Mesquite, Wm. E. Abbott.

NOTICE OF APPLICATION FOR PATENT

Mineral Application No. 07203

In the United States Land Office at Carson City, Nevada.

United States Land Office, Carson City, Nevada August 5, 1912.

NOTICE IS HEREBY GIVEN that in pursuance of the act of Congress approved May 10, 1872, and of the act of Congress entitled "An Act Extending the Mining Laws to Saline Lands" approved January 31, 1901, W. P. McGonigle, J. I. McGonigle and J. P. McGonigle, the Postoffice address of each of whom is Ventura, Ventura County, California, by and through their duly authorized Agent, LEVI SYPHUS, who resides, and whose Postoffice address is St. Thomas, Clark County, Nevada, have made application for a mineral patent for the Last Chance salt placer mining claim situate in St. Thomas Mining District in Clark County, Nevada, and being the South half of Lot 1 of Section 16 and all of Lot 1 in Section 21 Township 19 South of Range 68 East M. D. M., and including all that portion of mineral survey No. 37 (lying in said sections 16 and 21) which lies within the exterior boundaries of the Southeast quarter of the Southeast quarter of said Section 16 and the Northeast quarter of the Northeast quarter of said Section 21; containing sixty (60) acres; and that all of said land for which patent is hereby applied is public lands of the United States.

W. P. McGonigle
J. I. McGonigle
J. P. McGonigle

By Levi Syphus, their duly authorized agent.

Louis J. Cohn,
Register

First publication August 10, 1912
Last publication October 12, 1912

Delinquent Notice

MUDDY VALLEY IRRIGATION COMPANY
Location of principal place of business, Overton, Nevada. Location of Irrigation system and works, Moapa Valley, Clark County, Nevada.

NOTICE

THERE ARE DELINQUENT upon the following described Prefered capital stock on account of assessment No. 21, levied on the 2nd day of March 1912, the several amounts set opposite the names of the respective shareholders as follows:

No. of cif.	Name	Shares	Amt.
321	W. L. Batty	5	$ 2.00
344	Chas. Cobb	41½	41.50
261	Moapa Imp. Co.	97	
312	"	3	
686	"	41	141.00
606	Moapa Garden Co.	56½	24.58
360	A. N. Leonard &	5	
361	E. S. Hinckly	46½	51.50
590	J. A. Lytle	1	1.00
455	St. Joe School Dist	1 3-5	2.45
341	H. S. Tengvall	5	2.50
540	S. H. Wells	51 4-5	51.80

There are also delinquent upon the following described common stock on account of assessment No. 22, levied on the 2nd day of March 1912 the several amounts set opposite the names of the respective shareholders as follows:

6	Chas. Cobb	150	$22.50
51	Moapa Imp. Co.	263½	66,67
78	A. N. Leonard &	17	
90	E. S. Hinckly	216½	54.38
109	S. H. Wells	85 9-10	13.01

And in accordance with law and an order of the board of directors made on the 7th day of Sept, 1912, so many shares of each parcel of each class of such stock as may be necessary will be sold at public auction at the office of the company in Overton, Clark County, Nevada, on the 26th day of Oct. 1912, at the hour of 4 o'clock p. m., of said day, to pay the delinquent assessment together with cost of advertising and expense of sale.

Overton, Nevada, Sept. 16, 1912,

ISAAC E. LOSEE,
Secretary

First publication Sept. 21, 1912.
Last publication Oct. 12, 1912.

BORN IN 56 IS NOW 56

Senator Massey Celebrates His Birthday on Monday in Moapa Valley

Senator Massey received numerous telegrams Monday last reminding him that, having been born in '56 he is therefore 56 years "young." The day was spent by the senator among his friends of the famous Moapa Valley, where, in the evening, he spoke at Overton.

Few men have undergone the hardships and trying experiences in the remote districts of Nevada at all seasons of the year, facing every danger known to the desert and mountains, undergoing all the hardships of the miner and stockman, to still retain at his age such remarkable vigor of both mind and body.

Thousands of Nevadans join in wishing for the junior senator many more years of active and useful life and especially that he may round out the measure of a life rich in achievement, by serving his state in his declining years in the Senate of the United States, where already, with the service of but a few weeks to his credit, he stands a notable character before the nation.

CLARK COUNTY FINANCES

The Facts and Figures Concerning Your Taxes and the County Treasury.

There has been recently considerable discussion regarding the condition of the county treasury and the county business generally. In the search for a grievance, a certain disgruntled element has finally discovered a wrong to be righted—a condition of cruel indignity put upon the suffering taxpayers, which calls for a courageous champion of the people for righting.

The people have been wronged! By an excessive tax rate? No. By graft on the county treasury? No. By the reckless squandering of money through unnecessary expenditures? No, not so. Through extravagance in the county offices? No. Through hiring unnecessary deputies while the county officers take things easy? No, not that. Then by the embezzlement of the county funds? No, not so. The county officials have deliberately, wantonly, shamelessly and cruelly piled up a surplus in the county treasury!

Now, the people's champions want to remedy that awful condition by electing themselves or their tools to office. The remedy will, we may be sure, effective should the ones who are loudest in their condemnation of the present county government be given a chance to get their hands on the surplus.

The AGE has taken pains to find out the exact condition of the county treasury, the past expenditures and probable expenditures for next year, as well as the tax rate and the amount of assessed property. We will lay the facts down as clearly as possible so that people may judge for themselves as to conditions instead of taking the words of those who either through ignorance or malice are misstating the facts.

In the first place, if there were a large surplus unexpended in the county treasury, we would consider that the very best kind of a platform for a bunch of office holders to make a campaign for re-election on. However, the statement is made, varied apparently to suit the credulity of the victim, that the county treasury has a surplus of $60,000, or $100,000. The facts are as follows:

The financial condition of the county funds on June 30th, 1912, showed a balance of cash on hand of $57,003.22.

(Concluded on second page.)

Out of this the state, school and special funds contain $20,060.11, leaving a balance of $36,943.11 available for county government purposes. This amount must run the county for the six months from July 1st, 1912, to January 1st, 1913. The total county expenses for the first six months from January 1st, 1912, to June 30th was $15,015 01. The expense from July 1st, 1912, to January 1st, 1913, will be the same with an extra expense of election of about $5,000, making the total expense approximately $20,000 for the last six months of the year. This, deducted from the $36,943.11, will, if no unforeseen expenses arise, leave a cash balance or surplus of about $17,000 on hand January 1st, 1913.

The total expenses for the year 1912 will amount to about an even $35,000 as shown by the above figures. The total amount that will be raised on the 1912 assessment for county purposes will be $24,820 together with the licenses and fees from the various offices of $11,000,

making a total of $35,820, leaving at the end of the year 1913 practically the same cash surplus as we have on hand at the conclusion of this year, or approximately $17,000, provided no unusual expense occurs.

It would be well for the people of Clark to compare the condition of their county with that of Lincoln, from whom she was divorced three years ago in July. Although Lincoln's assessment roll foots nearly as much as Clark's the business of her court house is much less. Yet she has a tax rate of almost twice what we pay.

Clark County began business without a dollar in her treasury. Owing to the careful and economical manner in which her affairs have been carried on it has been possible to reduce the tax rate steadily and at the same time accumulate a small surplus, just enough so that the county business may be maintained on a cash basis, even

should some unforeseen expenses make an unusual drain on the treasury.

The county tax rate of $2.00 as fixed by the commissioners Monday shows a reduction from last year of sixty cents. It is made up as follows:

State fund	.60
Jury fund	.05
Contingent	.05
Indigent	.05
General county	.52
High school	.15
General county school	.30
Interest fund	.28
Total	$2.00

Las Vegas school special, .30; Las Vegas city special, .70; Goodsprings school special, .15; St. Thomas school special, .25; Overton school special, .25; Moapa school special, .60.

The general county, contingent, indigent and jury funds which go to pay all county government expenses, make a total rate of 67 cents, which will raise approximately $24,000.

The licenses and fees from all the county offices will amount to about $11,000, making a total collection for the use of the county government for the year 1912 of $35,000.

The total amount collected from taxes for general county purposes is $24,000, out of which the railroad company, Western Union Tel. Co., Pacific Fruit Co., and subsidiary companies pay a little over 60 per cent or about $14,000, leaving the individual taxpayer the balance or $10,000 for the running of the county government.

The difference between the 67 cent rate for county purposes and the total $2.00 levy for state and county is $1.33 and is a special levy for state, schools and interest funds over which the commissioners have no power or authority, except to levy as required by law for the purposes named. This reasonable rate is made possible on account of the increased valuation and equalization of the assessments and the healthful condition of the funds at the present time, which is due to the economical and prudent management of the various offices together with the fact that the county has no expensive litigation to prosecute.

It would seem that in the face of the facts as clearly presented above, the taxpayer should thank his stars that he has had a bunch of sober, sensible, hardworking, conscientious men running his county affairs instead of some of those who are now so anxious to help reduce the surplus.

YOUR TAXES NOW FIXED

Board of Equalization Completes Work Last Monday.

The county board of equalization completed its work Monday, the 7th. There were practically no complaints made before the board, there being a few corrections in descriptions and a few transfers of property.

The rates as established in March were changed and the following ones take effect for the year 1912 taxes:

County and state, $2.00.

County, state and Las Vegas school, $2.30.

County, state, Las Vegas school and Las Vegas city, $3.00.

County, state and Moapa school, $2.60.

County, state and Goodsprings school, $2.15.

County, state and Overton school, $2.25.

County, state and St. Thomas school, $2.25.

Some interesting information comes from the comparison of the rates and assessments of the last three years.

In 1910 the assessment roll was $2,380,336. In 1912 it is $3,549,927, an increase of $1,169,591, or in other words, just about an even third of the total roll at the present time is increase over the 1910 roll. As compared with this the rate for county purposes in 1910 was $2.40 on each $100 of valuation, while at this time it is $1.40. The rate has therefore gone down in about the same proportion as the roll has gone up.

One of the most interesting things about this comparison is that the most of this increase comes from the railroads and corporations. In 1910 the railroad assessment was $783,556. Now it is $1,707,198, an increase of $923,642. The increase on the Western Union is $19,804. The increase in the Las Vegas Land & Water Co. is $51,940. The increase on the Pacific Fruit Express Co. is $14,740, making a total increase on the corporations of $1,010,126, which does not include an increase of several thousand dollars on the Pullman company that was on the rolls and the taxes collected by the treasurer in 1910, but is collected this year by the

(Concluded on last page.)

284

Your Taxes Now Fixed.

(Concluded from first page.)

assessor as personal property.

This increase of $1,010,126 on the corporations taken from the total increase of the rol leaves a balance of increase assessed to the tax payers of $159,465. It therefore becomes plain to the tax payer that he is not burdened with taxation that should be paid by the corporations in this county.

The personal property tax collected by the assessor in the years 1909 and 1910 amounted to $672; in 1911 and 1912 it is approximately $2,017.

The bullion tax collected in 1909 and 1910 was $441.70; in 1911 and 1912 it is $1,838.91, with two quarters to be heard from yet—that is, two more reports quarterly yet to come in this year, both of which promise to be good.

The poll taxes collected by the assessor in 1909 and 1910 was $3,081; in 1911 and 1912 it will be approximately $6,500.

The fact that none of the corporations made any complaint before the board of commissioners may be construed to mean that they are not paying more taxes than they should on the amount of property they have invested in the county.

Overton, Oct 16 —Stake confer ence of the Primary association was held here Sunday Pres Louie B Felt Sister May Anderson and Miss Vera Felt were in attendance from Salt Lake City On Monday they visited St Thomas where Sister Felt and her husband Jos H Felt made their first home 46 years ago having been called to come to this valley by Pres Brigham Young They left Moapa Tuesday enroute to southern California on a vacation

Among the visitors to the state fair and conference in Salt Lake City the following have returned home Mrs Sarah Perkins Miss Sylvia Shurtliff Mr and Mrs S D Conger Mr and Mrs Jos Robinson Pres and Mrs W L Jones Wm Perkins Frank and Wallace Jones Mis Rebecca Murphy and son Melvin Murphy

Among the visitors to the stake primary conference were Mrs Eva Lee of Panaca Mr and Mrs O D Leavitt Mrs Iuella Leavitt Harold Earl Nettie M Earl Lovica Leavitt and Mabel Leavitt of Bunkerville ward St Thomas ward was also well represented and all of the brethren of the stake presidency, were present

E J Milne of Salt Lake City president of the Rocky Mountain Insurance Agency and Adjustment Co is here in the interest of his company He gave a public lecture last evening on the Boy Problem which was much appreciated and well attended

Among the newest residents of Overton are a son born to Mr and Mrs Fay Perkins a son to Mr and Mrs W L Batty and a daughter to Mr and Mrs Fred Bischoff

A carload of wagons and buggies was shipped in last week by Warren Cox of St George W L Jones having them in charge

Willard Iverson and family of Morelos Mexico have moved here for the winter and will probably make their home here

The lady friends of Mrs Eliza Ingram give her a surprise party on the 16th the event being her 41st birthday

Mrs Patience Lee and family of Morelos Mexico arrived here last week They will make their home here

C. F. Feldt of Overton, with his wife and child, was registered at the Overland this week.

John Hopden and Engineer Charles Gallaway returned Friday evening from Moapa Valley where they have been enjoying excellent sport hunting duck the past few days.

MOAPA VALLEY NEWS ITEMS

Overton the Scene of Considerable Activity Recently.

(S ecial correspondence.)

Overton, Oct. 17.—Stake Primary Conference was held here last Sunday, Stake President Eliza Ingram in charge. General President of the Primary Associations Louie B. Felt and Miss May Anderson, editor of The Children's Friend, were in attendance from Salt Lake City. The following ward organizations were represented: Panaca, Overton, St. Thomas and Bunkerville.

E. J. Milne, president of the Rocky Mountain Insurance Agency, is here this week in the interest of life insurance. Mr. Milne has been connected with the Utah State Industrial School, also athletic work in the University of Utah and the L. D. S. University. He gave a public lecture Wednesday evening, his subject being "The Boy Problem."

Friends of Mrs. Eliza Ingram gave her a surprise birthday party on the 16th.

Mr. Warren Cox has recently shipped in a car of wagons and buggies. They are in charge of W. L. Jones.

Mrs. Patience Lee of Morelos, Mexico, and family arrived here last week and will make her home here until peace is restored in Mexico.

The Overton basket ball team left this afternoon for Bunkerville, where they will have a contest game of basket ball tomorrow with the B. V. boys. Leon Hickman is in charge of the Overton team.

The newest residents of Overton are baby boys at the home of Mr. and Mrs. Fay Perkins, Mr. and Mrs. Wm. Batty and a daughter at the home of Mr. and Mrs. A. F. Bischoff.

Overton Oct 30 — Born, October 30 to Mr and Mrs Sylvester Nay a daughter all concerned doing well

Mrs O J Van Pelt came over from Las Vegas with her husband Friday and spent several days here visiting friends during Mr Van Pelt's absence at the river settlements

Elder Martin A Bunker and Bp Robt Gibson of St Thomas occupied the time in Sunday's services as home missionaries

Pres W L Jones and J P Anderson spent Saturday and Sunday visiting the Mesquite and Bunkerville wards

Miss Ethelyn Bennion and her mother of Taylorsville Utah are here to spend the winter

Mr and Mrs Clifford Cochran leave on the 1st for Salt Lake City to reside

The young ladies will give a Hallowe en ball here Oct 30th

Mrs Patience Lee and family have moved to Kaolin

Miss Effie Angell has gone to Salt Lake City for a visit

288

Death by Shooting

J A Swapp of Overton Nevada was here the latter part of last week on business leaving for his home Saturday afternoon Mr Swapp has recently suffered a great bereavement in the death of his son Steven A Swapp a young man in his twenty third year The young man was accidently shot while out about six miles from the Grand Gulch mine Sept 20th a charge of buck shot entering the left leg just above the knee shattering the bone The young man was driven to St Thomas thence by train to Las Vegas where surgical aid was secured it being thirty hours before he received this attention after being shot on account of distance After being attended to the young man appeared to be getting along nicely till the 28th ult when lockjaw set in and he succumbed the same day

Funeral services were held at Overton on the 30th ult

The gun from which the young man received his death wound was lying loaded in the bed of the rig in which he was riding and it is believed that in moving the things in the rig something struck the hammer of the gun discharging it

H. H. Sparks of Overton has been in Vegas several days.

W. W. Angell of Overton was registered at the Overland Tuesday last.

County Assessor Whitehead came came down from Overton Thursday evening.

MOAPA VALLEY HAPPENINGS

Items of Personal Interest from Northern Part of Clark County.

(Special Correspondence.)

Overton, Oct. 30.—A Democratic rally was held here Friday evening. Harley Harmon, Hon. Clay Tallman and Senator Levi Syphus were the speakers. Assessor S. R. Whitehead acted as chairman and local Democratic candidates occupied seats on the stage. The latter spoke here Wednesday evening.

Pres. W. L. Jones and James P. Anderson returned Monday from a visit to Bunkerville and Mesquite wards.

Miss Effie Angell went to Salt Lake City last week for a visit.

Bishop Robt. Gibson and Martin A. Bunker of St. Thomas were here to Sunday afternoon services as home missionaries.

BORN. October 30 to Mr. and Mrs. Sylvester Nay, a daughter.

Mrs. O. J. Van Pelt came over Friday with her husband and has spent the time visiting her many friends here while Mr. Van Pelt was campaigning over on the Rio Virgin.

Mrs. Patience Lee and family have moved to Kaolin to live.

Mr. and Mrs. Clifford Cochran leave on the first for Salt Lake City, where they intend to make their home.

Miss Ethelyn Benion and her mother are here from Taylorsville to enjoy our sunny winter climate.

The ladies of the Y. L. M. I. A. gave a basket Wednesday evening as a Hallowe'en ball. The hall was decorated with jack-o'lanterns.

The local county candidates held forth here last evening in an interesting Democratic rally.

290

Overton Nov 6 —The Young Men and Young Ladies M I A gave a concert here Sunday evening the numbers being given is a contest between the two associations The Judges were J P Anderson, Mrs W A Whitehead and our Primary teacher Miss Sundry They decided in favor of the young men

Election day passed off very quietly here and all are anxiously awaiting returns from the rest of the county

A circus was here Wednesday which was well attended from all parts of the valley

Mr and Mrs Luman Shurtliff of Idaho are visiting relatives here

Correct spelling should be Andersen

291

THE CIRCUS "HAS CAME"

Stupendous Aggregation of Irresistable Grandeur Exhibiting Today.

"Hark, hark, the dogs do bark,
The beggars are coming to town.
Some in rags, and some in tags,
And some in velvet gowns."

The shades of night were falling faster than really seemed necessary as the first light rigs of the stupendous aggregation of consolidated grandeur drove into town Friday evening. To say that every living creature, human or otherwise, was tired and hungry, is mild indeed.

Again, as the stroke of midnight echoed through the ambient atmosphere, the sound of strenuous voices, from which the strenuousity seemed from which the strenuousity seemed about to depart, was heard adjuring in concise terms more active movements on the part of the tired mules.

It was the circus. Oh, the gay, free, happy life! Nothing to do Friday but leave Overton before daylight and drive and pound and swear at the tired animals until they came gaily into town at all hours between midnight and morning.

Yet, with all the hardship, the bunch came to life Saturday morning and pulled the ragged tents into shape to show this evening. M. L. Clark & son are the owners, and the spirit that can combat the terrors of untraveled desert roads in addition to the usual vicissitudes of circus business, is an admirable one, even if misdirected in its energy. The outfit showed at St. George, Utah, and Bunkerville and Overton, Nevada, and will proceed from here to southern California.

The owners are gentlemen and are giving the public the worth of its money in a performance which, considering the circumstances, is very good.

293

NEWS LETTER FROM OVERTON

Death of Mrs. Sylvester Nay, Respected Resident of the Valley.

Overton, Nov. 13,—Miss Armelia Ingram left yesterday for Salt Lake City.

The primary association gave the children a Chrysanthemum Dance in the hall Friday evening. The little people attended the party in such numbers as almost to overcrowd the hall, each child wearing bouquets or wreaths of Chrysanthemums.

Mr. and Mrs. Joseph H. Jones of Delta, Utah, are here to spend the winter.

Abram Woodbury of Mesquite, Nev., was a visitor here last week.

Solon Huntsman of Mesquite was here this week with raisins for sale.

Mrs. Chas. Felt of Moapa is here this week the guest of Mrs. Racie King.

Mr. and Mrs. Horace Jones have gone to Panaca for the winter.

Mrs. Wm. McDonald of Pima, Ariz., is here visiting her parents Mr. and Mrs. John Thomas.

Mrs. Mary Lorena Nay of this place departed this life Nov. 12 and was buried today in the city cemetery. The services were held at ten o'clock today under the direction of Bishop W. A. Whitehead. Elders Fred Bischoff, Crayton Johnson and Stake Pres. W. L. Jones spoke at the services.

Mrs. Nay was the wife of Sylvester Nay and the daughter of William Perkins, Sr. and Rachel Laub and was born Oct. 4, 1888, at St. George, Utah.

On June 4, 1906, she married Sylvester Nay, and three children have been born to them, Vesta, Sylvester Burdette and Mary Ellen the youngest, being but twelve days old at the time of her death.

She is survived by her father, three sisters and six brothers, all of whom reside here. She was not thought to be seriously ill until the day before her death and her death comes as a surprise and shock to her many relatives and friends.

She was an excellent wife and mother and was loved and respected by all who know her. Mr. and Mrs. Morley Nay of Las Vegas were over to attend the funeral and will take care of the infant for the present.

294

SUMMONING THE JURORS

Sheriff Gay Serving Notice on Those Who Will Act the Next Term.

The list of grand jurors and trial jurors as drawn is published below. The Grand jury is called for November 25, on which day Judge Taber will open court. One week later, December 2, the trial jury will appear for the purpose of sitting in the trial of several criminal charges pending. The term of court will probably be a busy one, there being several important cases to be tried, one of them, at least, on a charge of murder.

Following is the grand jury, called for November 25:

J. I. Earl, Ed. Bunker, Jr., Bunkerville; A. J. Barnum, Sr., W. G. Potter, Jr., Mesquite; M. A. Bunker, St. Thomas; Aug. Koenig, Willard L. Jones, Jas. P. Anderson, Overton; Geo. C. Baldwin, Moapa; Bert Mills, Logan; A. J. Robbins, Goodsprings; Wm. C. Bright, Crescent; C. E. Burdick, J. E. Emerson, H. A. Wallbrecht, Searchlight; David Farnsworth, Jas. G. Givens, W. E. Hawkins, J. D. Kramer, Wm. Laubenheimer, D. J. O'Leary, W. S. Park, Geo. Swadener, M. C. Thomas, Las Vegas.

The following compose the trial jury, called for December 2:

Maximillian Weiss, Clark M. Alvord, Wm. J. Crozier, John Truax, Nelson; Chas. B. Huff, Chas. S. Stark, Alfred Peterson, Alfred Bley, William Kirwin, Searchlight; Chas. M. White, Jeff Davis, Crescent; A. E. Thomas, N. B. Hunter, John R. Williams, A. E. Buys, Goodsprings; David Mowery, Wm. P. Sprunt, David Conger, Moapa; Harrison Anderson, Jas. H. Robinson, Perry D. Huntsman, Logan; Albert F. Bischoff, Thomas Johnson, Fred J. Rushton, Geo. E. Perkins, Sanford A. Angell, Isaac E. Losee, John M. Lytle, Mendis D. Cooper, James W. Huntsman, Overton; Alfred L. Syphus, Robert O. Gibson, R. E. Bunker, St. Thomas; Benj. Bunker, Hector Bunker, Thos. L. Adams, Daniel L. Leavitt, Alma D. Leavitt, Harmon Wittwer, Albert Hafen, Bunkerville; Jas. E. Hughes, Edgar Leavitt, Frank S. Leavitt, Walter A. Hughes, Mesquite; B. F. Boggs, Jr., Wm. L. Helm, W. G. Morse, John S. Wisner, Robt. A. Ferguson, Warren H. Lester, A. L. J. Clark, Chas. C. Corkhill, Henry Squires, J. T. McWilliams, J. E. Westlake, Geo. R. Garwood, B. R. Jefferson, Frank Weaver, P. J. Sullivan, D. Petty, C. P. Ball, C. P. Squires, Daniel Hickey, Wm. L. Aplin, U. W. Beckley, Las Vegas.

Miss Laura Gentry of St Thomas is home from the Las Vegas high school on account of ill health

Fred Bischoff has recently completed an addition to his home of two rooms on the front

Born Nov 14 a daughter to Mr and Mrs O B Grissom all concerned doing nicely

296

Some Sweet Spud.

Willard L. Jones brought down from Overton some famous sweet potatoes, one speciman weighing six pounds and another five. The five pound tuber may be seen in the window at the Age office. These beautiful specimens from the vegetable kingdom are astonishing to those who are not informed on the wonderful productiveness of the soil of the Moapa Valley and of various portions of Clark County.

Albert F. Bischoff of Overton, is a member of the jury in attendance on court this week.

John M. Lytle of Overton, who is in this city on jury duty is registered at the Overland.

Geo. E. Perkins, one of the best known of Overton's citizens, is spending the week in this city greeting his many friends and attending court as a juryman.

Thomas Johnson and James W. Huntsman of Overton, are among those serving on the trial jury panel this week.

Levi Syphus, former state senator from Lincoln County, was in this city Friday night, leaving for St. Thomas this morning.

Basket Ballers Still Jubilating Over Their Victory at Las Vegas.

(Special Correspondence.)

Bunkerville, Dec. 2.—The high school students are very much elated over their victory at Las Vegas Thanksgivings day. The boys were given a chocolate supper on their return by the high school girls. They are working hard to keep in shape for the coming game with Overton.

Ira J. Ear returned home last night from Logan, Utah, where he has been attending the agricultural college for the past two years.

J. M. Whiting, principal of the district school here, and Miss Irene Cox Whiting of this place have just returned from St. George, Utah, where they were married Friday, Nov. 29.

Funeral services were held here Sunday morning over the remains of an infant son of Mr. and Mrs. J. N. Hunt. Measles were given as the cause of the death. The other cases in the town are about all well. It is hoped that there will be no more deaths.

The quarterly conference of the Moapa Stake is to held at Overton instead of Bunkerville December 7 and 8, on account of the sickness at the latter.

The water is still out and people are hauling water from the river for drinking purposes.

A light shower fell last night, just enough to settle the dust and liven the grain, which is just beginning to show above the ground.

298

NEWS NOTES FROM OVERTON

Items of interest of Doings in the Moapa Valley Community.

(Special Correspondence.)

BORN: November 17, a daughter, to Mr. and Mrs. O. B. Grissom, all concerned doing nicely.

Fred Bischoff has recently completed an addition to his home of two rooms on the front.

Mrs. Louisa Nay was here a few days last week. She returned Friday to Las Vegas, taking with her the two older children of her son, Sylvester Nay.

Miss Laura Gentry of St. Thomas is home from the Las Vegas high school on account of ill health.

Mr. McQuaid of Searchlight is here visiting his sister-in-law, Mrs. Martha Fleming. He will probably bring his family here for the winter.

Prof. Hickman of the B. Y. U. at Logan, Utah, was here several days last week to visit his son, Leonidas Hickman, who is principal of our schools, and to deliver a series of lectures. He spoke here Saturday evening on "The Effects of Stimulants;" to the Parents' Class Sunday morning on "The Development of the Child;" Sunday evening on "The Early History of the Mormon People;" Monday afternoon to school children, parents and visitors from the Logan school on "The Inventions of the Last One Hundred Years," and on Monday evening he gave an answer to I. C. Riley's book, "Joseph Smith an Epileptic." On Sunday afternoon he spoke at St. Thomas. His lectures were well attended and very much appreciated.

Overton Dec 9 —The quarterly conferei ce of the Moapa Stake con vened here last Saturday and Sun day It was to have been held in Bunkerville but was change l owing to an epidemic of measles in that place Dr James Talmage and Bp O P Miller were in attendance from Salt Lake City The attendance from all parts of the valley was very good considering the cold windy days of the confuence but very light from other war ls of the Stake All wards except the Alamo w nd were reported by mail bishops ex cept the Mesquite ward which was represented by Lewis Pulsipher Patriarch Tho J Jones the presi l ency of the stale and a majority of the members of the high council were in attendance Four sessions of the conference were held al o a priesthood meeting and a Sunday evening session The instructions given were timely and appreciatel as may be realized when it is known that some of our people have lived here to see a visit from a member of the quorum of the Twelve once in twenty seven years. Dr Talmage returned on Monday but Bp Miller remained over one day on business connected with the Church land at Kaolin

The Mutual Improvement Assn put on a play here Saturday evening "Jack Travers" the following having a part in it: Misses Clara Perkins and Mildred Anderson Mr and Mrs W A Whitehead Leon Hickman Clayton Johnson Ben Robinson and N Ray Pixton

Francis N Bunker lately of old Mexico came down last week from Delta Utah and has spent several days visiting relatives and friends in the valley. He went over to Bunkerville Monday with Bp Cox of that place

The following were here Saturday and Sunday to attend State Conference: Bp Edward Cox of Bunkerville Lewis Pulsipher of Mesquite Bp Robt Gibson of St Thomas and Bp Wadsworth of Panaca

A number of the jurors who have been in Las Vegas this week attending court were over Saturday to attend one day of conference returning to Las Vegas Sunday

Mrs Henry Henzie and Miss Henzie of northern Utah have moved down to Kaolin. Mr Henze has been there for some months

Mrs Ellen Gentry of St Thomas is in Salt Lake with her two children Laura and Osborne for medical treatment

Mr and Mrs Jos H Jorgane are located at the K enig ranch where they have employment

Mrs Baldwin of the upper Muddy spent several days here last week the guest of Mrs Joe F Perkins

Albert Jones and Sherman Thomas are out on the Grand Gulch road and have been for some time

Warren Cox of St George is here on business this week.

301

Correct Spelling should be Andersen

Sundry Cases in Court.

Several minor matters came before the court at various times the past week as follows:

In Estate of W. W. Lowe, deceased; on petition of W. R. Thomas, administrator, decree of distribution was entered, distributing to Belle M. Lowe a life interest, with the remainder in fee to Vinnie M. Heartwell, the following:

S.E. 1-4 section 2, 20 S. 61 E. and lots 17, 18, 19 in block 6 Clark's Las Vegas Townsite.

In Estate of Jos. M. Woodward deceased,

On petition of J. E. Emerson administrator of said estate, the final account was settled and allowed.

Hass, Baruch & Co., vs Moapa Investment Co.

Demurrer overruled and defendant ordered to answer forthwith.

In re. writ of Certeroria against A. L. F. MacDermott, Justice of the Peace of Overton township. The witnesses were examined and the case was argued and submitted.

302

WHAT'S DOING AT OVERTON

Budget of News Items from the Moapa Valley Section.

(Special Correspondence.)

Mrs. Baldwin of the upper Muddy spent several days here last week, the guest of Mrs. Joe F. Perkins.

A number of jurors who have been in Las Vegas this week attending court were over Saturday to attend one day of conference, returning to Las Vegas Sunday.

The Mutual Improvement put on a play here Saturday evening, "Jack Travers," the following taking part in the play: Misses Clara Perkins and Mildred Anderson, Mr. and Mrs. W. A. Whitehead, Leon Hickman, Crayton Johnson, Ben Robinson and N. Ray Pixton.

Mrs. Patience Lee of Kaolin has recently purchased a carpet loom and is prepared to do weaving at her home.

Albert Jones and Sherman Thomas are out on the Grand Gulch road and have been for some time.

Miss Henzie and Mrs. Henry Henzie of northern Utah have moved down to Kaolin. Mr. Henzie has been there for some months.

The following were here Saturday and Sunday to attend stake conference: Bishop Edward Cox of Bunkerville, Lewis Pulsifer of Mesquite, Bishop Robert Gibson of St. Thomas and Bishop Wadsworth of Panaca.

Warren Cox is here on business this week.

Mr. and Mrs. Jos. H. Jones are located at the Koenig ranch, where they have employment.

Francis N. Bunker, lately of old Mexico, came down from Delta, Utah, and has spent several days visiting relatives and friends in the valley. He went over to Bunkerville Monday with Bishop Cox of that place.

Miss Ellen Gentry of St. Thomas is in Salt Lake City with her children, Laura and Osborne, for medical treatment.

The quarterly conference of the Mo-

303

apa Stake convened here last Saturday and Sunday. It was to have been held in Bunkerville, but was changed owing to an epidemic of measles in that place. Dr. James Talmage and Bishop O. P. Miller were in attendance from Salt Lake City.

The attendance from all parts of the valley was very good, considering the cold windy days of the conference, but very light from the other wards of the stake. All wards except the Alamo ward were reported by ward bishops except the Mesquite ward, which was represented by Lewis Pulsifer. Patriarch Thos. J. Jones, the presidency of the stake, and a majority of the members of the high council were in attendance.

Four sessions of the conference were held, also a priesthood meeting and a Sunday evening session. The instructions given were timely and appreciated, as may be realized when it is known that some of our people have lived here to see a visit from a member of the quorum of the Twelve, once in twenty-seven years.

Dr. Talmage returned on Monday, but Bishop Miller remained over one day on business connected with the church land at Kaolin.

OVERTON

Overton Dec 18 —For the ac
commodation of travel in and out of
the valley, the railroad company is
running a motor car daily between
Moapa and St Thomas which con
nects with both the north and south
bound trains at Moapa

W H McDonald and brothers
Clarence and Charles arrived here
this week from Pima Ariz and
will remain for some time to work
on land which they have here

Jos I Earl and daughter Winona
passed through here Saturday The
latter is returning home from Las
Vegas where she has been attending
the county high school

Mr and Mrs John Perkins are
in Salt Lake where they went last
week to take their daughter Jessie
for medical treatment

A son was born Dec 12th to Mr
and Mrs S R Wells at St Thomas
all concerned doing nicely

Miss Zilla Peterson has returned
home for the Christmas holidays
from Las Vegas

305

WHAT'S DOING AT OVERTON

Budget of News Items from the Moapa Valley Section.

(Special Correspondence.)

Overton, Dec. 18.—For the accomodation of travelers in and out of the valley the railroad company is running a motor car daily between Moapa and St. Thomas, which connects with both the north and south bound trains at Moapa.

A son was born December 12 to Mr. and Mrs. S. R. Wells at St. Thomas. All concerned are doing nicely.

W. H. McDonald and brothers, Clarence and Charles, arrived from Pima, Ariz., and will remain for some time to work on land which they have here.

Jos. I. Earl and daughter, Winona, passed through here Saturday. The latter is returning home from Las Vegas where she has been attending the county high school.

Miss Zilla Peterson has returned home for the Christmas holidays from Las Vegas.

Mr. and Mrs. John Perkins are in Salt Lake where they went last week to take their daughter, Jessie, for medical treatment.

Judge A. L. F. MacDermott of Overton spent several days this week in Las Vegas on business.

306

Overton Dec 26 — The usual midwinter excitement about mines in this locality has come a little stronger than usual this time Crayton Johnson and some others have found a prospect about eight miles west of town which gives rich returns in silver and some gold and for several days excitement has run high The ledge for miles and adjacent property is fast being covered by locations and a crowd of prospectors are constantly in the vicinity There are also a number of other claims that bid fair to bring rich returns

The motor car is giving us service which is very much appreciated although a ride in an open car is rather cold at this season On Dec 24th it was necessary to make two trips down from Moapa to accommodate all the passengers about 15 in number Among those coming in on that day were Mis Harry Gentry and daughter Laura and son Osborne also Mr and Mis John Perkins who were returning home from Salt Lake City

George Lytle and Miss Clara Perkins both of this place surprised their friends last week by slipping over to the county seat and being married on the 23rd They returned the following day Miss Perkins place as Hello Girl in the telephone office is being filled by her sister Miss Sadie Perkins

The primary children were treated to a dance on Monday evening the donors being the McDonald orchestra and the Shurtliff Bros The little people enjoyed the dance and were out enmasse

Ellis Turnbeaugh left Monday for northern Nevada where he has employment He was released as stake clerk at the December conference and N Ivy Pixton was chosen to fill the vacancy

Don McFate of Pima Ariz came up with the McDonald boys and is a member of the McDonald orchestra that is furnishing us some splendid music for the Christmas parties and dances

Mrs Emma Cox of Logan Utah and her daughters Mis Lu Emma Clark and Miss Virginia also her son David are visiting old friends and their many relatives here

Miss Ruby Laub of St George and Miss Booth who is teaching school

days Miss Booth is the guest of
Miss Ethelin Bennion

On Christmas night there was a
dance in the hall There was a
huge crowd out and everybody had
a merry time

Jos Hatch of Tropic Utah, is
here to spend holidays with his sis
ters Mrs Etta Swapp and Parmela
Losee

Mis Lottie Hansen Miss Alice
Lewis and Ralph Leavitt went over
to Bunkerville to spend the holidays

The Overton Relief society gave a
program and lunch in the school
house on Christmas eve

Miss Mattison of Payson Utah
is here the guest of her brother in
law Fred Rushton

George Whitney and son are here
from St George Utah

Las Vegas Age Newspaper
December 28, 1912

Exhibit of Products.

In the exhibit maintained by the
Chamber of Commerce at the depot
there is a wide variety of products.
Even a resident of Vegas, familiar as
he may be with the possibilities of this
section, is astonished at what is from
time to time shown there. A few days
ago we observed the following things,
all Vegas grown and of a quality to
equal the best of any country.

Peaches, apricots and figs in glass
jars, prepared by Mrs. C. P. Ball.

Beautiful apples from the Cottonwood ranch.

Kaffir corn from the Park ranch.

Broom corn of fine quality.

Lettuce, cauliflower and tomatoes
from the Ed. VonTobel ranch.

Pears from the Stewart ranch.

Field corn (second crop raised on same soil) from D. F. Watson's Colorado river ranch.

Sweet potatoes, ten pounds to one plant, raised by W. S. Park.

Chile peppers by Mrs. Gamble.

Three exhibits of cotton raised by Helen J. Stewart, Mrs. G. H. French and Mrs. J. G. Givens respectively.

Apples by Ira MacFarland at Indian Springs.

Sweet potato weighing 6 pounds, by Willard L. Jones at Overton.

Two varieties of kaffir corn state experiment station at Logan.

Also two varieties of corn, cucumbers, squash, watermelons and pomegranates not labeled.

This exhibit is in charge of Mr. C. P. Ball, who is taking much interest in keeping it in shape. Any one having products to show should notify Mr. Ball.

MOAPA VALLEY NEWS ITEMS

Happenings of the Holiday Week. Young Couple Steal a March.

(Special Correspondence.)

Overton, Nev., Dec. 26.—Miss Lottie Hansen, Miss Alise Lewis and Ralph Leavitt went over to Bunkerville to spend the holidays.

Ellis Turnbaugh left Monday for northern Nevada, where he has employment. He was released as stake clerk at the December conference and N. Ray Pixton was chosen to fill the vacancy.

George Lytle and Miss Clara Perkins, both of this place, surprised their friends last week by slipping over to the county seat and being married on the 23rd. They returned the following day. Miss Perkins' place as "hello girl" in the telephone office is being filled by her sister, Miss Sadie Perkins.

Jos. Hatch of Tropic, Utah, is here to spend the holidays with his sisters, Miss Etta Swapp and Parmela Losee.

Miss Mattison of Payson, Utah, is here, the guest of her brother-in-law, Fred Rushton.

Don McFate of Pima, Ariz., came up with the McDonald boys, and is a member of the McDonald orchestra, which is furnishing us some splendid music for the Christmas parties and dances.

Miss Ruby Laub of St. George and Miss Booth, who is teaching school at Bunkerville, are here for the holidays. Miss Booth is the guest of Miss Ethelin Bennison.

Mrs. Emma Cox of Logan, Utah, and her daughters, Mrs. Lu Emma Clark and Miss Virginia, also her son, David, are visiting old friends and their many relatives here.

The motor car is giving us service which is much appreciated, although the ride in an open car is rather cold at this season. On December 24 it was necessary to make two trips down from Moapa to accomodate all the passengers, about fifteen in number. Among those coming in on that day were Mrs. Harry Gentry and daughter, Laura, and son, Osborne, also Mr. and Mrs. John Perkins, who were returning home from Salt Lake City.

George Whitney and son are here from St. George, Utah.

The primary children were treated to a dance on Monday evening, the donors being the McDonald orchestra and the Shurtliff brothers, the owners of the hall. The little people enjoyed the dance and were out en masse.

The Overton Relief Society gave a program and lunch in the school house on Christmas eve.

On Christmas night there was a dance in the hall. There was a large crowd out and everybody had a merry time.

The usual midwinter excitement about mines in this locality has come a little stronger than usual this winter. Crayton Johnson and some others have found a prospect about eight miles west of town which gives rich returns in silver and some gold and for several days the excitement has run high. The ledge for miles and adjacent property is fast being covered by locations and a crowd of prospectors are constantly in the vicinity. There are also a number of other claims that bid fair to bring rich returns.

VIRGIN VALLEY NEWS NOTES

Cupid Again Invades Ranks of School Teachers at Bunkerville.

(Special Correspondence.)

Bunkerville, Jan. 6.—Hoder (the blind god of winter) has not forgotten to visit this sunny land. The thermometer stands at 12 and 18 degrees below freezing. Every one seems to have a cold. The river is almost frozen over and great blocks of ice are floating down the small channel that remains unfrozen.

The holidays passed off quietly here. There were plenty of dances and day sports for those who wished to attend them. Perhaps the most interesting game of the holidays was the one played between the married men and the single boys of the two towns, Bunkerville and Mesquite, the score being 17 to 18 in favor of the married men.

Leroy Haffen, who has been attending school at St. George, came home for the holidays, bringing with him his sister, Miss Ella Haffen of Santa Clara. They returned home last Thursday.

Young men with ability to teach wishing to get married apply at once to the school trustees of Bunkerville, for it seems that those who come here single never leave alone. Mr. Paul Miner, the high school teacher, and Miss Ethel Bunker of this place were married at St. George December 20th and spent their holidays and honeymoon at the bridegroom's home in Springville, Utah.

The stork and Santa made a joint visit to the home of W. C. Bowman Christmas day, leaving among other presents a baby boy.

J. I. Earl leaves this week with fifty colonies of bees, which he intends to locate at Overton.

312

Overton, Feb 7.—The stockholders of the Moapa Valley Irrigation Co. met here Feb 1 and the following were elected board of directors: Robert O Gibson, F F. Heintz, W W. Muir, Mr. Foxley and W. L Jones,

Mr and Mrs Warren Cox of St. George left here the 1st enroute to the coast.

S H Wells is in Salt Lake City on business.

Overton, Feb 15.—The many friends here of Sylvester Nay were pained to learn that his infant daughter May, died from pneumonia Monday last at Las Vegas, where Mr. Nay had taken his children to the care of his mother, since the death of his wife last November

Mrs Sanford Angell is in southern California to visit her son Bert and daughter, Mrs Minnie Koenig A baby girl has recently come to the home of the latter.

Mrs Isaiah Cox of the upper Moapa valley came down Sunday for a few days to visit with friends She was the guest of Mrs Martha Fleming while here.

Mr. and Mrs Albert Jones have sold their home in "Strington" and will move onto their farm east of Overton townsite soon

Leland, the infant son of Mr and Mrs. W. L Batty, has been very sick with pneumonia this week but is now much better

Mr and Mrs. Orrn Jarvis have a son, born last week in Las Vgas All concerned doing nicely.

There was a Valentine dance here on the 14th.

Edwin Jones of Gunlock was here this week.

313

AGRICULTURAL DEMONSTRATION

Train Will be in Las Vegas on Tuesday the 25th of February.

The annual tour of the demonstration train operated jointly by the Utah Agricultural College and the Salt Lake Route will commence its journey this year on February 18th at the city of Tooele. From there the tour will extend westward as far as Las Vegas, stopping at all principal points along the line of the Salt Lake Route and making a detour over the new branch of railway into the Moapa Valley, with a day's stop at Overton, Nevada.

On Tuesday, February 25th, this train will be at Las Vegas, where it will be open to public inspection and where a series of meetings will be held to which everyone who is interested in the development of our section of the state is invited to be present.

The personnel of the party accompanying this train comprises several of the most experienced demonstrators and lecturers along the various lines of western development. The principal representative of the agricultural college will be Dr. E. G. Peterson, director of the college's extension division, who will be heard both in lectures and demonstrations.

The live stock features will be attended to by Prof. John T. Caine, III, superintendent of farmers' institutes and professor of animal husbandry.

Mr. H. E. McCartney, dairy expert of the college's extension division, will give daily demonstrations and lectures.

Hon. Ben R. Eldredge, president of the Utah Dairymen's Association, will present the dairying question from its practical side.

Mr. Edward W. Bowling, the college demonstrator, will make his third tour with the demonstration train and will be in charge of the exhibits. Mr. Gottlieb Smith, of the college staff, will have charge of the selected live stock which the train will carry.

The Salt Lake Route will be practically represented on the train by Professor S. E. Merrill, who has lately entered this railroad's official family as agricultural expert of the Clark system of railways.

Professor Merrill, in addition to his various lectures on the tour, will devote his time to the dissemination of information and advice regarding agricultural and horticultural possibilities of the various sections visited.

The train will be in charge of Mr.

314

Douglas White, industrial agent of the Salt Lake Route.

Dr. J. A. Widtsoe, president of the Utah Agricultural College, has promised to devote sufficient time to visit several of the important points at which the train will stop.

The train itself will be one of the most complete exhibits that has ever been sent over the lines of the Salt Lake Route, particular attention being given during the present tour to the question of "More and Better Live Stock."

The cars of the train will contain exhaustive exhibits of feeds, forage, complete modern dairy equipment, models of farm buildings, including barns, dairy, milk house, hog house, a model silo with silage, butter and cheese exhibit, "a clean dairy" demonstration, an exhibit of bacteria of the dairy, together with many other features, every one of which will be of deep interest to all visitors. There will also be illustrations and charts for the demonstration of all practical dairy questions.

During the day when the train will be at Las Vegas the cars will be open for constant inspection and demonstration except during the hours when lectures are being given either in the lecture coach accompanying the train or in a place selected by the local committee of arrangements.

The various tours of the Salt Lake Route demonstration train have been most successful along the line of practical education and information and the 1913 tour with all of its new special features will add materially to the good work which has been done in the past.

Las Vegas Age Newspaper
February 22, 1913

Joe F. Perkins of Overton spent several days in this city during the week, being registered at the Overland.

BABCOCK BOOSTS BASKET BALL

Clark County Candidate's Championship Cup Contemplates Continued Competion.

"Bab" sure made good, even if some small number of unfeeling voters did put the little stamp in the wrong place. During his campaign for the assembly last fall Mr. J. E. Babcock announced that he intended to present a handsome silver cup to the schools of the county to promote competition among the basket ball teams.

Last Friday night "Bab" arrived from Eldorado Canyon and the big part of his baggage consisted of one silver cup too large for a suds scuttle and just too small for a hoisting bucket. Closer inspection develops the fact that the affair sports three handles, which, in either of the above cases, would seem to be unnecessary.

The cup is a beautiful and artistic silver affair, standing upon a large ebony base, the whole being about 18 inches high. The three sides of the cup are handsomely inscribed, the principal face reading:

"EMBLEMATIC OF THE BASKET BALL CHAMPIONSHIP OF CLARK COUNTY."

On another side is the dedication:

"DEDICATED TO CLEAN SPORT AND CLEAN LIVING."

The terms of the competition are briefly set forth on the third face as follows:

"To be held each year by the winner of the Annual County Series and to become the Permanent Trophy of the team which shall so win it thrice."

Below this is left space for the inscription of the name of winning team each year.

The cup will be known as the Babcock Basket Ball Cup and is now on exhibition in the window of the Bank. It will surely prove a strong incentive to the young people of the Clark County schools to promote "clean sport and clean living."

This incident will doubtless go down in history as the one case where a defeated candidate carried out his pre-election promises just the same as though he had been elected (and a democrat at that.)

The Overton High School, Bunkerville and the Clark County High are the three schools composing the Basket Ball League. Players, according to the rules adopted, must be under 21 years age, must abstain from intoxicants and tobacco during the year he plays, and those in high schools must conform to inter-scholastic scholarship requirements.

316

O. W. Jarvis, superintendent of the state experiment farm at Logan, came down last night to visit the wife and new baby, Gordon Young Jarvis. He happily finds them so much improved that he plans to take them home with him tomorrow. Incidentally Mr. Jarvis has left with the editor of the AGE a few pounds of selected Dwarf Milo seed for free distribution to those who desire it. A full description of this product will be printed in the AGE of next week through the courtesy of Mr. Jarvis.

N. Ray Pixton of Overton came down to the county seat Friday last.

NEWS ITEMS FROM OVERTON

Chronicle of Happenings in the Hustling Muddy Valley Community.

(Special Correspondence.)

Overton, Feb. 21.—The weather has changed considerably the past week, slight snow falling and cold north winds continuing.

Joe F. Perkins and Bryant Whitmore have returned from Las Vegas, where they went on business.

Doctor Beale from Utah has purchased a lot in the heart of our beautiful little town and intends locating here. We are glad to welcome such a useful and clever man into our valley.

The Young Ladies M. I. A. presented a play on the 20th, entitled, "Dr. Danby," which was a decided success and gave credit to the actors for their high talent. Those who took part were Misses Sadie and Vivien Perkins, Armelia Ingram, Mildred Anderson, Mrs. P. Losee and Chicken Dotson. Following the play was a farewell party in honor of Richard Cooper, who leaves for a mission to the southern states on the 26th. Lunch was served at 11:30 and an enjoyable time was had by the large crowd in attendance.

Mrs. Guy Gardner of St. Thomas has been very ill, but by the aid of our able physician she is now on the road to recovery.

Whitmore Bros. are shipping some fine ore from their Copper and Silver Belt, near Gold Butte.

In spite of the week of cold weather the trees are putting on their green mantle and fruit trees are blooming. It is feared that some fruit will be frozen.

Our daily motor system is doing good business, with many passengers to and fro daily.

A number of strangers are among us for the purpose of renting and buying land on which to raise cantaloupes.

317

Overton, Mar. 1.—The Salt Lake Route Industrial and Educational Train came in last Sunday evening, Feb 23 There was a short meeting held that evening and one the next afternoon and evening On the morning of the 24th the train went to St Thomas, returning at noon; it was met by the school children and a large company of farmers who visited the exhibit and witnessed the stock judging at the train The lectures were well attended from all parts of the valley and surrounding towns

Harold and Milton Earl, Hugh Bunker, Thos. D Leavitt and Mr Darling were over from Bunkerville to attend the lectures and exhibits of the Industrial Train

Mr. and Mrs E. I Cox were here a few days this week, the guests of Mr and Mrs. W. L Jones

Mrs Guy Gardner, who has been seriously ill for several weeks, is now much better.

Mrs. Brig Whitmore is here from Centerville, Utah, visiting relatives

S H Wells is ill with pneumonia at his home in St Thomas

We were favored with a fine rain this week

FROM OVER OVERTON WAY

Valley is Throbbing With the Impulse of Returning Spring.

(Special Correspondence.)

Beautiful spring weather is with us; fruit trees are blooming and fields getting green. The nights are somewhat chilly, but the days are warm with sunshine.

Truman O. Angell with his bride of three months is at home again greeting his many friends after an absence of several months.

Mrs. George Whitney is slowly recovering from a severe attack of pneumonia.

Mrs. Minerva Cochran recently returned from Salt Lake City and is visiting with relatives and friends and enjoying the old home again.

Doctor Beale is kept very busy of late, as considerable sickness prevails in our valley in the nature of colds and pneumonia. Mrs. Beale is expected to arrive soon.

S. R. Whitehead with several of his employees returned from the Copper Mountain mine, where they are busy getting out ore and shipping the same as fast as teams can haul it to the shipping point at St. Thomas.

Mrs. Brig Whitmore and children from Centerville, Utah, are visiting relatives here. Mr. Whitmore is out near Gold Butte working his mine. He has shipped several loads of ore and expects to do greater work soon.

Samuel H. Wells of St. Thomas has been so ill with pneumonia it was necessary to call Dr. Beale in several times to handle the case. He is reported to be convalescing nicely.

Overton, Mar 18.—The cosy little cottage recently built by Mrs Rachel King on Main street burned to the ground last evening Mrs. King and the children were at her father's home nearby when the fire was first noticed It was impossible by the time help arrived to save anything as the flames had gained such headway fanned by the wind from the south All houses in the path of the wind for two blocks had to be watched from the burning brands that flew in the wind. A small millinery shop nearby, also belonging to Mrs King, was burned. It was a six room frame building with bath and porches, One of the most modern homes in the valley. Mrs King carried insurance to the amount of $1600 on the building, which will not cover the entire loss

320

Ruben, The little son of W. L Batty, was cut on the wrist by a piece of glass last Saturday, making a gash that bled quite badly. Mr. and Mrs Batty were at Cane Springs ranch at the time A doctor was called who put in five stitches in closing up the wound The parents returned home Saturday.

The Panaca basket ball team arrived here Friday evening to play a matched game with the Overton team. They played Saturday evening, the score being 39 to 9 in favor of Overton. The game was followed by a dance.

Dr. John T. Miller, editor of the Character Builder, was here last week and delivered a number of lectures He also spent a couple of days at St. Thomas

Bp Wm Whitehead is out to Copper Mountain on business connected with the mine, which has been leased to the Whitehead Bros

Bp Jos. I Earl and son Marion are over from Bunkerville doing work on their lot here and looking after their bees

The ladies of the Relief society gave a surprise party on the 17th to Mrs. Susan Johnson.

Miss Thirza Leavitt is here from Bunkerville

ACTIVITIES IN MOAPA VALLEY

Preparations Being Made to Build a Flour Mill at Overton.

(Special Correspondence.)

Overton, March 17.—In spite of the cold nights which still prevail the days are warm and beautiful, causing the alfalfa fields to become green and vegetables more plentiful. It is feared that the freezing point the past few nights has destroyed some fruit.

Mrs. Horace Jones of Jean, Nevada, is visiting with relatives and many friends in the valley.

W. A. Whitehead is out at Copper Mine, looking after his mining property in that section. He now has about ten employees getting out ore for shipment.

Jim McQuaid and Crayton Johnson left for Copper Mountain to work recently. The silver strike west of town is now something of the past, and the owners seek riches elsewhere.

A successful operation was performed on the hand of Fay Perkins at 10:30 Sunday morning by Doctor Beale, assisted by Mrs. Beale and Mrs. Virginia Lytle. The hand was badly infected, but at present is improving nicely.

Friday and Saturday nights were quite interesting features of the week, a basket ball game and dance being the event of Friday evening. The game was played between the scrub team and the regulars, the latter being winners.

Saturday night an interesting game between the Panaca, Lincoln County, team and the Overton regulars was played, with a score of 39 to 9 in favor of Overton. The game passed off nicely, followed by a grand ball in which a large and merry crowd participated. The Panaca team not being used to indoor playing, and on a ball room floor, stood no show with the Overton leaders in winning the game. However, their visit was enjoyed, and we hope they will come again.

322

Strangers from the north country are in and around town making surveys for a flour mill site. Much rumor is reported to the effect of the same, and hands are busy clearing land for that purpose. The people are delighted with the idea of a flour mill, so badly needed in this section of the country.

Fay Anderson is home again greeting his many friends after an absence of seven months, which time he has spent at school studying music in Manti, Utah.

The little son of W. L. Batty severed an artery by falling on broken glass while at Moapa. The wound was a deep one on the wrist. Dr. Beale was called and dressed the wound, and the little lad is feeling fine so far.

The ladies of the Relief Society Club gave a nice party on St. Patrick's Day at the home of Annie J. Cooper in honor of her invalid mother, Mrs. Susan Johnson. The crowd took lunch, and a dainty meal was enjoyed by all present, and a social good time. Mrs. Johnson has been paralized in the left side for ten years, but enjoyed the faces of the kind donors.

Overton. Apr. 6 —The planting of cantaloupes is about through with in the valley now; a very large acerage has been planted. The asparagus crop is now being harvested. A daily service on the railroad is very much needed for this crop It is expected that a large gasoline car will soon be put on the line, for a week or more the passenger traffic has made it necessary to make as many as four trips in one day.

The Overton basket ball team went to Panaca for a game on the 29th of March. They again scored a victory, the score being 14 to 10 in favor of Moapa Valley. The boys stayed over Sunday to attend Y. M. and Y. L M. I A. convention there Leon Hickman, N. Ray Paxton, and the Misses Sadie and Vivian Perkins accompanied the ball team.

The following are in Salt Lake City during conference week, Mrs Ellen Gentry and son Osborne, Mrs Lizzie Gibson, Albert Frehner and son, Pres L Jones, Bp Jos I Earl and Mrs. Sevilla H. Jones The latter is a member of the stake primary board and will remain to take the primary course; also Bp F Hienze and daughter Florence of Kaolin

Mrs John Thomas of Logan, who has had poor health for some time left Tuesday for Salt Lake City for treatment Dr. Beal, her husband and her daughter and Mrs Nora McDonald, accompanied her.

Benjamin Robison and Miss Mildred Anderson also Ralph Leavitt and Miss Alise Lewis were among those who left for Salt Lake City on the 1st The young couples will be married before returning.

Fred Rushton and his sister-in-law Miss Vetus Mattison have gone to Salt Lake City; the latter is returning to her home in Payson after having spent the winter in the valley.

Milton Earl of Bunkerville and Leo Hardy of Mesquite returned to their homes last week The latter has been freighting on the Gulch road.

The young ladies have put up a basket ball outfit and expect to practice regularly these fine spring days

Jos. Ingram of this place was married this week at Kanarra, Utah, to Mrs Woods of that place.

Norman Shurtliff and his sister Miss Sylvia are in Moapa to teach the Indian school there.

Sylvester Nay came over from Las Vegas last week and is working at Capalapa

The Primary association gave an entertainment Thursday evening in the hall.

James Huntsman has recently added a couple of rooms to his home.

Las Vegas Age Newspaper
April 12, 1913

MacDermott Affirmed.

Judge Taber has handed down a decision in certiorari in the case of W. M. Smith, plaintiff and petitioner, vs. A. L. F. MacDermott, justice of the peace of Overton township, defendant and respondent, affirming the proceedings in the justice court in the case of J. R. McDonough vs. W. M. Smith.

Stevens & Van Pelt appeared for plaintiff and petitioner and Richard Busteed for defendant and respondent.

Washington County News
April 25, 1913

Overton, April 25.—The family and friends of Benson W. West were very much surprised by his sudden death on Tuesday afternoon. He had not been ill, except a touch of rheumatism in his right side and was irrigating in the lot by his home when he fell dead, caused by rheumatism of the heart. No one of the family was at home at the time, but his little son, Averett returning from Primary found him lying there with the shovel on his arm. He had only been dead a short time as he saw seen in one of the stores down town about an hour before his death. Mr. West came here in November, 1912, with his wife and family of seven children from Blackfoot, Idaho, where he has resided for 17 years, for a number of years he had worked in the hardware store of Niel F Boyle & Co They moved to Moapa Valley thinking the change of climate would better the health of his wife and oldest son. Funeral services were held on the 23rd, Elder Jesse F. Cooper and Bp Whitehead being the speakers. Interment was made in the Overton cemetery. Mr

West was an affectionate husband and father and an examplary citizen and has made many friends during his short stay in Moapa valley who sympathize with the bereaved family.

A number of the lady friends of Mrs Elizabeth Anderson, president of the ladies relief society, gave her a pleasant surprise on Thursday afternoon

Mrs Sarah Thomas is much improved in health since her return from Salt Lake City several weeks ago.

Pres John M. Bunker and Stake Clerk N. Ray Pixton have gone to visit the Alamo ward.

Elmer Losee and S R Whitehead returned Monday from a visit to Panaca ward.

Frank Spencer, jr., late of Provo, Utah, but now of Los Angeles is here

Correct spelling should be Andersen

325

Overton vs. Vegas.

Base ball will again be instituted in Vegas when the Overton nine meets the Vegas aggregation at the ball grounds Sunday afternoon. The game bids fair to be a good one. The Overton boys will make an effort to keep their string of victories intact, they having beaten the Vegas boys on the visit of the latter to Overton a year ago.

It is hoped that this game may arouse sufficient interest so that a team may be organized in Goodsprings, in which case a series of games would be played by the Southern Nevada League, consisting of the teams at Goldfield, Tonopah, Overton, Goodsprings and Las Vegas. Let everybody turn out in the interest of good base ball.

326

Las Vegas Age Newspaper
May 3, 1913

NEWS LETTER FROM OVERTON

Highly Respected Resident of the Moapa Valley Dies Suddenly.

(Special Correspondence.)

Overton, April 25.—Mrs. Sarah Thomas is much improved in health since her return from Salt Lake City several weeks ago.

Pres. John M. Bunker and Stake Clerk N. Ray Pixton have gone to visit the Alamo ward.

A number of the lady friends of Mrs. Elizabeth Anderson, president of the Ladies' Relief Society, gave her a pleasant surprise on Thursday afternoon.

Elmer Losee and S. R. Whitehead returned Monday from a visit to the Panaca ward.

Frank Spencer, Jr., late of Provo, Utah, but now of Los Angeles, is here soliciting stock for a company to manufacture and sell the Little Wonder Button Sewer, an attachment for a sewing machine which will sew on buttons, hooks and eyes, etc.

The family and friends of Ransom W. West were very much surprised by his sudden death on Tuesday afternoon. He had not been ill except for a touch of rheumatism in his right side, and was irrigating in the lot by his home when he fell dead, caused by rheumatism of the heart. No one of the family was at home at the time, but his little son, Averett, returning from primary found him lying there with the shovel on his arm. He had only been dead a short time, as he was seen in one of the stores down town about an hour before his death.

The correct spelling should be Andersen

Mr. West came here in November, 1912, with his wife and family of seven children from Blackfoot, Idaho, where he had resided for seventeen years. For a number of years he worked in the hardware store of Niel F. Boyle & Co. He moved to Moapa Valley thinking the change of climate would better the health of his wife and oldest son. Funeral services were held on the 23rd. Elder Jessie F. Cooper and Bishop Whitehead were the speakers. Interment was in the Overton cemetery.

Mr. West was an affectionate husband and father and an exemplary citizen and has made many friends during his short stay in Moapa Valley who sympathize with the bereaved family.

School Notes.

An event of interest in Goldfield school circles was the declamation contest held last Wednesday at the high school. The winner in the contest will have the honor of representing the school in the state contest to be held at the University in Reno on May 9.

The children of the Mason schools are to give the operetta, "Gyp Junior," on May 9 for the benefit of the children's playground.

State Superintendent John Edwards Bray visited the Fernley schools recently. He advised enlarging the present building to accommodate high school students who would otherwise be obliged to leave home for their education.

St. Thomas district, in Clark County, intends to issue $15,000 bonds to build a handsome new school house.

The Bunkerville branch high school has nearly thirty pupils finishing the second year work and prepared to enter the high school in Las Vegas next fall.

Overton district has issued $15,000 bonds and will build one of the most attractive school houses in Clark County.

THE GAME WAS GOOD

Vegas Nine Defeats Overton at Base Ball on Sunday Afternoon.

A game full of interest from start to finish was contested Sunday afternoon by the Overton and Las Vegas teams, the latter winning by a score of 10 to 4. Up to the fifth honors were even and the score stood goose eggs all around. In the fifth Overton started the trouble by scoring one, Vegas retaliating by bringing four men around the bases in her half of the inning. From that time on McDonald, the Overton pitcher, was hit hard. A feature of the game was the home run by Jones in the last half of the fifth, bringing in two men for Vegas.

LAS VEGAS.

	AB	R	BH	BOB
Getshine, 1b	5	2	2	1
Ullom, lf	4	0	0	1
Houck, 2b	5	0	1	0
Black, c	5	0	0	0
Johnson, 3b	4	1	1	0
Jones, cf	4	2	2	0
Thomas, rf	5	2	0	3
Henderson, ss	5	2	1	1
Emrick, p	4	1	2	1

Score, 10.

OVERTON.

	AB	R	BH	BOB
Ralph Leavitt, 3b	5	1	1	0
Chas. McDonald, ss	5	0	0	1
W. H. McDonald, p	4	1	2	0
Dave Conger, 1b	4	1	1	0
Lamon Thomas, cf	4	0	1	0
C. McDonald, 2b	4	1	1	1
Wood Perkins, rf	4	0	1	0
Frank Jones, lf	5	0	1	0
Leon McDonald, cf	5	0	0	1

Score, 4.

BY INNINGS.

	1	2	3	4	5	6	7	8	9
Overton	0	0	0	0	1	2	0	0	1
Las Vegas	0	0	0	4	4	1	1	-	

Mr. W. A. Rogers umpired the game in a manner acceptable to all.

Overton, May 15 —There is a number of cases of measels in Kaolin in the Hardy, Iverson and Hientze families and owing to a delay in quarantine regulation a number of Overton children have been exposed County Physician Martin authorized J. F. Perkins to quarantine the families having the disease and he did so on Monday last.

Miss Ethelyn Bennion and her mother, Mrs. Heber Bennion, left Tuesday for their home in Taylorsville after having spent the winter here Miss Bennion returned to her home much improved in health.

Mrs. Eliza Ingram, president of the stake board of primary officers, left this morning to visit the Bunkerville and Mesquite organizations Mrs. Etta Swapp, stake aid, accompanied her.

Mrs. Clifford Cochran has returned to northern Utah to join her husband after a visit of several months with her parents, Mr. and Mrs John Swapp.

Mrs Orin Jarvis is in Salt Lake City for medical treatment, she is reported to be getting along nicely.

Leon Hickman has been joined here by two of his brothers and the trio are raising cantaloupes.

Mrs. Bryant Whitmore has gone to spend the summer with her father in northern Utah

The 1-year old daughter of Calvin Nay is very sick with typhoid fever

Bp W. A. Whitehead is out to the Copper mountain on business

R. L. Shurtliff of Overton was an interested spectator at the high school track meet Monday last. He remained in Vegas several days.

COUNTY EXHIBIT AN EYE OPENER

Products of Clark County Shown at Reno Astonish the Beholders.

Las Vegas and Clark County made a hit in Reno during the recent G. A. R. encampment and Grand Lodge sessions with an exhibit of products that surprised the natives and visitors to the northern city.

The exhibit was arranged by Mr. E. W. Griffith for the Las Vegas Chamber of Commerce and was first placed in the city hall and later, by invitation, in the handsome rooms of the Reno Commercial Club.

There were several varieties of grains and forage, including wheat three feet high, harvested May 4; rye four feet high, harvested May 1st; barley 30 inches high, fully headed and well filled; corn six and a half feet high six weeks after planting, and alfalfa from the second cutting four feet high cut June 6th. It should be borne in mind that in the northern valleys two cuttings per season is the limit and often only one good cutting is secured, while here in the Vegas and Moapa Valleys, the alfalfa has already furnished two full cuttings and will easily provide four more, the third cutting being now well on its way to maturity.

Ripe peaches from the Moapa Valley were also an attractive feature, astonishing to the northern people. Other fruits in various stages of maturity were apples, figs, grapes, prunes, plums apricots, almonds and English walnuts.

In the vegetable line there were squash (two varieties), turnips, cabbages, onions, beets, lettuce and radishes all ready for the table.

The exhibit was inspected by many who were amazed that Nevada contained any locality which would produce such things at this season. The Chamber of Commerce expresses its thanks to the Reno Commercial Club for the hospitality shown in allowing the exhibit to be shown in its rooms and for many courtesies to the visitors.

Thanks are also due to those contributed the various exhibits, among them being Wm. Laubenheimer, F. E. Matzdorf, A. Matteuci and Geo. Crouse of this city and Messrs. Lytle and Shurtliff of Overton and others in that locality.

County School Census.

The school census has been completed throughout the county and reports turned in to Deputy Superintendent B. G. Bleasdale and approved by him.

The total for the county numbers 763, divided among the districts as follows: Eldorado, 3; Goodsprings, 23; Warmsprings, 14; St. Joe, 31; Searchlight, 23; Moapa, 16; Kaolin, 17; St. Thomas, 51; Las Vegas, 290; Bunkerville 107; Mesquite, 107; Virgin (Overton), 81.

Washington County News
June 24, 1913

Overton, June 24.—A son was born recently to Mr. and Mrs Andrew L Jones. Mrs. Jones is in Salt Lake City to spend the summer with her parents while the proud father is pursuing his labors as watermaster here in the valley

The ladies of Overton met at the home of Mrs Ethel Perkins on the afternoon of the 18th in honor of Mrs. Emeline B Wells, to celebrate "Aunt Em's Day." They report an enjoyable time

Miss Winona Earl, Mrs Rose C Bunker and Miss Etta McMullin came over last week from Las Vegas where they had been to take the teachers' examination

The McDonald Brothers have leased the Shurtliff hall and will conduct a series of dances The McDonald orchestra will furnish music

James McWade and Crayton Johnson have returned from the Copper mountains where they have been at work for several months

Ripe fruit in a scant quantity, owing to late frosts, is on hand now, and consists of apricots, peaches, plums, figs and blackberries.

Trehner & Sons threshing machine is at work threshing near Kaolin this week and will continue up the valley

Ellis Turnbeaugh is home for a few days from northern Nevada, where he has been since January last

Elmer Lossee has completed the building for his ice plant and will install the machinery this week.

Deo Hickman had the misfortune to break his arm a few days ago He is getting along nicely now.

Mrs Racie King and family are spending the summer in northern Utah.

332

MOAPA VALLEY HAPPENINGS

Budget of Interesting Items From Our Correspondent at Overton.

(Special Correspondence.)

Overton, June 24.—Trehner and sons' threshing machine is at work threshing the recently harvested grain. They are threshing near Kaolin this week and will continue up the valley.

Mr. Dee Hickman had the misfortune to break his arm a few days ago. He is getting along nicely with it now.

Miss Winona Earl, Mrs. Rose C. Bunker and Miss Etta McMullen came over last week from Las Vegas, where they have been to take the teachers' examinations.

Mrs. Racie King and family are spending the summer in northern Utah.

The ladies of Overton met at the home of Mrs. Ethel Perkins on the afternoon of the 18th in honor of Mrs. Emeline B. Wells, to celebrate "Aunt Em's Day." They report an enjoyable time.

The McDonald brothers have leased the Shurtliff Hall and will conduct a series of dances. The McDonald orchestra will furnish music.

Elmer Losee has completed the building for his ice plant and will install the machinery this week.

James McQuaid and Crayton Johnson have returned from the Copper Mountain, where they have been at work for several months.

Ellis Turnbaugh is home for a few days from northern Nevada, where he has been since January last. He will open his ice cream parlor while here and leave it for Mrs. Turnbaugh and Miss Perkins to operate after his return to his position.

A son was born to Mr. and Mrs. Andrew L. Jones. Mrs. Jones is in Salt Lake City to spend the summer with her parents, while the pround father is still pursuing his labors as water master here in the valley.

Ripe fruit in a scant quantity is on hand now, owing to the late frosts. It consists of apricots, peaches, plums, figs and blackberries.

Correct spelling should be Frehner

IMPORTANT WORK UNDER WAY

Water Reservoiring for Moapa Valley Makes Good Progress.

The Nevada Land & Livestock Co., owner of the land at Kaolin and vicinity, some three miles below Overton, is going ahead steadily with the work of constructing reservoirs with which to impound the surplus flow of Moapa creek, together with such flood waters as may come from time to time.

Two of these reservoirs are situated in the foot hills immediately adjoining the company's present extensive alfalfa fields and a short distanse from Koalin town. Some four feet of water is held in the smaller of these, and boating and bathing have been enjoyable sports there for some time past.

Iron headgates, with corrugated iron piping attached, ranging from sixteen to twenty-four inches in diameter, are being put in. When filled, these two reservoirs will hold something like 15,-000,000 cubic feet of water, but flood waters will have to be caught to secure anything like this amount.

The third and larger of the reservoirs will be situated some three miles west of Kaolin at a point where water from the Las Vegas side of the country sheds through a narrow gorge in a ridge of conglomerate into the Moapa Valley. Here a breastwork of reinforced concrete is to be built. The gorge is only fifteen or eighteen feet wide, but the wall will be built forty feet high. The country lying back of it is clover leafed in shape, three water sheds coming into one at that point.

Flood waters are all that can be relied upon here. If they occur in sufficient volume it is estimated that approximately 15,000,000 cubic feet of water can be impounded at this point. Less than half this quantity will be sufficient to thoroughly irrigate all the valley lands lying in and around Kaolin through to St. Thomas and the Virgin River.

The work is in charge of F. F. Hintze, manager of the Kaolin Company, who says the proposition can easily be rounded out to the point of making that part of the valley attractive to winter visitors, and he expects to be in a position to bid for a portion of that trade during the coming winter season.

334

OVERTON NOTES MOAPA VALLEY

Melon Crop is Moving in Good Earnest---Packing Sheds Busy Places.

(Special Correspondence.)

Overton, July 16.—Mrs. Willard L. Jones and children have gone to Provo for a visit with relatives during the hot spell.

Isaac E. Losee has put in operation at Overton a small ice manufacturing plant. It is of a ton a day capacity.

The packing sheds at Overton and Logan sidings are busy places these days. Melons have been going out from both places by the car for the past ten days. The Moapa Improvement Co., located at the head of the lower valley, also began shipping by the car last Wednesday.

The cantaloupe crop of the valley is a good one this year, though ten days late. No aphis has yet developed, and in the absence of rains perhaps none will. This being the case, a good shipping season ought to result.

Mrs. Walter E Morrison, whose home is east of Overton, has gone to Los Angeles, where she will visit relatives until September.

Hereafter the Muddy Valley Irrigation Co. will be the sole distributor of water from the Moapa River at Overton and points below. The Nevada Land & Live Stock Co. recently assigned to the irrigation company all its rights obtained from the state engineer, and one system of distribution will be in effect hereafter.

The spur to the new gypsum plant being built south of the railroad in the Narrows is about finished. A car of machinery was sent in Tuesday. There is only one piece of up-grade on the railroad in going from Moapa to St. Thomas. This is at a point where the road leaves the valley in the Narrows, or canyon, and cuts through some hills of gypsum. At a point about half way up this grade the spur cuts out and runs to the west.

OVERTON

Overton, July 22 — The Stork has paid two recent visits to Overton, leaving a girl on the 12 of July at the home of Tom and Gertie Ander son, and a boy on the 20 of July at the home of Elmer and Nellie Losee

Mary V Lytle has gone to the Gyp camp to visit with her husband, John A. Lytle

Mrs Hannah L Jones has gone to Idaho to visit relatives

Correct spelling should be Andersen

336

Overton Outlook.

(Special Correspondence.)

Overton, July 23.—Mrs. Hannah Jones has gone to Idaho to visit with relatives.

Mrs. Mary V. Lytle has gone to the gypsum plant to visit with her husband who is working there.

The stork has made two recent visits to Overton, leaving a tiny girl on the 12th of July at the home of Tom and Gertie Anderson and on the 20th a ten-pound boy at the home of Elmer and Nellie Losee.

The weather is not so extremely hot now as it has been, but continues cloudy and threatening. The farmers are hoping it will not storm for a few more weeks. Storm now would be ruin to cantaloupes and alfalfa seed.

The correct spelling should be Andersen

W. W. Angell of Overton was a welcome visitor at the AGE office Friday morning. He is on his way home from the Death Valley country, where he has been driving one of the famous 20-mule teams.

Overton, Aug 29 —The weather has been hotter the latter part of August than was the first weeks The local ice plant has been running day and night to supply ice in the valley.

The Ladies Relief society will give a program and dance Friday evening. They will also have cake and ice cream for sale

Mrs. Ellen Gentry and Miss Eleanor Syphus returned Tuesday from a visit to the Relief Society association of Alamo.

Mrs. Martha Fleming is clerk in Anderson's store taking the place of Mrs Mildred Robinson who has moved to Logan

Frank Jones and Woodruff Perkins have gone to Logan, Utah They will attend school there this winter.

Dee Hickman of Provo and Miss Vivian Perkins of this place will be married this week in St George.

Mrs. Ellen Perkins and Mrs Sarah Perkins are spending a few days in St George this week.

Mrs. John Thomas and Mr. and Mrs. Bert Mills are visiting on the coast a few weeks.

Miss Naomi Henderson of Salt Lake City is visiting her sister, Mrs. Andrew L. Jones.

Miss Winona Earl of Bunkerville is here, the guest of her sister, Mrs. W. L. Jones.

Dr. and Mrs Beal are visiting relatives in Leeds, Utah.

J. M. Lytle of Overton, who has been spending some time at the California coast resorts, is in this city, a guest at the Overland.

Overton, Sept. 6 —Pres. J. M. Bunker and Pres S H. Wells, Bishop Robert Gibson, Mrs Ellen Gentry and daughter, Miss Laura, Martin Bunker, Milton Earl, Mrs Lizzie Gibson, Miss Doris Syphus and Bert Murphy were among the conference visitors from St. Thomas who passed through here Friday morning on a train that came down the evening before and will connect at Moapa with the noon train for Caliente from which place they will be driven by team to Panaca, where the quarterly conference of the Moapa stake will convene Sept. 6 and 7, followed by a mutual convention on the 8. Pres W. L. Jones, Stake Clerk, N. Ray Pixton, Mrs Eliza Ingram, Miss Sylvia Shurtliff, Miss Armelia Ingram, Anthony Perkins, Wm. Perkins jr, and George Ingram joined the party. Apostle David O. McKay and Patriarch Hyrum G. Smith are expected to be in attendence from Salt Lake City.

Mrs. Sarah Perkins entertained Thursday evening in honor of the wedding of her daughter, Vivian, and Mr. E. Dee Hickman. A large crowd was entertained, the grounds being well lighted for the occasion and ice cream and cake were served during the evening. The happy couple received many beautiful presents as tokens of the good wishes of their many friends here.

Bp. Jos I. Earl came over from Bunkerville on the 5th bringing with him Mrs. William A. Whitehead and Miss LoRen Watson of St. George. Miss Watson will clerk in Whitehead Bros. store; the former clerk, Miss Sadie Perkins, will attend school in Las Vegas the coming winter.

Brig. Whitmore of Centerville came down last week on business connected with the Capalapa and Overton ranches which he sold to the Moapa Fruit Lands company several years ago

There was a dance in the hall last evening in honor of a number of Overton and St Thomas students, who will leave next week to attend school this winter.

Prof C. E. Overman, principal of the Las Vegas high school was here yesterday in the interest of the school which will open on Sept. 8th.

Mr. and Mrs. Horace Jones have moved into their new home recently built for them by A. F. Bischoff.

Mrs Patience Lee has returned from a trip to Bunkerville.

Norman Shurtliff left yesterday for Salt Lake City

Overton, Sept. 15 —District school opened on the 15th with Warren Losee as principal, Miss Edna Wadsworth of Panaca teacher in the intermediate grades and Miss Mary Berkstrom of Cedar City in the Primary grades.

Agent Thomas was here last week representing the Daynes-Beebe Music Co. of Salt Lake City. He placed a piano in the home of Ute. V. Perkins also left a player piano temporarily at the Swapp hotel.

Stake counselor Mrs Sevilla Jones of the primary association, who attended the primary class in Salt Lake City last June, is giving a course of lessons on primary work turned from St George last week. Mr. Hickman and Mrs Dora Lee of Las Vegas will teach the Logan schools this winter.

Prof. L. A Merrill of the Salt Lake Route was here on the 9th and spoke to the farmers here and at St. Thomas, encouraging them along agricultural lines.

Warren Losee and family have returned from Tropic, Utah. Mr. Losee's mother, also his sister, Miss Olive, came with him and will spend the winter here.

Alonzo Huntsman has sold his home here to Mrs. Mary West. He will move his family to St Thomas soon where he is engaged in farming

to stake and local officers here

Mrs J, C Jones returned Saturday from a visit to her daughter, Mrs Ella Callister, in Blackfoot, Idaho She also visited relatives in Provo and Delta, Utah, before returning.

Pres T. J. Jones who has spent the summer in Delta left on the 11th for Lincoln, Nebraska, to visit relatives there and in that vicinity where he spent his boyhood days

J. M. Lytle has recently returned from Los Angeles, bringing with him a car of building material and some furniture He will erect a new home in the near future.

Mr. and Mrs Leon Hickman re

Mr. and Mrs. Alex Swapp and family and Mr. Swapp's sister, Miss Hatch, returned on the 14th from a visit to Tropic, Utah

Miss Addie Ingram and George Ingram have gone to Las Vegas to attend the county high school this winter.

O. B. Grissom and family have moved to Logan, Nev., where Mr. Grissom has charge of the Benson farm

Wm. McDonald, sr, and wife have returned from their summer outing in Idaho and Utah

Fay L Anderson is attending school in northern Utah this winter.

340

HIGH SCHOOL OPENED MONDAY

Enrollment Exceeds Expectations. Will Probably Reach Sixty.

With an enrollment at the opening of 48 it is very probable that the total attending Clark County High School this term will reach 60 pupils.

Among the number are 21 entering for the first time this year and about one third of the total have registered in the new commercial course, just added to the course.

The branches are divided among the instructors as follows:

Principal C. E. Overman, sciences and mathematics; Miss Evelyn M. Sinn, history and geometry, in addition to which she occupies the responsible position of dormitory matron; Miss Pauline J. Hayes is in charge of the new Commercial department and girls athletics. Miss Anna T. Alexander has music, English and sewing.

The senior class this year numbers seven. The school now occupies a general assembly room and three recitation rooms besides the business office.

Considerable new equipment has been added this year, including five typewriters and five bookkeeping tables each for three students for the commercial work.

The library is increased to about 600 volumes, half of which are new this year. Eight of the best magazines have been subscribed for and will be kept regularly on file.

The enrollment at this time is as follows:

Las Vegas—Floyd Ashman, Gladys Boggs, Hazel Bray, Wanda Ball, Norma Brockman, Harold Cragin, Lester Cragin, Francis Coughlin, Joseph Coughlin, Vernon Delameter, Martha Ferris, Robert Griffith, Louise Hertil, Margaret Hinge, Helen Hinge, Margaret Ireland, Clara Kiernan, John Kramer, Martha Kramer, Pearl Laravey, Nellie McWilliams, Nila Meade, Ed Marshall, Christine McDonald, Carl Noblitt, Nora Noblitt, Edward Rogers, Leon Ronnow, Harry Siegmund, Andrew Small, Marie Sheppard, Rosie Taylor, Clarence Van Deventer, Luella Wengert.

St. Thomas—Helen Bunker, Bryan Bunker, Carrie Hannig, Verda Hannig, Mary Syphus, Fay Syphus, Everet Syphus.

Overton—Effie Angel, Sadie Perkins, Zilla Peterson.

Logan—Charles Hewett.

Bunkerville—George Leavitt.

Goodsprings—Clay Robbins, Reynold Robbins.

NEWS FROM MOAPA VALLEY

Large Number Attend Stake Conference at Panaca Sept. 6 and 7.

(Special Correspondence.)

Overton, Sept. 8.—Norman Shurtliff left yesterday for Salt Lake City.

Bishop Jos. I. Earl came over from Bunkerville on the 5th, bringing with him Mrs. William A. Whitehead and Miss Lo Ren Watson of St. George. Miss Watson will clerk in Whitehead Bros. store. Miss Sadie Perkins, the former clerk, will attend school in Las Vegas the coming winter.

President J. M. Bunker, President S. H. Wells, Bishop Robert Gibson, Mrs. Ellen Gibson and daughter, Miss Laura, Martin Bunker, Miller Earl, Mrs. Lizzie Gibson, Miss Doris Syphus and Bert Murphy were among the conference visitors from St. Thomas, who passed through here Friday morning on a train that came down the evening before and will connect at Moapa with the noon train for Caliente, from which place they will be driven by team to Panaca, where the quarterly confer-ence of the Moapa Stake will convene September 6 and 7, followed by a mutual convention on the 8th. Pres. W. L. Jones, Stake Clerk N. Ray Pixton, Mrs. Eliza Ingram, Miss Sylvia Shurtliff, Miss Armelia Ingram, Anthony Perkins, Wm. Perkins, Jr., George Ingram, joined the party. Apostle David O. McKay and Patriarch Hyrum G. Smith are expected to be in attendance from Salt Lake City.

Mrs. Sarah Perkins entertained Thursday evening in honor of the wedding of her daughter Vivian and Mr. E. Dee Hickman. A large crowd were entertained, the grounds being well lighted for the occasion and ice cream and cake were served during the evening. The happy couple received many beautiful presents as tokens of the good wishes of their many friends here.

Mr. and Mrs. Horace Jones have moved into their new home recently built for them by A. F. Bischoff.

Prof. C. E. Overman, principal of the Las Vegas high school, was here yesterday in the interest of the school which will open on September 8.

Brig. Whitmore of Centerville came down last week on business connected with the Capalapa and Overton Ranches which he sold to the Moapa Fruit Land Company several years ago.

There was a dance in the hall last evening in honor of a number of Overton and St. Thomas students who will leave next week to attend school this winter.

Mrs. Patience Lee has returned from a trip to Bunkerville.

CLARK COUNTY WILL EXHIBIT

Collection of Products of Orchard, Field and Mine Sent to State Fair.

A collection of products of the soil from nearly every portion of the county was assembled at Las Vegas during the past week and shipped Friday morning to Reno, where it will be placed on exhibition at the State Fair next week. Mr. E. W. Griffith, president of the Chamber of Commerce, has put in much time and hard work in securing the material for the exhibit, and to make sure that it was properly arranged and cared for, accompanied the exhibit to Reno, where he will remain in charge of it during the fair.

The products collected are principally from the Moapa and Vegas Valleys. The Moapa Valley is represented by exhibits from St. Thomas, Overton, Logan and from the state experiment farm at Logan, under the direction of Superintendent Jarvis.

The products shipped comprise corn, Kaffir corn, milo maize, peanuts, sweet potatoes, alfalfa and alfalfa seed, bamboo, sugar cane, sugar beets, pumpkins, squash, apples, pomegranates, peaches, pears, figs, water melons, cantaloupes, casabas, and others.

Samples of lime and lime rock from the quarry at Sloan, as well as a few samples of ores, petrified wood and things of that nature were also taken.

While the shipment is not as large and as full in representation of the various communities as could be desired, yet it is believed it will compare favorably with any other county in the state.

Owing to the great distance and the necessary expense, no live stock was shipped from this county.

Miss Adelaide Ingram of Overton is a new pupil at the Clark County High School. She came Monday.

NEWS LETTER FROM OVERTON

Interesting Budget of Events in the Muddy Valley Metropolis.

(Special Correspondence.)

Overton, Sept 15.—Miss Addie Ingram and George Ingram have gone to Las Vegas to attend the county high school this winter.

Fay E. Anderson has gone to attend school this winter in northern Utah.

Our district school opened on the 15th with Warren Losee as principal, Miss Edna Wadsworth of Panaca teacher in the intermediate grades, and Miss Mary Berkstrom of Cedar City in the primary grades.

Agent Thomas was here last week representing the Daynes-Beebe Music Co. of Salt Lake City. He placed a piano in the home of Ute V. Perkins, also left a player piano temporarily at the Swapp Hotel.

Stake Councilor Mrs. Sevilla Jones of the primary association, who attended the primary class in Salt Lake City last June, is giving a course of lessons on primary work to stake and local officers.

Wm. McDonald, Sr., and wife have returned from their summer outing in Idaho and Utah.

Mrs. J. C. Jones returned Saturday from a visit to her daughter, Mrs. Ella Callister, in Blackfoot, Idaho. She also visited relatives in Provo and Delta, Utah, before returning.

Pres. T. J. Jones, who has spent the summer in Delta, left on the 11th for Lincoln, Nebraska, to visit relatives there and in that vicinity, where he spent his boyhood days.

Alonzo Huntsman has sold his home here to Mrs. Mary West. He will move his family to St. Thomas soon, where he is engaged in farming.

J. M. Lytle has recently returned from Los Angeles. He brought with him a car of building material and some furniture. He will erect a new home in the near future.

Mr. and Mrs. Alex Swapp and family and Mrs. Swapp's sister, Miss Hatch, returned on the 14th from a visit to Tropic, Utah.

Warren Losee and family have returned from Tropic, Utah. Mr. Losee's mother, also his sister, Miss Olive,

The correct spelling is Andersen

344

came with him and will spend the winter here.

Prof. L. A. Merrill of the S. P., L. A. & S. L. R. R. was here on the 9th, and spoke to the farmers here and at St. Thomas, encouraging them along agricultural lines.

O. B. Grissom and family have moved to Logan, Nev., where Mr. Grissom has charge of the Benson farm.

Mr. and Mrs. Leon Hickman returned from St. George last week. Mr. Hickman and Mrs. Dora Lee of Las Vegas will teach the Logan schools this winter.

Las Vegas Age Newspaper
September 27, 1913

BARCLAY-ANGELL: Charles Sheldon Barclay to Effie Christina Angell. So reads the marriage license issued by Cupid Harmon Thursday. Both the young people are residents of the Moapa Valley, and we understand the marriage will take place at Overton Monday. All extend congratulations.

Overton, Oct. 13 —The Y. M. M I. A began their winter's work last Sunday evening with Andrew L Jones as president, Ralph Leavitt and Horace Jones as counselors, and D O. Beal as class leader in the senior department. The Y. L M I. A also began Sunday evening, Mrs Clara Lytle, Mrs Nora Mc Donald and Mrs. D. O. Beal as the presidency.

Orin Jarvis, manager of the experiment farm, returned Thursday from Salt Lake City. His mother, Mrs Eleanor Jarvis of St. George, returned with him and will visit in the valley a few days

Miss Armelia Ingram entertained a party of her lady friends at a social and luncheon Thursday evening. Miss Ingram left Sunday for Las Vegas where she will attend school this winter.

Stake Pres. of the Primary, Mrs. Eliza Ingram and counselor, Nellie Losee left today to visit the Primary association of the Alamo ward I. E Losee accompanied the ladies as driver.

Mrs Lytle and her daughter, Miss Nell Lytle, from Arizona who have been here visiting the former's sons, George and John A. Lytle, left Friday for Barclay, Nevada

The first frost for this season came on the 6th; the weather soon changed, however, and we now have bright, sunny days and pleasant nights.

Dr. Martin and Sheriff Sam Gay of Las Vegas were here this week to look after the sanitary condition of the valley and of the Muddy river

Miss Cornelia Whipple of Pine Valley, Utah, is visiting here, the guest of Miss Lydia Cooper.

The school at Kaolin commenced Monday with Miss Ella Hafen of Santa Clara as teacher.

Born, Oct 12, a daughter to Mr. and Mrs Clifford Cochran; all concerned doing well.

County Assessor S. R. Whitehead is in Carson City on business this week.

Mr. and Mrs John Ingram came over from Mesquite Saturday.

346

HAPPENINGS AT OVERTON

Items, Personal and Impersonal, From the Valley of the Muddy.

(Special Correspondence.)

Overton, Oct. 13.—Miss Cornelia Whipple of Pine Valley is visiting here, the guest of Miss Lydia Cooper.

Mrs. Lytle, also her daughter, Miss Nell Lytle, from Arizona, who has been here visiting her sons, George and John A. Lytle, left Friday for Barclay, Nevada.

Miss Armelia Ingram entertained a party of her lady friends at a social and luncheon Thursday evening. Miss Ingram left Sunday for Las Vegas, where she will attend school this winter.

County Assessor S. R. Whitehead is in Carson City on business this week.

Dr. Martin and Sheriff Sam Gay of Las Vegas were here this week to look after the sanitary condition of the valley and the Muddy River.

Orin Jarvis, manager of the experiment farm, returned Thursday from Salt Lake City. His mother, Mrs. Eleanor Jarvis of St. George, returned with him and will visit in the valley a few days.

Mr. and Mrs. John Ingram came over from Mesquite Saturday.

Born, October 12, a daughter, to Mr. and Mrs. Clifford Cochran. All concerned are doing well.

The first frost for this season came on the 6th. The weather soon changed, however, and we now have bright, sunny days and pleasant nights.

Stake President of the Primary Eliza Ingram and Councilor Nellie Losee left today to visit the Primary Ass ciation of the Alamo Ward. I. E. Losee accompanied the ladies as driver.

The school at Kaolin commenced Monday with Miss Ella Hafin of Santa Clara as teacher.

The Y. M. M. I. Association began its winter's work last Sunday evening with Andrew L. Jones as president, Ralph Leavitt and Horace Jones as councilors, and Dr. D. O. Beal as class leader in the senior department.

The Y. L. M. I. Association also began Sunday evening with Mrs. Clara Lytle, Mrs. Nora McDonald and Mrs. D. O. Beal as the presidency.

347

Washington County News
October 20, 1913

Overton, Oct 20 —The stork visited Overton during the past week and left new comers to the following couples Mr. and Mrs Van Rensellar, a girl; Mr. and Mrs Bryant Whitmore. a son, Mr. and Mrs Sherman Thomas, a girl, and Mr. and Mrs Alonzo Huntsman, a son.

Thomas Anderson left here Monday to fill a mission in the Northwestern States A farewell dance was given Saturday in his honor. A purse was raised as an offering from his friends to help him on his mission.

Albert Frehner is threshing grain here this week. His threshing machine is run by a gasoline engine which he has recently purchased for that purpose.

Orin Jarvis has gone to Modena to purchase sheep which he expects to fatten for the market at the experiment farm

Mr and Mrs Fred J Rushton went over to Bunkerville for a visit last Friday.

Warren Cox of St George is here on business

Las Vegas Age Newspaper
October 25, 1913

Married.

CONNELLY—LOSEE: At Overton, Nevada, John Larken Connelly and Olive Thankful Losee were united in marriage this week. The happy young couple have the congratulations and the best wishes of the AGE.

NEWS ITEMS FROM OVERTON

Population Rapidly Increasing In the Valley of the Moapa.

(Special Correspondence.)

Overton, Oct. 20.—Thomas Anderson left here Monday to fill a mission in the northwestern states. A farewell dance was given Saturday in his honor. A purse of dollars was raised as an offering from his friends to assist him on his mission.

Albert Frehner is threshing grain here this week. His threshing machine is run by a gasoline engine which he has purchased for that purpose.

Orin Jarvis has gone to Modena to purchase sheep, which he expects to fatten for the market at the Experiment Farm.

Mr. and Mrs. Fred J. Rushton went over to Bunkerville for a visit last Friday.

Warren Cox of St. George is here on business.

John M. Lytle is building a new house on his farm west of town.

The stork visited Overton during the past week and left newcomers to the following couples. Mr. and Mrs. Van Rensellar, a girl; Mr. and Mrs. Bryant Whitmore, a boy; Mr. and Mrs. Sherman Thomas, a girl, and Mr. and Mrs. Alonzo Huntsman, a boy.

349

Spelling should be Andersen

Overton, Oct 29. — Mr. John Connelly of Logan and Miss Olive Lossee were married at Kaolin last week, Justice of the Peace McDermont performing the ceremony. Mr Connelly has resided here for a number of years and Miss Lossee, who is a daughter of Isaac and Mary Lossee of Trovic, Utah, has recently moved here   The young couple have the best wishes of their many friends. They will make their home for the present in Logan at the Rice farm.

Whitehead Brothers have recently received a car of lumber which has been ordered for a number of persons who expect to build soon, also a car each of coal and flour, a number of cars of hay is being loaded to be shipped out of the valley. A car of hogs recently sent out from the Koenig ranch brought 8 cents on foot in Salt Lake City.

A number of families of refugees from Mexico are here looking over the valley with a view of locating, they include members of the Naegle, Harris and Aldrich families

Miss Florence Thayne, who has been working at the Swapp hotel for some time, has returned to her home in Washington, Utah

Miss Chechew Dotson is home again after several months' spent at the home ranch in Moapa

The schools are planning a celebration of Hallowe'en Friday night

Mrs. Sophie Cooper and her daughter, Miss Lydia, came down from Overton Tuesday evening to spend a few days in this city. They are guests at the Overland.

NEWS ITEMS FROM OVERTON

Mexican Refugees May Locate in Valley --- Building Is Active---Local Notes

(Special Correspondence.)

Miss Florence Thayne, who has been working at the Swapp Hotel for some time past, has returned to her home in Washington, Utah.

Miss Chechew Dotson is home again after several months spent at the home ranch near Moapa.

A number of families of refugees from Mexico are here looking over the valley with a view of locating here. They include members of the Naegli, Harris and Aldrich families.

S. R. Whitehead has gone to St. George on business.

The schools are planning a celebration of Hallowe'en Friday night.

Mr. John Connelly, of Logan, and Miss Olive Losee were married at Kaolin last week, A. L. F. McDermot, justice of the peace, preforming the ceremony. Mr. Connelly has resided here for a number of years, and Miss Losee, who is a daughter of Mr. and Mrs. Izaac Losee, of Tropic, Utah, has just recently moved here. The young couple have the best wishes of their many friends here. They will make their home for the present in Logan, at the Rice farm.

Whitehead Brothers have recently received a car of lumber which had been ordered for a number of persons who expect to build soon; also a car each of coal and flour. A number of cars of hay are being loaded to be shipped out of the valley. A car of hogs recently sent out from the Koenig ranch brought 8 cents on foot in Salt Lake City.

351

Overton, Nov. 12 —Mrs Eliza Ingram and Mrs Sevilla Jones of the stake presidency of the Primary association visited the settlements on the Virgin river last week in the interest of the associations

Mrs Mary Batty is here from Toquerville, where she has spent the summer. She has returned on business connected with the sale of the Batty home and farm here

Ute V Perkins has moved his family into town for the winter They are occupying the Turnbeau home Mr. Perkins has purchased a lot here

Mr and Mrs Jos, I. Earl came over from Bunkerville last week bringing their son Harold for medical treatment

Mrs Pearl Turnbeau and family have gone to Mina, Nevada, where her husband has employment

Crayton Johnson is suffering from a broken leg, caused by a gate striking it

Mrs Winnie Gann is visiting relatives in Alamo.

352

Busy Firm

The A. A. Clark Company, engineering contractors of Salt Lake City, are reaching out in this direction for business. They already have the $100,000 contract for building the rock-filled dam for the Rio Virgin Irrigated Fruit Lands Co., above Mesquite, and for building a new school house at Overton. They have now a force of men ready to press the latter building to completion before hot weather arrives. The firm will also submit bids on the new Clark county court house, with a good prospect, in view of their large experience in this county, of landing the prize.

News Items from Overton

(Special Correspondence.)

Crayton Johnson is suffering from a broken leg, the accident being caused by a gate striking his leg.

Mrs. Mary Batty is here from Toquerville, where she spent the summer. She has returned on business connected with the sale of the Batty home and farm here.

Mrs. Pearl Turnbeau and family have gone to Mina, Nevada, where her husband has employment.

353

Las Vegas Age Newspaper
November 22, 1922

School Notes

Among the pupils to go home for the Thanksgiving holiday are the following: Misha Potter and Clay and Reynolds Robbins to Goodsprings Friday evening; Helen Bunker and Mary Syphus to St. Thomas, and Adeline Ingram, Sadie Perkins and Lorna Perkins to Overton this morning.

Washington County News
November 26, 1913

Overton, Nov. 26 —Prof. J. E. Hickman of Logan, Utah, was here last week and delivered two lectures On Saturday evening his subject was "The Emotions," and Sunday evening, "The Temptations of Christ."

Nephi Hunt of Bunkerville and a number of Sunday school workers were here Sunday to hold a union meeting of officers of all the Sunday schools of the valley.

Misses Sadie and Lenora Perkins and Miss Addie Ingram are over from the Los Vegas High School for a visit at home during institute week.

Miss Edna Wadsworth left this evening for her home in Panaca to attend institute at Pioche and spend Thanksgiving day.

John M. Lytle has recently returned from Utah with a flock of sheep which he will fatten for the market

Mr and Mrs Joseph Ingram are here from Kanarra, Utah, to make their home

Mrs Williams returned Tuesday from a visit to her mother in Salt Lake City

Ira J. Earl came in Wednesday from Arden, Nevada, to visit relatives here

OVERTON ITEMS

Misses Sadie and Lorna Perkins and Addie Ingram are over from Las Vegas for a visit at home during Institute week.

Prof. J. E. Hickman of Logan, Utah, was here last week according to arrangements made by the Ward Amusement Committee, and delivered two lectures. On Saturday evening his subject was "The Emotions," and Sunday evening "The Temptations of Christ."

State Sunday School Supt. Nephi Hunt of Bunkerville and a number of Sunday school workers were here Sunday to hold a union meeting of officers of all the Sunday schools of the valley.

Miss Edna Wadsworth left Wednesday for her home in Panaca to attend Institute at Pioche and spend Thanksgiving day.

Ira J. Earl came in Wednesday from Arden, Nevada, to visit relatives here.

John M. Lytle has recently returned from Utah with a flock of sheep which he will fatten for the market.

Mr. and Mrs. Joseph Ingram are here from Kanarra, Utah, to make their home.

Mrs. Williams returned Tuesday from a visit to her mother in Salt Lake City.

Ira Earl, of Bunkerville, was in Vegas early in the week, visiting his sister, Mrs. Newell Leavitt. He left Wednesday morning for Overton, where his brother Harold is lying very ill

355

Overton, Dec. 3 —Thanksgiving day passed very pleasantly here the time being given over to family dinners There was a splendid ball in the evening, about the best attended of the season

Mr. and Mrs N. Ray Pixton have returned from a visit at Las Vegas where they went to attend the contest game of basket ball between the Bunkerville and Las Vegas high school boys

Milton and Kenneth Earl of the Bunkerville basket ball team came down from Moapa Friday on their way home from Las Vegas and will spend the week here

Miss Ella Hafen will not be able to finish the winter at the Kaolin school on account of defective eyesight Her successor has not been announced

S R Whitehead came over from Las Vegas Wednesday accompanied by his friend, C C. Wylie, in an auto to spend Thanksgiving day at his home.

S R Whitehead came over from Las Vegas Wednesday accompanied by his friend, C C. Wylie, in an auto to spend Thanksgiving day at his home.

Warren Losee, Edna Wadsworth and Mary Berkstrom, the Overton school teachers, are in attendance at the institute in Pioche this week.

Messers Meckum and Hatch and their families came in last week from Tropic, Utah, and will spend the winter here.

Harold Earl, who has been very sick for several weeks, is improving. He is here under a doctor's care.

Daughters have been added recently to the families of Brigham Hardy and Roy Bundy, both of Kaolin.

Miss Maggie Iverson of Littlefield, Ariz , is visiting friends in the valley this week

356

COURT CONVENES NEXT MONDAY

Judge Taber Will Open Regular Term in Botkin Building ...Jurors Drawn

Monday morning next, Judge E. J. L. Taber will open district court in the Botkin building in this city. The 24 citizens who have been served with summons to appear as grand jurors will be present to take up the work of hearing criminal charges against those awaiting grand jury action, and to investigate the manner in which the public business is being conducted.

Monday, the 15th, the 60 men summoned as trial jurors will be present to try any cases demanding a jury.

Trial Jurors Summoned for December 15, 1913, at 10 a. m.

SEARCHLIGHT

J. R. Booth	Sellick W. Waring
C. E. Burdick	H. Patrick
John Howe	Walter M. Brown
Steve Hayduck	

OVERTON

Clifford Whitmore	Ransom L. Shurtleff
Andrew L. Jones	Crayton Johnson
Wm. A. Whitehead	David Conger
Alonzo R. Leavitt	

NELSON

C. E. Hastings	Louis L. McCarthy
J. B. Hoffman	

LAS VEGAS

J. J. Tuckfield	Roy C. Thomas
Frank Quereau	Minor E. Cheney
W. H. Elwell	Alfred F. Ferlin
R. E. Robinson	Henry Jackson
Joseph L. Smith	O. D. Hicks
J. W. Seiders	John Becwar
L. H. Rockwell	J. A. Delameter
C. C. Howard	W. J. Baldwin
Earl Eglington	

BUNKERVILLE

Thos. D. Leavitt Jr.	Edwin L. Knight
Harold B. Earl	Conrad Adams
George H. Hunt	Ithamar Sprague
A. M. Thompson	John A. Leavitt

CRESCENT

Samuel Spencer	G. H. Morrison
Dennis Callahan	

GOODSPRINGS

Charles H. Clark	S. C. Root
Geo. Beacham	Matt. Finley
Fred A. Hale	Max Silva
J O. Kemple	Thomas Williams

LOGAN

Edwin Marshall	W. R. Gann
James Thomas	W. J. McBurney

357

OVERTON ITEMS

Messrs. Meekum and Hatch and their families came in last week from Tropic, Utah, and will spend the winter here.

Miss Maggie Iverson of Littlefield, Ariz., is visiting friends in the valley this week.

Daughters have been added recently to the families of Brigham Hardy and Roy Bundy, both of Kaolin.

Warren Losee, Edna Wadsworth and Mary Berkstrom, the Overton teachers, are in attendance at the Institute in Pioche this week.

Thanksgiving day passed very pleasantly here, the time being given over to family dinners. There was a splendid ball in the evening, which was about the best attended of the season.

Stephen R. Whitehead came over from Las Vegas Wednesday in an auto accompanied by his friend, C. C. Wylie, to spend Thanksgiving day at his home.

Mr. and Mrs. N. Ray Pixton have returned from a visit to Las Vegas, where they went to attend the game of basketball between the Bunkerville and Las Vegas high school boys.

Milton and Kenneth Earl, of the Bunkerville basketball team, came down from Moapa Friday on their way home from Las Vegas and will spend the week here.

Harold Earl, who has been very sick for several weeks, is improving. He is here under the care of Dr. Beal.

Miss Ella Hafen will not be able to finish the winter at the Kaolin school on account of defective eyesight. Her successor has not been announced.

MESQUITE

David A. Abbott   M. D. Abbott
John A. Barnum

Grand Jurors Summoned December 9, 1913, at 10 a. m.

LAS VEGAS

David Farnsworth   R. B. Sproul
Henry G. Helm   G. H. French
George Crouse   E. W. Griffith
F. E. Matzdorf   P. J. Sullivan
I. C. Johnson   A. D. Bishop
John F. Miller   C. C. Corkhill
John S. Park   W. D. Worrell
Peter Buol

ST. THOMAS

John Perkins   M. A. Bunker

OVERTON

Brigham T. Hardy   Ute V. Perkins

LOGAN

Orrin Jarvis   Henry Rice

MESQUITE

C. S. Knight

BUNKERVILLE

J. I. Earl

GOODSPRINGS

A. J. Robbins

Team to Overton

The Clark County H. S. basket ball team will go to Overton next Saturday. A pleasant time is anticipated.

Overton, Dec. 8 —The quarterly conference of the Moapa stake convened in Overton Dec 6 and 7, with an excellent attendance from different wards of the stake. Apostle Rudger Clawson and Pres Charles H Hart of the first council of the seventies were in attendance from Salt Lake City. The train came down from Moapa Friday evening bringing the visitors from Panaca and the north. We were also favored with a train Monday morning to carry the visitors back to Moapa. This service was very much appreciated. The choir at St Thomas, under the leadership of Francis Bunker furnished the music for Sunday's session of conference. The Overton choir under the management of N. Ray Pixton furnishing the music for the Sunday meetings. Good work was done by both choirs

Mrs Sarah J. Cannon and Mrs. Doctor Wilcox of the general board of the Relief society were here from Salt Lake city. They spoke in the Saturday afternoon session of the conference also holding a special session of Relief society workers

Sunday.

The following were among those summoned to Las Vegas this week on the Grand Jury: Jas I. Earl, M. A. Bunker, Ute V. Perkins B. H. Hardy and L. W. Syphus.

Miss Mary Beckstrom who has been teaching the primary grade of the district school was obliged to return to her home at Cedar City on account of ill health.

On Friday night a carload of ore and a caboose broke loose at Moapa and ran down to the end of the track at St. Thomas. No serious damage was done.

Henry Leavitt had the misfortune to cut his lip by running against a barb wire in the dark. He returned home to Bunkerville Sunday.

Dr Bracken and his brother, Walter Bracken, of Salt Lake City came down the valley Monday on a hunting trip.

Mr. and Mrs Dick Kirkham of Moapa were down to attend the ball Saturday evening also Sunday's conference.

A reunion of the seventies was held Friday evening. Lunch was served and a program rendered.

Henry Cannon of St George is here with the intention of making his home in the valley.

W. H. McDonald has recently received a shipment of cement and expects to build soon.

S R. Whitehead is now making cement blocks for his new home.

There was a dance in the hall Saturday evening

OVERTON ITEMS

The quarterly conference of the Moapa Stake convened in Overton Dec. 6 and 7, with an excellent attendance from the various wards of the Stake. Apostle Rudger Clawson, also Charles H. Hart of the First Council of Seventies, were in attendance from Salt Lake City.

The train came down from Moapa Friday evening bringing the visitors from Panaca and the north. We were also favored with a train Monday morning to carry the visitors back to Moapa. This service was very much appreciated.

The following persons were in attendance from Panaca: Bp. Wm. Edwards; Frank Lee, Stake Pres. of the Y.M.M.I.A.; E. R. Phillips, Chas. Mathews, Marion Keele, Mrs. W. T. Morris, Stake Aid of the Y.L.M.I.A.; Shanette Blad, Mrs. Wm. Mathews, Mrs. Lizzie Edwards, Miss Nell Lytle and her mother. The latter will remain here for some time to visit relatives.

On Friday night a car loaded with ore and a caboose broke loose at Moapa and ran down to the end of the track at St. Thomas. No serious damage was done.

The following were among those summoned to Las Vegas this week to serve on the grand jury: Jos. I. Earl, Martin A. Bunker, Ute V. Perkins, Brigham H. Hardy, Levi Walter Syphus.

Dr. Bracken and his brother, Walter R. Bracken, came down the valley Monday on a hunting trip.

A reunion of the Seventies was held Friday evening. Lunch was served and a program rendered.

Bp. Udell Schofield and Jos. Foremaster were here from Alamo to attend conference.

The St. Thomas choir, under the leadership of Francis Bunker, furnished the music for Saturday's session of the conference, and the Overton choir, under the management of N. Ray Pixton, furnished music for the Sunday conference meetings. Good work was done by both choirs.

Bp. Abbott of Mesquite ward and 21 members of his ward were here to attend conference.

Mrs. Sarah J. Connor and Mrs. Dorton Wilcox of the general board of the Relief Society were here from Salt Lake City. They spoke at the Saturday afternoon session of the conference, also holding a special session of Relief Society workers Sunday.

Miss Mary Berkstrom, who has been teaching the primary grade of the district school, was obliged to return to her home at Cedar City on account of ill health.

A dance was held at the hall Satururday evening.

Henry Leavitt had the misfortune to cut his lip by running against a barbed wire fence in the dark. He returned home to Bunkerville Sunday.

Bp. Edw. Cox, Nephi Hunt and wife, James Abbott, Mr. and Mrs. Dudley Leavitt, Misses Winona Earl and Lovica Leavitt, William Wittwer, Hugh Bunker, Hector Bunker, Albert Leavitt and a number of others were here this week from Bunkerville.

S. R. Whitehead is now making cement blocks for his new home.

W. H. McDonald has recently received a shipment of cement and expects to build soon

Henry Cannon of St. George is here with the intention of making his home in the valley.

Mr. and Mrs. Dick Kirkham of Moapa were down to attend the ball Saturday evening and Sunday's conference.

Overton, Dec 16 — On Saturday afternoon a game of basket ball was played between the Las Vegas high school and the Overton basket ball team. The line up being as follows —Las Vegas· Capt. Vernon Delameter, Leland Ronnow, Lamond Thomas, Bryan Bunker and Howard Elwell; score 22. Overton: Capt, Evan Lee, Clarence McDonald, Frank Jones, Wallace Jones, Murray Williams; score 7. Referee, Ben J. Robinson; Umpire, Leon Hickman. Prof. C E Overman accompanied the Las Vegas team. The game was followed by a dance. There was a good crowd out to see the game and the gate receipts was sufficient to meet the expenses.

Elmer Losee has been ill with mumps this week Clarence, the six year old son, of Crayton Johnson, has also been very ill with mumps There have been a number of other cases but all very light

The weather to date is very mild· the leaves are autumn colored, but many of the chrysanthemums and roses and fall gardens are yet untouched by frost

Mrs Sherman Thomas has been very ill but is some improved at present Mrs J. P. Anderson has also been ill with the grip this week.

Andrew L. Jones, Bp Wm Whitehead and Crayton Johnson were summoned to Las Vegas this week on the jury.

Ira J. Earl returned this week to the Potosi mine, near Arden, where he has employment.

Miss Della Prince of Washington, Utah, is visiting here, the guest of Miss Lydia Cooper.

Mr. and Mrs John Ingram came over from Mesquite recently and will locate here.

Born, to Mr. and Mrs. Truman Angell, a daughter; all concerned doing nicely.

Warren Cox was here this week from St. George, Utah, on business.

363

OVERTON ITEMS

Last Saturday afternoon a game of basketball was played between the Las Vegas high school team and the Overton basketball team, the line-up being as follows:

Las Vegas—Vernon Delameter, captain; Leland Ronnow, Lamond Thomas, Bryan Bunker, Howard Elwell.

Score 22.

Overton—Evan Lee, captain; Clarence McDonald, Frank Jones, Wallace Jones, Murray Williams.   Score 7.

Referee, Ben. J. Robinson.

Umpire, Leon Hickman.

Prof. C. E. Overman accompanied the Las Vegas team. The game was followed by a dance. There was a good crowd out to see the game and the gate receipts were sufficient to meet the expenses.

Miss Dell Prince of Washington, Ut., is visiting here, the guest of Miss Lydia Cooper.

Ira J. Earl returned this week to the Potosi mine near Arden, where he has employment.

Mrs. Sherman Thomas has been very ill but is somewhat improved at present.

Mrs. S. P. Anderson has been ill with la grippe this week.

Born, to Mr. and Mrs. Truman Angell, a daughter. All concerned are doing nicely.

Mr. and Mrs. John Ingram came over from Mesquite recently and will locate here.

Elmer Losee has been ill with mumps this week. Clarence, the six-year-old son of   nson, has also been very   us. There have been   r cases, but all very
r

Andrew L. Jones, Bp. Wm. Whitehead and Crayton Johnson were summoned to Las Vegas this week on the jury.

Jabez Haig, Divine Scientist and lecturer, spoke here Saturday and Sunday evenings on "Self Government and Bodily Sanitation."

Warren Cox was here this week on business.

The weather to date has been very mild. The leaves are autumn colored, but many of the chrysanthemums and roses and fall gardens are yet untouched by frost.

Overton, Nev , Dec 21 —A horse thief was captured here Monday evening by Deputy Sheriff Joe F. Perkins The horse he had stolen from Samuel Leavitt of Mesquite was returned to the owner who had followed the thief. He was handcuffed and chained to a carriage wheel for the night and given a bed near by, but in the night he dragged the buggy to a work-bench and with a vise and hammer broke the chain and escaped still wearing the handcuffs He has not been recaptured.

The Overton basket ball team returned today from Bunkerville where they played with the high school boys a game of basket ball The score was 13 to 9 in favor of Bunkerville. The score remained even until the last few minutes of the game. Mr. and Mrs Leon Hickman and Miss Naomi Henderson accompanied the boys on the trip.

The Misses Armelia and Addie Ingram, Zilla Peterson, Lorna and Sadie Perkins have returned from the Las Vegas high school for the Christmas holidays.

Overton, Nev , Dec 26. — On Christmas eve the Home Dramatic Co. played "The Next Door," a pleasing comedy. The parts were taken by Mr. and Mrs Leon Hickman, Mr. and Mrs. D. O. Beal, Mrs. Geo Lytle, Mrs Wm Whitehead, Norman Shurtliff, Ray Weber and Crayton Johnson.

The Shurtliff Amusement Co. have installed roller skates in their dance hall. The floor soon cut up so badly that there will be no more dancing in the hall.

Born, recently, a son to Mr. and Mrs. James Huntsman, all concerned doing nicely.

Thomas Johnson came in Wednesday from his work out in Nev.

Martin Lewis of Las Vegas is spending Christmas week here.

Mrs N L Leavitt of Las Vegas is here visiting relatives

Get a Postoffice

The postoffice department has arranged a series of examinations for the position of postmaster at fourth class postoffices. Those of interest to this section will be held at Goldfield and Tonopah Feb. 7; Caliente, Feb. 14; Moapa, Feb. 16; Las Vegas, Feb. 17; Rhyolite, Feb. 19; Mina, Feb. 21.

Among the postmasters to be appointed from those taking the examinations are those at Alamo, Arden, Beatty, Blair, Bonnie Clare, Bunkerville, Goodsprings, Johnnie, Mary Mine, Millers, Mina, Moapa, Nelson, Overton, Rhyolite, St. Thomas, Tecoma;

Any person may be examined at any of the examinations held, but an applicant for a postoffice must reside within the territory supplied by that office.

366

OVERTON ITEMS

The Overton basket ball team returned today from Bunkerville where they played with the high school boys a game of basket ball. The score was 13 to 9 in favor of Bunkerville. The score remained even until the last few minutes of the game. Mr. and Mrs. Leon Hickman and Miss Naomi Henderson accompanied the boys on the trip.

A horsethief was captured here Monday evening by deputy sheriff Jos. F. Perkins. The horse he had stolen from Samuel Leavitt, of Mesquite, was returned to the owner who had followed the thief. He was handcuffed and chained to a buggy wheel for the night and given a bed near by, but in the night he dragged the buggy to a work bench and with a vice and hammer broke the chain and escaped still wearing the handcuffs. He has not been recaptured.

The Misses Armelia and Addie Ingram, Zilla Peterson, Lorna and Sadie Perkins have returned from the Las Vegas High School for the holidays.

On Christmas eve., the Home Dramatic Co. played "The Next Door" a pleasing comedy. The parts were taken by Mr. and Mrs. Leon Hickman, Mr. and Mrs. D. O. Beal, Mrs. George Lytle, Mrs. Wm. Whitehead, Norman Shurtliff, Ray Weber and Crayton Johnson.

Mrs. N. L. Leavitt, of Las Vegas, is here visiting relatives.

Thos. Johnson came in Wednesday from his work out in Nevada.

Martin Lewis, of Las Vegas, is spending the holidays here.

The Shurtliff Amusement Co. have installed roller skates in their dance hall. The floor cut so badly that there will be no more dancing in the hall.

Born recently, a son to Mr. and Mrs. James Huntsman. All concerned doing nicely.

Overton, Nev., Jan 5.—The people of St. Thomas were here for New Year's day and a game of base ball and ladies basket ball was played between teams from the two settlements, the Overton teams winning the games.

Mr and Mrs Williams of Kanarra, Utah, were here to spend the holidays and visit relatives, Mr. and Mrs George Ingram and family also Mr. and Mrs Crayton Johnson. They left for their home Monday.

Miss Edna Wadsworth and Quincy Keele came down from Panaca Sunday; the latter will teach school at Kaolin Miss McDonald arrived here Saturday from Missouri to teach the primary school.

368

Pres Mark Austin of Sugar City, Idaho, was here several days last week and addressed the farmers of Logan, Overton and St. Thomas on agricultural subjects

Mr and Mrs Lemuel Leavitt and Miss Lovica Leavitt came over from Bunkerville Sunday; they will return Tuesday.

Geo. F. Jarvis and family have recently moved here from St. George, they are refugees from Mexico

Mrs. Kelly of the Bunkerville school gave an excellent recital here during Christmas week.

Pres W. L. Jones and J. M. Bunker left Friday to visit the Pánaca ward.

Lafe Matthews and Dale Edwards came down from Panaca Saturday.

Alfred Tobler came over from Bunkerville Saturday.

H. S. Athletics

Activity in high school athletics is on the increase. With the victories at Goldfield and Tonopah to encourage them, the Clark County High School team is reaching out for new worlds to conquer.

They will visit Bunkerville and play the team which has regularly defeated them Saturday, Jan. 17th. There is much interest attached to the result.

Bunkerville and Overton meet at Overton today. Overton has made up a strong team and is considered to have an even chance with Bunkerville.

Overton will meet C. C. H. S. in this city Saturday, Jan. 24th. The Vegas boys expect this to be the game of the season in public interest. However, in order to win the silver cup this year the Vegas lads must beat both Overton and Bunkerville and Overton must also defeat Bunkerville, making the situation rather complicated and uncertain.

370

OVERTON ITEMS

Mrs. Kelly, of the Bunkerville school, gave an excellent recital here during Christmas week.

Pres. W. L. Jones and J. M. Bunker left Friday to visit the Panaca Ward.

Miss Edna Wadsworth and Quincy Keele came down from Panaca Sunday. The latter will teach the school at Kaolin. Miss McDonald arrived here Saturday from Missouri to teach the primary school.

Mr. and Mrs. Lemuel Leavitt and Miss Lovica Leavitt came over from Bunkerville Sunday, returning Tuesday.

Lafe Mathews and Dale Edwards came down from Panaca Saturday.

Alfred Tobler came over from Bunkerville Saturday.

Geo. F. Jarvis and family have recently moved here from St. George. They are refugees from Mexico.

Pres. Mark Austin of Sugar City, Idaho, was here several days last week and addressed the farmers of Logan, Overton and St. Thomas on agricultural subjects.

Mr. and Mrs. Williams of Kanarra, Utah, were here to spend the holidays with their relatives, Mr. and Mrs. Geo. Ingram and family, also Mr. and Mrs. Crayton Johnson. They left for their home Monday.

The people of St. Thomas were up for New Year's day, and a game of baseball and a ladies' basketball game were played between teams from the two settlements, the Overton teams winning both games.

Game Postponed

On account of the stormy weather the basket ball game between Overton and Vegas, scheduled for today, will be postponed to Sunday afternoon at 2:30.

Mrs. Perkins of Overton is here visiting her daughter Sadie.

Mrs. Joe F. Perkins of Overton is in Vegas visiting her daughter Lorna, who is attending the high school.

The Misses Armelia and Adeline Ingram, of Overton, who were obliged by illness to leave school two weeks ago, are improving and hope to be here again in a short time.

Mrs. Willard L. Jones of Overton is reported to be seriously ill at her home in Overton.

SCHOOL MONEYS APPORTIONED

Clark County Receives $5,681.76 To Be Divided Among the Various Districts

John Edwards Bray, superintendent of public instruction, has completed the first semi - annual apportionment of school moneys for the year 1914. Under the present system schools of a given number of school children get the same amount of state money in every county of the state.

The amount coming to Clark county is $5,681.76, which is in turn apportioned among the school districts as follows:

Las Vegas	$1942.48
Mesquite	754.50
Bunkerville	754.50
Overton	567.75
St. Thomas	371.00
St. Joe (Logan)	321.00
Goodsprings	179.25
Searchlight	179.25
Kaolin	164.25
Moapa	161.75
Warm Springs	156.75
Eldorado	129.25
	$5681.76

Overton, Feb 10 —Funeral services was held at Kaolin, Feb 2nd for Frances J. Iverson, who died Jan. 31 leaving a husband and daughter 3 years old, also many friends to mourn her loss Mrs Iverson was the daughter of Samuel W. Jarvis and Frances Godfrey Defrieze Jarvis and was born Mar 2, 1885, at Colonia Diaz, Chihuahua, Mexico, being the first girl born of Latterday Saint parents in the Mormon colonies of Mexico. Her frontier life among the natives of Mexico acquired for her the staunch and brave character of the pioneer; she acquired a good knowledge of the Spanish language and having lived in a number of colonies was widely known and loved both by the natives and the colonists In 1907 she came with her father to visit relatives in St George, Utah, and during her stay there she was married to Willard Iverson of Littlefield, Arizona. In 1909 Mr. and Mrs. Iverson returned to Old Mexico and remained until they with the other Mormon colonists were driven out at the beginning of the war in Mexico

Funeral services was presided over by Bp Wm Whitehead, the Overton choir assisting with the music, Orin W. Jarvis and Pres W. L. Jones were the speakers. A line of 18 vehicles followed the remains to Kaolin cemetary where she was the first person to be burried.

Work is progressing nicely on the new school house. It is being built of cement blocks on a five acre tract of land recently purchased of James P. Anderson and Willard L Jones in the western part of town. It, however, will be in the center of the town when the lots are all occupied A A. Clark of Salt Lake City has the contract for erecting the building A car load of appliances has been received here for use in erecting the building

The Overton Dramatic Co. put on a play here Saturday evening which was well attended The Shurtliff Amusement Co have recently put a hardwood floor in their dance hall.

A carload of fruit trees arrived here last week from Utah. They have been distributed among the farmers of the valley.

Ephraim Peterson of Idaho is here this week looking over the valley with a view of investing here.

Messrs. Mitchel and Taber came in some time ago with a carload of bees from Utah

374

EARL: In Overton, Nevada, Wednesday, Feb. 5, 1914, Harold Earl, beloved son of Joseph I. Earl, after a lingering illness of many months.

The young man gave promise of an active and vigorous manhood up to the time when heart trouble began to sap his strength. While his death was not unexpected, it brings no less regret to the many friends of the deceased and his family. The family has the heartfelt sympathy of all in their bereavement.

375

OVERTON ITEMS

(Special Correspondence.)

The Overton Dramatic Co. put on a play here Saturday evening which was well attended.

The Shurtliff Amusement Co. has recently put a hardwood floor in the dance hall.

Work is progressing nicely on the new school house. It is being built of cement blocks on a five-acre tract of land recently purchased of James P. Anderson and Willard L. Jones in the western part of town. However, it will be in the center of the town when the lots are all occupied. A. A. Clark of Salt Lake City has the contract for erecting the building. A carload of appliances has been received here for use in the work.

Fred J. Rushton has charge of the laying of cement blocks in the S. R. Whitehead home now being erected.

Correct spelling should be Andersen

Dr. Mitchell and Mr. Taber came in some time ago with a carload of bees from Utah.

A carload of fruit trees arrived here last week from the Davis Co. Nursery Company of Roy, Utah. They have been distributed among the farmers of the valley.

Ephraim Peterson of Idaho is here this week looking over the valley with a view of investing here.

Funeral services were held at Kaolin Feb. 2d for Frances J. Iverson, who died Jan. 31st. She leaves a husband and a daughter three years old, also many friends to mourn her loss. Mrs. Iverson was the daughter of Samuel W. Jarvis and Frances Godfrey Defriez Jarvis and was born March 2d, 1885, at Colonia Diez, Chihuahua, Mexico, being the first girl born of Latter Day Saint parents in the Mormon colonies of Mexico. Her frontier life among the natives of Mexico acquired for her the staunch and brave character of the pioneer; she acquired a good knowledge of the Spanish language, and having lived in a number of the colonies was widely known and loved, both by natives and colonists. In 1907 she came with her father to visit relatives in St. George, Utah, and during her stay there she was married to Willard J. Iverson of Littlefield, Ariz. In 1909 Mr. and Mrs. Iverson returned to Mexico and remained until they, with other Mormon colonists, were driven out at the beginning of the war in Mexico, when they located in the Moapa Valley. The funeral was presided over by Bp. Wm. Whitehead, the Overton choir assisting with the music. Orin W. Jarvis and Pres. W. Jones were the speakers. A line of 18 vehicles followed the corpse to the Kaolin cemetery, wherein she was the first person to be buried.

Overton, Feb. 16 —Harold V. Earl passed away on the 11th inst after an illness of several months of leakage of the heart. Ira J. Earl and Andrew L Jones left with the corpse the next day for Bunkerville, where funeral services were held Friday afternoon. Mr. and Mrs Jos I Earl also acompaning the remains to Bunkerville. He was a son of Jos I Earl and Calista Bunker and was born in October, 1891, ar Bunkerville. He was a 3rd. year student at the Bunkerville high school, a young man of excellent habits. He had filled a number of positions in the Sunday school and M. I Assns, and during his long illness exhibited wonderful patience, faith and courage. He leaves a host of sorrowing relatives and friends, his mother and two sisters having preceded him to the great beyond.

Work on the school house has been stopped for lack of cement; a carload is expected in soon.

The March conference of the Moapa stake will be held on the 7th ,and 8th at Bunkerville.

OVERTON ITEMS

(Special Correspondence.)

Work on the school house has been stopped for lack of cement. A carload is expected in soon.

The March conference of the Moapa stake will be held on the 7th and 8th at Bunkerville.

Harold V. Earl passed away on the 11th of February after an illness of several months of leakage of the heart. Ira J. Earl and Andrew L. Jones left the next day with the corpse for Bunkerville where funeral services were held Friday afternoon. Mr. and Mrs. Jos. I. Earl also accompanied the remains to Bunkerville. He was the son of Jos. I. Earl and Calista Bunker and was born in October 1891 at Bunkerville. He was a 3d year student at the Bunkerville High School. A young man of excellent habits, he had filled a number of positions in the Sunday school and Mutual Improvement Associations, and during his long illness exhibited wonderful patience, faith and courage. He leaves a host of sorrowing relatives and friends, his mother and two sisters having preceded him to the great beyond.

Overton, Feb 24.— Last Saturday afternoon a flood, the equal of the big flood of Jan. 1910, both in volume of water and in damage done, came down the valley. Many acres of grain and alfalfa land were flooded, also lots of land in shape to plant cantaloupes and some asparagus crops that would have been ready to market next month. A number of families living in the flood district were forced to abandon their homes Among them the families living at Capalapa and Mr. and Mrs Wm Marshall, the latter had a babe two days old when they had to move out They are now staying at the Koenig ranch The railroad track between here and Moapa was not seriously damaged if any.

Owing to some of the players living across the creek the play, Lady Darrel, which was advertised for Washington's birthday was postponed till the last of the week.

Mrs Clem Cochran came down last week from Salt Lake City to join her husband who has been here several months

An eleven pound boy was born Sunday to Mr. and Mrs Ralph Leavitt

MOAPA VALLEY SUFFERS LITTLE

Flood Waters Do Less Damage Than First Reports Indicated

The first reports of the flood following the storms of last week were to the effect that the rush of waters down the Meadow Valley Wash into the Moapa Valley had caused greater damage than occurred in the big flood of 1910. This happily was not so, the reports being corrected by County Assessor Whitehead upon his arrival from Overton Wednesday.

The flood began to assume serious proportions Saturday morning and was at its highest point Sunday morning. At that time the water covered a large area but owing to favorable conditions did not wash the land so much as expected.

The largest damage was done at Logan. The State Experiment Farm lost its fences as in the former big flood and considerable of its area was covered with silt and sand, damaging growing crops and orchards. The Moapa Improvement Co.'s property was considerably damaged in the same manner, the levee constructed at a cost of $3,000 breaking and covering the asparagus and grain fields with silt. Much loose soil was washed from the fields which had been prepared for planting to cantaloupes.

The Moapa Valley branch railroad suffered very little, one fill having been washed out for a width of about 10 feet and 3 or 4 feet deep.

Las Vegas Age Newspaper
March 7, 1914

J. A. Lytle of Overton has been spending several days in Vegas this week. He is much impressed with the advance made by the city since his last visit here.

Moapa Valley Building

Contractor Wm Marschall was down from Overton the first of the week arranging to ship his cement block machine to the Moapa Valley. He reports considerable work in view there, among the buildings under way and contemplated being the fine residence of S. R. Whitehead, the $15,000 school building and a 20x100 one story and basement store building for Gunn, all at Overton, and a $12,000 school building and a $6,000 residence for S. H. Wells at St. Thomas.

MUDDY VALLEY IRRIGATION COMPANY

(Incorporated.)

OVERTON, · · · NEVADA

Notice of Assessments Nos. 1 and 2 for 1914

Muddy Valley Irrigation Company, Location of principal place of business, Overton, Clark County, Nevada, location of works, Moapa Valley, Clark County, Nevada.

Overton, Nevada, March 2, 1914.

Notice is hereby given that at a special meeting of the Board of Directors held on the 2nd of March, 1914, an assessment of 75 cents per share was levied upon the subscribed and outstanding preferred stock of the corporation, payable on or before the 15th day of April, 1914, to the secretary-treasurer of said corporation at its office in the residence of Isaac E. Losee, in the said town of Overton; also, notice is hereby given that at a special meeting of the Board of Directors held on the 2nd day of March, 1914, an assessment of 15 cents per share was levied upon the subscribed and outstanding common stock of the corporation, payable on or before the 15th day of April, 1914, to the secretary-treasurer, at his office in the residence of Isaac E. Losee, in the said town of Overton, Clark County, Nevada.

Any stock upon which this assessment shall remain unpaid the 1st day of June, 1914, will be delinquent and advertised for sale at public auction, and unless payment is made before, so many shares of each parcel of such stocks as may be necessary will be sold at the company's office, on Saturday, July 18, 1914, at the hour of 3 o'clock p. m., to pay the delinquent assessment, together with cost of advertisement and expense of sale.

By order of the Board of Directors,

ISAAC E. LOSEE,
Secretary-Treasurer.

First pub. Mar. 7, 1914.
Last pub. April 4, 1914.

Where Your Money Goes

The following is the tax rate set by the county commissioners at their last meeting, subject to revision when they meet again next fall as a board of equalization. It is probable that on that date the rate will be decreased to some extent by reason of the increase in the assessed valuation of property. The figures below are the same as last year with the addition of 17 cents to cover the court house bonds interest and sinking fund.

	Annual Budget
State fund	$ 66
General interest	25
Interest	23
County high school	20
General county school	30
Jury fund of county	05
Indigent fund	05
General county fund	21
Contingent fund	05
Court house bond interest	10
Court house bond sinking fund	07
	$2.17
St Joseph school	$ 25
Moapa school	25
Bunkerville school	25
Overton school	25
St Thomas school	25
Searchlight school special	50
Las Vegas school sinking	12
Las Vegas school interest	12
Goodsprings school interest	12
Warm Springs school interest	90
Searchlight City	2.00
Las Vegas City	1.00

Overton, Mar. 3 —The home dramatic club played "My Lady Darrel" to a crowded house Saturday night, Those having parts in the play were. Dr and Mrs Beal, Mr. and Mrs Leon Hickman, Mr and Mrs Elmer Losse, Mrs Myrtle Whitehead, Mrs Clara Lytle. Crayton Johnson, N. Ray Pixton, Ray Weber and A. L. F. McDermott. It was exceptionally well played

A basket ball game was played Saturday afternoon between the young ladies of Overton and St. Thomas, the St. Thomas girls winning the game The school boys of the two towns played a game also

Under the management of the Parents' class, a program and social was given in the school house Friday evening Lunch was served during the evening The party was a very enjoyable one

Stake Sunday School Aids, Parley S. Hunt and Jesse Cooper returned Saturday from a visit to the Alamo and Panaca Sunday schools They visited the Overton school Sunday.

A laborer at the Gann ranch stole a valued watch and gold pin and made his escape last week, he cut the phone line on his way to Moapa to avoid being caught

Apostle George F. Richards and Bp O P Miller have been appointed to attend stake conference on the 7th and 8th which will be held in Bunkerville.

The first dance on the new hardwood floor in the Shurtliff hall was given Thursday night and was well attended

Mr. and Mrs John Ingram have moved to the Weiser ranch to live for a time.

The primary will give the children a dance in the hall tonight.

386

Overton, Mar 17.—Jos I Earl and daughter, Winona, came over from Bunkerville Thursday. He has rented the Crosby farm here and will try raising cantaloupes as well as honey in the valley.

Those who attended conference from Overton, thirty-three in number, returned home Monday. Everyone enjoyed a pleasant time while there

Dr. Robert C. Smedley of Salt Lake City is here looking over the valley. Mrs Smedley is with him.

Mr. and Mrs. Joseph Wall left Kaolin last week to make a home at Delta, Utah.

The Kaolin Dramatic club played "The Iron Hand" here Wednesday evening

387

OVERTON ITEMS

Those who attended conference from Overton, thirty-three in number, returned home Monday. Everyone enjoyed a pleasant time while there.

The Kaolin Dramatic Club played "The Iron Hand" here Wednesday evening.

Jos. I. Earl and daughter, Winona, came over from Bunkerville Thursday. He has rented the Crosby farm here and will try raising cantaloupes as well as honey.

Mr. and Mrs. Joseph Wall left Kaolin last week to make a home in Delta, Utah.

Dr. Robert C. Smedley of Salt Lake City is here looking over the valley. Mrs. Smedley is with him.

MUDDY VALLEY IRRIGATION COMPANY

(Incorporated.)

OVERTON, · · · NEVADA

Notice of Assessments Nos. 1 and 2 for 1914

Muddy Valley Irrigation Company, Location of principal place of business, Overton, Clark County, Nevada, location of works, Moapa Valley, Clark County, Nevada.

Overton, Nevada, March 2, 1914.

Notice is hereby given that at a special meeting of the Board of Directors held on the 2nd of March, 1914, an assessment of 75 cents per share was levied upon the subscribed and outstanding preferred stock of the corporation, payable on or before the 15th day of April, 1914, to the secretary-treasurer of said corporation at its office in the residence of Isaac E. Losee, in the said town of Overton; also, notice is hereby given that at a special meeting of the Board of Directors held on the 2nd day of March, 1914, an assessment of 15 cents per share was levied upon the subscribed and outstanding common stock of the corporation, payable on or before the 15th day of April, 1914, to the secretary-treasurer, at his office in the residence of Isaac E. Losee, in the said town of Overton, Clark County, Nevada.

Any stock upon which this assessment shall remain unpaid the 1st day of June, 1914, will be delinquent and advertised for sale at public auction, and unless payment is made before, so many shares of each parcel of such stocks as may be necessary will be sold at the company's office, on Saturday, July 18, 1914, at the hour of 3 o'clock p. m., to pay the delinquent assessment, together with cost of advertisement and expense of sale.

By order of the Board of Directors,

ISAAC E. LOSEE,
Secretary-Treasurer.

First pub. Mar. 7, 1914.
Last pub. April 4, 1914.

Overton, Mar. 24.—The Bunkerville high school came over Friday bringing their high school band and the play "East Lynn." They gave a dance Friday evening and "East Lynn" was played to a crowded house Saturday evening It was a success as a social event and they also netted a neat sum from the receipts of their play for use in their school

Arthur Hughes, stake superintendant of religion classes, of Mesquite and Elder Wm A. Morton of the general board of religion classes visited here several days this week and held a meeting in Overton Friday evening in the interest of this work At the Saciament meeting Sunday Elder Morton spoke, his subject, "Was Joseph Smith an impostor?" being ably treated

Among those going out on Thursday's train were Miss Vida Tibbitts to her home at Benjamin, Utah, Joe Hatch to Tropic, Utah, and Dr and Mrs Robert C Smedley to Salt Lake City

Mrs Mary Losee and son, Donald, who came here last fall from Tropic, Utah, purchased a lot in the southern part of town and has moved into a little home recently built for her.

Ralph and Joe Perkins have returned from southern California Mrs Joe Perkins and children will remain for a month visiting relatives near San Diego

Mrs Loella Leavitt and Mrs Thos Leavitt, jr , were here Saturday on thair way to Las Vegas

Miss Roxie Leavitt who has been visiting here for several weeks returned home Sunday.

Elmer Losee has recently received machinery for the enlargement of his ice plant

A car of cement has been received for use on the new school house.

Mr. and Mrs Wm Bowman of Bunkerville are visiting here.

Born, last week, a son to Mr. and Mrs Joseph Ingram.

Meeting at Moapa

Representatives of the Moapa Valley towns met at Moapa Tuesday to consider the matter of county roads. Those present were E. H. Syphus and County Commissioner Bunker, of St. Thomas, Mr. Merrill of Kaolin, Dr. Beale of Overton, O. W. Jarvis and L. M. Grant of Logan, J. T. Sprague of Moapa, Geo. Baldwin of the upper valley, W. E. Abbott of Mesquite, Ed. I. Cox of Bunnkerville, who, with Ed. W. Clark of this city, comprised the committee. E. W. Griffith and C. P. Squires of Las Vegas representing the Las Vegas Chamber of Commerce were also present and presented the Vegas view of the matter. Although the desire for a permanent automobile highway through the heart of the Moapa Valley was practically unanimous, the decision was arrived at that this is not the proper time for undertaking that matter. The plan of building the highway from Vegas to St. Thomas and from St. Thomas to Bunkerville according to the original report of the road committe was left in the hands of County Commissioner Bunker for execution.

OVERTON ITEMS

(Special Correspondence.)

Among those going out on Thursday's train were Miss Vida Tibbitts, to her home in Benjamin, Utah; Mr. Joe Hatch to Tropic, Utah, and Dr. and Mrs. Robert C. Smedley to Salt Lake City.

A car of cement has been received for use on the new school house.

Elmer Losee has recently received machinery for the enlargement of his ice plant.

Born, last week, a son to Mr. and Mrs. Joseph Ingram.

Miss Roxie Leavitt, who has been visiting here for several weeks, returned home Sunday.

Mr. and Mrs. Wm. Bowman of Bunkerville are visiting here.

Ralph and Joe Perkins have returned from Southern California. Mrs. Joe Perkins and children will remain for a month visiting relatives near San Diego.

391

Stake Supt. of Religion Classes Arthur Hughes of Mesquite and Elder Wm. A. Morton of the General Board of Religion Classes visited here several days this week, and held a meeting in Overton Friday evening in the interest of this work. At the sacrament meeting Sunday Elder Morton spoke; his subject, "Was Joseph Smith a Impostor?" being ably treated.

The Bunkerville high school came over Friday, bringing their high school band. They gave a dance Friday evening and the play "East Lynne" was given to a crowded house Saturday evening. It was a success as a social event and they netted a neat sum from the performance for use in their school.

Mrs. Loella Leavitt and Mrs. Thos. Leavitt Jr. were here Saturday on their way to Las Vegas.

Mrs. Mary Losee and son Donald, who came here last fall from Tropic, Utah, purchased a lot in the southern part of town and have moved into a little home recently built for them.

Overton, Apr 2 —We are favored now with a service of three trains a week down the valley which makes it very convenient for farmers and also for travelers The trains come down Sunday, Tuesday and Thursday.

Mr. and Mrs Wm Flowers of Rexburg, Idaho, have spent the week looking over the valley and have purchased a lot in the western part of town and expect to return soon and make their home here They went out on Thursday's train.

Miss Winona Earl returned on Thursday's train from a short visit to Las Vegas Her brother, Ira, who accompanied her will remain for some time at Moapa in the employ of F. F. Gunn.

F. W. Clemens of Rexburg, Ida.,

who has spent the winter here, left this morning for Idaho   Mr Clemens has purchased the Wm Batty home and lot and will return in the fall with his family.

Among those who left today to attend April conference in Salt Lake City were Pres W L Jones and Counselor S H. Wells and F. F Hienze of Kaolin.

Mr Taber, who has been here for several months in the employ of Mr. Mitchel in the bee business was an outgoing passenger on Thursday's train

The Misses Thirza and Rachel Leavitt who have been working in the valley for some time left this morning for a short visit at Las Vegas

Born, last week, a son to Mr. and

Born, last week, a son to Mr. and Mrs John A. Lytle, and a daughter to Mr. and Mrs Albert L. Jones, all concerned doing nicely

Mrs Lytle and daughter, Miss Nell Lytle, who have been visiting relatives here, returned this week to Arizona.

Four cars of lumber have been received here this week, two of them for use in the district school building

State Supt of Schools Bray and District Supt Bleasdale visited the schools of the valley this week

Mrs Sophie Cooper and daughter, Miss Lydia, are visiting relatives in Mesa City, Arizona

Pres T. J. Jones has gone to Delta, Utah, where he will spend the summer

Mr. Bray Here

State Superintendent of Public Instruction, John Edwards Bray, arrived in Vegas Tuesday accompanied by Deputy Superintendent B. G. Bleasdale. They have just visited the schools in Panaca, Pioche and Caliente, in Lincoln county and Bunkerville, Mesquite, St. Thomas, Kaolin, Overton, Logan and Moapa in this county. They report the schools generally in a very satisfactory condition.

Mr. Bray left Thursday morning for the north over the L. V. & T. road. Mr. Bleasdale left by auto Thursday afternoon for Goodsprings, Beatty, Rhyolite and various schools in Nye and Esmeralda counties. He expects to be gone a month or more and travels in his Ford.

Overton Items

(Special Correspondence.)

Born, last week, a son to Mr. and Mrs. John A. Lytle, and a daughter to Mr. and Mrs. Albert L. Jones. All concerned are doing nicely.

Mrs. Lytle and daughter, Miss Nell Lytle, who have been visiting relatives here, returned this week to their home in Arizona.

We are favored now with a service of three trains a week down the valley, which makes it very convenient for farmers who are shipping early garden stuff and also for travelers. The trains come down Sunday, Tuesday and Thursday.

Miss Winona Earl returned on Thursday's train from a short visit to Las Vegas. Her brother Ira, who accompanied her, will remain for some time at Moapa in the employ of F. F. Gunn.

396

Among those who left today to attend April Conference in Salt Lake City were Pres. W. L. Jones and Councilor S. H. Wells, and F. F. Hienze of Kaolin.

Mr. Foxley of St. Thomas left this morning on a business trip to Carson City.

Pres. T. J. Jones has gone to Delta, Utah, where he will spend the summer.

Misses Thirza and Rachel Leavitt, who have been working in the valley for some time, left this morning for a short visit at Los Angeles.

Four cars of lumber have been received here this week, two of them for use in the district school building.

Mrs. Sophie Cooper and daughter, Miss Lydia, are visiting relatives at Mesa City, Arizona.

State Supt. of Schools Bray and District Supt. Bleasdale visited the schools of the valley this week.

Mr. Taber, who has been here for several months in the employ of Mr. Mitchell in the bee business, was an outgoing passenger on Thursday's train.

F. W. Clemens of Rexburg, Idaho, who spent the winter here, left this morning for Idaho. Mr. Clemens has purchased the Wm. Batty home and lot and will return in the fall with his family.

A new player piano was received here this week by the Shurtliff Amusement Cor for use in their hall.

Mr. and Mrs. Wm. Flowers of Rexburg, Idaho, have spent the past week looking over the valley and have purchased a lot in the western part town. They left on Thursday's train, but expect to return soon and make their home here.

BOARD OF COUNTY COMMISSIONERS

Bridge Across the Virgin and Furniture for New Court House Acted Upon

At the regular meeting of county commissioners Monday last, chairman C. C. Rennow presided, member Geo. A. Fayle being present and J. M. Bunker absent.

After the minutes of the last meeting were read and approved and reports of officers received and filed, the usual bills were allowed.

The claim of J. Earnest for refund on taxes of $2.42 was rejected, not being a legal claim against the county.

The bill of Dr. D. O. Beal for $22.00 for duties as quarantine officer was laid over awaiting the presence of Commissioner Bunker.

The claim of the Sterling Borax Co. for refund of taxes was laid over for further investigation.

J. T. Sprague of Moapa, McMurry & Ricketson Moapa, J. E Keate Moapa, Yount & Fayle Jean, Yount & Fayle Goodsprings, John Traux Nelson and Burdick & Clements, Nelson, were granted retail liquor licenses for the quarter. Arthur Woods of Roach, was granted a rural liquor license.

The county surveyor was instructed to get in touch with Commissioner Bunker and report on building a pile bridge across the Rio Virgin between St. Thomas and Bunkerville.

J. I. Earl was advised by the board to make such inspection of the bees of the county as he considered necessary.

The request for $1500 for use on the road in the Newberry mining district near Searchlight was laid over.

The petition for the appointment of a constable for Overton was laid over.

The assessment of Stratford Gold Mining Co. of $70.75 on patented claims was ordered cancelled, the claims not being patented.

The board ordered advertisements for bids for furniture for the new court house prepared as published in full in another column of this issue. The specifications and designs for the same are to be prepared by Architect F. J. DeLongchamps.

Bunkerville Notes

(Special Correspondence.)

Bunkerville for the first time in its history has been honored with a visit from the State Superintendent of Public Instruction, and notwithstanding the long hard drive from Moapa he gave a spirited address on "Practical Education" Saturday evening to a large, appreciative audience. Nevada has chosen well in getting the services of this grand man. Dept. Supt. B. G, Bleasdale accompanied him and added to the interest of the occasion with an instructive talk. We feel like saying to them, "Come again, road or no road."

The birds and bees are singing and soon the reapers and the mowers will commence their song.

The school campus has been enlarged and fenced and we expect to make a first class campus of it with a baseball diamond, basket ball and volley ball grounds, tennis court, track and swiming pool.

The Parents Class has set aside a day for the planting of shrubs and flowers. They believe in making the idea of "beautifying the home" materialize into actual improvements.

The high school greatly appreciates the cordial support given the band and "East Lynne" by Overton last week. Notwithstanding their high expenses they cleared a nice little sum to add to their student body fund.

Chas. Yandell, supertinendent of the work done by the Rio Virgin Fruit Land Co., with Contractor Wattis have filed on two large tracts of land below here on the Virgin River. They have now put one and one-half cars of stock to work clearing off brush, levelling the land and preparing to put in crops.

Isaac E. Losee of Overton, secretary of the Muddy Valley Irrigation Company, was among the Vegas visitors early in the week. He was a welcome caller at the AGE office.

Contractor Wm. Marschall was down from Overton Monday. He reports the Whitehead residence as about completed and work ready to proceed on the new school building and on the store of the Gunn Mercantile Co.

Overton, Apr. 10.— Under the management of the Parents class of the Sunday school, this week has been known as "clean up week." The merchants have co operated with them by offering a number of prizes for the best showing made in the surroundings of a home in a given time

Thos Johnson who has been working at Searchlight for some time came in this week to be at the bedside of his mother, Mrs. Susan Johnson, who has been quite ill the last few days Mrs Johnson has been an invalid for 12 years from the effects of paralysis.

The Wonderland Amusement Co gave a couple of picture shows here this week. Mr. Hannig of St. Thomas also gave one this week.

Jesse F. Murphy left Thursday to fill a mission. A farewell party was held in his honor Tuesday evening at St Thomas.

Mr. and Mrs Benjamin Robinson have a baby girl, born on the 4th of April, all concerned doing nicely

Washington Leavitt is in the valley from Bunkerville working at the gypsum mine.

Work has begun on a new store to be erected here by F. F. Gunn of Moapa.

S. R. Whitehead left Tuesday for Salt Lake City on business

T. J. Osborne came down from Pioche Thursday.

403

Overton, Apr. 13 —Stake M I A. day was held here on the 11th, the Mutual Improvement Assns of the Panaca, St Thomas and Overton wards participating The junior girls' chorus of the Panaca ward won first prize The blue ribbon for the best story was awarded to Miss Clara Whitney of St Thomas who told the "Vision of Sir Launfall" The Overton ward had a number of parts for which there was no contestant, and the ladies basket ball game between Panaca and Overton was a very even game, the Overton team winning by one point.

John Swapp and Andrew L Jones are each building a cement cistern to store water for culinary use

The Misses Carrie and Verda Hannig were over from Las Vegas for the M I A day sports

Solon Huntsman and Lewis Pulsipher of Mesquite were here Sunday as home missionaries

I E Losee is installing a 20 horse power engine in his electric light plant this week

The dances Friday and Saturday evening were well attended

J K W Bracken of Las Vegas is here this week

Overton Items

(Special Correspondence.)

Thos. Johnson, who has been working at Searchlight for some time, came in last week to be at the bedside of his mother, Mrs. Susan Johnson, who has been quite ill for some days. Mrs. Johnson has been an invalid for 12 years as the result of paralysis.

Mr. and Mrs. Benjamin Robinson have a baby girl, born on the 4th of April. All concerned doing nicely.

S. R. Whitehead visited Salt Lake City last week on business.

Work has begun on a new store building to be erected here by F. F. Gunn of Moapa.

T. J. Osborne came down from Pioche last week.

Washington Leavitt is in the valley from Bunkerville working at the gypsum mine.

Jesse F. Murphy left last week to fill a mission. A farewell party was held in his honor at St. Thomas.

The Wonderland Amusement Co. gave a couple of picture shows here last week. Mr. Hannig of St. Thomas also gave one here.

Under the management of the Parents' Class of the Sunday school last week was known as "clean-up week." The merchants co-operated with them by offering a number of prizes for the best showing made in the surroundings of a home in a given time.

Stake M. I. A. Day was held here on the 11th, the mutual improvement associations of the Panaca, St. Thomas and Overton wards participating. The Junior Girls' Chorus of the Panaca ward won first prize. The blue ribbon for the best story was awarded to Miss Clara Whitney of St. Thomas, who told the "Vision of Sir Launfal." The Overton ward had a number of parts for which there were no contestants, and the ladies' basket ball game between Panaca and Overton was a very even game, the Overton team winning by one point.

I. E. Losee is installing a 20 horsepower Wittle engine in his electric light plant this week.

J. K. W. Bracken of Las Vegas was here this week.

Misses Carrie and Verda Hannig were over from Las Vegas for the M. I. A. sports.

John Swapp and Andrew L. Jones are each building a cement cistern to store water for culinary use.

Solon Huntsman and Lewis Pulsipher of Mesquite were here Sunday as home missionaries.

The dances Friday and Saturday evenings at the hall were well attended.

Overton, April 28.—At a meeting of the stockholders of the irrigation company held here Saturday, a bond of $50,000 was voted to be used to install a new irrigation system in the valley.

The District school here closed on Friday with an outing to the Whitewash canyon in which many parents joined. On Thursday afternoon the intermediate grades under Miss Edna Wadsworth and the primary grades under Miss Dolly McDonald gave an entertainment consisting of drills, songs, recitations and folk dances which showed excellent training. Miss McDonald and Miss Wadsworth left Saturday for their homes at Panaca, Nev., and Marysville, Missouri.

A number of members of the Stake Sunday School board from Bunkerville and Mesquite visited the four Sunday schools at Overton, Logan, Kaolin and St. Thomas Sunday morning and held a Union meeting at Overton in the afternoon in which all the above named schools took part.

Bishop Thos Judd of St. George was here on the 20th to attend a meeting of the telephone company, of which he is a director.

M. D. Cooper of Overton is in this city for a few days.

Muddy Valley Irrigation Co. Votes $60,000 Bonds for New System

(Special Correspondence.)

Overton, April 28, 1914.

Bp. Thos. Judd of St. George was here on the 20th to attend a meeting of the telephone company, of which he is a director.

The district school here closed on Friday with an outing to the Whitewash canyon in which many parents joined. On Thursday afternoon the intermediate grades under Miss Edna Wadsworth and the primary grades under Miss Dollie McDonald gave an entertainment consisting of drills, songs, recitations and folk dances which showed excellent training.

Misses McDonald and Wadsworth left Saturday for their homes in Panaca, Nevada, and Marysville, Missouri.

At a meeting of the stockholders of the Irrigation Co. held here Saturday a bond issue of $60,000 was voted, to be used to install a new irrigation system in the valley.

A number of members of the Stake Sunday School board from Bunkerville and Mesquite visited the four Sunday schools at Overton, Logan, Kaolin and St. Thomas Sunday morning and held a union meeting at Overton in the afternoon in which all the above named schools took part.

409

OBITUARY

Overton, May 5 —Mrs Susanah Johnson, who departed this life May 3, 1914, was the daughter of James Veater and Dianah Baber. She was born in Bedminister, Bristol Co, England, Dec 23, 1844 At the age of 22 she joined the Church of Jesus Christ of Latter-day Saints and on her way to Utah lived two years at Pittsburg, Pa, later coming out west and living in Sevier county, Utah. She was the the first Primary president in the Venice ward there, and was also first councilor in the Stake Primary presidency for ten years From Glenwood, Sevier Co, she and her husband, Thomas Johnson, moved to Overton, Nevada, where she acted as president of the Relief Society from Mar 1892 till Feb 1897, also working as a teacher in the Sabbath school and doing much good among the sick as a nurse She suffered a paralytic stroke twelve years ago and has been a patient sufferer until relieved by death. At her death bed were her three children who have so faithfully cared for her during her long illness, Crayton Johnson, Thomas Johnson and her daughter, Mrs M. D Cooper, and Mrs Thos Anderson, an orphan whom she raised. She was the mother of seven children and a faithful Latter day Saint.

Mrs Mary Crosby Thomas, who died May 3, 1914, was the daughter of Jesse W. Crosby, Sr, and Minnie Bauer Crosby, and was born in Overton, Nevada, Mar 27, 1883 In 1901 she married Sherman A. Thomas in the St George temple and five children have been born to them, the youngest being a babe of six months Besides her husband and family and a host of friends, she leaves the following brothers and sisters Alvin C. Crosby, Salt Lake City, Nephi Crosby, Aurora, Nevada, and Mrs Lena Rule, Las Vegas, Nevada. She was an exemplary mother and a consistent Latter-day Saint. She has suffered from a complication of female troubles for the past two years and her death followed an operation in an attempt to save her life, which owing to her serious condition was unsuccessful.

410

Last week we had several days of rain which beside the good it did some crops, spoiled a good many acres of hay for the farmers, the Koenig ranch and Perry Huntsman being among the heavy losers with 40 and 30 acres respectively of hay in the field ready to haul.

The Relief society met Thursday at the home of Mrs Sanford Angell where after the usual program, a delicious lunch was served by Mrs Angell and her daughter, Mrs J M Lytle

Joe McDonald and family also Mrs Maud Le Barron and her two children are visiting at the home of their parents, Mr. and Mrs. W. W. McDonald.

An operation was performed on Thursday on Mis Harry Howell. Mrs Howell is progressing nicely

Commissioner J. M Bunker, Jos I. Earl and M. Cooper were over to the county seat this week.

A little son of Mr. Aldrich at Kaolin had the misfortune to break his arm Sunday.

Miss Chewchew Dotson left last week for a visit to friends in Idaho

I E. Lossee put out his first batch of ice for this season last week.

Mrs U. V. Perkins has been very ill for the past few days

OBITUARY

Mrs. Mary Crosby Thomas who died May 3, 1914, was the daughter of Jesse W. Crosby, Sr., and Minnie Bauer Crosby and was born in Overton, Nevada, Mar. 27, 1888. In 1901 she married Sherman A. Thomas in the St. George temple and five children have been born to them, the youngest being a babe of 6 months. Besides her husband and family and a host of friends she leaves the following brothers and sister: Alvin C Crosby, of Salt Lake City, Nephi Crosby, Aurora, Nevada, and Mrs. Lena Rule, Las Vegas, Nevada. She was an exemplary mother and a consistent Latter Day Saint. She has suffered from a complication of female troubles for the past two years and her death followed an operation in an attempt to save her life which, owing to her serious condition, was unsuccessful. Her surviving children are Nevada, aged 11 years; Helen, 9; Magnolia, 7; John, 5, and Louise, 7 months.

————————

Mrs. Susannah Johnson who departed this life May 3, 1914, was the daughter of James Venter and Diana Baber. She was born in Bedminister, Bristol, England, Dec. 23, 1844. At the age of 22 she joined the Church of Jesus Christ of Latter Day Saints, and on her way to Utah lived in Pittsburg, Pa., later coming out west and living in Sevier county, Utah. She was the first primary president in the ward there and was also first councilor in the stake primary presidency for two years.

From Glenwood, Sevier county, she and her husband, Thomas Johnson, moved to Overton, Nevada. Here she acted as president of the Relief Society from March, 1892, until February, 1897, also working as a teacher in the Sabbath school and doing much good among the sick as a nurse. She suffered a paralytic stroke twelve years ago and was a patient sufferer until relieved by death. At her death bed were her three children who have so faithfully cared for her during her long illness, Crayton Johnson, Thomas Johnson and her daughter, Mrs. M. D. Cooper, and Mrs. Thomas Anderson, an orphan whom she raised. She was the mother of seven children and was a faithful Latter Day Saint.

Overton Items

(Special Correspondence.)

Overton, Nevada, May 5, 1914.

Miss Chewchew Dotson left last week for a visit to friends in Idaho.

A little son of Mr. Aldrich at Kaolin had the misfortune to break his arm Sunday

Last week we had several days of rain, which, beside the good it did some crops, spoiled a good many acres of hay for the farmers. The Koenig ranch and Perry Huntsman were among the heavy losers, with 40 and 30 acres respectively in the field ready to haul.

I. E. Losee put out his first batch of ice for this season last week.

Commissioner J. M. Bunker, Jos. I. Earl and M. D. Cooper were over at the county seat this week.

Mrs. U. V. Perkins has been very ill for the past few days.

An operation was performed Thursday on Mrs. Harry Howell, and Friday one was performed on Mrs. Sherman Thomas, Dr. D. O. Beall and Dr. Sharp of Salt Lake City doing the work. Mrs. Howell is progressing nicely, but Mrs. Thomas being in a very critical condition, little hope was held out for her recovery, even at the time of the operation. The best of medical skill and the faith and prayers of her many friends were of no avail and on Sunday evening she passed away, leaving a sorrowing husband and five small children.

Mrs. Susan Johnson, who has been very ill for several weeks and an invalid for 12 years, passed away on May 3d surrounded by her family who have so faithfully cared for her during her long and patient suffering. On May 4 a double funeral was held in the Shurtliff Hall for Mrs. Johnson and Mrs. Thomas which was the largest ever held here, many friends from all over the valley having gathered to pay their respects to these noble women. Bp. W. A. Whitehead presided over the services. The choir under the direction of W. Ray Pixton rendered "O, My Father;" "The Beautiful City," the solo part being sung by Miss Lo Ren Watson; "I Know That My Redeemer Lives." A Quartette "My Soul is Full of Peace and Love" was rendered by Mrs. Warren Losee, Grace Bischoff, Jean Anderson and Lo Ren Watson. At the graves the choir sang "Somewhere." The speakers were Bp. Robert Gibson, Elder Samuel H. Wells, Pres. W. L. Jones and Elder Wm. Perkins who paid many beautiful tributes to the characters of the two sisters and offered many consoling remarks to the bereaved families. Many and beautiful were the floral offerings.

Mr. Joe McDonald and family also Mrs. Maud LeBarron and her two children are visiting at the home of their parents, Mr. and Mrs. W. W. McDonald.

The Ladies Relief Society met Thursday at the home of Mrs. Sanford Angell where after the usual program a delicious lunch was served by Mrs. Angell and her daughter Mrs. J. M. Lytle.

Routine Matters of County Business Transacted at Regular Meeting

With Chairman C. C. Ronnow presiding and Commissioners Geo. A. Fayle and John M. Bunker present, the county board cleared up the routine county business Monday.

The minutes of the last meeting were read and approved and reports of officers received.

The Clerk was instructed to notify the health officer for Moapa Valley that all expenditures by him must first have the approval of the resident commissioner, Bunker.

Overton school district was permitted to issue warrants to the amount of $400 and Searchlight district $425 in excess of the amounts standing to their credit on the books of the auditor.

The petition of Jack Reynolds for the sale by the county treasurer of lots 5 and 10, block 18 of the original townsight of Las Vegas, and of Mrs. V. A. Brewer for the sale of lot 24, block 4, original town of Searchlight, were granted.

Geo. E. Perkins was appointed constable of Overton township, subject to his filing a bond for $1,000.

Bee Inspector J. I. Earl was also made quarantine officer for bees.

Overton, Nev., May 10 —Word was received here last week by the Huntsman family of the death of their sister, Mrs Florence Adair Sweeney, in Salt Lake City on May 3rd. Mrs Sweeney has lived most of her life in this section and has many friends who will be pained to learn of her demise.

The Shurtliff Amusement Co have installed a moving picture machine in their dance hall and have given several picture shows the last few weeks.

Under the management of the Stake Primary Assn a troupe of sixteen girls played "Rebecca's Triumph" here Friday evening

Mrs Esther Arwin of Milford, Utah, who has been visiting relatives here the past week, returned to her home last Saturday.

Mrs Joe P. Perkins and children returned from California Saturday where they have been for some time visiting relatives

President W. L Jones and Elder Wm Perkins, jr, left Saturday to visit the Bunkerville and Mesquite wards

On May 5th, a daughter was born to Mrs. John Perkins and a son to Mr and Mrs. Albert Frehner

Mr. and Mrs Wm Flowers came in from Idaho this week, they expect to make their home here.

Pres S H. Wells and Elder Harry Gentry have gone out to visit Alamo ward

Mrs Nephi Crosby came in Wednesday from Arena, Nevada

417

418

L. N. Shurtliff and daughter of Overton came over Thursday for a few days stay.

Mr. and Mrs. O. J. Van Pelt and daughter Virginia are spending a few days in Overton.

Overton Items

(Special Correspondence.)

Overton, Nevada, May 10, 1914.

Under the management of the Stake Primary Association a troupe of 16 girls played "Rebecca's Triumph" here Friday evening.

The Shurtliff Amusement Co. has installed a moving picture machine in the dance hall and has given several picture shows in the past few weeks.

Mr. and Mrs. Wm. Flowers came in from Idaho this week. They expect to make their home here.

Pres. W. L. Jones and Elder Wm Perkins Jr. left Saturday to visit the Bunkerville and Mesquite wards.

Pres. S. H. Wells and Elder Harry Gentry have gone to visit the Alamo ward.

Mrs. Joe F. Perkins and children returned Saturday from California, where they have been for some time visiting relatives.

419

Mrs. Nephi Crosby came in Wednesday from Aurora, Nevada.

Word was received here last week by the Huntsman family of the death of their sister, Mrs. Florence Adair Sweeney, in Salt Lake City on May 3rd. Mrs. Sweeney had lived most of her life in this section and had many friends here who will be pained to learn of her demise.

Mrs. Esther Arwin of Milford, Utah, who has been visiting relatives here the past week, returned to her home last Saturday.

On May 5th a daughter was born to Mr. and Mrs. John Perkins and a son to Mr. and Mrs. Albert Frehner.

Overton, Nev, May 18 —Luke Whitney came in Friday from his ranch east of St Thomas with 84 baskets of delicious strawberries which found ready sale in the valley.

Mr and Mrs John Wittwer came down recently from Caliente, Nev., and are located at the experiment farm, where Mr. Wittwer has imployment

Mrs Sarah Perkins had the misfortune to break her arm near the wrist last week with a blow from the handle of a wringer she was turning

Mrs. Lena Rule, Miss Sylvia Shurtliff and Lyman Shurtliff left Thursday for Las Vegas; the latter for a short visit to the county seat

The mason work on the school house is about complete and the builders are putting on the roof

Mrs Mary West has recently given her cottage a coat of paint adding much to its appearance

Mr and Mrs Henry Kocherhans have gone to Wyoming to spend the summer.

John Swapp has gone on a business trip into southern Utah.

Ira J Earl returned Sunday from a short trip to the coast

Overton Items

(Special Correspondence.)

Overton, Nevada, May 18, 1914.

Mrs. Lena Rule, Miss Sylvia Shurtliff and Lyman Shurtliff left Thursday for Las Vegas. The latter will return after a short visit.

Mr. and Mrs. Leon Hickman have gone to St. George, Utah.

Mrs. Sarah Perkins had the misfortune to break her arm near the wrist last week with a blow from the handle of a wringer she was turning.

Mr. and Mrs. John Wittwer came down recently from Caliente and are located at the Experiment Farm, where Mr. Wittwer has employment.

John Swapp has gone on a business trip into Southern Utah.

Mr. and Mrs. Henry Kocherhans have gone to Wyoming to spend the summer.

Mrs. Mary West has recently given her cottage a coat of paint, adding much to its appearance.

Ira J. Earl returned Sunday from a short visit to the coast.

Luke Whitney came in Friday from his ranch east of St. Thomas with 84 baskets of delicious strawberries, which found ready sale in the valley.

The masonry work on the school house is about completed and the builders are putting on the roof

On the Job

Mr. E. C. Kenyon, of Sacramento, Cal., one of the engineers of the contracting firm of Campbell & Turner, arrived this week to assist in looking after the construction of the court house. The work is progressing now in a very satisfactory manner. The work of pouring the concrete for the second story walls and the third floor is now practically completed. The terra cotta partitions are being put in place and plastering will be under way next week.

Mr. Turner will remain in Clark county for a time, the firm also having the construction of the store of the Gunn Mercantile Co. at Overton under way. Mr. Turner promises that every effort will be made to advance the court house work so that the building may be completed as near to schedule time as possible.

DISTRICT COURT HOLDS SESSION

Judge Taber Clears Spring Docket in Busy Term of Two Days

Judge E. J. L. Taber, Judge of the District Court in and for the Fourth Judicial district, arrived in Las Vegas on schedule time and opened the spring term Monday morning at 10 o'clock.

The first business before the court concerned the two individuals who were in the county jail awaiting trial.

In the case of the State vs. George Lorenzi, charged in the bill of information with assault with a deadly weapon, the prisoner was arraigned and pleaded guilty. His sentence was deferred until 4:30 p. m. of the same day when Judge Taber let him off with a sentence of 1 year to 15 months in state's prison. Lorenzi is the man who posed as a deaf mute and who stabbed Wm. McCoy in a drunken brawl which started at the Lincoln Hotel bar recently.

The case of the State vs. Ed. Bell was next called. Bell also pleaded guilty to the charge of assault with intent to kill as charged in the information filed against him by the district attorney. He, also, was sentenced at 4:30 Monday to serve 1 year to 15 months in the state's prison. Bell stabbed a man named Erickson March 23d at Nelson. He is known as a dangerous criminal in the southwest and this is by no means his first time behind the bars.

S. P., L. A. & S. L. R. R. Co. vs. G. Holmes et al. Upon report of the commission consisting of W. E. Hawkins, W. R. Thomas, Isaiah Cox and Geo. Baldwin, heretofore appointed to as-

ss the compensation due to defendant
plaintiff, the report was confirmed
d judgment for $458 less costs was
tered for defendant.

S. P., L. A. & S. L. R. R. Co. vs.
m. H. Short et al. Order condemn-
right of way and awarding compen-
tion of $42.75 to defendant.

S. P., L. A. & S. L. R. R. Co. vs.
m. E. Wilkes et al. Order condemn-
right of way and awarding compen-
tion of $3.50.

S. P., L. A. & S. L. R. R. Co. vs.
rence J. Osgood et al. Order con-
nning right of way and ordering com-
sation of $16 to defendant.

Cordelia May Knight vs. Perry C.
ight. Decree of divorce for plaintiff
order restoring to her her maiden
ne Cordelia May Charlton.

(Continued on last page)

DISTRICT COURT HOLDS SESSION

(Continued from Page 1)

Estate of Fredolin Hartman, deceased. Final decree of distribution to Katherine Hartman, the whole of the residue of said estate.

Estate of James G. Givens, deceased. Order assigning to the widow, Esther K. Givens, 1800 shares of the capital stock of the Fidelity Company.

Estate of Joseph H. Spires, deceased. Order appointing O. J. Van Pelt administrator of said estate.

J. B. Jensen vs. Alfred Bley. Suit to recover on promissory note. Judgment entered for plaintiff for $1088.18, with attorney's fees of $75 and costs of suit.

426

Ada M. Perkins vs. Claude F. Perkins. Decree of divorce to plaintiff on grounds of cruelty and desertion.

Wilma A. Boghens vs. George Boghens. Decree of divorce for plaintiff on grounds of cruelty and desertion.

M. L. Cook vs. John F. More. Decree entered quieting title in plaintiff to the Lloyd and Marion mining claims in Eldorado Canyon.

Estate of Samuel Pixton, deceased. Final decree of distribution, to Nellie M. Van Pelt, the whole of the residue of said estate, consisting of 40 acres in the Moapa Valley between Logan and Overton with water rights.

Tuesday, May 26th, the Court acted upon the following matters: A. D. Bishop vs. Winterwood Land Company. Suit to recover $4500 alleged to be due for commission on the sale of property of said defendant. Submitted on briefs.

Julius P. Martin vs. Elizabeth Martin Action for divorce. Dismissed on motion of defendant.

Jasper E. Crandall vs. Riverside Dairy & Produce Co., C. N. Gary and G. L. Gary. On motion of plaintiff suit dismissed as to defendants Gary and default judgment entered against Riverside Dairy & Produce Co. for $2828.86 and costs.

Wong Kee vs. H. M. Lillis. On motion of Stevens & Van Pelt, attorneys for H. M. Lillis, a motion to retax costs was taken under advisement by the court.

Moapa & Salt Lake Produce Co. vs. Moapa Live Stock Co. Demurrer to amended complaint ordered submitted on briefs within 30 days, with 20 days additional to answer.

Estate of Isaac Rennolds, deceased. Order of Court appointing Harry Trehearne administrator.

In guardianship of Frank Murphy Buol, a minor, permission granted guardian to sell all interest of said minor, being und. ½ of W. ½ of S. W. ¼ E., 20 acres.

There being no further business the Court thereupon adjourned.

Wm. Marschall came down from Overton Saturday last for a period of rest and recreation. He is now on a trip to the timbered mountains near the old sawmill, where he will stay for a short time for the benefit of his health.

Overton Items

(Special Correspondence.)

Overton, Nevada, May 25, 1914.
Mr. and Mrs. Leon Hickman returned Sunday from a short visit at St. George.

Mrs. Hickman's mother, Mrs. Mary Whitehead, returned with them.

Marion Earl, Misses Ida Earl, Leah Leavitt, Kathleen Cox and Barlow, of Bunkerville, are in the valley this week.

S. R. Whitehead and family have moved into their new home.

Mrs. Elizabeth Anderson is visiting at Whitney's Ranch this week.

Mr. and Mrs. Wm. McDonald entertained Friday evening in honor of Miss Grace Bischoff, who will leave soon to take the nurses' course at the L. D. S. Hospital in Salt Lake City.

Mrs. Rachel King came down Thursday from Logan, Utah, where she had been for some time. She will keep house for her father this summer.

Miss Lorna Perkins is clerking in

Whitehead Bros.' store.

Ward conference was held here Sunday, all the stake presidency being in attendance.

Miss Winona Earl is visiting at St. Thomas.

Mrs. Sheldon Barclay is here visiting her parents, Mr. and Mrs. Sanford Angell.

Mrs. Heber Bennion and daughter, Mrs. Ray Pixton, left Thursday for Taylorsville, where they will spend the summer.

Mrs. Frank Williams has gone to Salt Lake to join her husband, who has work there.

Overton, Nev, May 25 —Mr. and Mrs Leon Hickman returned Sunday from a short visit at St. George Mrs Hickman s mother, Mrs Mary Whitehead, returned with them.

Mrs Heber Bennion and daughter Mrs Ray Pixton left Thursday for Taylorsville where they will spend the summer. Mrs Frank Williams also went to Salt Lake to join her husband who has work there

Mr and Mrs Wm. McDonald entertained Friday evening in honor of Miss Grace Bischoff who leaves soon to take a nurse's course at the L D. S hospital at Salt Lake City

Mrs Rachel King came down Thursday from Logan, Utah, where she has been for some time She will keep house for her father this summer.

Marion and Miss Vida Earl, Miss Leah Leavitt, Miss Barlow and Miss Kathleen Cox of Bunkerville, are in the valley this week.

Ward conference was held here Sunday, all the stake presidency being in attendance.

Mrs Shelton Barclay is here visiting her parents, Mr and Mrs Sanford Angell

Mrs Elizabeth Anderson is visiting at Whitney's ranch this week

S. R Whitehead and family have moved into their new home.

Miss Lorna Perkins is clerking in Whitehead Bros store

Miss Winona Earl is visiting at St Thomas.

Overton, June 2 —The quarterly conference of the Moapa stake will be held here June 6 and 7 in the new district school building, which though not completed will be in good condition for use then and will afford ample room for the conference in the assembly room, which is on the upper floor. Elder James E Talmage and Patriarch Hyrum G. Smith have been appointed to attend the conference.

On May 30 a celebration of May was held under the management of the Sunday school There was a program in the morning, games and a children's dance in the afternoon and a dance for adults at night. In the morning Decoration day was observed by a large crowd that assembled at the cemetery at 8 30 to decorate the graves.

Wm. Perkins, jr., has sold his ranch at Logan to Mr. Egbert and with his family will spend the summer at Riverside, Cal , where Mr. Perkins has employment He has purchased land at Overton and will eventually locate here. He left last Thursday.

Elder LeBarron of Mesa City, Ariz , came last week, his wife who was Miss Maude McDonald, has been here for some time visiting her parents, Mr and Mrs W. W. McDonald. Mr. and Mrs. LeBarron will go on to Salt Lake City next week.

Misses Sadie Perkins, Addie Ingram, Helen Bunker, Mary Syphus, Carrie Hannig and Veda Hannig; Lamond Thomas and Averett Syphus came home last week from Las Vegas where they have been attending High school.

W. H. McDonald left Thursday for Salt Lake city where he will remain a few weeks on business Miss Grace Bischoff also left on Thursday's train to enter the nurse training department of the L. D. S hospital there.

A number of shipments of peaches and apricots have been made the past 16 days. Blackberries are also ripe and some enterprising farmers have ripe tomatoes.

Edw. Cox, Heber Hardy, Jesse Waite, Lee Cox and others are here this week delivering cattle. Two car loads were loaded today at St. Thomas.

Mrs. Echart and children came last week to join Mr. Echart who has charge of the school building being erected here.

Mr. and Mrs. Orin Jarvis were at Panaca last week to attend the closing exercises of the Lincoln Co high school.

Frank Snow of Salt Lake City is here on business connected with the Utah-Moapi Distributing Co.

The two-year old child of Samuel B Gentry has been very sick this week with pneumonia.

Mr. Stallman, a professional queen bee breeder is here working in the apiary of J. I. Earl.

Miss Clarissa Cannon of St. George has employment at Whitehead Bros. store here

Mrs. Warren Losee has taken charge of the ice cream parlor.

Overton Items

(Special Correspondence.)

Overton, Nevada, June 2, 1914.

Misses Sadie Perkins, Addie Ingram, Helen Bunker, Mary Syphus, Carrie and Verda Hunnig and Lamond Thomas and Averett Syphus came home last week from Las Vegas where they have been attending high school. Zilla Peterson and Armelia Ingram returned home on Monday.

Wm. Perkins, Jr., has sold his ranch at Logan to Mr. Egbert and with his family will spend the summer at Riverside, Cal., where Mr. Perkins has employment. He has purchased land at Overton and will eventually locate here. He left last Thursday.

435

W. H. McDonald left Thursday for Salt Lake City, where he will remain a few weeks on business.

Miss Grace Bischoff left on Thursday's train to enter the nurses' training department of the L. D. S. Hospital there.

Mr. Stahlman, a professional queen breeder, is here working in the apiary of J. I. Earl.

A two-year-old child of Samuel B. Gentry has been very sick this week with pneumonia.

Edward Cox, Heber Hardy, Jesse Waite, Lee Cox and others are here this week delivering cattle; two carloads were loaded today at St. Thomas.

On May 30th a celebration of May was held under the management of the Sunday school. There was a program of games in the morning and children's dances in the afternoon and a dance for adults at night. In the morning Decoration Day was observed by a large crowd that assembled at the cemetery at 8:30 to decorate the graves.

Mrs. Warren Losee has taken charge of the Turnbeau ice cream parlor.

Mrs. Eckhart and children came last week to join Mr. Eckhart, who has charge of the school building being erected here.

Elder LeBarron of Mesa City, Ariz., came last week. His wife, who was formerly Miss Maud McDonald, has been here for some time visiting her parents, Mr. and Mrs. W. W. McDonald. Mr. and Mrs. LeBarron will go on to Salt Lake City next week.

A number of shipments of peaches and apricots have been made within the past ten days. Blackberries also are ripe, and some enterprising farmers have ripe tomatoes.

Miss Vinda Waite of Bunkerville is here working for Mrs. Grissom.

Miss Clarissa Cannon of St. George has employment at Whitehead Bros.' store here.

Frank Snow of Salt Lake City is here on business connected with the Utah-Moapa Distributing Co.

Mr. and Mrs. Orin Jarvis were at Panaca last week to attend the closing exercises of the Lincoln county high school.

The Quarterly Conference of the Moapa Stake will be held here June 6 and 7 in the new district school building, which though not completed will be in good condition by that time for use and will afford ample room for the Conference in the assembly room, which is on the upper floor. Bro. James E. Talmage and Patriarch Hyrum G. Smith have been appointed to attend the Conference.

Washington County News
June 9, 1914

Overton, Nev., June 9 —The quarterly conference of the Moapa stake convened here Saturday and Sunday with a good attendance from the St Thomas, Bunkerville and Mesquite wards and a number from the Panaca and Alamo wards. Patriarch Hyrum G. Smith and Apostle Heber J. Grant were in attendance from Salt Lake City. The weather was ideal during the days of conference, which was held in the assembly hall of the new school building, now nearing completion.

A convention of Relief society and Primary workers was held in connection with the conference, Sisters Janett A. Hyde and Belle S. Ross being in attendence from Salt Lake City. On Saturday evening a social was held under the management of the Stake Primary officers at which ice cream was served and an exhibit of children's handiwork made.

Bishop Wm. A. Whitehead and wife and also his mother, Mrs. Mary Whitehead of St George, have gone to Salt Lake City, to attend the June conference and visit relatives

June conference and visit relatives in the north for some time.

Mr. and Mrs. Leon Hickman have gone to Salt Lake City, where the former will attend the summer school at the University of Utah. Miss LoRen Watson has also gone to Salt Lake City.

The visitors to the conference from the north were accommodated with train transportation from Overton to Moapa on Monday morning by train.

Mrs. Wm Perkins, jr , and family left last Thursday to join her husband in California where they will spend the summer.

Mr. and Mrs Stolbell Whitney. (the latter was Miss Isabell Frehner) have recently returned from a honeymoon trip to the coast.

Mr Clarence McDonald and Miss Jean Anderson have gone to St. George, Utah, where they will be married this week.

Saturday afternoon at 5 o'clock a reunion of the seventies of the stake was held

439

Overton Items

(Special Correspondence.)

Overton, Nevada, June 9, 1914.

Mrs. Wm. Perkins, Jr., and family left last Thursday to join her husband in California, where they will spend the summer.

Warren Cox of St. George was here on business last week.

Mr. and Mrs. Leon Hickman have gone to Salt Lake City where the latter will attend the summer school at the University of Utah. Miss LoRen Watson has also gone to Salt Lake City.

The quarterly conference of the Moapa stake convened here Saturday and

440

apa stake convened here Saturday and Sunday with a good attendance from the St. Thomas, Bunkerville and Mesquite wards and a number from the Panaca and Alamo wards. Patriarch Hyrum G. Smith and Apostle Heber J. Grant were in attendance from Salt Lake City. The weather was ideal during the days of the conference which was held in the assembly hall of the new school building now nearing completion here.

A convention of relief society and primary workers was held in connection with the conference, Sisters Janette A. Hyde and Belle S Ross being in attendance from Salt Lake City. On Saturday evening a social was held under the management of the stake pri-

trip to the coast.

Clarence McDonald and Miss Jean Anderson have gone to St. George, Utah, where they will be married this week.

mary officers at which ice cream was served and an exhibit of children's handiwork made.

Saturday afternoon at 5 o'clock there was a re-union of the seventys of the stake held.

The visitors to the conference from the north were accommodated with transportation from Overton to Moapa Monday morning by train.

Bishop Wm. A. Whitehead and wife and also his mother, Mrs. Mary Whitehead of St. George, have gone to Salt Lake City to attend the June conference and visit relatives in the north for some time.

Mr. and Mrs. Stowell Whitney have recently returned from a honeymoon trip to the coast.

Clarence McDonald and Miss Jean Anderson have gone to St. George, Utah, where they will be married this week.

Miss Jean Anderson should be spelt Andersen

Logan News

(Special Correspondence.)

Logan, Nev., June 18, 1914.

The Rex Plaster Company has closed down for the hot weather after shipping 24 cars of gyp. This gypsum is the finest entering the Los Angeles market, some cars going 99 per cent pure.

The melon season is close at hand. Dave Conger, of Overton, has been getting ripe melons for five days. The melons average much better this year than ever before, poor patches being scarce.

The flood caused Logan so much damage last spring that it looks as if Overton might lead in melon production for the first time.

The bee men have already shipped out one car of bees.

Mr. Duffield, owner of potash claims near here, has also ceased work for the summer, although there is considerable interest being taken in potash and other places are being tried out.

The Hinckley ranch has again changed hands, a Mr. Georgeson being the new owner.

School Census

Deputy Superintendent of Public Instruction B. G. Bleasdale has received the reports of the census marshals of all districts in the county. The various districts have school children of school age, that is between the ages of 6 and 18, as follows:

Searchlight	24
Goodsprings	22
Las Vegas	308
Moapa	19
Warm Springs	18
St. Joe (Logan)	47
Overton	92
Kaolin	25
St. Thomas	61
Bunkerville	113
Mesquite	101
Eldorado	1

Arden now has ten children and the district there will be re-established this fall.

443

Overton, June 30 —Elders Levi Syphus and Harry Gentry, jr., of St Thomas were here Sunday as home missionaries and spoke at Sacrament meeting Elder Gentry has recently returned from a mission to the Tiahitian Islands and gave us some of his experiences in that land He was released after an absence of about 20 months on account of weak eyes

A fine program has been prepared for the 4th and Overton will fittingly celebrate our nation's birthday. Under the direction of Joseph Mc-Donald, a band has been organized and is working hard to prepare for July 4th.

Mr. and Mrs Clarence McDonald returned recently from a trip to relatives in Blackfoot, Idaho They were married in Salt Lake City June

444

... .
10.

Mrs Eliza Ingram and Mrs. Nellie Losee returned Friday from a visit to the Primary associations of the Bunkerville and Mesquite wards

N. Ray Pixton and Brigham Hardy were over to Bunkerville Sunday to fill home missionary appointments

The reservoir at Kaolin has been fitted up with bath rooms and has become a popular bathing resort for the valley.

A number of farmers are shipping cantaloupes now and we will have daily train service till the crop is over.

Afternoon service on Sunday has been changed to 8 o'clock p m. during the hot weather

CANTALOUPE SEASON OPEN

Moapa Valley Towns Now Scene of Melon Shipping Activity

(Special Correspondence.)

Overton, Nevada, June 30.

A number of farmers are shipping cantaloupes now and we will have daily train service until the crop is over.

The reservoir at Kaolin has been fitted up with bath rooms and has become a popular bathing resort for the valley.

A fine program has been prepared for July 4th and Overton will fittingly celebrate our nation's birthday.

Under the direction of Joseph McDonald a band has been organized and the members are working hard to pre-

446

pare for July 4th.

N. Ray Pixton and Brigham Hardy went over to Bunkerville Sunday to fill a home missionary appointment.

Mr. and Mrs. Clarence McDonald returned recently from a visit with relatives in Blackfoot, Idaho. They were married in Salt Lake City June 10.

Mrs. Eliza Ingram and Mrs. Nellie Losee returned Friday from a visit to the primary associations of the Bunkerville and Mesquite wards.

Sunday afternoon service has been changed to 7:00 p. m. during the hot weather.

Elders Levi Syphus and Harry Gentry, Jr., of St. Thomas, were here Sunday as home missionaries and spoke at sacrament meeting. Elder Gentry has recently returned from a mission to the Tahitan Islands and gave us some of his experiences in that land. He was released on account of weak eyes after an absence of about 20 months.

DELINQUENT NOTICE.

MUDDY VALLEY IRRIGATION COMPANY.

Location of principal place of business, Overton, Clark Co., Nevada.

Location of irrigation system and works, Moapa Valley, Clark Co., Nevada.

NOTICE

There are delinquent upon the following described preferred capital stock on account of assessment No. 1, levied on the 2nd day of March, 1914, the several amounts set opposite the names of the respective shareholders as follows:

No. ctf.	Name	Shares	Amt.
344	C. Cobb	41½	$ 1.13
683	W. W. Muir	10	1.21
641	James G. Foxley	8	6.00
480	Moapa Farm and Orchard Co.	50	37.50
261, 312, 634,	Moapa Improvem't Co.	131	98.25
496	Moapa Garden Co.	50½	37.88
374	Wm. F. Murphy	46 4 5	35.10
461	Hyrum Murphy	28 2 5	17.50
612	Guy Gardener	2	1.50
651	E. H. Syphus	9	5.80
427	Christiana Syphus	4	3.00
622	Francis Johnson	3	2.25

There are also delinquent upon the following described common stock on account of assessment No. 2, levied on the 2nd day of March, 1914, the several amounts set opposite the names of the respective shareholders as follows:

221	A. J. Avey	36	$ 5.40
76	Chas. Cobb	150	22.50
37	H. H. Church	16	2.40
131	J. S. Gordon	25	3.75
129	Moapa Farm & Orchard Co.	63½	9.50
51	Moapa Improvement Co.	266⅔	40.00
97	Moapa Garden Co.	54½	8.18
92	Wm. F. Murphy	36 9-10	6.54
117	Chas. Murphy	28 7-10	4.31
119	Hyrum Murphy	16 4-10	2.46
78		80	
79		80	
80		80	
81		80	
82	T. J. Osborne	40	54.00

And in accordance with law and an order of the Board of Directors made on the 2nd day of March, 1914, so many shares of each parcel of each class of such stock as may be necessary will be sold at public auction at the office of the Company, in Overton, Clark County, Nevada, on the 18th day of July, 1914, at the hour of 3 o'clock p. m. of such day, to pay the delinquent assessments together with cost of advertisement and expense of sale.

Overton, Nevada, June 1st, 1914.

By order of the Board of Directors.

ISAAC E. LOSEE, Secretary.

First publication, June 13, 1914.

Last publication, July 11, 1914.

Overton, Nev , July 10 —Every body is busy these days in the Moapa valley. The melons are ripening nicely and this morning's shipment consisted of six carloads, careful supervision is made at the various packing sheds that nothing but good cantaloupes are shipped out.

On the 1st of July there was a change in the mail service down the valley; the contract for carrying the same having been let to George Perkin of St. Thomas The mail now goes up to Moapa and returns the same day each Tuesday, Thursday and Saturday.

Bp O. P. Miller and Mr Nebeker came down from Salt Lake City Thursday on business connected with the church property at Kaolin. F. F. Hienze who has charge there returned also from a short trip to Salt Lake City.

Chas. Osborne came down from Pioche this week to take charge of his property here He and his father, T J. Osborne, each own tracts of land here.

450

COUNTY BOARD HOLDS MEETING

Varied Items of Important Business Come to Attention of the Commissioners

The county commissioners' meeting held July 6th found Chairman C. C. Ronnow presiding and Commissioners Geo. A. Fayle and John M. Bunker in their usual places.

After the routine business of reading the minutes of the previous meeting and receiving the reports of officers, the usual grist of monthly bills was passed.

A request was made by the trustees of the Bunkerville school district that the county transfer $5,000 from the county general funds to the Bunkerville school district funds for the purpose of carrying on high school work in that district. The matter was laid over until a report as to the standing of the school should be received from Deputy Superintendent of Public Instruction B. G. Bleasdale.

I. C. Johnson was appointed public administrator in the place of J. D. Kramer, resigned, to fill the unexpired term, the appointment to take effect upon filing a bond for $2,000.

Campbell and Turner, contractors for the court house, were granted an extension of 45 days from the first day of July for completing the new courthouse.

The sum of $10 per month was allowed the Harvey family from the indigent fund.

The matter of applications for permits for liquor licenses coming up, and upon statements made by Dr. E. G. Murtaugh and Sheriff Sam Gay, permits were refused to C. L. Ricketson and J. T. Sprague of Moapa.

Permits for liquor licenses were granted as follows: J. E. Keate, Moapa; Crescent Mercantile Co., Crescent; John Truax and Burdick & Clements, Nelson; Yount & Fayle, for Jean and Goodsprings.

Inspectors for election were appointed for the primary and general elections as follows:

Mesquite—Wm. E. Abbott, John H. Barnum, Louis J. Pulsipher.

Bunkerville—Parley Hunt, Edw. I. Cox, Harmon Wittwer.

St. Thomas—M. A. Bunker, Edw. Syphus, Frank Bonelli.

Overton—Elmer Losee, J. P. Anderson, Wm. A. Whitehead.

Logan—Fred Rushton, J. M. Thomas, O. W. Jarvis.

Correct spelling should be J. P. Andersen

453

Moapa—J. E. Keate, J. T. Sprague, Ira Earl.

Las Vegas—J. T. McWilliams, Jack Tuck, David Farnsworth.

Indian Springs—Al McCausland, Jimmie McMahn, Ira MacFarland.

Arden—J C. Gorin, T. H. Garnett, C. M. McLeod.

Goodsprings—Fred A Hale, Jr., Henry Robbins, Jos. Ashbaugh.

Crescent—Jeff Davis, C. H. Sheerer, J. Horne.

Searchlight—Frank Haine, Jas. Cashman, J. E. Emerson.

Nelson—Victor Troise, I. W. Allcock, Wm. Burke.

C. N. Irwin of Searchlight was granted a license as stationary engineer.

Clark Alvord was appointed registry agent for Nelson precinct.

No further business appearing the board adjourned to Aug. 3.

Not Returning to School

Misses Armelia and Adeline Ingram and Miss Sadie Perkins will not, we are sorry to hear, return to the high school next fall.

Misses Sadie Perkins and Adeline Ingram will both leave their home in Overton Aug. 20 for Salt Lake City to take a nurse's training course in the L. D. S. Hospital. Miss Armelia Ingram will open a dressmaking establishment for the benefit of the Moapa Valley people at Overton in September. The young ladies will all be missed in Clark County High school.

Washington County News
July 18, 1914

Overton, Nev., July 18 —It has been very warm here the past week. The farmers are very busy with the cantaloupe crop The shipments running to about 15 cars a day. Today St. Thomas furnished 3 cars and Overton 6

Joseph Webb of St George was here this week in the interest of the Utah's Dixie Nursery Co at Hurricane Utah.

Dr. and Mrs D O. Beal have gone for a two weeks visit to relatives in Ephraim, Utah.

Bishop J. Jones who is spending the summer in Delta, Utah, is very sick with pneumonia.

455

OBITUARY

Overton, Nev., July 24.—Funeral services were held here July 23 for Patriarch Thomas Jefferson Jones, who died July 18 at Delta, Utah, where he was visiting members of his family who have homes in Millard Co. He was 75 years of age having been born in Pittsfield, Pike Co, Ill, in 1838, a son of James Hart Jones and Parthena Davis. In 1852 he came by ox team to Utah locating in Centerville, Davis Co, Utah, later moving to Willard, Box Elder County. In 1860 he visited the old home in Illinois and while there married Emily Miller who came with him to Utah the following year. He was called by Pres Young to the southern mission, reporting to Apostle Erastus Snow at St George who sent him to Panaca, Nevada.

Here he helped survey the townsite and the land occupied by the Latter-day Saints there and presided as bishop, also serving two years as county commissioner. In 1875 he was called by Pres Brigham Young to Washington, Utah, to take charge of the Rio Virgin Manufacturing factory as its Supt. in which position he served six years. During that time he also served two years as county commissioner, four years as bishop of Washington and also acted as first counselor to Pres J. D. T. McAllister in the presidency of the St. George Stake. By appointment from Pres John Taylor, he moved to Parowan in March 1882 to be president of the Parowan Stake of Zion; this position he occupied for eleven years also serving Iron county as county commissioner. In

456

1878 he married Johanah C Larson and in 1879 he also married Alice Hall and during the "raid" he moved part of his family to the Moapa Valley in Nevada, locating at Overton; here he was set apart as bishop by Apostle Lyman In June 1890 he was released from serving a six-months term in the Utah penitentary for polygamy In June 1912 he was ordained a patriarch in the Moapa Stake of Zion by Apostles Francis M. Lyman and George F. Richards Of his family, two wives and twenty children survive him, one wife and six sons having died. He has 55 grandchildren and 12 great-grandchildren. Funeral services were in charge of Bp W. A Whitehead, Pres. John M. Bunker of St. Thomas, Patriarch Jos I. Earl of Bunkerville and Bp William Abbott of Mesquite were the speakers, each paying many tributes of respect to him for his long and usefull life and sterling qualities Mrs. Mary V. Lytle and Mrs Jean McDonald sang "O, My Father;" N. Ray Pixton sang, "Sometime We'll Understand," and the choir rendered "When First the Glorious Light of Truth" and "I Know That My Redeemer Lives ' Interment was made in the Overton cemetery, Robert Bunker dedicating the grave. The funeral was well attended from all parts of the Valley, his daughters, Mrs A. C. Christenson and Mrs W. L Batty of Oasis, Utah, and Miss Louisa Jones and sons, Calvin and Jefferson Jones of Delta, Utah, and daughters Mrs. O. P. Callister of Blackfoot, Idaho, and Mrs. Annie Cox of Bunkerville, Mrs. Patience Lee of Kaolin and his family residing in Overton all being in attendance.

Miss Kathleen Cox who has been here working in the home of Dr. Beal for some time, left this morning for the Home ranch in the upper Moapa valley.

On the 22nd of July there had been 210 cars of cantaloupes shipped this season It is estimated that 300 cars will be shipped before the season is over.

John Averett of Logan is very sick with stomach trouble and his son, John, jr., left with him today for Salt Lake City.

Miss Laprele Wait of Bunkerville is here employed in the Johnson home.

DIED

JONES: In Delta, Utah, Saturday July 18, 1914, Bishop Thomas Jefferson Jones, of Overton, Nevada, of pneumonia. The deceased was aged about 87 years and has been one of the most active of the early pioneers of the Moapa Valley. He leaves a large family and mony friends who regret the passing of a good man. His remains were brought to Overton for burial Thursday.

Overton Items

(Special Correspondence.)

Overton, Nev., July 17, 1914.

Dr. and Mrs. D. O. Beal have gone for a two weeks' visit to relatives in Ephriam, Utah.

Bp. Thos. J. Jones, who is spending the summer in Delta, Utah, is very sick with pneumonia.

Jos. Webb of St. George was here this week in the interest of the Southern Nursery at Hurricane, Utah.

It has been very warm here the past week. The farmers are very busy with the cantaloupe crop, the shipments running about 15 cars a day. Today St Thomas furnished three cars and Overton six.

Overton, Nev., Aug 3 — The cantaloupe crop has practically all been harvested The Farmers association quit shipping last week and it is reported that daily service on the railroad will not be continued down the valley after this week

Wm Perkins, jr and sons, Maynard and Lewis, have returned from California Mrs Perkins will remain at the coast a few weeks longer.

Jos I Earl went over to Las Vegas Sunday to attend the county commissioners meeting, in the interest of the Bunkerville high school.

Contractor Eckart and family left last week for their home in Salt Lake City, his work on the district school house being finished

Joe F. Perkins and family have gone for a trip to the Timber mountain where Mr. Perkins has cattle on the range

Elmer Losee was over to Bunkerville last week to set the ice plant there in operation.

Born, July 30, a daughter to Mr. and Mrs O B Grissom at the Benson farm in Logan.

Mrs W A Whitehead is visiting relatives in St George, Utah.

MARRIED

ANDERSON — HANNIG: In this city, Monday evening, August 3, 1914, Fay E. Anderson and Miss Carrie S. Hannig, both of Overton, Nev. The ceremony was performed by Chas. C. Ronnow, elder in the church of Jesus Christ of Latter Day Saints, and was witnessed by Newell Leavitt and Mary Crosby.

The groom is the son of J. P. Anderson, the Overton merchant, and will be remembered as a member of the crack Overton basketball team of last winter. He is highly respected by a large circle of friends.

The bride is a charming young lady who is a favorite in the Moapa Valley. She attended Clark county high school here last year and her winning ways and cheery disposition made her many friends in Vegas. We take pleasure in extending our most hearty congratulations to the happy pair.

Correct spelling should be Andersen

Overton Items

(Special Correspondence.)

Overton, Nev., Aug. 3, 1914.

Contractor Eckart and family left last week for their home in Salt Lake City, his work on the district school house being finished.

Mrs. W. A. Whitehead is visiting relatives in St. George, Utah.

Born, July 30, a daughter to Mr. and Mrs. O. B. Grissom at the Benson farm in Logan.

Wm. Perkins, Jr., and sons, Maynard and Lewis, have returned from California. Mrs. Perkins will remain at the coast and visit a few weeks longer.

Jos. I. Earl went to Las Vegas Sunday to attend the county commissioners' meeting in the interest of the Bunkerville high school.

The cantaloupe crop has practically all been harvested. The farmers' association quit shipping last week and it is reported that daily service on the railroad will not be continued down the valley after this week.

Joe F. Perkins and family have gone for a trip to the Timber mountain where Mr. Perkins has cattle on the range.

Elmer Losee was over to Bunkerville last week to set the ice plant there in operation.

461

School Apportionment

Carson City, Nevada, July 18, 1914.
To the County Auditor and the County Treasurer, Clark County.

Gentlemen: The following is a statement of the second semi-annual apportionment of county school moneys for Clark county for the calendar year of 1914. The county treasurer reported the amount in the county school fund to be $4,996.36. Forty per cent of this sum is divided among 18 teachers on the basis of $118.7431 per teacher, and 60 per cent is divided among 830 school census children on the basis of $3.86273 per child.

DISTRICTS	CENSUS CHILDREN	CO. SCHOOL FUNDS
Las Vegas	308	$1,611.84
Bunkerville	113	608.89
Mesquite	101	566.75
Searchlight	24	190.31
Goodsprings	22	183.29
Warmsprings	18	169.24
Moapa	19	172.75
St. Joe	47	271.08
Overton	92	535.14
St. Thomas	61	320.25
Kaolin	25	193.82
Totals	830	$4,823.36

To the Auditor and the Treasurer of Clark County, Nevada.

Gentlemen: Following is a statement of the second semi-annual apportionment of state school money for Clark county for the calendar year 1914. The amount set apart for Clark county is $6,374.65. Seventy per cent of this is apportioned among 33 teachers, allowing one teacher for every 30 school census children or fraction thereof, making $128.38562 for each teacher. Thirty per cent is apportioned among 830 school census children, making $2.57589 for each school census child.

DISTRICTS	CENSUS CHILDREN	STATE FUND
Las Vegas	308	$2,205.60
Bunkerville	113	804.61
Mesquite	101	779.70
Searchlight	24	190.20
Goodsprings	22	185.05
Warmsprings	18	174.75
Moapa	19	177.33
St. Joe	47	377.83
Overton	92	750.52
St. Thomas	61	542.28
Kaolin	25	192.78
Totals	830	$6,374.65

Respectfully,
JOHN EDWARDS BRAY,
Superintendent of Public Instruction.

462

Overton, Aug 11.—A dance was held August 4 in the assembly room at the new school house which was well attended from all parts of the valley The building is well lighted, cool and airy; the fine hardwood floor and the splendid music by the McDonald brothers added to the pleasure of the evening

Benj Robinson, Clarence McDonald, Fay Anderson and their wives, Mrs W W. McDonald and others have gone to the mountains, most of the campers will be in the neighborhood of Whitney's ranch in the Bunkerville mountains

Will McDonald and family returned last week from a month's stay in Salt Lake City. They with Jos McDonald and family have gone for an outing in the mountains

Mr. and Mrs Warren Losee will leave this week for Panguitch lake. Later they will go on to Logan, Utah, where Mr. Losee expects to attend the A. C the coming winter.

Lorin Prisbrey and Miss Lydia Cooper surprised their friends last week by being married here by Justice A. L F. McDermott and leaving the same evening for Idaho.

U. V Perkins left Monday for St. George, Utah, where his wife has been visiting her parents, Mr. and Mrs George Whitney for some time.

Dr. and Mrs. D. O. Beal returned Sunday from a visit to Ephriam, Utah, where Dr. Beal's parents reside

Fay Anderson and Miss Carrie Hannig were married August 3 in Las Vegas by Bp Chas. Ronnow.

Laylette Mathews has returned to his home in Panaca after a year spent working here in the valley.

Overton Items

(Special Correspondence.)
Overton, Nev., Aug. 11, 1914.

A dance was held August 4th in the assembly room at the new school house, which was well attended from all parts of the valley. The building is well lighted, cool and airy. The fine hardwood floor and the excellent music by the McDonald brothers added to the pleasure of the evening.

Lorin Prisby and Lydia Cooper surprised their friends, being married here by Justice A. L. F. McDermott and leaving the same evening for Idaho.

U. V. Perkins left Monday for St. George, Utah, where his wife has been visiting for some time with her parents.

L. Mathews has returned to his home in Panaca after a year spent working in the valley.

Fay Anderson and Carrie Hannig were married Aug. 3rd in Las Vegas by Bishop Chas. Ronnow.

Will McDonald and family returned last week from Salt Lake, where they have been for the past month. They have gone for an outing in the mountains with Jos. McDonald and family.

Benj. Robinson, Clarence McDonald, Fay Anderson and wives, Mrs. W. W. McDonald and others have gone to the mountains. Most of the campers will be in the neighborhood of Whitney's ranch in the Bunkerville mountains.

Two car loads of merchandise is being placed on the shelves at the new Gunn store this week. Ira J. Earl is in charge during Mr. Gunn's absence in Chicago, selling cantaloupes. He is expected to return soon as the shipping season is now practically over.

Dr. and Mrs. D. O. Beal returned Sunday from a visit to Ephriam, Utah, where Dr. Beal's parents reside.

Mr. and Mrs. Warren Losee will leave this week for Panguich Lake. Later they will go on to Logan, Utah, where Mr. Losee expects to attend the A. C. College the coming winter.

465

Correct spelling should be Andersen

Overton, Aug 21 —Mrs Geo. Pearson, who has been here at the Dr Beal home for some time under the care of a special nurse, returned to her home at St Thomas last week much improved in health The nurse, Mrs. Edwards left for Salt Lake City Saturday.

A social was given Monday evening for Mr. and Mrs George Lytle who left the next morning for Eager, Arizona, where they expect to make their home Their city lot here was purchased by Wm. Perkins, jr.

The doors at the new Gunn store were thrown open here today for business. Their store is in a fine new concrete building and is well supplied.

Robert Bunker and Horace Jones and their families returned Friday from an outing in the mountains near Whitney's ranch.

Born, Aug 10, a son to Mr. and Mrs Fred Bischoff, all concerned doing nicely.

Pres S H. Wells and family have returned from a visit to Salt Lake City.

Mr. and Mrs. Elmer Losee left Thursday for a trip to the Pacific coast

Miss Naomi Henderson is now employed in the telephone office.

Miss Winona Earl came over from Bunkerville Monday.

466

PREPARING FOR STATE FAIR

Chamber of Commerce Will Send Carload of Products From Clark County

The Chamber of Commerce held its meeting Tuesday evening at the Chamber headquarters, and important action was taken in the matter of making a big showing at the state fair at Reno, Sept. 21st to 26th.

C. P. Squires, as special committee to ascertain the feasibility of securing the shipment of the Clark county exhibits in a through car, thus doing away with the necessity of having the materials loaded and unloaded at several points of transfer, was called upon for a report. He presented authority from the Salt Lake road, the Las Vegas & Tonopah and Bullfrog & Goldfield, the Tonopah & Goldfield and Southern Pacific roads, showing that a through car would be handled by those roads if approximately a carload of exhibits should be shipped.

Arrangements have been made with the Salt Lake Route whereby the car will be placed at St. Thomas for the loading of any products there, and stopped in turn at Overton, Logan and Moapa. At Las Vegas the loading will be finished. It is the intention of the Chamber to include several blooded horses, one or two or more fine bulls, hogs, chickens and whatever is available in the livestock line, in the exhibit, this to use one end of the car. The agricultural products will be packed in

467

able in the livestock line, in the exhibit, this to use one end of the car. The agricultural products will be packed in the other end and should reach Reno in a much better condition than last year.

The railroads have united in providing free transportation to and from the fair. This is a most generous action and is thoroughly appreciated by the people of Clark county. It will readily be seen that the cost to the roads of transporting a carload of exhibits from St. Thomas to Reno and return, a distance of over 1000 miles, is no small item and the spirit of co-operation which the officials have shown in the matter of handling the exhibits is most commendable.

Frank Clark, Peter Buol and M. M. Riley were appointed a committee to raise $200 for use in preparing the exhibit.

The matter of the difficulty of establishing a market for Clark county cantaloupes, water melons and fruits in Tonopah and Goldfield was discussed. The freight and express rates were considered and W. R. Thomas, chairman of the Committee on Transportation, was requested to get such information as possible for the benefit of the Chamber.

The secretary was instructed to obtain all information possible as to the amount of vegetables, fruit etc. raised in and about Las Vegas, the amount shipped in for local consumption and the possibility of establishing a local market of some nature for local products.

The meeting was a profitable one, the earnest discussion of the important questions brought up indicating that the Chamber is doing excellent work. Especially to be commended is the orderly neatness of the rooms and the numerous things of interest there on exhibition as provided by Miss Thompson, the secretary. The pitchers of ice water also provided by her for the comfort of the members were also much appreciated. The attractive exhibit which the new secretary is also maintaining at the depot was also noted most favorably.

468

Busy Sheriff

Sheriff Sam Gay is having a busy time this week in getting the election supplies, ballot boxes etc. distributed to the various precincts. He returned Thursday from the southern portion of the county where he visited Goodsprings, Crescent, Searchlight and Nelson.

He reports that there is new activity in the southern camps and that the mining interests are looking well.

Sheriff Gay is now making the trip to Moapa, Logan, Overton and St. Thomas. Robert Ferguson has been deputized to make the trip to Bunkerville and Mesquite, this being necessary by reason of the short time remaining after the receipt of the supplies from the north.

469

Overton Items

(Special Correspondence.)

Overton, Nev., Aug. 21, 1914.

Mrs. Geo. Pearson, who has been at the Dr. Beal home for some time, under the care of a special nurse, returned to her home at St. Thomas last week much improved in health. The nurse, Mrs. Edwards, left Saturday for Salt Lake City.

Miss Naomi Henderson has accepted a position as operator in the telephone office.

Born, August 10th, to Mr. and Mrs. Fred Bischoff, a son. Mother and child are doing nicely.

A social was given Monday evening for Mr. and Mrs. George Lytle, who left the next morning for Eager, Ariz., where they expect to make their home. Their city lot here was purchased by Wm. Perkins, Jr.

Miss Winona Earl came over from Bunkerville Monday.

Mr. and Mrs. Elmer Losee left Thursday for a trip to the Pacific coast.

Robert Bunker and Horace Jones, with their families, returned Friday from an outing in the mountains near Whitney's ranch.

Pres. S. H. Wells and family have returned from a visit to Salt Lake City.

The doors of the new Gunn's store were thrown open today for business. Their store is in a fine new concrete building and is nicely furnished and supplied with a good stock of general merchandise.

470

STATE FAIR GETS ATTENTION

Entire State to Compete---Clark County's Exhibit Will Be Second to None

The State Fair to be held at Reno Sept. 21 to 26 is receiving attention from nearly every county in the state. According to present appearances a most interesting collection of the products of the state will be shown this year.

Clark county, although nearly 500 miles from the fair grounds, will be right there with a carload of her best. E. W. Griffith, president of the Chamber of Commerce, reports that St. Thomas, Overton, Logan and the upper Moapa Valley will furnish a wonderful variety of grains, vegetables and fruits, some of the latter being semi-tropical in their nature. Horses, cattle, hogs and chickens will indicate what Clark county may do in livestock. Hay and forage plants will also contribute to the excellence of our exhibit.

Every person in the county who has produced anything of especial excellence is urged to send a portion of the best. A special through car will carry everything without any reloading, thus making it possible for Clark county to make a better show than ever before. A splendid collection of minerals will also make our northern neighbors open their eyes. Let everybody get busy and boost for Clark county.

Washington County News
September 3, 1914

Overton, Nev., Sept. 3.— The Moapa Stake conference will be held Sept. 4 and 5 at Panaca, Nevada. Elders Anthony W. Ivins and George Albert Smith of the Quorum of the Apostles have been appointed to attend the conference. Special service was secured on the branch line to St. Thomas for the accommodation of those who went to Panaca to attend the conference About 25 in number left the valley this morning and will return by train Tuesday.

Sunday services were held in the new school house which has recently been fitted up with seats for school on the lower floor. A general contribution has been made by the people of the ward to buy seats for the assembly room

Born, Aug. 25, a daughter to Mr. and Mrs W. L Jones; and Aug. 29, a daughter to Mr. and Mrs. Alex Swapp.

Geo Ingram, jr., and the Misses Armelia and Adeline Ingram have gone for a visit to Kanarra, Utah.

Mr and Mrs Frank L Cox of St George, Utah, are visiting relatives here

Las Vegas Age Newspaper
September 12, 1914

Wallace Jones of Overton is among the arrivals to attend Clark county high school this year.

472

Overton Items

(Special Correspondence.)
Overton, Nev., Sept. 3, 1914.

The Moapa stake conference will be held Sept. 4th and 5th at Panaca. Elders Anthony W. Ivins and George Albert Smith of the quorum of the twelve apostles have been appointed to attend the conference.

Special service was secured on the branch line to St. Thomas for the accommodation of those who went to Panaca to attend the conference, numbering about 25. They left the valley this morning and will return by train Tuesday.

Sunday services were held in the new school house, the lower floor of which has recently been fitted up with seats for school. A generous contribution has been made by the people of the ward to buy seats for the assembly room.

Baby daughters were born last week to Mr. and Mrs. W. L. Jones, and to Mr. and Mrs. Alex Swapp.

Samuel H. Wells has moved his family to Kaolin, where he has charge of the church property. F. F. Heinze, formerly in charge there, has been released and has moved his family to Murray, Utah.

Mr. and Mrs. Frank L. Cox of St. George, Utah, are visiting relatives here.

Geo. Ingram Jr. and the Misses Armelia and Adeline Ingram have gone for a visit to Kanarra, Utah.

(From Another Correspondent)

A Sunday school party given at Logan last evening was well attended by the young people of Overton.

Mr. Lewis, who has been located at Capalpa for several years past, is now putting up a frame cottage on his lot in town and will move his family down soon.

Sadie Perkins is comfortably located in the L. D. S. hospital in Salt Lake City, enjoying her course in nursing. The second day after her arrival found her in the typhoid division, which was very interesting to her.

It is reported that a fine electric plant is soon to be established at Rioville on the Colorado river. The system will extend the entire length of the valley. The old ferry there, which was handled so long and well by Daniel Bonelli, will also be put in again. This will be done under the management of his son, George A. Bonelli, of Kingman, Arizona, who is already placing engines and machinery on the grounds.

Dee Hickman has gone to San Juan county, Utah, on a business trip. While away he will visit relatives in Provo and Salt Lake City.

Wallace Jones left Sunday to attend Clark county high school at Las Vegas.

An epidemic of sore throat and fever is quite prevalent throughout the valley, also a number of cases of malaria and other diseases, which are thought to be caused by the impure water that we are forced to drink. Election day is near and it is hoped that the officers elected will help the people in keeping the stream of water through the valley more sanitary.

473

Isaac E. Losee, secretary of the Muddy Valley Irrigation Co., and owner of the electric light plant and ice factory at Overton, is spending a day or two in Vegas on business.

County Candidates Meet at Court House Tuesday According to Law

The Republican county candidates met at the court house Tuesday as provided by law and the work of formulating a county platform was taken up This is in the hands of a committee which will get the suggestions in shape and report the result to another meeting for adoption.

Republican county central committeemen were also chosen as follows:

Nelson—I. W. Allcock.

Searchlight—B. Frank Miller, Jr.

Crescent—S. C. Whipple.

Goodsprings—O. J. Fiske.

Arden—J. T. Boyd.

Indian Springs—Ira MacFarland.

Las Vegas—R. W. Martin.

Moapa—J. T. Sprague.

Logan—Bert Mills.

Overton—S. A. Angell.

St. Thomas—B. F. Bonelli.

Bunkerville—S. W. Darling.

Mesquite—Jas. E. Hughes.

474

Overton, Nev, Sept 22.—The district school commenced here on the 14th, in the new school building with the following teachers: Primary, Miss Florence Beal; Intermediate, Leonidas Hickman; Principal, A. E Jones.

Mrs. W. A. Whitehead returned last week from a visit to St. George. Mrs. Joseph Judd came down with her to visit relatives here Mrs Judd taught our primary school here when she was Miss Effie Whitehead and has many friends who will appreciate her visit.

Supt Nephi Hunt and the members of the Stake Sunday school board were here Sunday to visit the Sunday schools of the valley in the forenoon In the afternoon the officers of all the schools met at Overton for a union meeting.

Among the newest arrivals are a daughter to Mr and Mrs. George Perkins, a son to Mr and Mrs. John Connelly, and a daughter to Mr. and Mrs Van Pelt, at Logan, where Mrs Van Pelt is visiting her parents.

Under the management of the Stake officers here a farewell party was given Friday evening for N. Ray Pixton, who is to leave soon for Salt Lake valley where he will make his home.

Mrs Martha Fleming is visiting her parents in Leeds, Utah.

District Attorney Van Pelt returned Thursday from Logan and is receiving the congratulations of his many friends upon the arrival of a fine little daughter, who was born at Logan on the 8th of September.

Purchases Auto

I. E. Losee, of Overton, has purchased a new Ford from J. W. Woodard. Mr. Losee will use the car in making trips through the Moapa Valley where he is interested in irrigation work.

Overton Items

(Special Correspondence.)
Overton, Nev., Sept. 22, 1914.

The district school commenced here on the 14th, in the new school building, with the following teachers; Primary, Miss Frances Beal; Intermediate, Leonidas Hickman; Principal, A. E. Jones.

Among the newest arrivals are a daughter to Mr. and Mrs. George Perkins, a son to Mr. and Mrs. John Connelly and a daughter to Mr. and Mrs. Van Pelt at Logan, where Mrs. Van Pelt is visiting her parents.

Mrs. Martha Fleming is visiting her parents in Leeds, Utah.

Mrs. W. A. Whitehead returned last week from a visit to St. George. Mrs. Joseph Judd came down with her to visit relatives here. Mrs. Judd taught our primary school when she was Miss Effie Whitehead and has many friends here who will appreciate her visit.

Under the management of the Stake officers here, a farewell party was given Friday evening for Stake Clerk N. Ray Pixton, who is to leave soon for Salt Lake Valley where he will make his home. There was dancing, games and a general hand shake also a short program. The ladies served cake and punch.

Supt. Nephi Hunt and the members of the Stake Sunday school board were here Sunday to visit the Sunday schools of the valley in the forenoon. In the afternoon the officers of all the schools met at Overton for a union meeting.

Overton, Nev., Oct 5 —The Y. M M. I A. was reorganized Sunday with D Hickman president and Fay Anderson and Clarence Mc-Donald as counselors The Y. L A was also reorganized with Mrs Nellie Losee as president, Mrs William Hickman and Dora Jones as counselors, Mrs. Marie Flowers senior girls' class leader and Mrs Myrtle Whitehead junior girls' class leader.

Mrs Laura J Cannon, representing the Nevada Equal Franchise society, spoke here Sunday evening Her lecture was very interesting. A sufferage committee was organized among the Overton ladies with Mrs. W. L. Jones as chairman.

The ladies of the Relief society gave a weight ball Tuesday evening in which the gentlemen drew for partners and paid one-half cent a pound for his lady. Lunch consisting of cake and punch was served

Mr. and Mrs. William Flowers and Mr and Mrs. A. L Jones returned Tuesday from Alamo, where the ladies went in the interest of the Primary association. They report a pleasant trip

Goldeen, the little daughter of Mrs Mary West had the misfortune to break her arm by a fall on the playground at school last week.

Elmer Losee returned last week from Las Vegas with an auto, the first one to be owned by an Overton citizen

Whitehead Bros store, which was taken over by a receiver some time ago, has been sold to Mr Sloan of Moapa

Miss Adeline Ingram and her brother, George Ingram, jr , are attending the B A. C. at Cedar City, Utah

Mr and Mrs Henry Kockerhans returned Thursday from Wyoming, where they spent the summer.

477

Overton Items

(Special Correspondence.)

Overton, Nev., Oct. 5, 1914.

The ladies of the Relief Society gave a "Weight" ball Tuesday evening in which the gentlemen drew for partners and paid one-half cent a pound for his lady. Lunch consisting of cake and punch was served.

Elmer Losee returned last week from Las Vegas with an auto, the first one to be owned by an Overton citizen.

Miss Adeline Ingram and her brother, George Ingram, Jr., are attending the branch agricultural college in Cedar City.

Mr. and Mrs. Henry Kocherhans returned Tuesday from Alamo, where they spent the summer.

Mr. and Mrs. Wm. Flowers, with Mr. and Mrs. A. L. Jones, returned Tuesday from Alamo, where the ladies went in the interest of the Primary association. They report a pleasant trip.

Whitehead Bros. Store, which was taken over by a receiver some time ago, has been sold to Mr. Sloan of Moapa.

Mrs. Laura J. Cannon, representing the Nevada Equal Franchise Society, spoke here Sunday evening, Sept. 27. Her lecture proved very interesting. A suffrage committee was organized among the Overton ladies with Mrs. Jones as chairman.

Among those going out on Thursday's train for Salt Lake City to attend the fair and conference were Mr. and Mrs. Fred Bischoff, Mrs. John A. Lytle, Mr. and Mrs. Lyman Shurtliff, Mrs. Sarah Perkins, Pres. W. L. Jones and Wm. Perkins, Jr.

The Young Men's Mutual Improvement Association was reorganized Sunday with Edwin Dee Hickman as president and Fay Anderson and Clarence McDonald as councilors. The young ladies' association was reorganized with Mrs. Nellie Losee as president, Mrs. Winnie Hickman and Dora Jones as councilors, Mrs. Marie Flowers, senior girls' class leader, and Mrs. Myrtle Whitehead, junior girls' class leader.

Goldeen, the little daughter of Mrs. Mary West, had the misfortune to break her arm by a fall on the playground of school last week.

Overton Items

(Special Correspondence.)

Overton, Nev., Oct. 19, 1914.

Funeral services were held Oct. 11th at the home of Mr. John Averett at Logan, Nev., for his daughter, Mrs. Vina Cooper, who died on October 10th after a long illness.

Elmer Losee has gone to St. George, Utah, making the trip in his auto. Mrs. Joseph Judd and Mrs. Leon Hickman accompanied him.

Mrs. Martha Fleming has returned from a visit to Leeds, Utah. Miss Alice Sterling came down with her and will visit here for some time.

Ralph Perkins returned from a trip to Salt Lake City Thursday with his bride, who was Miss Ethel Sunderland, of Sunnyside, Utah.

Overton, Nev., Nov. 4 —George and Wilford Ingram came in from Utah last week. Ansel Huntsman has also returned from California, where he has been working for some time

Mr. and Mrs Fay Anderson and Mrs D O Beal have gone to St. George, Utah. Mrs Beal will visit relatives at Leeds, Utah, for some time.

Bishop Edwards and Arthur V. Lee of Panaca, Nevada, were here as home missionaries Sunday. They spoke at St Thomas Sunday evening.

Mrs Myrtle Whitehead has gone to Las Vegas, Nev., to join her husband who is working there.

The ladies gave a sufferage rally here Friday evening which was a very interesting one

The stake Primary association gave a Halloween ball Friday evening

Bryant Whitmore and Wm J Flowers are each erecting new houses here.

480

MOAPA VALLEY DRAINAGE SYSTEM

County Commissioners Pass Resolution Creating District as Petitioned

Quite a party of the Moapa Valley people who are interested in promoting the building of the proposed drainage canal, designed to carry off the flood waters, were in this city Monday to urge the matter before the county commissioners. Those who appeared before the board were Messrs. W. W. Muir, J. H. Averett, Henry Rice, M. Jorgenson, W. J. McBurney, Bert Mills and W. H. Gann of Logan, U. V. Perkins of Overton and D. H. Livingston of Salt Lake City.

After a full discussion of the drainage matter, the board granted the application and made the order creating the drainage district. The expenditure will not be less than $50,000, which will be made a lien against the lands included in the district.

This move is a very necessary one to bring to the Moapa Valley the prosperity which the richness of her lands and the abundance of irrigating water would entitle her to.

It has been most unfortunate in the past that winter floods would sweep down the Meadow Valley Wash into the Moapa Valley nearly every winter, covering much land with loose sand and destroying much of the year's crop.

These floods could be kept from sweeping over the cultivated lands by building a large drainage canal to carry off the floods. This will now be done. In conjunction with this work, it is understood that the Muddy Valley Irrigation Company will remodel their water system and that a road the length of the valley will be constructed on the embankment of the drainage canal.

481

Overton Items

(Special Correspondence.)

Overton, Nev., Nov. 4, 1914.

The women held a suffrage rally here Friday evening which proved very interesting.

The Stake Primary Association gave a Hallowe'en ball Friday evening.

Mr. and Mrs. Fay Anderson and Mrs D. O. Beal have gone to St. George, Utah. Mrs. Beal will visit relatives at Leeds, Utah, for some time.

Bryant Whitmore and Wm. J. Flowers are erecting new houses here.

Mrs. Myrtle Whitehead has joined her husband in Las Vegas, where he has employment.

Bishop Edwards and Arthur V. Lee of Panaca, Nevada, were here as home missionaries Sunday. They spoke at St. Thomas Sunday evening.

Mrs. Era Jones entertained a party of ladies at a sewing bee Wednesday.

George and Wilford Ingram came here from Utah last week.

Ansel Huntsman has returned from California, where he has been working for some time.

Correct spelling should be Andersen

Moapa Valley Map

J. T. McWilliams has compiled a new map of the Moapa valley from the county assessor's records. It is invaluable to land owners in the valley and is for sale at $4.00 per copy. Send your orders to J. T. McWilliams, Las Vegas, Nevada.   tf

482

Overton, Nev , Nov 18 —Miss Margaret Mathews of Panaca, Nev., passed through here Monday on her way to visit her sister, Mrs Robert Bunker of St Thomas Mr and Mrs Bunker have a son born last week; all concerned doing well

Fay Anderson is in St George to take the short course in athetics given there for Y. M. M. I. associations.

Pres, W L Jones and M. D Cooper were at Bunkerville Sunday on Church business

Mr. and Mrs Lorin Prisbee have returned from spending the summer in Idaho

Joseph Hatch and family of Tropic, Utah, are here to spend the winter.

Dick Prince and family have moved to St Thomas

Overton Items

(Special Correspondence.)

Overton, Nev., Nov. 18, 1914.

A dance, which included a wrestling match between Ray Weber and Mr. Bryson, was given Friday evening under the management of the Y. M. M. I. association. The match was preceded by an exhibition of scientific wrestling. These young men have volunteered their services in teaching the boys of the Moapa Athletic Association, under the leadership of A. E. Jones, principal of schools.

Dr. D. O Beal has gone to Leeds, Utah, and will return with Mrs Beal, who has been visiting there for some time.

Pres. W. L. Jones and M. D. Cooper were at Bunkerville Sunday on church business.

Miss Margaret Mathews of Panaca passed through here Monday on her way to visit her sister, Mrs. Robert Bunker of St. Thomas. Mr. and Mrs. Bunker are parents of a son born last week.

Joseph Hatch and family of Tropic, Utah, are spending the winter here.

Mr. and Mrs. Lorin Frisbee have returned from Idaho, where they spent the summer.

Dick Prince and family have moved to St Thomas.

Fay Anderson is in St. George, Utah, to take the short course in athletics given there for the Y. M. M. I. Associations.

Mrs. Mar'e Flowers and Sevilla Jones will visit the Bunkerville and Mesquite wards this week on business connected with the primary associations.

A public celebration of Thanksgiving day is being planned.

484

Correct spelling should be Andersen

(Special Correspondence.)

Overton, Nev., Nov. 27, 1914.

Miss Minerva Cochran returned from Salt Lake City this week.

Mr. and Mrs. John Averett, Jr., were here for Thanksgiving.

Thanksgiving day was celebrated here by the following program in the school house, from 12 till 1 p. m.

Hymn—"We Thank Thee."

Prayer—J. P. Anderson.

Hymn—"America."

Address—W. W. Perkins, Jr.

Thanksgiving Story—Mrs. Lois E. Jones.

Recitation, "Thanksgiving Quarrel" —Bertha Shurtliff.

Girl's Chorus, by a group of small girls.

Recitation—Raymend Mills.

Hymn—"Doxology."

Prayer—A. L. Jones.

By appointment, a number of boys were out with buggies from 10 until 11 o'clock to give the old folks a morning drive.

Tables were set for dinner in one of the class rooms and under the management of W. J. Flowers as chef and a dozen or more Boy Scout aids, dinner was served to every body present. Under the management of Andrew L. Jones, a dance was given the children in the assembly hall following the dinner.

At three o'clock a game of basket ball was played between the Overton and Bunkerville teams. A dance in the evening concluded the day's festivities.

Correct spelling should be Andersen

DELINQUENT NOTICE.

MUDDY VALLEY IRRIGATION COMPANY.

Location of principal place of business, Overton, Clark Co., Nevada.

Location of irrigation system and works, Moapa Valley, Clark Co., Nevada.

NOTICE

There are delinquent upon the following described preferred capital stock on account of assessment No. 3, levied August 1st, 1914, the several amounts set opposite the names of the respective shareholders as follows:

No. ctf.	Name	Shares	Amt.
374	Wm. F. Murphy	46 4 5	46.80
461	Hyram Murphy	23 2 5	23.40
662	Harry Gentry	31¼	12.50
585	Levi Syphus	9	9.00
375		15 3-5	
556		1	
559	Whitehead Bros.	2	21.40
601		2	
663		1	
480	Moapa Farm and Orchard Co.	60	11.60
427	Christiana Syphus	4	4.00

There are delinquent upon the following described common stock on account of assessment No. 4, levied on the 1st day of August, 1914, the several amounts set opposite the names of the respective shareholders as follows:

No.	Name	Shares	Amt.
92	Wm. F. Murphy	36 9-10	12.92
119	Hyrum Murphy	16 4-10	5.74
17		10	
140		16	
142	Levi Syphus	13	31.40
182		28	
217		22	
91	Whitehead Bros.	13 3-10	39.81
192		100	

And in accordance with law and an order of the Board of Directors made on the 7th day of Nov., 1914, so many shares of each parcel of each class of such stock as may be necessary will be sold at public auction at the office of the Company in Overton, Clark County, Nevada, on the 31st day of December, 1914, at the hour of 8 o'clock p. m. of said day, to pay the delinquent assessments together with cost of advertisement and expense of sale.

Overton, Nevada, Nov. 25th, 1914.

By order of the Board of Directors.

ISAAC E. LOSEE,

Secretary-Treasurer.

First publication, Dec. 5, 1914.
Last publication, Dec. 26, 1914.

486

Basket ball

On Monday, Dec. 15, Mr. J. M. Whiting of Bunkerville, Leonidas Hickman of Overton and Mr. Street of Las Vegas met at the Overland Hotel and made out the following basket ball schedule for the teams competing for the cup presented by Mr. Babcock a year ago:

Jan. 8.—Overton and Bunkerville at Bunkerville.

Jan. 23.—Las Vegas and Bunkerville at Las Vegas.

Jan. 30.—Bunkerville and Las Vegas at Bunkerville.

Feb. 1.—Overton and Las Vegas at Overton.

Feb. 6.—Bunkerville and Overton at Overton.

Feb. 13.—Overton and Las Vegas at Las Vegas.

Lemond Thomas spent New Year's at Overton.

Teachers Here

Deputy Superintendent of Public Instruction B. G. Bleasdale has been very busy the past week conducting the examinations of teachers. Fourteen have presented themselves for examination. They are the Misses Elizabeth Vaughn and Gladys Peck of Logan; Frances Beal, of Overton; Winona Earl, Bunkerville; Hannah Crosby, Mesquite; Kate Dunphy and Georgia English of Caliente; Elizabeth M. Perkins of Goodsprings; Rose Coughlin, Olive Lake and C. E. Mable, of Las Vegas; Mrs. Dora E. Lee of Las Vegas and Messrs. Leonidas Hickman of Overton and John M. Whiting of Bunkerville. The trouble took place in the deputy's new office in the court house.

INSTITUTE AT BUNKERVILLE

Interesting Meeting of Farmers Lasting Five Days, Very Profitable

(Special Correspondence.)

The Farmers' Institute last week continued five days with three sessions each day, two of them being divided into sections. The ladies met at the high school assembly room, and the men met at the church. The evening sessions were conjoint.

The total attendance exceeded seventeen hundred with an average of about one hundred fifteen. We considered this an excellent response, and our visiting speakers were of the same opinion. The interest was very good throughout, and all feel that it will result in much good to these two communities.

Prof. Scott and Miss Davis arrived Monday evening. Each gave a number of demonstrations along with the lectures. The people received their work enthusiastically. Miss Davis demonstrated, by cooking before the women, the principles of cooking different classes of food. She followed her lecture on fabrics by a demonstration of the removal of stains from different fabrics. She organized home economics clubs among the girls and the women. Mrs. Edward I. Cox was made matron for the girls and Mrs. A. L. Kelly was chosen president of the women's club.

Prof. Scott talked on the following subjects:

Different Breeds of Cattle.

Feeding Farm Animals.

Poultry Raising.

Dairy Sanitation.

Co-operation Among Farmers.

Breeds and Breeding of Dairy Stock.

He gave a demonstration in the testing of milk and spent one afternoon judging horses and another in judging dairy cattle.

Mr. J. I. Earl talked on the possibilities in bee culture. The average yield per colony in Nevada for 1914 was 50 pounds. Mr. Earl showed that by proper care he had received an average of 75 to 80 pounds for the last ten years. This is higher than the average of any state in the Union for 1914.

Mr. Fred Rushton and Mr. William McDonald of Overton spoke on the possibilities and methods of winter gardening. Mr. McDonald exhibited some fine samples of radishes, turnips, carrots, beets, onions and head lettuce just pulled from his garden at Overton.

Mr. John Bunker discussed good roads.

Prof. Baker talked on soil fertility, how plants feed, pruning, etc., and gave a demonstration on the latter.

Mr. Douglas White was unavoidably detained and could not be present.

The institute ended with a rousing social Friday night. Refreshments were served. Dancing, games, singing and speech-making kept the large crowd very busy until midnight.

All pronounce it a very successful and profitable week, and express the hope that it may be made an annual affair. Mesquite people supported loyally. Only a very few from Moapa valley were present.

488

OVERTON HAS ATHLETIC CLUB

Wrestlers Furnish Good Sport-- Challenge to Wrestlers Under 160 Pounds

(Special Correspondence.)
Overton, Nev., Feb. 2, 1915.

Again the Moapa Athletic Club put on some good stunts last Saturday night, when the gong sounded for the commencing of hostilities between some dozen wrestlers.

First, the "bantams" went to the mat for one fall, which happened when Jacob Lee succeeded in pinning the shoulders of Ether Bischoff in 3½ minutes of clever work. Lee weighed in at 79 pounds and Bischoff at 70 pounds. These two later gave an exhibition of a dog fight, which Bischoff succeeded in winning.

Next, two clever men weighing about 133 pounds each, went to the mat. They were Fay Anderson of Overton and Duane Walsh of Logan. These two men were to have gone for two out of three falls, but after an hour's wrestling, neither of them had gotten a fall, although Anderson was on the offensive and had the shade of the match. The match was then a draw because Walsh was ill and could not continue. They may meet again soon.

For fast work, you should have seen Clarence McDonald and Willard Lee play at "Hercules." They weighed about 152 pounds. The first fall went to McDonald in six minutes. Lee took the second and third falls in 3½ minutes and 3 minutes reepectively.

The final event was a handicap. Bryson, our star, guaranteed to throw four of his pupils in 30 minutes. The boys who thought themselves lucky were Tom Perkins, John Lewis, Amicy Lee and Ben Robinson. For about 12 minutes these boys put up a game fight and kept Bryson alert and active, but at the end of that time Bryson seemed to be the hero, but not without showing much evidence of having been at work.

We now have our club well organized. We have an excellent punching bag, tights and other equipment for our welfare and growth. Watch us, for we are alive and doing. In the near future we intend putting on some boxing bouts.

We also have two men here who will meet any man or men in the state under 160 pounds. If you think you have something, get in touch with us and we will be glad to give you a meeting.

Yours for good, clean sport,

Moapa Athletic Club.

Correct spelling should be Andersen

489

Logan News

(Special Correspondence)

Logan, Nevada, March, 17, 1915.

This town feels keenly the loss of one of it's most valued members Mr. Walt Muir, who passed away on the 12th of this month. Mr. Muir injured himself jumping a ditch, causing a kink in one of his intestines. Dr. Allen came down from Salt Lake City and assisted by Dr. Beal of Overton performed two operations. The kink was taken out but the intestines were chilled during the operation apparently as all action ceased, causing death.

Mr. Muir was one of Salt Lake City's crack gardeners having had much experience in the vegetable and commission business. He had been in charge of the Moapa Improvement Co's. ranch here for two years.

The remains were taken to Salt Lake City by his family

Mr. Allen is in temporary charge of the ranch and is rushing in 20 acres of melons and getting ready to ship the 30 acres of asparagus which are ready to start cutting.

J. H. Robinson is moving from the old Mills Ranch to his new residence.

The pupils here getting their diplomas from the 8th grade are Alta Marshall, Juanita Robinson, Frank Allen, Clay Rushton and Ray Mills

Vegas Strawberries

Mr. E. G. McGriff marketed strawberries from the ranch south of Vegas this week. The berries were fine in shape and color and delicious in flavor, being in the latter respect in marked contrast to the insipid fruit often brought in from Los Angeles.

We also received from Mills and McDonald of Overton a sack of green peas, the finest in flavor we ever ate. For the bnelfit of our northern neighbors we would say that we have had our table lettuce, radishes, asparagus, green peas and strawberries all grown in Clark County and as fine as the world can produce. By the way, did you ever see finer radishes than those coming in from the Jake Beckley ranch? And new potatoes too!

Miss Dodson of Overton is visiting school chums in Vegas.

Miss Clara Coleman of Overton, has been spending the week in Vegas.

Mrs. Racie King returned to her home in Overton this week after a few weeks visit with her aunt Mrs. Nay.

W. J. McBurney and wife of Logan, passed through Vegas Thursday evening on number one on their way to visit the expositions.

491

U. V. Perkins of Overton is spending a few days in Vegas, a guest at the Overland.

Las Vegas Age Newspaper
June 5, 1915

ST. THOMAS GIVES ROYAL WELCOME

Auto Excursionists From Vegas Shown Good Time By Valley People

Early Sunday morning the sound of the eager automobile broke the slumbers of the Vegas Valley as about fifty of our citizens started the long planned trip over the new road to St. Thomas.

The road being new, was not in the best of condition, but the trip of 57 miles was made in a little more than four hours and without mishap.

The St. Thomas people met the tired crowd with a hearty welcome. Tables were prepared under a bower of green branches in the yard of Mr. and Mrs. Harry Gentry and here all gathered for a picnic luncheon. Plenty of ice water and lemonade were provided and the occasion made a happy one for all. The children especially enjoyed the event, Mr. M. M. Riley and Mr. C. P. Ball taking many of them for auto rides.

C. C. Ronnow, chairman of the board of county commissioners and one most active in securing a system of good roads for Clark county presided at the exercises. He introduced Levi Syphus who delivered an address appropriate to the occasion. He was followed by E. W. Griffith, one very active in behalf of the St Thomas route, who spoke upon the matter of good roads. Miss McAllister, of St George, Utah, gave a vocal solo very delightfully. J. I. Earl of Bunkerville spoke of the advantages of the through road to the Moapa and Virgin valleys. Mrs. A. L. Kelley of Bunkerville gave a very well rendered reading which was much enjoyed. Joe Banner entertained with a solo on the baratone horn.

County Commissioners S W. Darling and C. C. Ronnow closed the speaking with an account of what the county has accomplished. Mr. Ronnow especially made a plea that the citizens co-operate with the county in making small repairs and assisting to keep traveled roads in good condition. The meeting closed with the audience singing "The Star Spangled Banner" and "America." on the piano by Mrs. R. W. Martin.

A pleasant and unexpected feature was music by the Moapa Valley band which added just the necessary strain of patriotism appropriate to Memorial day.

492

wife, W. J. Flowers and wife and Mr. Flowers' sister, Geo. Perkins and wife, I. E. Losee and wife, Dr. Beale and wife, Horace Jones and wife and Mrs. S. R. Whitehead.

From Las Vegas, C. C. Ronnow, F. A. Clark, J. W. Horden, E. S. Sheppard, C. P. Ball, Robt. Ball, David Farnsworth, Dr. Roy. W. Martin, W. H. Elwell, M. M. Riley, Harley A. Harmon and W. R. Bracken were properly chaperoned by their respective wives. Among the unattached were Ed. W. Clark, Miss Marie Thomas, E. F. Heinecke, Henry Albright, Miss Zoe Thompson, Wm. B. Leonard, C. D. Breeze, Will Beckley, Ed. Von Tobel, O. D. Hicks, D. J. O'Leary, E. W. Griffith, Robt. Griffith, R. S. Cheney, Mrs. Emery, Mrs. C. C. Bray, Mrs. C. J. Martin, Mrs. Geo. Mueller, A. S. Henderson, Arthur Richards and Chas. Hitt.

The day was a notable one for the Moapa Valley and for the whole county. Such gatherings do much toward creating the spirit of co-operation so necessary in the work of developing our natural resources. The development of the Moapa Valley is and should be a matter of vital interest to every citizen of Las Vegas, and it is hoped that the new auto road will still further strengthen the ties which bind all together.

Among those present from various portions of the county were as follows:

From Bunkerville; A. L. Kelly and wife, Ed. I. Cox and J. I. Earl.

From Overton; U. V. Perkins and

Prof. J. F. Mayes and Mrs. Mayes left Wednesday morning for Whittier, Cal., where they will visit for a couple of weeks with Mr. Mayes' brother, after which they will spend the summer at Berkley.

W. J. McBurney of Logan, was a Vegas visitor for a portion of the week. He has recently purchased a ranch in California and anticipates moving there in the near future.

We acknowledge with pleasure the receipt of a box of beautiful fruit, —apricots and peaches—from the Ingram ranch at Overton. Such products of the orchard are surely appreciated.

NEVADA'S HONEY WINS GOLD MEDAL

Apiarists Highly Commended For Exhibits at the Exposition

In competition with enormous quantities of honey from all parts of the world, Nevada is able to command a gold medal of honor for a general honey display, with a very small exhibit.

The exhibitors whose honey made up the winning exhibit were:

J. I. Earl	Overton
G. M. Bower	Lamoille
Charles McLeod	Yerrington
William Penrose	Yerrington
C. G. Swingle	Hazen
H. Warren	Wabuska
Lovelock Honey Co	Lovelock
E. C. Grahme	Reno
R. M. Gurthrie	Reno
I. Jensen	Reno

An award for a collective display of strained honey among the same contributors was made to Nevada in the way of a bronze medal. Nevada also was given a silver medal for 1914 comb honey.

The beemen of this state now have an opportunity of using the publicity of this great world's fair for their commercial uses and thus extend the market for their products.

This exhibit was prepared by L. B. Patrick, a graduate of the University of Nevada, under the direction of Dean Charles S Knight of the College of Agriculture, and has been complimented personally by a great many of the International Jury of Awards It is hoped that a new display of 1915 honey may be had to take the place of the prize-winning 1914 crop.—Gazette.

Chamber of Commerce

Mr. Laubenheimer presented us with a very fine onion weighing one pound.

Mr. Pasno brought in some very fine spuds from his ranch.

Mr. D. Petty presented branches of fine peaches ripened May 26 for preseving. Mr. Von Tobel gave fine apricots and Jake Beckley brought branches of plums and apricots which cannot be rivaled for size and beauty. Peas and turnips from Winterwood Ranch have also been added to the collection.

Fruit intended for the Expositions must be picked when turning and each piece well wrapped with paper, in fact several thicknesses would be better. The express must be prepaid and will be refunded later. Some fruit sent from Overton reached its destination badly crushed and unfit for use as it had not been well packed

We have plenty of fine jars and want to have them filled with fruit and vegetables of all kinds for our permanent display and ask the owners of ranches and gardens to bring us enough for a jar.

We want a sample of ore from each and every mining claim in Clark county no matter of what value. Mining men look over the exhibit and a few clams have been optioned on the strength of samples displayed. Mail them to us. Care of the Secretary of the Las Vegas Chamber of Commerce.

Dead Man Found Seven Miles From St. Thomas Short Distance from Water

Wednesday evening about 8:15, Dr. R. W. Martin discovered the dead body of a man on the road from Las Vegas to St. Thomas, and close by, still tied to a bush, the dead body of a horse. The doctor had been called to St. Thomas to attend the daughter of John F. Perkins who has been seriously ill.

He traveled in his Ford runabout a n d was accompanied by Arthur Richards o f this city.

As the machine turned a slight bend in the road the headlights showed a camp beside the road a short distance ahead As they approached they could see the buggy and under it a man as if asleep. A few feet away lay the horse as if resting after the day's drive. Almost, it seemed, they could see the traveler turn toward them to see who was coming. About to pass the quiet camp, t h e stench of decaying flesh came to their nostrils, but even then they scarcely suspected anything wrong. After passing by a few rods, Dr. Martin thought it best to investigate. He stopped the machine and walked back. As he came near in the darkness and about to speak the stench again smote him. Lighting a match, he approached the quiet figure beneath the buggy and as the rays lighted up the face he saw the busy stream of bugs moving in and out of the staring eyes and realized that he was face to face with another of the almost numberless desert tragedies.

Making but a superficial examination, he found that the body of the man was partially mummified by the action of the sun and wind. The horse was also dead, still tied where his master had placed him and with grain in a pan before him.

The traveler had been dead for several days, but less than a week, the

496

road having been traveled the week before. He had passed through Las Vegas, coming here from the direction of Jean. The buggy was light and carried a large umbrella on which were the advertisements of Bakersfield, Cal., firms. The man's clothing and blankets were torn to strips as though he had died in a frenzy of delerium. The ground where the horse was tied was torn up as though the animal had also struggled to escape his fate.

There was no water in the rig, but there were an empty demijohn and canteens which would hold altogether three and a half gallons of water. This had evidently been insufficient to keep them alive. Probably already possessed of the halucinations which crowd the mind when the blood becomes thickened from lack of water, the traveller had stopped to camp, not realizing the situation. But a quarter of a mile from where he stopped was a spring which would have furnished the life giving fluid had he but known, and but seven miles beyond was the green oasis of St. Thomas in the Moapa Valley, with its streams of running water.

Dr. Martin proceeded on his journey to St. Thomas and Coroner MacDermott of Overton was notified and a party formed to return and hold an inquest and bury the body. At the time of writing this, nothing is known here as to the identity of the dead man, nor, to a certainty, the cause of his death.

It seems that it will be necessary to place signs at intervals to show the direction and distance to water. It should also be arranged to place temporary signs to warn against depending on certain springs and water holes which in the heat of summer are empty as at present.

497

Overton News

The thermometer has been registering over the hundred mark the past week but with no ill effects. Cantaloupes are ripening and are being shipped out by the trainload. Indications are that we shall have big returns from the crop. Bishop R. O. Gibson will go to Salt Lake to look after the cars. Manager S. R. Whitehead will remain in the valley to see that the melons are properly packed and shipped.

Harold Sparks will look after the crop to be handled by the Utah Moapa Distributing Company which is headed by Frank Snow of Salt Lake City.

Crayton Johnson and wife are rejoicing in the birth of a son while the John Averetts have a little daughter.

W. W. McDonald and family have moved to California.

The high price of copper has opened up many of the claims in this vicinity and everyone is busy.

ROBERT MASON'S LONELY DEATH

Aged Prospector Killed in Mountains by Accidental Discharge of Gun.

Miles away from civilization, among the rugged mountains he loved well, Robert Mason met his lonely death July 13th.

When word that the body was found reached the Moapa Valley, A. L. F. MacDermott, justice of the peace at Overton, impanelled a coroner's jury and engaged I. E. Losee and S. B. Gentry to take the party to the scene of the tragedy. When they arrived it was evening. After examining the body they went to the Whitney ranch, two miles distant, where they remained all night. In the morning they held the inquest.

George L. Whitney testified that on Tuesday morning, July 14, he went over to the camp of Robert Mason to see how he was, Mason having been staying at the Whitney ranch off and on for two months. As he rode down the trail near the camp, the horse suddenly stopped. Looking down he saw the body lying against the hill below him, with the top of the head gone, apparently blown off by a shotgun. Without touching the body, he rode home, about two miles, and sent his son Fenton on horseback 20 miles to St. Thomas to notify the authorities.

After examining into the circumstances, the coroner's jury returned the following verdict:

We, the undersigned jury impanelled to inquire into the time and cause of the death of Robert Mason there lying dead, do find that the deceased came to his death by the accidental discharge of the right barrel of his 10-gauge shotgun, probably on the 13th day of July, 1915.

ISAAC E. LOSEE, Foreman.
REINHOLD HANNIG.
SAM B. GENTRY.
W. C. JONES.
PARK L. WESTOVER.
ROXTON WHITMORE.

Whereupon, the body being in a terrible condition from the blood having run down and soaked the clothing, the coroner directed the immediate burial of the remains. A coffin was constructed from the materials brought and deceased, wrapped in his bedding, was buried under a large pinon tree close to his tent and the grave marked with a headboard, the grave being dedicated by Elder Whitney. Thus runs the simple story as related in the report of the coroner.

Whatever strange circumstances brought about the passing of our old friend, Robert Mason, it seems fitting that death should find him amid the sublime solitude of the mountains he loved so well and his mortal remains be buried beneath the moaning pines far from the haunts of man.

Although about 80 years of age, it has been the habit of this rugged character to spend much of his time traveling through the mountains and desert—doing work on his claims here, taking samples of ores and minerals there, seeking out the treasures which nature has so well hidden. And he loved his work, although we fear nature has not always provided him with the good things of life. Be that as it may, he lived his life. As we have known him here, cheery and sociable in his nature, active and energetic to a degree far beyond his years, so doubtless he died, buoyed up to the last by a sublime courage and the hope of a better life hereafter.

Las Vegas Age Newspaper
August 8, 1915

An Overton Affair.

At 4 o'clock on the afternoon of August 4, Miss Sylvia Shurtliff was given a surprise china shower by about fifteen of her friends. The party was gotten up by the Pampas club of which Miss Shurtliff is vice president, anticipating her marriage on the 12th to Mr. Timberline W. Riggs, who is manager of the Moapa Valley division of the Ogden Bee & Honey Co.

The affair was one of the most successful of its kind ever held in the valley, the attendance being exceptionally good and every one having an enjoyable time. Miss Shurtliff was presented with sufficient china and glasses to last her a lifetime—that is, if they don't break.

Marriage Licenses

ECORD—ORTEGA: July 16, Andrew Jackson Ecord of Kelso, Cal., aged 25 to Francell Ortega of Bard, Nev., aged 18.

BLACK—CAMPBELL: July 20, 1915, Parley Black of Goodsprings, aged 40, Dora Bell Campbell of Erie, aged 17. Bishop C. C. Ronnow of this city performed the ceremony.

RIGGS—SHURTLIFF: August 5, 1915, Timberline W. Riggs, of Overton, aged 24, to Sylvia Shurtliff, of the same place, aged 21.

500

MEETING OF COUNTY BOARD

Usual Grist of County Business Transacted by Commissioners Thursday.

The Board of County Commissioners held its regular monthly meeting Thursday, August 5, with Chairman C. C. Ronnow and members Geo. A. Fayle and S. W. Darling present.

After the reading and approval of the minutes of the previous meeting and receiving reports of officers, the usual bills were allowed. The bill of Joe Sparacino as interpreter in the Italian stabbing case at Moapa, was reduced from $10 to $5.

The report of the state controller was received, allowing Lincoln and Clark counties' claim to the amount of something over $2600 on account of the overpayment to the state by Lincoln county. Approved as to the proportion to be received by Clark county upon condition that Lincoln county should also approve such settlement.

The bill of Mr. O'Donnell of Overton was ordered returned for his affidavit.

The application of C. E. Barler and H. A. Hanna for a liquor license at Platina was approved.

The application of J. S. Wisner and E. F. Addis for a liquor license at the proposed ferry across the Colorado at the mouth of Eldorado canyon was approved.

Stationary engineers' licenses were granted to Harry K. Williams of Goodsprings and to Walter Schauss.

George Perkins was appointed constable at Overton and C. M. Peterson constable at Moapa, subject to the approval of their bonds.

The sale by the county for taxes of lot 4, block 4, original townsite of Searchlight, to C. E. Burdick was approved.

There being no further business, the board adjourned to meet Monday, August 9, when it will meet as a board of equalization.

501

MOAPA VALLEY SENDS PRODUCTS

Cantaloupes, Grapes, Almonds and Honey on Exhibition at S. F. Exposition.

Moapa Valley is making a good showing at the San Francisco exposition, as evidenced by the following letter to The Age from Mr. Lloyd B. Patrick, who is in charge of the Nevada exhibit in the Agricultural building. The letter says in part:

"We are today in receipt of some very elegant Muddy Valley products, comprising cantaloupes, grapes and almonds, all of them 1915 crop and very fine goods. These are the earliest products on display in the Agricultural building.

"These products have been collected by Mr. Ed. H. Syphus of St. Thomas and Mr. A. V. Lord. Bishop Earl of Overton has just sent in the first 1915 comb honey yet seen at the great exposition.

"We wish to congratulate the people of Clark county on their pride in their exhibit here and the way they have shown their pride by sending in the products they produce.

"We are still urging our friends and loyal Nevadans in southern Nevada to see that we receive a weekly supply of assorted products from at least two districts in Clark county. Your valued assistance toward this end will surely aid us in presenting those products to visitors that they think impossible of growth in Nevada. Mr. Pinger and myself will at all times be more than willing to do our part.

"Very truly yours,
"LLOYD B. PATRICK,
"Nevada Exhibit Ag'l Bldg."

We can bear witness that the Nevada exhibit is attracting its share of the attention. People by the thousands are searching for those raw materials which Nevada has in abundance, out of which to build farms. But few, comparatively, realize that Nevada in large part is just the same as California in climate, soil, water conditions and products. The best way to prove the case is to keep a supply of what we raise at both expositions.

Strange as it may seem, the most

502

difficult thing those in charge of the exhibits have to contend with is the seeming reluctance of those who are raising stuff to send a little of it to the expositions to show to those seeking information. There is an apathy on the part of the larger portion of the public, especially with those who would profit most by an increasing population and better markets. In the Vegas valley there is little interest shown, but in the Moapa Valley the people are sending in something of their products from time to time. We strongly urge those who have anything good to see that a sample of their best is sent to the expositions.

Las Vegas Age Newspaper
August 14, 1915

Recovering.

Leon Wilson, who was operated on for a very serious case of appendicitis at Moapa, July 28, is reported as entirely out of danger and now able to be up. The operation was performed by Dr. Beal of Overton, assisted by Dr. Martin of Vegas and by Mrs. Beal, who administered the anesthetic, and much of the credit for the patient's quick recovery is due to the careful nursing of Mrs. Beal.

In our issue of July 31 we failed to give proper credit to Mrs. Beal, inadvertantly crediting another with her share in the affair. Mrs. Beal is a trained nurse, and after the operation the patient was removed to Overton, where he received the care of both Dr. and Mrs. Beal

I. E. Losee of Overton was in Vegas Monday. He has just returned from Los Angeles where he went to purchase a new compressor for his ice plant to take the place of the one put out of commission recently.

Fancy Cattle

Joe. F. Perkins of Overton has just purchased 35 head of pure blood Hereford cattle in San Diego County. He has shipped them to Moapa and placed them on the J. M. Pickett ranch which he has bought and where he will engage in breeding cattle for beef.

Mr. Perkins has sold off all his range cattle and says that only good breeds will give good results when it comes to making beef.

In the bunch just imported is included the registered bull Hero 152,296. The purchase was made from D. H. Ogden who is prominent in the cattle business in San Diego county.

Joe. F. Perkins of Overton was a Vegas visitor Monday, stopping off here after a two month's stay at San Diego.

ROUSES INTEREST

Citizens From Every Portion of County Will Visit Vegas For Two Days Celebration

Program of Arrangements Practically Completed

The Labor Day Sports Carnival to be held Monday and Tuesday September 6 and 7 has met with the approval of the people of every portion of the county and hundreds will visit Vegas to take part in the two days celebration. Reports from Goodsprings, Jean, Crescent, Searchlight, Nelson, Moapa, Logan Overton, and St. Thomas all indicate a large attendance from those points and it is believed that there will be a few from Bunkerville and Mesquite.

The two days will be filled with interest and excitement. The two events which are exciting the most interest are the drilling contest, to which Potosi, Goodsprings and Searchlight are sending their best men as contestants, and the wrestling match in which Walter Brison of Overton, the Moapa Valley favorite, is matched against Mike Varney of Nelson, the champion of the Southern mining camps.

The automobile races are exciting considerable rivalry on the part of the owners of cars and both the Ford and the free for all events promise to make the dirt fly.

To fill in between the larger events, numerous interesting contests have been arranged and the whole will wind up with an open air street dance and carnival of fun on Tuesday evening on Fremont street at which frivolity will reign, with masks, fancy costumes, music and confetti to add to the fun.

505

The following is the program:

MONDAY Sept. 6th.

10:00 a.m.　Hard Rock Drilling Contest, at intersection of First and Fremont Streets. 1st Prize $150. 2nd Prize $75.

2:00 p.m.　100 yard foot race, on Fifth near Fremont. Prize $25.

2:15 p.m.　Burro Race

3:00 p.m.　Horse Races—Running
One-half mile dash, Prize $100.
One-fourth mile dash, Prize $75.
300 yard dash, Prize $50.

7:00 p.m.　At Airdome, Third and Fremont streets.
Wrestling match, Walter Brison vs Mike Varney.

TUESDAY Sept. 7th.

10:30 a.m.　Ford Automobile race, prize $75.

1:30 p.m.　Small Sports.

3:00 p.m.　Automobile race, free for all, prize $100.

4:00 p.m.　Water contest, Volunteer Fire Companies.

5:00 p.m.　Trap Shoot.

8:00 p.m.　Open Air Street Dance and Carnival of Fun, by all citizens with or without masks, on Fremont street between First and Second. Music by the Band.

High School

Clark County High School will open Tuesday morning, Sept. 7 at 8:30 for the enrollment of pupils. The opening session will last about 1½ hours during which books will be distributed and lessions assigned. The regular work will begin Wednesday. All pupils are required to be on hand at the opening session.

Prof. Bernard Street visited the Moapa valley during the week in the interest of the high school and reports that there will be several enrollments from that section, including probably the following; Bryan Bunker, Fay Syphus, Galdys and Dorris Syhus, Stella and Verda Hannig, all of St. Thomas, and Armelia Ingram and Zilla Peterson of Overton. Some others are also considering attending.

The dormitory has been undergoing general repairs the past week to fit it for the young ladies coming to school. All indications point to an increased attandance and a most successful year's work for Clark County High School.

507

BOARD MET LABOR DAY

County Commissioners Transacts Grist of Business Monday and Tuesday

The board of county commissioners met Monday morning with Chairman C. C. Ronnow and S. W. Darling, present assisted by District Attorney Henderson and Clerk Harmon.

The minutes of the last meeting were read and approved, reports of officers received and filed and the monthly bills passed upon, after which the board adjourned on account of the Labor Day celebration.

Tuesday morning pursuant to adjournment, the board met again to take up miscellaneous business.

Applications for licenses were received for the establishment of saloons at Goodsprings from the following: L. Groesbeck, Conner & Schwanbeck and Wm. A. Taylor. All were laid over until the next meeting, for action.

The applications for the sale of property bid in by the county, were approved and the treasurer instructed to offer for sale to the highest bidder the following:

Lot 8, block 1, with improvements, of the Arizona addition of Searchlight, and lot 3, block 3, original townsite of Searchlight.

C. M. Carry, motor truckman of the Potosi mine, was granted permission to carry a gun.

The bond of George Perkins, as constable of Overton township was approved.

A letter was received from S. R. Whitehead, secretary of the Moapa Valley Commercial League, informing the board that the people of the valley were ready to co-operate with the county in road building, and asked what amount of money would be available from the county. The clerk was instructed to reply that the board would visit the valley to consider the road matter in the near future.

The resignation of C. L. Aug. Mahn was received, and he was notified that it would be accepted to take effect when his successor should be appointed and qualified.

The application of the sheriff for additional deputies during the coming term of court was granted.

Mrs. Kessler and Mrs. Rosa Neju were each allowed $15 per month under the Mother's Pension Act.

The district attorney was allowed a deputy to assist him during the term of court.

CARNIVAL WAS GREAT SUCCESS

Big Crowd of Visitors Well Entertained, and Interest in Various Events was Keen

Everybody Happy, and No Mishaps Mark Two Days Celebration

From Monday morning until midnight Tuesday, the streets of Vegas were filled with people who came from all portions of the county, to unite with us in the greatest celebration the county has ever enjoyed. From the beginning of the drilling contest Monday morning, until the last carnival dancers left the street, Tuesday night, the interest of the pleasure seekers never flagged and merriment reigned supreme.

Many are the words of commendation and good will spoken by the visitors, and in all the big throng, there was no dissatisfaction expressed. To be sure some of the boys bet on the wrong side, but what would you? Not all can win, and a little careful thought will convince us that as many bets were won as lost.

Good humored and orderly was the crowd at all times and never have we seen a celebration of equal magnitude, where there was so little drunkeness and disorder on the streets, and no accidents to mark the occasion with regret.

The general committee, composed of H. M. Lillis, George Swadener, Harley A. Harmon, J. E. Keate and Frank A. Waite, put in much time and hard work on the carnival; and to them and members of the fire department, is due the great success achieved.

The drilling contest was the first event and the rivalry between the camps of Potosi, Goodsprings and Searchlight was high. Unforfortunately the steel used by the Potosi was not tempered for the very hard rock, the drills coming out of the hole badly blunted after a few strokes. The team was a good one and but for the defective steel would have made a far better showing. In the betting the Goodsprings team was probably the favorite, and when they finished their magnificent work it was really believed by many that the contest was ended. But not so. When Jack Remol and Hughey McDonald were fairly started in their great drive, the excitement began to burn. As they increased their stroke, working together like parts of a great machine, with never a lost stroke or a break on the change it was seen that they were strictly in the race, and when the judges announced them as the winning team, they received an ovation. It will will be long before a prettier contest will be seen than that in which Searchlight and Goodsprings, took first and second prize.

Of the Goodsprings team, Blair was badly handicapped by having his hand severely cut by a piece of steel from a drill, early in the contest.

Potosi Team—R. E. Roberts and A. Tavelli, record 17 11-16 inches.

Timekeeper, F. W. Stephens. Coach, Robert Groves.

Goodsprings Team—Clyde Blair and George Kemple, record 24 13-16 inches.

Timekeeper, F. A. Hale. Coach, John Kemple.

Searchlight Team—Jack Remol and Hughey McDonald, record 26 1-8 inches.

Timekeeper, F. M. Black. Coach, Chas. Huff.

Judges, R. B. Sproal, P. J. Sullivan and F. A. Doherty.

Official Timekeeper, John F. Miller.

(Continued on page 2)

510

Ford, by M. C. Thomas.
  Driver, Young.
  Mechanican, Bingham.
  Car wrecked.
Buick, by Wm. Ball.
  Driver, Ball.
  Mechanician, Mathews.
  Broke water connections.
Dodge, by J. W. Woodward.
  Driver, Arthur Richards.
  Mechanician, Robinson.
  Time 16 min and 44 sec.

LABOR DAY CARNIVAL

(Continued from page one)

The 100 yard free for all foot race had eight entries, Mike Varney of Nelson, Dick Bundy of Kaolin, Sanderson of Goodsprings, Aldert Leavitt and Warren Hardy of Bunkerville and Lenord Ronnow and Newel Leavitt of Vegas. The Race was won by Bundy, with Newell Leavitt second and was a pretty contest.

The burro race was a walkover won by McDonald, theae being only two entries.

The horse races were to some extent dissapointing by reason of the failure of four horses which had been expected to enter. The race was between the five year old "Black Bart", entered by Keate ane the four year old "Mandy Girl" entered by Gann, of Logan.

The half mile dash was won by Black Bart in 49 seconds and the quarter

The water contest was short but entertaining. The team headed by Ernest Lake and Henry Lutz had the first stream; but Charles Brown and Joe Banner by the fierceness of their attack, until Lutz unwittingly stepped out of the ring, his team thus loosing the contest.

In the trap shoot, Goodsprings carried off the honors, E. J. Evans winning the match and W. E. Allen making the high run. It is hoped that the Goodsprings shooters will form a club so that frequent contests may be had.

The winners were E. J. Evans, of Goodsprings, first; Frank Ferris, second; J. J. Williams, third; W. E. Allen, high run.

The other entries were Roy Barnes, of Goodsprings, Dr. W. S. Parks, O. D. Hicks, Walter Houck, J. S. Fleming and J. W. Horden.

Tuesday evening all restraint of formality were cast aside and the carnival

The half mile dash was won by Black Bart in 49 seconds and the quarter mile by Mandy Girl in 23 seconds.

The wrestling match was short and sweet while it lasted. Mike Varney of Nelson was matched against Walter Bryson of Overton. The first fall was won by Bryson in three minutes and the second fall by the same in two minutes. Varney is a much older man than Bryson, and while the Nelson favorite put up a game fight, he was clearly out classed by his antagonist. A good crowe attended.

The Ford auto race was one of the prettiest events of the sports carnival. The two laps of the course figure slightly less than ten miles and in making the rounds the cars encountered every possible kind of road. The auto races proved more a contest of skillful driving than of fitness of machines. Although none of the drivers had ever been in a race before they drove like veterans. When young Bobbie Griffith came across thr line a winner by 48 seconds he was the hero of the day.

The following is a record of the Ford race.

Car No. 1. Entered by M.C. Thomas. Driver, Young, mechanician, Bingham. Time 18 min. 3 sec.

Car No. 2. Entered by C. P. Ball. Driver, Richards Mechanician, Robinson Time 18 min. 27 sec.

Car No. 3 Entered by E W. Griffith Driver R.Grffith; Mechanician, Brown.

Tuesday evening all restraint of formality were cast aside and the carnival spirit was supreme. Hundreds of dancers masked and in fancy costumes took up the grand march at 9 o'clock and Fremont street became for the first time a scene of mad merriment. The music of the band set all feet dancing on the pavements under the colored lights, and confetti filled the air like vari-colored snows. And in spite of the multitude of noise makers, ticklers, baloon squaker and nerve tormenters of every kind, everybody was happy, goodnatured and full of the joy of carnival night and there were no unpleasant happenings to mar the pleasure. At eleven o'clock the throng began to melt away and when the hour of midnight sturck there were only the drifts of confetti and the pleasant memories left to recall the happiest two days Vegas has seen in her ten short years of life. Tired? Uh-huh. But happy too!

512

The boy's and girl's races were held Tuesday afternoon on Fremont street. There were some close finishes and good sport was enjoyed by all. No record was kept by the judges and we regret that it is impossible to name the winners of these events.

The nail driving contest for women was some event as may be seen by the list of entries. There were no shirkers on the job and the winners had to work at a rate that would put the men to shame, to win. Mrs. Frazier was the winner, driving the 20 nails on 1 minute 25 seconds. Mesdames Tisdale and Alter tied for second place, time 2 minutes. The following ladies were in the contest, Mesdames Kelley, Ruder, Tisdale, Goodrich, Harkins, Buselle, Lake, Conley Ball, Shurtliff, Frazier, Van Nortwick, Wilson, Eazell, Nicholson and Alter, also the Misses Matteuci and Hooper.

The free for all auto race was full of excitement. Two cars were disabled on the first lap, leaving the contest between Roy Barnes, of Goodsprings, driving W. E. Allen's Studebaker and Arthur Richards, driving J. W. Woodard's Dodge. Roy Barnes is a daring driver and made a beautiful race in the Allen car. Had it not been for an unfortunate skid in rounding the the corner from Main onto Fremont street, during which the car turned entirely around without going over, the race might have been his.

The Thomas Ford went into the air when it struck a piece of soft ground going at 45 miles per hour and came down wrong side up. Fortunately Young and Bingham were thrown clear and escaped injury. The car was badly wrecked.

Billy Ballys powerful Buick, would have been in the race, had it not been for a broken water connection on the first lap, which flooded the magneto, putting the car out of the race.

Arthur Richards, the winner of the race, is a Vegas boy, and naturally was the favorite with the crowd, when the race was seen to be a close one. He drove with splendid judgment and skill, and the great burst of speed which he worked up on the straight-way Fremont street finish brought him home a winner, and earned him an enthusiastic ovation from the crowd. The popularity of the Dodge car and J. W. Woodard, the owner, also made the victory a very populer one.

ENTRIES:

Studebaker, by W. E. Allen.
  Driver, Roy Barnes.
  Mechanician, Fletcher

Marshal Gray Here

U. S. Marshal A. B. Gray, of Carson City, passed through Vegas last Saturday night on his way to Overton where he will remain until Monday next.

His business there is to sell the real and personal property of the Irrigation & Development company to satisfy two judgments rendered in the United States district court by Judge Farrington last July.

One judgment is in favor of James Ivers and is for $14,141.33 and costs of suit taxed at $32.70 and $500 allowed as counsel fees.

The other is in favor of James Armstrong, for $47,200 and costs taxed at $60.20 and the sum of $1,250 allowed as counsel fees.

Marshal Gray will sell all the interest of the Irrigation & Development company in both real property and the water stock and other personal property belonging to it to the highest bidder.

514

COURT CONVENES NEXT TUESDAY

Many Interesting Cases to Be Tried at Approaching Term of Court

Tuesday morning Judge Charles Lee Horsey will convene the regular fall term of the district court of the Tenth Judicial district. A venire of eighty jurors has been summoned from the county to try the cases on the docket requiring jury trials.

Wells and Steele, who made the sensational escape from the jail, after beating the deputy, Roy T. Lockett severely, will face three charges, They will be tried for an assault with intent to kill, for their attack upon Mr. Lockett. A charge of robbery has also been placed against them, for holding up the store at Moapa, and a third charge, that of jail breaking, has also been filed against them by District Attorney Henderson. McNamee & McNamee will conduct the defense.

Fred Ben, the Indian, will be tried for killing Indian Bismark, in a drunken carousal last Christmas day. Judge Peter J. Somer of Goldfield, will appear for the defendant.

J. E. Thayer is in jail in default of $3,000 bonds, charged with intent to kill, for his brutal assault upon a woman of the red-light district.

Charles A. Whitaker, James Craig and Douglas Craig of Searchlight will be tried upon the charge of stealing the plates of the Searchlight M. & M. company last July. R. H. Cabell will defend them.

Thomas H. Fitzgerald will be tried upon the charge of appropriating irrigation water of another and will be defended by Richard Busteed. This is an appeal from the Justice Court.

Louis Gandolfi will answer to the charge of an assault with a deadly weapon, for having carved his partner in a fight at Moapa.

L. D. Smith will appear to answer a charge of violating the law relating to the burial of the dead bodies of human beings, and will be defended by Judge W. R. Thomas.

J. C. Armstrong will also appear to answer to the charge of shooting Paul Coski last June at Goodsprings. The defense will plead self defense.

In addition to the criminal cases there are numerous civil cases which will be hard fought. Among are those the Moapa Valley water cases, in which former Judge George S. Brown will appear for the Muddy Valley Irrigation company.

The list of trial jurors drawn follows:

Mesquite—A. N. Woodbury, F. S.

515

Leavitt, John S. Barnum, L. R. Abbott, W. G. Peters, Jr., Wm. E. Abbott and William B. Hughes.

Overton—Frank N. Olend, Thomas Johnson and C. A. Simson.

Crescent—Joseph B. Horne.

Logan—Henry Pierce, C. S. Barclay, J. L. Connelly and E. E. Thompson.

Searchlight—John Howe, J. P. Vest, John W. Stark, A. S. Gains, Paul Barlock, W. S. Ball, S. F. Wilson and Wilford E. Cox.

Nelson—John Truax, Harry Weinecke, Wm. Burke, and Jos. P. Campbell.

Goodsprings—Frank S. Hall, H. J. Jarman, John Frederickson C. L. May, James Ashbaugh, A. A. Buys and Wm. Cramer.

St. Thomas—Robert E. Bunker, Wm. F. Murphy, and Robt. O. Gibson.

Bunkerville—Nephi J. Hunt, Jessie Waite, Alma D. Leavitt, Harmon Wittwer, Hector Bunker, and Henry D. Leavitt.

Las Vegas—W. G. Morse, Asher Helm, Peter Jost, Proctor Smith, E. F. Eglington, J. W. Woodard, John W. Horden, Roy Goodwin, L. A. Rockwell, W. I. Roberts, James Clark, William Laubenheimer, Jake Beckley, W. L. Aplin, J. L. Russell, Walter E. Seare, M. I. Newkirk, Ed. VonTobel, C. A. French, George E. Lane, Jr., Joseph Kutcher, Wm. Marshall, B. R. Jefferson, Merrit Pollard, John M. Miller, J. D. Richards, H. M. Nay, W. J. Reid, W. H. Elwell, Joseph May, John S. Wisner, R. E. Lake, Harry E. Mathews, Henry Bechtel, Frank Quireau, J. E. Westlake, and D. Petty.

Washington County News
September 25, 1915

Misfortunes

J. A. Swapp of Overton, Nevada, has been visiting here. One of his horses dropped dead when he was near the city enroute in, Thursday evening. His health, which has been very poor since he was struck by lightning shows no improvement—Washington County News (St. George, Utah.)

Las Vegas Age Newspaper
October 16, 1915

Joe F. Perkins of Overton is in Vegas on court business.

Las Vegas Age Newspaper
October 30, 1915

James C. Phelps of Goodsprings was an arrival at the Overland, Wednesday.

Lewis M. Grant of Logan, came to the county seat last night on legal business.

K. Tanner, Moapa Valley water commissioner, arrived in Vegas Thursday night.

Miss Adaline Ingram of Overton, has accepted a position as nurse in the Las Vegas Hospital.

Asst. Attorney General E.T. Patrick, who has been here this week representing the interest of the State in the Moapa Valley water case, left this morning for St. Thomas. After after a day or two there he will start for Los Angeles to enjoy a well earned vacation.

Miss Zilla Peterson left last evening for Overton to attend the convention of Sunday schools to be held there to-morrow.

Miss Armella Ingram has been spending the week at her home in Overton. She will resume her high school work next week.

Overton "Cotton Ball"

Last evening the Moapa Valley Chamber of Commerce gave a "Cotton Ball" in the Overton Hall. The invitations stated that any person wearing other than a cotton dress or suit would be fined by the committee not less than one dollar. Four spicey numbers were rendered on the program and refreshments were served. The hall was profusely decorated with flowers of the Valley and everybody was in high spirits.

A prize was given for the neatest cotton dress and suit. The affair was unique in its conception and greatly enjoyed by all. Such events are helpful in bringing the people of all portions of the valley together, promoting good-fellowship and the spirit of enterprise.

LOGAN FAIR GREAT SUCCESS

Splendid Showing of Agricultural Products Attracts Much Attention

The agricultural exhibit at the state experiment farm at Logan last Monday was a very successful one, besides being the occasion of a pleasant day for the valley.

Among the perfect products shown were almonds, olives, peanuts, apples, pears, pomgranates, new potatoes (second crop), cabbage, celery, lettuce (heads as big as a basket), radishes, Korean cabbages and radishes, turnips, beets and pumpkins. A display of Mexican giant Indian corn, a white dent which produced 50 bushels to the acre, was a wonder.

The livestock department included fine Percheron horses, Poland China hogs, Holstein cattle, both pure breds and grades of each kind.

Following the fair, a dance was enjoyed at Overton. The motor car was out of order on that day, and the people wish to thank the railroad company for furnishing a train and giving them every possible accommodation by running between the towns until a late hour at night.

A movement was inaugurated to hold a county fair at Las Vegas in September of next year, the Moapa valley being anxious to join in such an enterprise, provided they can get transportation for their products. If Las Vegas shall show the spirit which the Moapa Valley folks are showing, such an affair can be held here and will become a regular annual institution, which will be of wonderful value.

S. A. Angell of Overton was a welcome caller at the Age office Thanksgiving day. Mr. Angell has been at the Grand Gulch mines for some months and reports that section as very prosperous in a mining way.

Las Vegas Age Newspaper
December 4, 1915

Pres. Willard L. Jones of Overton, and Bishop Edw. I. Cox of Bunkerville, will be present at the services of the Latter Day Saints, Sunday.

J. M. Lytle of Overton was a welcome caller at the Age office Monday. He spent several days in this city, stopping at the Overland.

Las Vegas Age Newspaper
December 11, 1915

Pres. Willard L. Jones of Overton, and Bishop Edw. I. Cox of Bunkerville, will be present at the services of the Latter Day Saints, Sunday.

Bunkerville Game

Last week Friday, the Boys' Basket Ball Team of the County High School journeyed to Bunkerville to meet the team of the Virgin High School. The boys were given a good send-off by the rest of the school who accompanied them to the depot. After a continuous journey of ninety miles, nearly half of it by team, Bunkerville was reached a little after dark.

The game was called for 2 o'clock the following day. It started with a rush. Both teams played hard and fast. Except for the work of Layman Leavitt, who made five baskets against three by his opponents, the first half was practically a stand-off. Otto Westlake, the foul shooter for the C. C. H. S., converted three of the five fouls called on Bunkerville into points while Walte was able to throw but three out of nine chances. The half ended with the score 19 to 14 in favor of Bunkerville.

Vegas came back strong in the second half and by clever team work and accurate shooting, overcame the lead of their opponents. But the greater endurance of the Bunkerville quintet soon wore them out. Toward the last of the game Reynolds Robbins was disqualified for four personal fouls, a feature of the new rules. Fred Silk went in as substitute. McDonald and Ben Robinson of Overton officiated. The final score was 38 to 22.

Bunkerville has a strong, fast team, but the local five believe they can beat them in a return game in January. The boys all enjoyed the trip and speak in the highest terms of the hospitality of the Bunkerville people. Line-up:

Las Vegas: R. Robbins, center; H. Cragin, right forward; O. Westlake, left forward; B. Bunker, right guard; C. Van Deventer, left guard; Fred Silk, substitute.

Bunkerville: L. Leavitt, center; N. Walte, right forward; Huntsman, left forward; A. Leavitt, right guard; Earl Leavitt, left guard.

Made in the USA
San Bernardino, CA
07 July 2016